Principles of Heat Treatment of Steels

Romesh C Sharma
PhD
Ex-Professor
Department of Materials and Metallurgical Engineering
Indian Institute of Technology, Kanpur

NEW AGE
REFERENCE
An Imprint of
NEW AGE INTERNATIONAL (P) LIMITED, PUBLISHERS
LONDON • NEW DELHI • NAIROBI
Bangalore • Chennai • Cochin • Guwahati • Hyderabad • Kolkata • Lucknow • Mumbai
Visit us at **www.newagepublishers.com**

Published by New Age International (P) Ltd., Publishers
First Edition: 1996
Hardbound Edition: 2018

GLOBAL OFFICES

- **New Delhi** **NEW AGE INTERNATIONAL (P) LIMITED, PUBLISHERS**
  7/30 A, Daryaganj, New Delhi-110002, (INDIA)
  Tel.: (011) 23253771, 23253472, **Telefax:** 23267437, 43551305
  E-mail: contactus@newagepublishers.com • Visit us at www.newagepublishers.com
- **London** **NEW AGE INTERNATIONAL (UK) LTD.**
  27 Old Gloucester Street, London, WC1N 3AX, UK
  E-mail: info@newacademicscience.co.uk • Visit us at www.newacademicscience.co.uk
- **Nairobi** **NEW AGE GOLDEN (EAST AFRICA) LTD.**
  Ground Floor, Westlands Arcade, Chiromo Road (Next to Naivas Supermarket)
  Westlands, Nairobi, KENYA, **Tel.:** 00-254-713848772, 00-254-725700286
  E-mail: kenya@newagepublishers.com

BRANCHES

- **Bangalore** 37/10, 8th Cross (Near Hanuman Temple), Azad Nagar, Chamarajpet, Bangalore- 560 018
  Tel.: (080) 26756823, **Telefax:** 26756820, **E-mail: bangalore@newagepublishers.com**
- **Chennai** 26, Damodaran Street, T. Nagar, Chennai-600 017, **Tel.:** (044) 24353401
  Telefax: 24351463, **E-mail: chennai@newagepublishers.com**
- **Cochin** CC-39/1016, Carrier Station Road, Ernakulam South, Cochin-682 016
  Tel.: (0484) 2377303, **Telefax:** 4051304, **E-mail: cochin@newagepublishers.com**
- **Guwahati** Hemsen Complex, Mohd. Shah Road, Paltan Bazar, Near Starline Hotel
  Guwahati-781 008, **Tel.:** (0361) 2513881, **Telefax:** 2543669
  E-mail: guwahati@newagepublishers.com
- **Hyderabad** 105, 1st Floor, Madhiray Kaveri Tower, 3-2-19, Azam Jahi Road, Near Kumar Theater
  Nimboliadda Kachiguda, Hyderabad-500 027, **Tel.:** (040) 24652456, **Telefax:** 24652457
  E-mail: hyderabad@newagepublishers.com
- **Kolkata** RDB Chambers (Formerly Lotus Cinema) 106A, 1st Floor, S N Banerjee Road
  Kolkata-700 014, **Tel.:** (033) 22273773, **Telefax:** 22275247
  E-mail: kolkata@newagepublishers.com
- **Lucknow** 16-A, Jopling Road, Lucknow-226 001, **Tel.:** (0522) 2209578, 4045297, **Telefax:** 2204098
  E-mail: lucknow@newagepublishers.com
- **Mumbai** 142C, Victor House, Ground Floor, N.M. Joshi Marg, Lower Parel, Mumbai-400 013
  Tel.: (022) 24927869, **Telefax:** 24915415, **E-mail: mumbai@newagepublishers.com**
- **New Delhi** 22, Golden House, Daryaganj, New Delhi-110 002, **Tel.:** (011) 23262368, 23262370
  Telefax: 43551305, **E-mail: sales@newagepublishers.com**

ISBN: 978-81-224-0869-0
C-17-09-10731

Printed in India at Rashtriya Printers, Delhi.

NEW AGE INTERNATIONAL (P) LIMITED, PUBLISHERS
7/30 A, Daryaganj, New Delhi-110002
Visit us at **www.newagepublishers.com**
(CIN: U74899DL1966PTC004618)

PREFACE

This book is written as a text book for a senior level undergraduate course on Heat Treatment of Steels for students in metallurgical and materials engineering and mechanical engineering. The emphasis is on the basic principles underlying various heat treatment processes of steels, rather than on the engineering details, which are easily learned in industry. While writing this book, it has been assumed that the student has already been exposed to basic courses on phase equilibria, phase transformations and mechanical properties of materials. In this book, first seven chapters deal with phase diagrams, phase transformations and structure-property relationships in steels, relevant to the heat treatment of steels. The remaining chapters are devoted to hardenability of steels and various heat treatment and surface hardening processes of steels. The principles of heat treatment of tool steels and cast irons are essentially the same as heat treatment of low alloy steels. Hence, a brief discussion on tool steels and cast irons, and their heat treatment is also included in this book.

Though this book is primarily written as a text book for senior level undergraduate students, it should prove to be an useful reference book for post-graduate students and engineers working in industry.

I am indebted to Prof. A.K. Jena and Prof. M.L. Vaidya, my colleagues at I.I.T. Kanpur, for reviewing parts of the manuscript and giving helpful suggestions. I am also grateful to Mr. Yash Pal for typing the manuscript and to Mr. R.K. Bajpai for preparing the illustrations.

ROMESH C. SHARMA

ACKNOWLEDGEMENT

The author gratefully acknowledges the financial support provided by the Ministry of Human Resource Development, Government of India, under the Curriculum Development Scheme of the Quality Improvement Programme (QIP), for the preparation of the manuscript of this book.

ROMESH C. SHARMA

CONTENTS

CHAPTER 1

Transformations in Plain Carbon Steels

1 INTRODUCTION

Heat treatment processing of steels is based on the manipulation of their microstructures by suitable heating and cooling cycles to develop desired mechanical properties in steel components. To properly understand various processes of heat treatment of steels, it is imperative to have basic understanding of the development of various microstructures in steels and their effect on mechanical properties. This requires the knowledge of thermodynamics and kinetics of different solid state phase transformations that occur in steels as function of temperature and composition, and the understanding of relationship between microstructures, composition and mechanical properties. Phase transformations in steels cover a wide variety of transformations that occur in solids and have been a subject of many monographs and books due to their theoretical as well as practical importance. A comprehensive discussion on all aspects of these transformations is beyond the scope of this book; however, the essential features of these transformations have been covered. Phase transformations in plain carbon steels, i.e. Fe–C alloys, are covered in this chapter. The effect of different alloying elements on these transformations and the relationship between structure and properties will be discussed in the subsequent chapters.

2 IRON–CARBON PHASE DIAGRAM

Steels are basically iron–carbon alloys, with other alloying elements either incidentally present as a consequence of the steel making processes (i.e. small amounts of elements like Mn, Si, P, S, etc.) or intentionally added to improve their properties and/or their response to heat treatment processes. Figure 1.1 gives the binary Fe–C phase diagram. Iron alloys containing up to approximately 2% carbon[1] are generally classified as steels. Steels containing less than 0.3% carbon are referred to as low carbon steels, those containing between 0.3 and 0.8% carbon as medium carbon steels and the ones with higher carbon contents as high carbon steels.

Pure iron exists in two allotropic forms; as body centered cubic (bcc) up to 1185K (912°C) and between 1667K (1394°C) and its melting point at 1811K (1538°C); and

1. Unless otherwise specified, all compositions in this book will be in weight per cent.

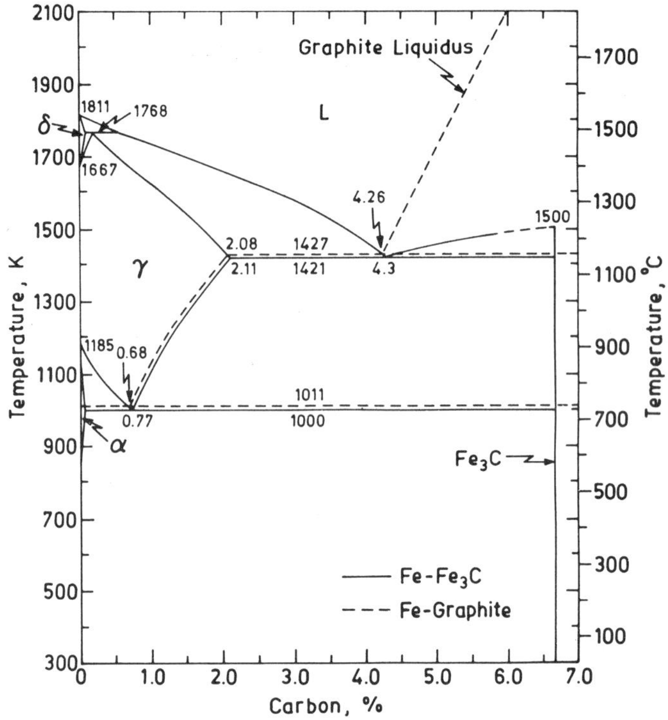

Fig. 1.1. Stable Fe-Graphite and metastable Fe–Fe_3C Phase Diagrams.

as face centered cubic (fcc) between 1185K (912°C) and 1667K (1394°C). The low temperature bcc phase is normally designated as α, the fcc phase as γ and the high temperature bcc phase as δ.

Carbon forms an interstitial solution in iron. The solubility of carbon in bcc iron (α as well as δ) is relatively small, whereas fcc iron (γ-phase) can dissolve substantial amount of carbon; the maximum solubility of carbon in γ-phase is 2.11% at 1421K (1148°C). The low temperature bcc phase in steels is also called ferrite and the fcc phase is known as austenite. At higher concentrations of carbon in iron, higher than the solubility limit of carbon in iron, an intermediate compound Fe_3C, called cementite (cm), containing 25 atomic percent carbon (~6.67%C) is formed in the Fe–C system. Cementite has an orthorhombic crystal structure and is a hard and brittle phase. Furthermore, the cementite phase is metastable with respect to iron plus graphite (pure carbon) equilibrium as seen in Fig. 1.1. However, in steels, on solidification and/or transformations from austenite, it is the metastable cementite phase that invariably forms and is stable under most conditions. Hence, for all subsequent discussions on phase transformations and heat treatment of steels, the metastable Fe–Fe_3C phase diagram will be considered.

Figure 1.2 shows a portion of the Fe–Fe_3C phase diagram relevant to the study of phase transformations in steels in an expanded form. In the Fe–Fe_3C system, an eutectoid point, $\gamma = \alpha + \text{cm}$, exists at 0.77%C and 1000K (727°C). Steels with carbon content lower than the eutectoid composition are called hypo-eutectoid steels, the

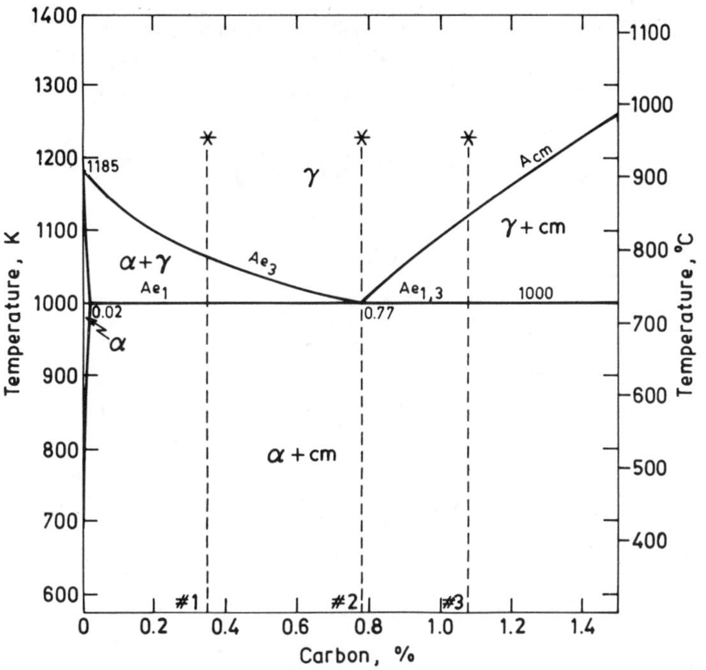

Fig. 1.2. A portion of the Fe–Fe_3C phase diagram in expanded form.

ones with a higher carbon content as hyper-eutectoid steels and those of the eutectoid composition as eutectoid steels. The $\gamma/(\alpha+\gamma)$ equilibrium line is normally referred to as Ae_3, $\gamma/(\gamma+cm)$ line as A_{cm} and the eutectoid temperature as Ae_1. An iron–carbon alloy containing less than ~2% carbon can be rendered completely austenitic by heating it to a suitable temperature in the austenite (γ) stability range. On slow cooling from the austenitic range, austenite phase transforms to different phases in accordance with the Fe–Fe_3C phase diagram. The typical room temperature microstructures obtained on slow cooling from austenite are shown in Fig. 1.3.

On slow cooling from the austenitic state, a hypo-eutectoid steel, of say composition #1 in Fig. 1.2, starts transforming to ferrite below Ae_3 temperature. Assuming the cooling rate to be sufficiently slow for the diffusional processes during the transformation to be essentially complete, the compositions of ferrite that is formed and of the untransformed austenite at any temperature between Ae_3 and Ae_1 are given by $\alpha/(\alpha+\gamma)$ and $(\alpha+\gamma)/\gamma$ phase boundaries, respectively, and their relative amounts by lever rule (mass balance). The ferrite transformation generally starts heterogeneously at the austenite grain boundaries and ferrite grows inwards from these boundaries with decreasing temperature. As temperature reaches Ae_1, the composition of untransformed austenite approaches eutectoid composition. On further cooling below Ae_1, the remaining austenite of eutectoid composition transforms simultaneously to a lamellar mixture of ferrite and cementite, called pearlite. The room temperature microstructure of such a steel is, then, ferrite plus pearlite, as seen in Fig. 1.3(a). Here the light regions are ferrite and the dark ones are pearlite. The amount of pearlite in a hypo-eutectoid steel is equal to the amount of untransformed

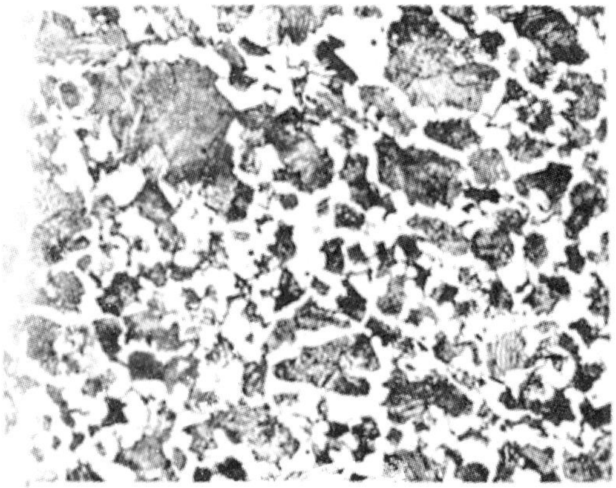

(a) × 500

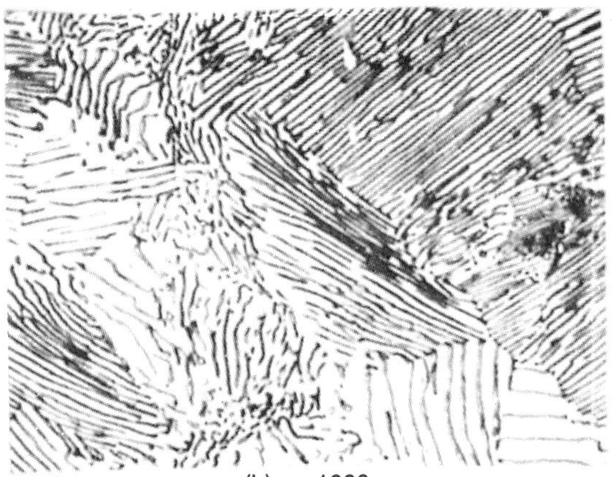

(b) × 1000

Fig. 1.3. Room temperature microstructures of slowly cooled (a) hypo-eutectoid, (b) eutectoid, and (c) hyper-eutectoid steels.

austenite (determined by the lever rule) just above the Ae_1 temperature. An eutectoid steel of composition #2 in Fig. 1.2 transforms, on slow cooling from austenite, to a structure of 100% pearlite below Ae_1 temperature. The room temperature microstructure of a eutectoid steel is shown in Fig. 1.3(b). It clearly reveals the lamellar nature of pearlite consisting of alternate lamellae of ferrite (light) and cementite (dark), essentially parallel to each other within a pearlite grain. The relative amounts of ferrite and cementite within the pearlite structure are given by the lever rule at a temperature just below the Ae_1 temperature. Finally, the room temperature microstructure of a hyper-eutectoid steel, obtained on slow cooling from the austenitic state, is shown in Fig. 1.3(c). In a hyper-eutectoid steel, of say composition #3 in Fig. 1.2, cementite starts forming at the austentite grain boundaries below A_{cm} temperature, the amount of cementite increases (according to lever rule) till Ae_1 temperature is reached, below which the remaining austenite (of eutectoid composition) transforms to pearlite.

3 CLASSIFICATION OF TRANSFORMATIONS IN STEELS

Instead of cooling slowly, when a steel of certain composition is quenched (i.e. cooled rapidly enough so that no diffusional transformations occur during cooling) from the austenitic range to some temperature below the equilibrium transformation temperature and held there isothermally, then metastable austenite decomposes to various products (phases) as shown in Fig. 1.4. At isothermal transformation temperatures higher than ~773K (500°C) austenite transforms to either ferrite, or pearlite, or cementite, or to a mixture of these products depending upon the composition of steel and the temperature of transformation. At lower isothermal transformation temperatures, below ~773K (500°C) and down to ~573K (300°C), austenite of all compositions transforms to a morphologically different product, called bainite. Bainite may be defined as a non-lamellar precipitation of cementite (or other iron carbides) in association with ferrite. During bainite transformation, austenite primarily transforms to ferrite and the carbides may precipitate either from austenite at the α/γ interfaces during the transformation, or within the ferrite phase behind the advancing α/γ interfaces. All these transformations involve redistribution of carbon by diffusional processes. Fig. 1.4 shows the general range of composition and temperature for the occurrence of different diffusional transformations under isothermal conditions. In the region marked "Ferrite" in Fig. 1.4, at temperatures higher than Ae_1, austenite only partially transforms to ferrite as the equilibrium phases at these temperatures are ferrite plus austenite, whereas, below Ae_1, austenite initially transforms to ferrite, enriching the remaining austenite in carbon, which at a later stage transforms to pearlite as its composition enters the "Pearlite" region in Fig. 1.4. Similarly, in the region marked "Cementite", the transformation is to cementite plus austenite (untransformed) above Ae_1 temperature and to cementite plus pearlite below the Ae_1 temperature. In the "Pearlite" and "Bainite" regions in Fig. 1.4, austenite, in general, fully transforms of these products.

Apart from the above mentioned diffusional transformations, if austenite (of any composition) is quenched to room temperature such that the diffusional transforma-

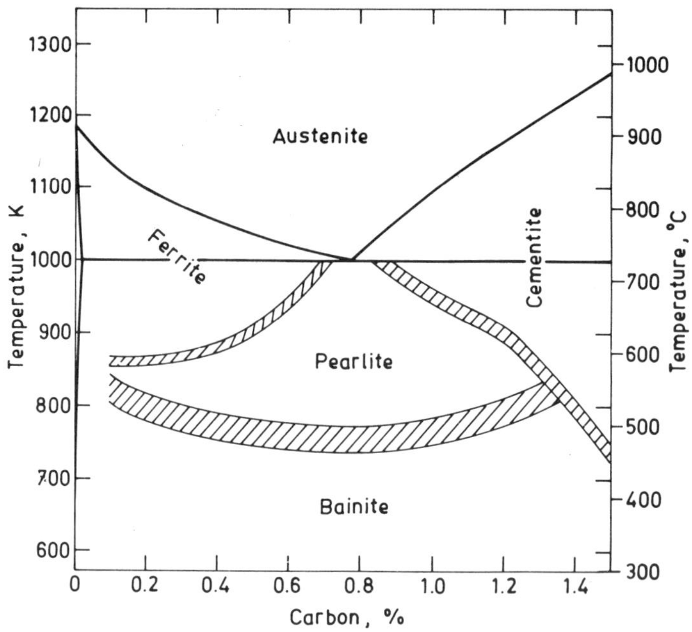

Fig. 1.4. Composition and temperature regions for the occurrence of different transformations under isothermal conditions.

tions cannot occur, then, it transforms athermally, by a diffusionless transformation, to a hard and brittle phase, called martensite. Martensite has a body centered tetragonal (bct) structure and is formed from austenite by a shear transformation at lower temperatures. Martensitic transformation does not involve any redistribution of carbon. Martensite has the same composition as original austenite. Martensite is metastable with respect to equilibrium phases, i.e. ferrite plus cementite. On heating, therefore, it decomposes into more stable phases. This is generally referred to as tempering of martensite and is usually carried out during the heat treatment of steels to increase the toughness of quenched steel components.

Different transformations that occur in plain carbon steels have been mentioned above. The thermodynamics and kinetics of these transformations are briefly discussed in the remaining part of this chapter, except the tempering of martensite, which is discussed later in a separate chapter.

4 FERRITE AND CEMENTITE TRANSFORMATIONS

4.1 MORPHOLOGY

The austenite to ferrite transformation in pro-eutectoid steels and the austenite to cementite transformation in hyper-eutectoid steels can be classified into few distinct morphologies, known as Dube' classification. These are schematically shown in Fig. 1.5a–f, as briefly described in the following.

(*a*) *Grain Boundary Allotriomorphs* are crystals which nucleate at the grain boundaries of austenite and then grow along these boundaries as well as

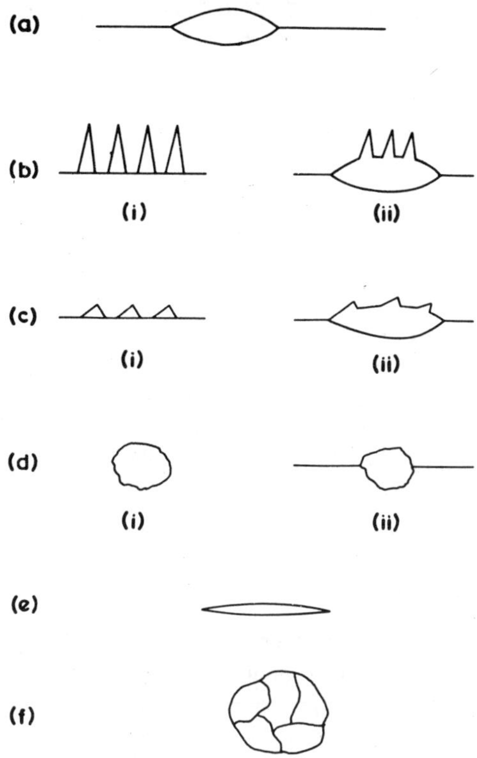

Fig. 1.5. Dube' classification of ferrite/cementite morphologies.

perpendicular to them. The growth rates along the grain boundaries are generally much faster compared to those normal to them.

(*b*) *Widmanstätten Side Plates* are plate shaped crystals which grow into the interior of austenite grains from the grain boundaries (primary side plates), or from the already existing grain boundary allotriomorphs (secondary side plates).

(*c*) *Widmanstätten Sawteeth* have triangular cross-section in the plane of polish. Like Widmanstätten plates, these grow either directly from the austenite grain boundaries or from the grain boundary allotriomorphs.

(*d*) *Idiomorphs* are roughly equiaxed crystals that are formed in the interior of the austenite grains.

(*e*) *Intragranular Widmanstätten Plates* are the plate shaped crystals formed within the interior of the austenite grains.

(*f*) *Massive Structure* is a result of the impingement of crystals from other morphologies, and of grain growth within the aggregate, to form bulky, roughly equiaxed polycrystalline masses in the microstructure.

Grain boundary allotriomorphs and Widmanstätten plates are the two most dominant morphologies that occur during the ferrite and cementite transformations in steels. Therefore, only these two morphologies are considered here. For more detailed discussion on this topic the reader is referred to [Ref. 1] given at the end of this chapter.

Ferrite and cementite transformations in steels (as also pearlite and bainite) occur by a process of nucleation and growth. The basic mechanisms of nucleation and growth of ferrite and cementite are essentially the same; hence, they are discussed in some detail for ferrite transformation, and the same, in general, would apply to cementite transformation.

4.2 NUCLEATION

Let us consider that a hypo-eutectoid Fe–C alloy of composition C_0 in Fig. 1.6 is quenched from austenite region to some temperature T below Ae_3 temperature and held there isothermally. At time $t = 0$, the alloy is then completely austenitic and it is metastable with respect to ferrite plus austenite equilibrium. Therefore, the austenite will partially transform to ferrite at this temperature. This would be true even if the isothermal holding temperature is below Ae_1 (see Fig. 1.4). Below Ae_1, the transformation occurs in accordance with the metastable (α+γ) equilibrium. The metastable phase boundaries may be obtained by extending the stable phase boundaries into the metastable region.

During the austenite to ferrite transformation, ferrite nucleates preferentially (heterogeneously) at the austenite grain boundaries and then grows along these boundaries as well as perpendicular to them. The thermodynamic driving force for the transformation is the decrease in Gibbs energy that accompanies the transformation. The Gibbs energy change per unit volume of the ferrite formed, ΔG_V, from

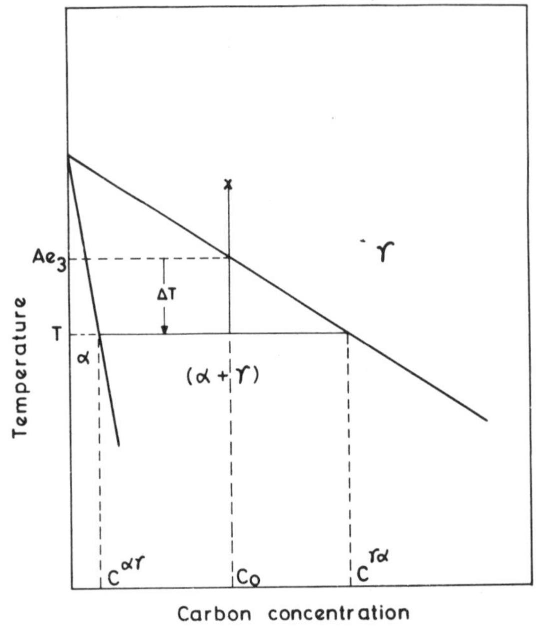

Fig. 1.6. Local equilibrium concentrations during austenite to ferrite transformation (schematic).

austenite of composition C_0, may be obtained from the Gibbs energy functions of ferrite and austenite at the temperature of transformation, as schematically shown in Fig. 1.7. The volume Gibbs energy change, ΔG_V, is negative below Ae_3. ΔG_V must be negative for the transformation to be feasible. When a nucleus/embryo of ferrite is formed in metastable austenite, apart from the appearance of a volume of ferrite (which decreases the Gibbs energy), new interfaces are created, which increase Gibbs energy of the system. Furthermore, as the specific volumes of austenite and ferrite are different, elastic strains are introduced into the system to accommodate this volume change which also increase Gibbs energy of the system. The volume Gibbs energy and the strain energy contributions to total change in Gibbs energy are proportional to volume of the embryo, whereas the interfacial energy contributions are proportional to area of the interfaces created and/or replaced. The nucleation of ferrite occurs heterogeneously at the austenite grain boundaries by forming part of the α/γ interfaces by replacing/eliminating the high energy austenite grain boundary regions. This minimizes the positive contribution of interfacial energy to total energy required for the formation of a nucleus of ferrite. Assuming the α/γ interface to be incoherent, the shape of the ferrite embryo/nucleus formed on an incoherent (high angle) austenite grain boundary would be as shown in Fig. 1.8. The embryo is lens-shaped in the form of two spherical caps of radius of curvature R. The enclosed grain boundary area equal to πr^2 is eliminated upon the formation of such an embryo.

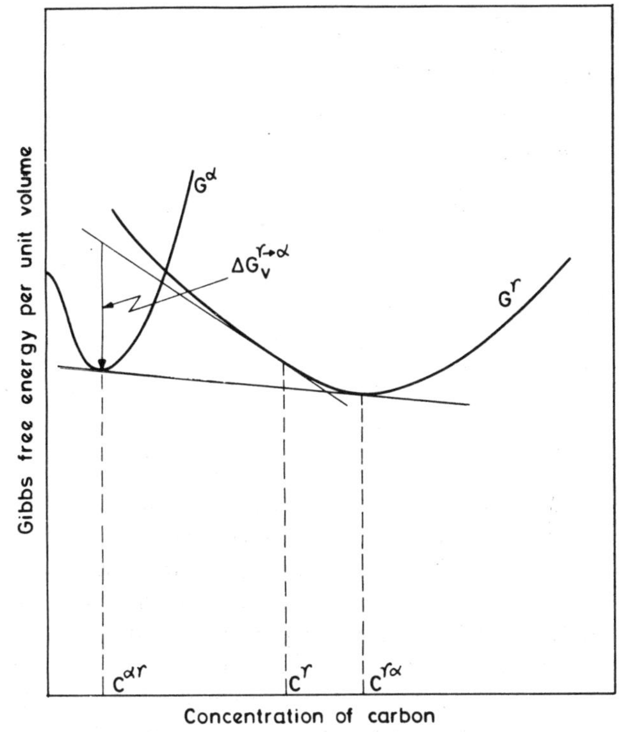

Fig. 1.7. Volume Gibbs energy change for austenite to ferrite transformation (schematic).

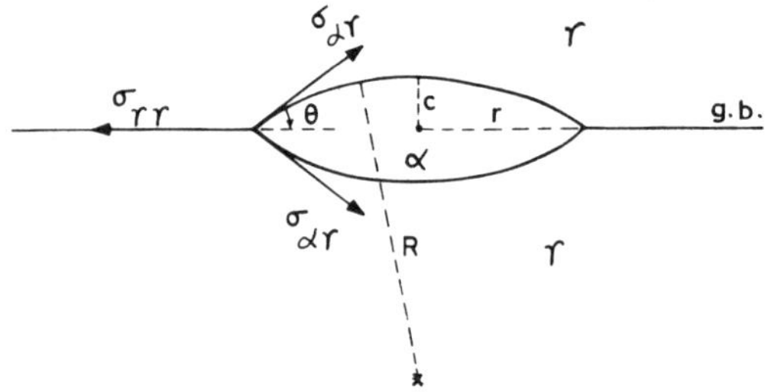

Fig. 1.8. Heterogeneous nucleus/embryo of ferrite at an austenite grain boundary (schematic).

The angle θ in Fig. 1.8 is determined by the balance of surface tension forces at the embryo/grain-boundary junction, i.e.

$$\sigma_{\gamma\gamma} = 2\sigma_{\alpha\gamma} \cos\theta \quad \text{or} \quad \cos\theta = \frac{\sigma_{\gamma\gamma}}{2\sigma_{\alpha\gamma}} \tag{1.1}$$

where $\sigma_{\gamma\gamma}$ and $\sigma_{\alpha\gamma}$ are interfacial energies of the austenite grain boundary and α/γ interface, respectively. The parameters *r* and *c* in Fig. 1.8 are related to the radius of curvature of the lens by:

$$r = R\,(\sin\theta) \tag{1.2}$$

and $$c = R\,(1 - \cos\theta) \tag{1.3}$$

The volume, *V*, of the embryo in Fig. 1.8 is given by:

$$V = \frac{2}{3}\pi R^3\,(2 - 3\cos\theta + \cos^3\theta) \tag{1.4}$$

and its total surface area, *A*, is:

$$A = 4\pi R^2\,(1 - \cos\theta) \tag{1.5}$$

The total Gibbs energy change, ΔG, accompanying the formation of the embryo can now be written as:

$$\Delta G = V(\Delta G_V + W) + A\sigma_{\alpha\gamma} - \pi r^2 \sigma_{\gamma\gamma}$$

or $$\Delta G = \frac{2}{3}\pi R^3\,(2 - 3\cos\theta + \cos^3\theta)\,(\Delta G_V + W) + \pi R^2\,[4\,(1-\cos\theta)\,\sigma_{\alpha\gamma} - (\sin^2\theta)\,\sigma_{\gamma\gamma}] \tag{1.6}$$

where *W* is strain energy per unit volume of embryo and all other terms are as defined earlier. The total Gibbs energy change, ΔG, consists of two types of terms, some proportional to R^3 (volume of the embryo) and others proportional to R^2 (interface area created and/or replaced). In Eq. (1.6), ΔG_V is always negative below Ae_3 temperature and is approximately proportional to the undercooling ΔT; $\Delta T = Ae_3 - T$; whereas, *W*, the strain energy due to the difference of ~4% in the specific volumes of ferrite and austenite is always positive. The volume term (i.e. the term proportional to R^3) in Eq. (1.6) is then negative whenever $(\Delta G_V + W)$ is negative. The transformation is possible only when this is the case. The term proportional to R^2 (the surface term) in Eq. (1.6) is always positive. Fig. 1.9 schematically shows the variation of these two terms and that of the total Gibbs energy change,

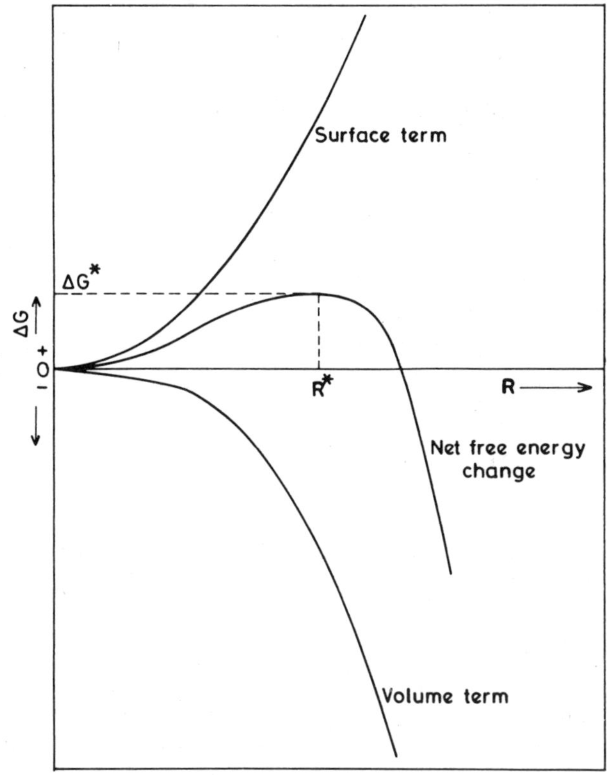

Fig. 1.9. Gibbs energy of the ferrite embryo formed heterogeneously at an austenite grain boundary as a function of its size (R) (schematic).

ΔG, of the embryo (the sum of these two terms) as a function of R. As R increases from zero, ΔG first increases, as the contribution due to the interfacial terms, proportional to R^2, dominates, goes through a maximum at $R = R^*$, and then, decreases as the volume term, negative and proportional to R^3, starts dominating. According to the second law of thermodynamics, at a given temperature and pressure, a process occurs spontaneously in a direction in which Gibbs energy decreases. Hence, an embryo of $R < R^*$ will spontaneously dissolve, whereas, the one with $R > R^*$ will spontaneously grow. The embryo of size $R = R^*$ is called critical nucleus and the Gibbs energy change, ΔG^*, required for the formation of critical embryo is called activation energy of nucleation. R^* may be obtained by finding the maximum of ΔG from Eq. (1.6), i.e.

$$\frac{\partial (\Delta G)}{\partial R} = 0, \quad \text{at } R = R^* \tag{1.7}$$

which gives:

$$R^* = -\frac{2\sigma_{\alpha\gamma}}{(\Delta G_V + W)} \tag{1.8}$$

and substituting this value of R in eq. (1.6), we obtain:

$$\Delta G^* = \frac{8\pi\sigma_{\alpha\gamma}^3}{3\,(\Delta G_V + W)^2}\,(2 - 3\cos\theta + \cos^3\theta) \tag{1.9}$$

As the formation of a critical nucleus involves an increase in Gibbs energy of the system (note that ΔG^* is always positive), it can form only through statistical fluctuations and the probability of its formation is proportional to $\exp[-\Delta G^*/(kT)]$, where k is Boltzmann's constant and T is temperature in degrees Kelvin. The critical nucleus becomes stable once its size exceeds R^*. This is achieved with the addition of one more atom to the critical nucleus. The probability of one more atom joining the nucleus is proportional to $\exp[-\Delta G_D/(kT)]$, where ΔG_D is activation energy for the addition of one more atom to the nucleus across the nucleus/matrix interface. The rate of nucleation, n, of ferrite at the austenite grain boundaries may then be written as:

$$n \propto \exp\left[-\frac{(\Delta G^* + \Delta G_D)}{kT}\right] \tag{1.10}$$

The proportionally constant in Eq. (1.10) depends on the number of nucleation sites available, n_s, and some other factors. Hence:

$$n = K(T)\,n_s \exp\left[-\frac{(\Delta G^* + \Delta G_D)}{kT}\right] \tag{1.11}$$

where the constant $K(T)$ is, in general, a function of temperature. However, its variation with temperature is negligible as compared to that of the exponential terms in Eq. (1.11); n_s (number of nucleation sites per unit volume) is essentially equal to the total number of atoms per unit volume at the austenite grain boundaries.

In Eq. (1.11), ΔG_D is essentially independent of temperature, whereas, ΔG^* strongly varies with temperature in accordance with Eq. (1.9). In Eq. (1.9), $\sigma_{\alpha\gamma}$ (interfacial energy) and W (strain energy) are both positive and approximately independent of temperature, $\cos\theta$ depends on the relative magnitudes of $\sigma_{\alpha\gamma}$ and $\sigma_{\gamma\gamma}$ [Eq. (1.1)], but is always positive and lies between 0 and 1, whereas, ΔG_V is negative and its magnitude increases with decreasing temperature, approximately linearly with undercooling ΔT ($\Delta T = Ae_3 - T$). As long as $(\Delta G_V + W)$ is positive, a net decrease in total Gibbs energy upon the formation of ferrite is not possible [see Eq. (1.6)] and no nucleation will take place. With decreasing temperature, when $(\Delta G_V + W)$ becomes zero, ΔG^* is infinite and the rate of nucleation, according to Eq. (1.11), is zero. With further decrease in temperature, ΔG_V becomes more and more negative, the magnitude of $(\Delta G_V + W)$ increases and ΔG^* decreases. The rate of nucleation, then, increases rapidly with decreasing temperature as long as ΔG^* is substantially larger than ΔG_D. At still lower temperatures, where ΔG^* becomes negligible as compared to ΔG_D, the rate of nucleation decreases with decreasing temperature and is essentially proportional to $\exp[-\Delta G_D/(kT)]$. At some intermediate temperature, where ΔG^* and ΔG_D are of comparable magnitude, the rate of nucleation would go through a maximum. Figure 1.10 schematically shows the variation of rate of nucleation with temperature.

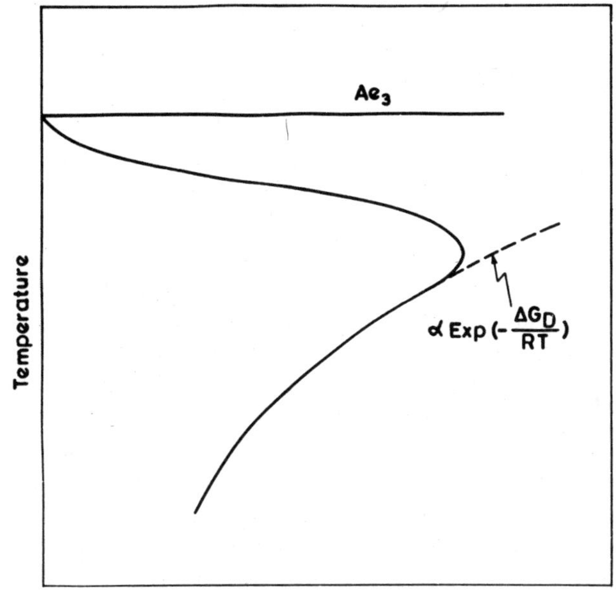

Fig. 1.10. Schematic variation of rate of nucleation of ferrite as a function of temperature.

In the above discussion, the nucleation of ferrite has been qualitatively discussed and general variation of the nucleation rate with temperature has been arrived at. The same would, in general, be applicable to the nucleation of cementite during austenite to cementite transformation in hyper-eutectoid steels. The theory of nucleation discussed above is in qualitative agreement with the experimental observations on ferrite and cementite nucleation. A more quantitative agreement between experiment and the theory of nucleation has generally not been possible for solid state transformations.

4.3 GROWTH OF GRAIN BOUNDARY ALLOTRIOMORPHS

Once nucleated at the austenite grain boundaries, the ferrite nuclei grow along the grain boundaries as well as perpendicular to them. As the carbon content of ferrite that is formed, $C^{\alpha\gamma}$ in Fig. 1.6, is lower than that of the original austenite concentration, C_0, carbon must diffuse away from α/γ interface for the ferrite to grow. When α/γ interface is incoherent (completely disordered), as in the case of grain boundary allotriomorphs, interface mobility is relatively high and the growth rate is essentially controlled by the rate at which carbon is removed (by diffusion) from the advancing α/γ interface. Under these conditions, the interface is essentially in local equilibrium, i.e. the carbon concentrations on either side of the interface are given by equilibrium phase boundary concentrations, $C^{\alpha\gamma}$ in ferrite and $C^{\gamma\alpha}$ in austenite (see Fig. 1.6).

The growth of ferrite allotriomorphs along the austenite grain boundaries (ie. lengthening of the allotriomorphs) is much faster than perpendicular to them (i.e. thickening of the allotriomorphs). Lengthening of allotriomorphs occurs mostly by carbon diffusion through the α/γ and γ/γ interfaces, as schematically shown in

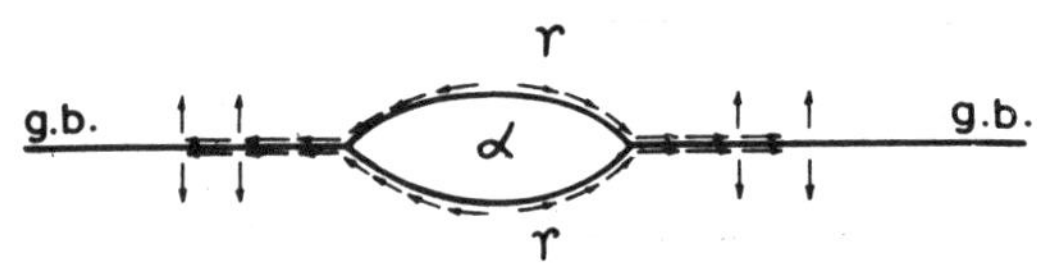

Fig. 1.11. Carbon diffusion paths during the lengthening of ferrite grain boundary allotriomorphs by interface diffusion.

Fig. 1.11. Diffusion through incoherent inerfaces is, in general, orders of magnitude faster than through the austenite matrix, and hence, the much faster lengthening rates of ferrite allotriomorphs along the austenite grain boundaries. The ferrite allotriomorphs, which nucleate randomly at the grain boundaries of austenite and grow relatively faster along them, soon impinge upon each other, forming a continuous ferrite film covering whole of the austenite grain boundaries before any susbstantial thickening of these allotriomorphs can occur. The overall rate of formation of ferrite is, then, controlled by the growth rate of ferrite allotriomorphs perpendicular to the austenite grain boundaries. The rate of thickneing (growth) of ferrite allotriomorphs in the early stages can then be treated as a one-dimentional diffusion problem, where, essentially planar α/γ interfaces grow normal to the austenite grain boundaries and can be approximately solved for as follows.

Let us consider that austenite of composition C_0 is quenched to a temperature T in the $(\alpha + \gamma)$ region, and held there isothermally (Fig. 1.6). It is assumed that the time taken for the ferrite to nucleate and completely cover the austentite grain boundaries (by lengthening of ferrite allotriomorphs) is negligible. Furthermore, in early stages of the thickening process, carbon concentration in austenite far away from the advancing α/γ interface may be considered to be same as original austenite concentration, C_0. This will not be true during the later stages of transformation, when carbon diffusion fields in austenite from the opposite sides of a grain start overlapping. Now, let the ferrite allotriomorph thickness from the original austentite grain boundary be equal to x at any time t greater than zero, starting from $x = 0$ at $t = 0$. Under the conditions of semi-infinite plane front growth (as described above) and assuming local-equilibrium at the α/γ interface, the carbon concentration distribution at any time t on either side of the austenite grain boundary can be approximated as shown in Fig. 1.12. Ferrite growth on other side of the austenite grain boundary would also occur in the same manner. In Fig. 1.12, the carbon concentrations, $C^{\alpha\gamma}$ and $C^{\gamma\alpha}$, on either side of the α/γ interface are given by the local equilibrium condition and may be obtained from the Fe–C phase diagram, as schematically shown in Fig. 1.6. The ferrite has uniform concentration of $C^{\alpha\gamma}$ and the carbon concentration in austenite is assumed to linearly decrease from $C^{\gamma\alpha}$ at the interface to C_0 at some distance y away from the interface. Now, during the transformation, if α/γ interface has a velocity v at time t, then, the consideration of mass balance at the interface gives:

$$v\,(C^{\gamma\alpha} - C^{\alpha\gamma}) = -D_C^{\gamma}\left[\frac{dC}{dx}\right]_x \tag{1.12}$$

where D_C^{γ} is carbon diffusion coefficent in austenite. $[dC/dx]_x$ is carbon concentration gradient in austenite at the interface and is given by:

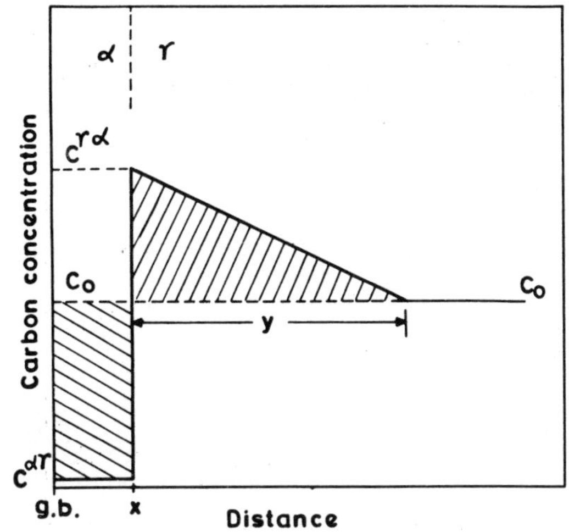

Fig. 1.12. Approximate carbon concentration profile during the thickening of grain boundary allotriomorphs (schematic).

$$\left[\frac{dC}{dx}\right]_x = -\frac{C^{\gamma\alpha} - C_0}{y} \tag{1.13}$$

Further considering the total balance of carbon, the two shaded areas in Fig. 1.12 on either side of the α/γ interface must be equal, i.e.

$$x\,(C_0 - C^{\alpha\gamma}) = \frac{1}{2}\,y\,(C^{\gamma\alpha} - C_0) \tag{1.14}$$

From Eqs. (1.12) to (1.14) and putting $v = \dfrac{dx}{dt}$, we get:

$$2x\,dx = \left[\frac{(C^{\gamma\alpha} - C_0)^2\, D_C^{\gamma}}{(C^{\gamma\alpha} - C^{\alpha\gamma})\,(C_0 - C^{\alpha\gamma})}\right] dt \tag{1.15}$$

which upon integration gives:

$$x = \left[\frac{(C^{\gamma\alpha} - C_0)^2\, D_C^{\gamma}}{(C^{\gamma\alpha} - C^{\alpha\gamma})\,(C_0 - C^{\alpha\gamma})}\right]^{1/2} t^{1/2} \tag{1.16}$$

or

$$x = \alpha\,\sqrt{t} \tag{1.17}$$

where

$$\alpha = \left[\frac{(C^{\gamma\alpha} - C_0)^2\, D_C^{\gamma}}{(C^{\gamma\alpha} - C^{\alpha\gamma})\,(C_0 - C^{\alpha\gamma})}\right]^{1/2} \tag{1.18}$$

The ferrite growth rate, v, is then given by:

$$v = \frac{dx}{dt} = \left(\frac{\alpha}{2}\right)\frac{1}{\sqrt{t}} \tag{1.19}$$

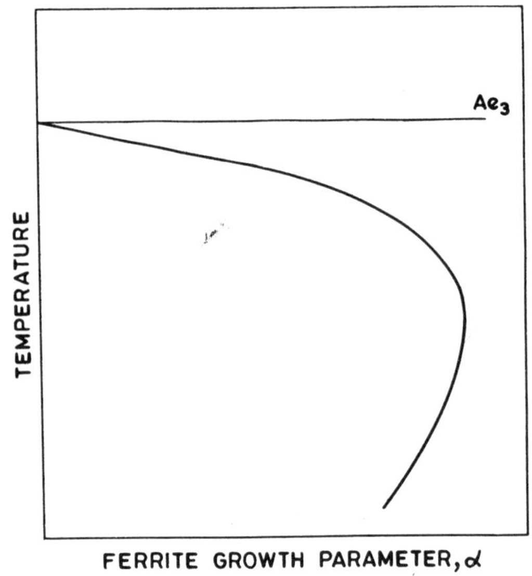

Fig. 1.13. Variation of the ferrite growth rate parameter, α, with the temperature of transformation (schematic).

where α is given by Eq. (1.18) and is known as ferrite growth rate parameter. Thickness of the ferrite allotriomorphs is, then, proportional to the square root of time (Eq. (1.17)] and their growth velocity is inversely proportional to square root of time [Eq. (1.19)]. Such a growth behaviour is normally referred to as parabolic growth and is typical of several diffusion controlled processes. In the above analysis, ferrite growth only on one side of the austenite grain boundary has been considered. Growth occurs symmetrically on the other side of the boundary also. Hence, Eq. (1.17) gives only half thickness of the ferrite grain boundary allotriomorphs.

The ferrite growth rate parameter α in Eq. (1.18) is a function of supersaturation of austenite, $(C^{\gamma\alpha} - C_0)$, (or undercooling ΔT) and the diffusion coefficient of carbon in austenite, D_C^γ. $(C^{\gamma\alpha} - C_0)$ is 0 at Ae_3. As the temperature is decreased below Ae_3, $(C^{\gamma\alpha} - C_0)$ increases approximately linearly with the undercooling, ΔT, whereas the diffusion coefficent D_C^γ decreases exponentially with decreasing temperature.* As a result, with decrease in the temperature of isothermal holding below Ae_3, the growth rate parameter, α, [Eq. (1.18)] first increases (from zero at Ae_3), goes through a maximum and then decreases, as schematically shown in Fig. 1.13.

---

* The diffusion coefficient of carbon in austenite is a function of temperature as well as concentration and is given by:

$$D_C^\gamma = D_0 \exp\,[-Q/RT]$$

where, $D_0 = 0.5 \exp\,[-30X]$ cm²/s

and, $Q = 160{,}250 - 7.95 \times 10^5 X + 2.3 \times 10^6 X^2$ J/mole

where X is carbon concentration in atomic fraction.

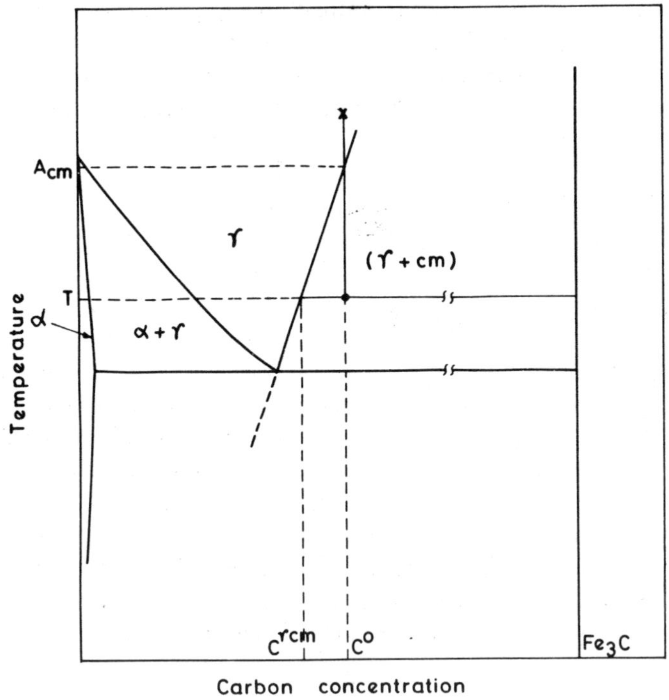

Fig. 1.14. Local equilibrium concentrations during the growth of cementite in a hyper-eutectoid steel (schematic).

A similar analysis of the growth of cementite grain boundary allotriomorphs in a hyper-eutectoid steel would give a growth rate equation similar to Eq. (1.19) with the growth rate parameter α as:

$$\alpha = \left\{ \frac{(C_0 - C^{\gamma cm})^2 \; D_c^{\gamma}}{(C^{cm} - C^{\gamma cm}) \; (C^{cm} - C_0)} \right\}^{1/2} \tag{1.20}$$

where, the concentration terms in Eq. (1.20) are as schematically shown in Fig. 1.14.

A more rigorous solution of the diffusion problem in plane front, semi-infinite, one-dimensional ferrite (or cementite) growth, with local equilibrium at the interface, gives the growth parameter α in Eq. (1.19) as:

$$\alpha = \frac{2}{\sqrt{\pi}} \frac{(C^{\gamma\alpha} - C_0)}{(C^{\gamma\alpha} - C^{\alpha\gamma})} \frac{\exp\,(-\alpha^2/4)}{erfc\;(\alpha/2)} \tag{1.21}$$

Equation (1.21) gives a more accurate solution but has to be solved for α by iterative methods. An equivalent equation for α parameter for camentite growth can be obtained by using appropriate concentrations from Fig. 1.14 in Eq. (1.21). Values of the growth parameter, α, calculated by using the approximate solution [Eq. (1.18)] are a good approximation to the actual solution [Eq. (1.21)], particularly at small supersaturations. Ferrite/cementite growth rates calculated by using the above discussed solutions agree well with the experimental data within the experimental error and uncertainty in the diffusion data. The solutions discussed above are only valid for the early stages of transformation. At later stages, when the carbon diffusion profiles in austanite from opposite sides of the grains start overlapping, the rate of carbon diffusion and consequently the ferrite growth rates are slower than given by the above equations.

4.4 GROWTH OF WIDMANSTÄTTEN SIDE PLATES

(i) Crystallography

The Widmanstätten side plates are formed due to inherent instability of planar α/γ interface during the plane front growth of grain boundary allotriomorphs. The theory of instability of plain front growth is rather involved and will not be discussed here. The Widmanstätten side plates are more likely to form under conditions of high supersaturation and/or large austenitic grain size. Widmanstätten side plates, either formed directly from the grain boundaries or from the grain boundary allotriomorphs, grow as plates into the austenite grains. Widmanstätten plates have a definite crystallographic orientation relationship with the austenite grains into which they grow. This may be seen from the fact that these plates grow only in certain specific directions within a given austenite grain. The specific crystallographic relationship that is observed is called Kurdjumov and Sachs relationship and is given by:

$$(111)_\gamma \parallel (110)_\alpha$$

and

$$[1\bar{1}0]_\gamma \parallel [1\bar{1}1]_\alpha$$

i.e. the close packed planes of crystal lattices of α and γ and the closest packed directions in these planes are parallel to each other. This relationship exists along the broad faces of the Widmanstätten side plates which are approximately parallel to each other. The interface between ferrite and austenite along these faces is semi-coherent, i.e. it consists of regions of complete one-to-one matching of atoms on either side of the interface separated by regions of interfacial dislocations. Such an interface, in general, has very low mobility. However, the interface at the tips of these plates is incoherent (completely disordered) and highly mobile.

(ii) Growth Kinetics

The sideways growth (thickening) of Widmanstätten ferrite plates is much slower as compared to the edgewise growth (lengthening). This is primarily due to difference in the nature of interfaces at the broad faces and at the tips of these plates. Interfaces at the broad faces of these plates are semi-coherent with the austenite matrix and have very low mobility. Such interfaces can only move either by coordinated movement of atoms across the interface (by some kind of interfacial dislocation motion), or by a ledge mechanism as shown in Fig. 1.15. The latter is a more likely mechanism for the sideways growth (thickening) of Widmanstätten plates. Ledges at the broad faces of these plates have incoherent interfaces with the austenite matrix. These ledges can move along the broad faces of the plates by carbon diffusion control, in a manner similar to the movement of incoherent α/γ interfaces during the growth of ferrite grain boundary allotriomorphs, as schematically shown in Fig. 1.15. The rate of thickening of these plates would, then, depend on the density and height

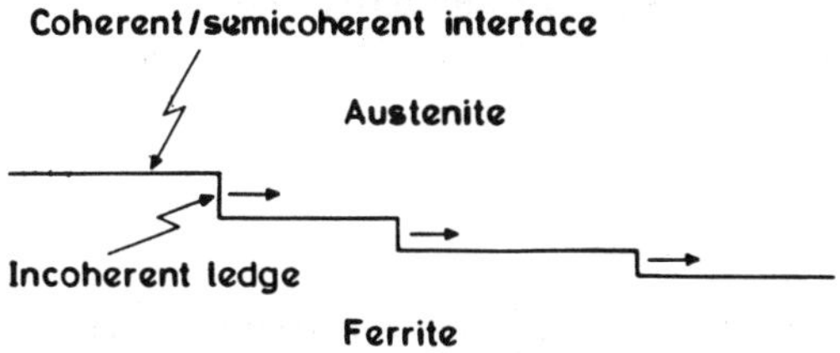

Fig. 1.15. Thickening of Widmanstätten plates by ledge mechanism.

of these ledges. In general, the overall thickening process is very much slower than the lengthening process.

Tip of a Widmanstätten ferrite plate is incoherent with the austentite matrix and it grows by carbon diffusion control. Let us consider the lengthening kinetics of Widmanstätten plates in a Fe–C alloy of composition C_0 in Fig. 1.6, quenched from the austenitic range to a temperature T below Ae_3. The high mobility incoherent interface at the tip is essentially in local equilibrium with the austenite matrix. However, as the interface at the tip is curved (Fig. 1.16), the local equilibrium concentrations across the interface are different than the ones given by the Fe–C phase diagram. The local equilibrium concentrations across a curved interface are a function of the radius of curvature of the interface due to Gibbs–Thompson effect and are equal to the ones given by the phase diagram only when the interface is flat. In the present case, since the solubility of carbon in ferrite is very small, the concentration of carbon in ferrite at all curvatures may be considered to be the same as given by the phase diagram, i.e. $C^{\alpha\gamma}$ in Fig. 1.6, whereas the local equilibrium concentration, $C_r^{\gamma\alpha}$, in austenite across the interface of radius of curvature r will be less than $C^{\gamma\alpha}$ and is given as:

$$C_r^{\gamma\alpha} = C^{\gamma\alpha}\left(1 - \frac{V\sigma_{\alpha\gamma}}{RTrk^{\gamma\alpha}}\right) \tag{1.22}$$

where V is molar volume of ferrite, $\sigma_{\alpha\gamma}$ is interfacial energy of the α/γ interface, $K^{\gamma\alpha}$ is a thermodynamic factor approximately equal to 1, R is gas constant and T is temperature in degrees Kelvin. As seen from Eq. (1.22), $C_r^{\gamma\alpha}$ decreases as the radius of curvature, r, decreases. There, then exists a critical radius of curvature, $r^{\#}$, such

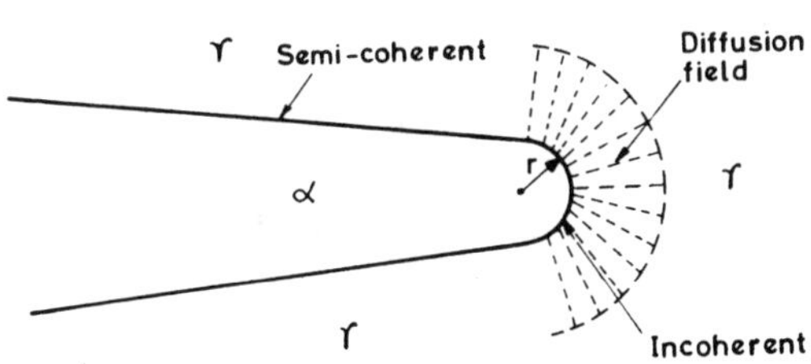

Fig. 1.16. Tip of a Widmanstätten plate growing into the austenite grain.

that $C_r^{\gamma\alpha} = C_0$, where C_0 is carbon concentration of original austentite. Therefore, when $r = r^{\#}$, tip of the ferrite plate is in equilibrium with austenite of composition C_0 and there is no carbon concentration gradient in austenite ahead of the inerface. Under these conditions, carbon does not diffuse away from the interface and the Ferrite plate does not grow. The critical radius of curvature, $r^{\#}$, from Eq. (1.22), is given by:

$$r^{\#} = \frac{V\sigma_{\alpha\gamma}\ C^{\gamma\alpha}}{RTk^{\gamma\alpha}\ (C^{\gamma\alpha} - C_0)} \tag{1.23}$$

The ferrite growth will, then, take place only when $r > r^{\#}$. The local equilibrium carbon concentration, $C_r^{\gamma\alpha}$, in austenite at the interface of radius of curvature r is given by Eq. (1.22). When $r > r^{\#}$, then $C_r^{\gamma\alpha} > C_0$. Carbon is now removed from the interface by carbon diffusion and the plate will grow. During the growth of the plate tip, diffusion of carbon in austenite can be approximated as radial diffusion in cylindrical coordinates (see Fig 1.16). and such a diffusion geometry gives a constant rate of growth. Here an approximate analysis is given to arrive at the growth rate of the tip, i.e. the lengthening rate of a Widmanstätten plate. The difference in carbon concentrations in austenite at the plate tip and far away from the interface, $(C_r^{\gamma\alpha} - C_0)$, from Eqs. (1.22) and (1.23) is given by:

$$(C_r^{\gamma\alpha} - C_0) = (C^{\gamma\alpha} - C_0)\left(1 - \frac{r^{\#}}{r}\right) \tag{1.24}$$

Now, if the average diffusion distance of carbon ahead of the interface is L and v is the edgewise growth rate of the plate tip, then, mass balance at the interface gives:

$$v\ (C_r^{\gamma\alpha} - C^{\alpha\gamma}) = D_C^{\gamma}\left[\frac{(C_r^{\gamma\alpha} - C_0)}{L}\right]$$

or $$v = \frac{D_C^{\gamma}\ (C_r^{\gamma\alpha} - C_0)}{L\,(C_r^{\gamma\alpha} - C^{\alpha\gamma})} \tag{1.25}$$

where D_C^{γ} is diffusion coefficient of carbon in austenite. Now, assuming $(C_r^{\gamma\alpha} - C^{\alpha\gamma}) \cong (C^{\gamma\alpha} - C^{\alpha\gamma})$ and substituting from Eq. (1.24), we get:

$$v = \frac{D_C^{\gamma}\ (C^{\gamma\alpha} - C_0)}{L\,(C^{\gamma\alpha} - C^{\alpha\gamma})}\left(1 - \frac{r^{\#}}{r}\right) \tag{1.26}$$

The detailed diffusion analysis gives $L = 2r$, and hence:

$$v = \frac{D_C^{\gamma}}{2}\ \frac{(C^{\gamma\alpha} - C_0)}{(C^{\gamma\alpha} - C^{\alpha\gamma})}\ \frac{1}{r}\left(1 - \frac{r^{\#}}{r}\right) \tag{1.27}$$

Equation (1.27) gives growth velocity v as a function of the radius of curvature r of the plate tip. The velocity at which the plate will actually grow, must then be determined by some additional criterion. The maximum growth rate criterion, suggested by Zener, is normally used. This states that the growth will take place at the maximum possible velocity. Such a maximum occurs at $r = 2r^{\#}$ and the growth rate is, then, given by:

$$v = \frac{D_C^{\gamma}}{8\,r^{\#}}\ \frac{(C^{\gamma\alpha} - C_0)}{(C^{\gamma\alpha} - C^{\alpha\gamma})} \tag{1.28}$$

Substituting for $r^{\#}$ from Eq. (1.23), we get:

$$v = D_C^{\gamma} \frac{RTk^{\gamma\alpha}}{8\,V\sigma_{\alpha\gamma}} \frac{(C^{\gamma\alpha} - C_0)^2}{C^{\gamma\alpha}\,(C^{\gamma\alpha} - C^{\alpha\gamma})} \tag{1.29}$$

Eq. (1.29) gives the lengthening rate of Widmanstätten plates under isothermal conditions. The temperature dependence of the growth rate of Widmanstätten plates is similar to that of the ferrite allotriomorphs (Fig. 1.13), i.e. at Ae_3 the growth velocity is zero, as $C^{\gamma\alpha} = C_0$, and with decreasing temperature, it first increases as $(C^{\gamma\alpha} - C_0)$ increases, goes through a maximum, and then, decreases with decreasing temperture as the effect of exponentially decreasing D_C^{γ} overtakes the effect of increasing undercooling.

5 PEARLITE TRANSFORMATION

5.1 NUCLEATION

Like ferrite and cementite transformations, the pearlite transformation also occurs by a process of nucleation and growth. Pearlite also nucleates heterogeneously at the austenite grain boundaries. In hypo-eutectoid and hyper-eutectoid steels, pearlite grows (at the later stages of transformation) from the already formed ferrite and cementite, respectively. In steels of eutectoid composition, the active nuclei for the formation of pearlite, i.e. the nuclei that form first and determine the nucleation rate, are either ferrite or cementite. Hence, the general theory for the nucleation of ferrite, presented in Sec.4.2, also holds good for pearlite nucleation.

5.2 GROWTH

Pearlite is a lamellar structure of ferrite (α) and cementite (cm). After nucleation, the cooperation between α and cm is soon set up and pearlite, consisting of essentially parallel alternate lamellae of ferrite and cementite of approximately uniform thickness, grows into austenite with a constant inter-lamellar spacing and a constant rate of growth. At low undercoolings, where the nucleation rate is low (and may be confined to grain corners), the nuclei of pearlite are far apart and they grow at a constant rate in all directions as spherical nodules of pearlite. However, at larger undercoolings, where the nucleation rate is high, pearlite nodules (nucleated at austenite grain boundaries) soon impinge on each each other, covering the grain boundary surfaces, and then grow with an essentially planar front into the austenite grains.

Though the average composition of pearlite is the same as that of austenite from which it grows, the growth of pearlite requires redistribution of carbon as the compositions of α and cm phases that constitute pearlite are very different. Figure 1.17 shows a schematic picture of the lamellar structure of pearlite. The α phase in pearlite has negligible carbon concentration, whereas the concentration of the cm phase (Fe_3C) is ~6.67%C. During the growth of pearlite into metastable austenite, the redistribution of carbon to ferrite and cementite may take place either by the diffusion of carbon in austenite matrix ahead of the γ/pearlite interface or by phase boundary diffusion through the γ/pearlite interface itself. In Fe–C alloys, the diffusion of carbon during pearlite growth essentially occurs through the austenite

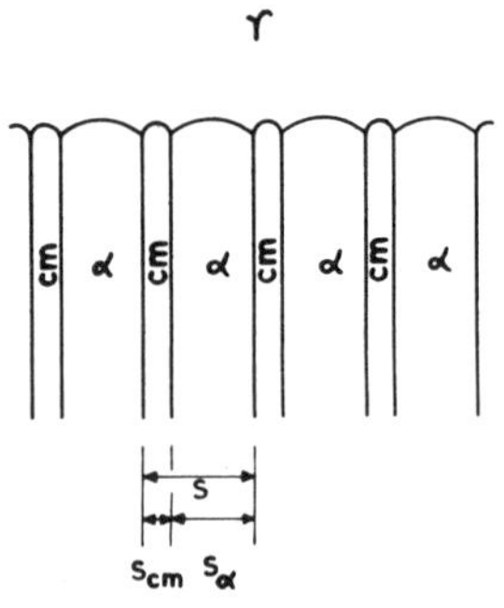

Fig. 1.17. Lamellar structure of pearlite (schematic).

matrix (volume diffusion control). Therefore, only the theory of volume diffusion-controlled pearlite growth will be discussed here.

Let us consider the isothermal growth of pearlite in an eutectoid steel at temperature T, ΔT below the Ae_1 temperature (Fig. 1.18). Let the inter-lamellar spacing of pearlite be S ; S_α of ferrite and S_{cm} of cementite with $S_\alpha + S_{cm} = S$; as shown in Fig. 1.17. We further assume the incoherent γ/pearlite interface to be in local equilibrium. The interface of α and cm phases of pearlite with the γ phase is curved and the curvature is maximum at the α–cm–γ three phase junction. For local equilibrium to exist at the α–cm–γ three phase junction, the local equilibrium concentration of carbon in austenite at this point must be C^γ, i.e. the carbon concentration of original austenite. Note that, due to Gibbs–Thompson effect, with increase in curvature the local equilibrium concentration in austenite at the α/γ interface decreases from a maximum of $C^{\gamma\alpha}$ (Fig. 1.18) at zero curvature and that at the cm/γ interface increases

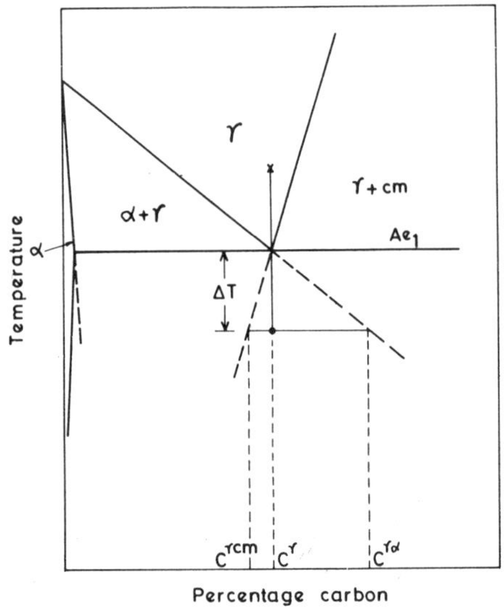

Fig. 1.18. Local equilibrium concentration during pearlite growth.

from a minimum of $C^{\gamma cm}$ (Fig. 1.18) at zero curvature. The interface curvature does not affect the equilibrium concentration of cementite, as it is a stoichiometric compound and has little effect on the equillibrium concentration of ferrite, as the solubility of carbon in ferrite is very small. The curvatures of α/γ and cm/γ interfaces at the three phase junction is such that a local equilibrium concentration of C^{γ} is obtained in austenite at this point. The interface curvature decreases as one moves away from the three phase junction and is minimum at the centres of ferrite and cementite lamellae. The local equilibrium concentration of carbon in austenite is, then, maximum at the centres of α lamellae and minimum at the centres of cm lamellae, as minimum curvature exists at these points. When curvature at these points is zero, local equilibrium concentrations would be $C^{\gamma\alpha}$ and $C^{\gamma cm}$, respectively (Fig. 1.18). The carbon can thus diffuse in austenite parallel to the γ/pearlite interface as well as perpendicular to it. The concentration profile of carbon in austenite ahead of the growing γ/pearlite interface is schematically shown in Fig. 1.19. The detailed diffusion analysis of the pearlite growth problem will not be discussed here; however, an approximate analysis is given in the following.

As pearlite grows into austenite, the total thermodynamic driving force, ΔG_V (Fig. 1.20), for the transformation is dissipated in two different ways: (*i*) in creating the α/cm interfaces in pearlite, behind the growing γ/pearlite inteface, and (*ii*) in the growth of pearlite by diffusion of carbon (dissipation by diffusion). The total area of α/cm interfaces increase with decreasing inter-lamellar spacing, S. Thus, there must exist a minimum spacing, S_0, at which all the thermodynamic driving force is spent in creating the α/cm interfaces and no pearlite growth takes place. At this spacing, the curvature along the γ/pearlite interface is such that the local equilibrium concentration in austenite is C^{γ} all along the interface. Thus there is no driving force for diffusion of carbon and consequently, the pearlite does not grow. The critical (minimum) inter-lamellar spacing, S_0, is related to the volume Gibbs energy change, ΔG_v, for the γ to pearlite transformation by:

$$\frac{2\sigma_{\alpha cm}}{S_0} = -\Delta G_V \qquad (1.30)$$

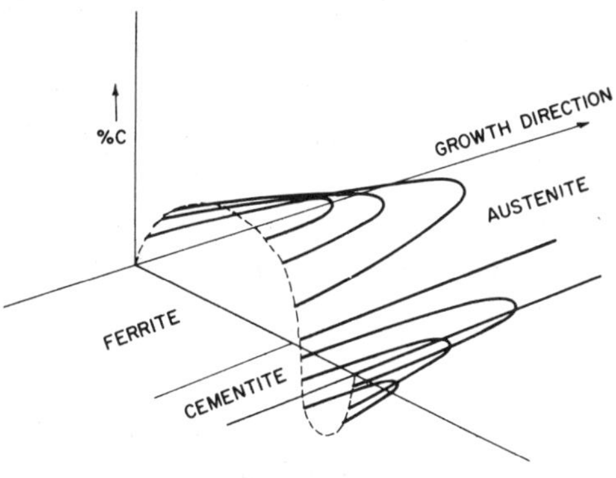

Fig. 1.19. Contours of equal carbon concentration ahead of the pearlite front growing by carbon volume diffusion control.

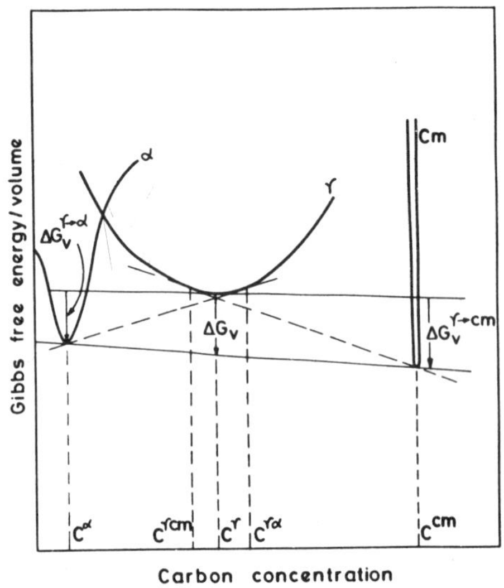

Fig. 1.20. Volume Gibbs energy changes for austenite to pearlite transformation.

where $\sigma_{\alpha cm}$ is interfacial Gibbs energy of the α/cm interface per unit area and $2/S_0$ is total area of the α/cm interfaces per unit volume of pearlite at spacing S_0. Left hand side of Eq. (1.30) is the total interfacial energy stored in α/cm interfaces per unit volume of pearlite of inter-lamellar spacing S_0. Note that ΔG_V is negative. From Eq. (1.30):

$$S_0 = -\frac{2\sigma_{\alpha cm}}{\Delta G_V} \tag{1.31}$$

Now, for any spacing S greater than S_0, the thermodynamic driving force in excess of what is required for creating the α/cm interfaces is $\Delta G_v (1 - S_0/S)$. To a first approximation, the total driving force, ΔG_V, is directly proportional to relative supersaturation, i.e. $(C^{\gamma\alpha} - C^{\gamma cm})/(C^{cm} - C^{\alpha})$,where all the concentration terms are as defined earlier and in Figs. 1.18 and 1.20. Thus, the thermodynamic driving force contributing to the growth of pearlite by diffusion is proportional to $(1 - S_0/S)(C^{\gamma\alpha} - C^{\gamma cm})/(C^{cm} - C^{\alpha})$. Furthermore, as the growth of pearlite requires redistribution of carbon, the pearlite growth rate is directly proportional to the diffusion coefficient of carbon in austenite, D_C^{γ}, and inversely proportional to the average diffusion distance, which as a first approximation may be taken as proportional to inter-lamellar spacing, S. Hence, the pearlite growth rate, v, may be written as:

$$v = K\frac{D_C^{\gamma}}{S}\frac{(C^{\gamma\alpha} - C^{\gamma cm})}{(C^{cm} - C^{\alpha})}\left(1 - \frac{S_0}{S}\right) \tag{1.32}$$

where K is a constant. A more detailed diffusion analysis of the pearlite growth problem gives the proportionality constant K in Eq. (1.32) as:

$$\frac{1}{K} = \frac{1}{\pi^3}\left(\frac{S^2}{S_\alpha S_{cm}}\right)^2 \sum_{n=1}^{\infty}\frac{1}{n^3}\sin^2\left(n\pi\frac{S_\alpha}{S}\right) \tag{1.33}$$

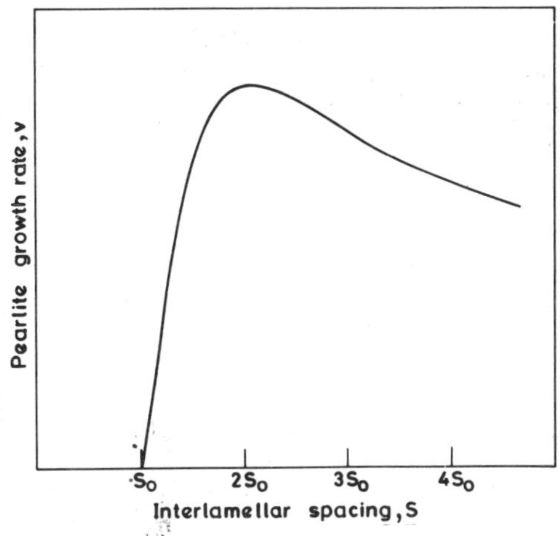

Fig. 1.21. Pearlite growth velocity according to eq. (1.32) as a function of inter-lamellar spacing at a given temperature (schematic).

According to Eq. (1.32), the pearlite growth rate v is a function of interlamellar spacing S, as schematically shown in Fig. 1.21. At a given temperature, pearlite actually grows at a constant rate and fixed inter-lamellar spacing. The actual rate at which pearlite grows must, then, be determined by using some additional optimization criterion. Zener has suggested that the growth would occur at the maximum possible rate, which according to Eq. (1.32) occurs at $S = 2S_0$. Accordingly, the pearlite growth rate is given by:

$$v = \frac{KD_c^{\gamma}}{4\,S_0}\,\frac{(C^{\gamma\alpha} - C^{\gamma cm})}{(C^{cm} - C^{\alpha})} \tag{1.34}$$

The volume Gibbs energy change, ΔG_v, for pearlite transformation is to a first approximation also proportional to undercooling ΔT (Fig. 1.18). Hence, according to Eq. (1.31) S_0 (and so also S) is inversely proportional to ΔT ($\Delta T = Ae_1 - T$). In agreement with this, the experimental results give a straight line relationship between $1/S$ and T, with the intercept along the T-axis at eutectoid temperature (Ae_1), as shown in Fig. 1.22. Furthermore, in Eq. (1.34) ($C^{\gamma\alpha} - C^{\gamma cm}$) to also approximately proportional to ΔT and ($C^{cm} - C^{\alpha}$) is essentially constant, and hence, Eq. (1.34) can also be written as:

$$v = K'\,D_C^{\gamma}\,(\Delta T)^2 \tag{1.35}$$

where K' is a constant. In Eq. (1.35) ΔT increases linearly and D_C^{γ} decreases exponentially with decreasing temperature. Thus, the pearlite growth rate initially increases with decreasing temperature (or increasing ΔT) from zero at Ae_1, goes through a maximum and then decreases at still lower temepratures, where the effect of exponentially decreasing D_C^{γ} dominates. Figure 1.23 shows experimental pearlite growth rates as a function of temperature for the eutectoid Fe–C alloy. These are in general agreement with Eq. (1.34), (or Eq. (1.35). The maximum in growth velocity

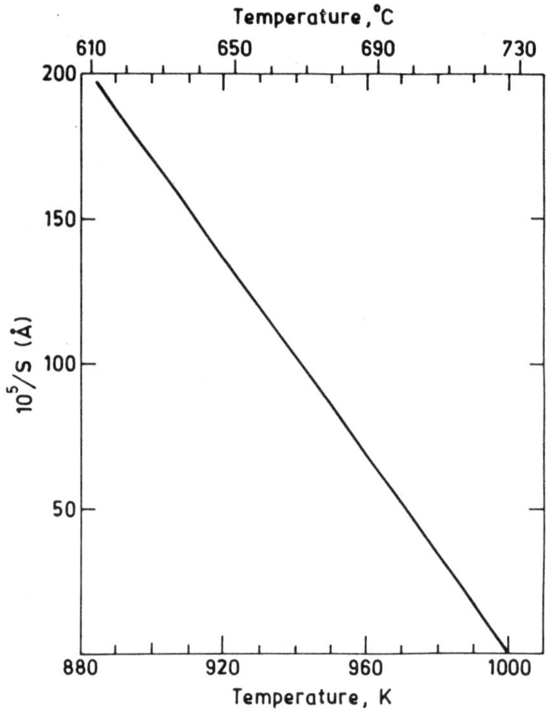

Fig. 1.22. Pearlite inter-lamellar spacing as a function of temperature in Fe–C eutectoid steel (experimental).

with decreasing temperature occurs at a still lower temperature than shown in Fig. 1.23.

6 BAINITE TRANSFORMATION

6.1 NATURE OF BAINITE

Bainite reaction, which occurs at temperatures lower than ~773K (500°C) in Fe–C alloys of all compositions (see Fig. 1.4), can be considered as a non-cooperative simultaneous precipitation of ferrite plus carbides. It is further classified, based on the microstructural features, into upper and lower bainite. Figure 1.24 shows typical microstructures of upper (a) and lower (b) bainite.

Upper bainite consists of laths (or plates) of ferrite with carbide (cementite) precipitation between these plates. A number of ferrite plates together, essentially parallel to each other,, form a packet. Within a packet, the plates are separated by small angle grain boundaries, whereas the boundaries between different packets are high angle boundaries. The growth of upper bainite is essentially controlled by the growth of ferrite plates, and cementite forms in the carbon-enriched regions adjacent to these plates. Furthermore, the bainitic plates may nucleate sympathetically next

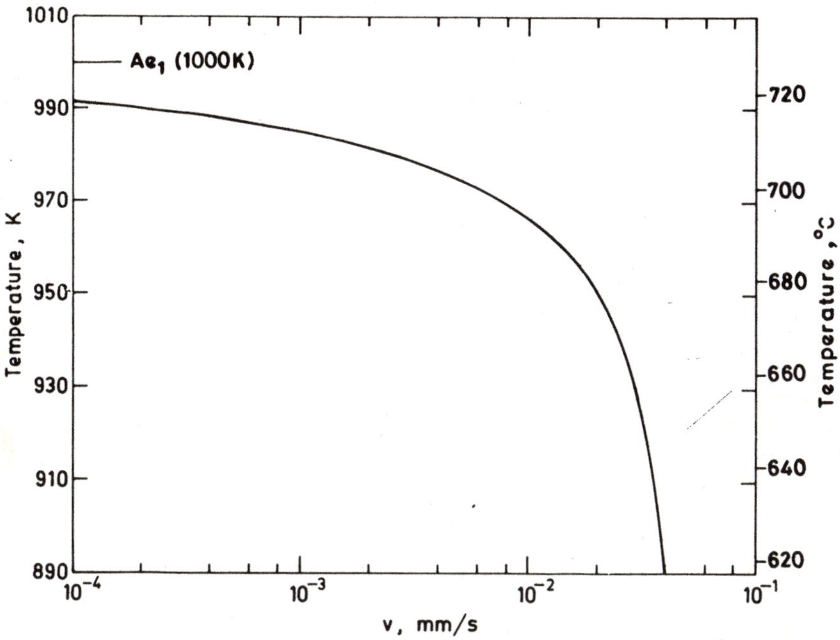

Fig. 1.23. Pearlite growth rate as a function temperature in Fe–C eutectoid steel (experimental).

to the existing plates. The overall transformation rate is then controlled by the frequency of sympathetic nucleation as well as the growth rates.

Lower bainite consists of accicular ferrite, with fine carbide precipitation occurring essentially within these plates. The carbide precipitates have specific crystallographic orientation relationships with the ferrite plates in which they form. In lower bainite, formed at relatively lower temperatures, the carbide that precipitates inside the ferritic plates could be hexagonal ε-carbide rather than cementite. The carbide precipitates in lower bainite are much finer and more uniformly distributed as compared to upper bainite, where cementite forms as thin films between essentially carbide-free ferritic plates.

The exact temperature ranges in which upper and lower bainite form upon isothermal transformation from austenite depend on the composition of steel. In general, upper bainite forms approximately between 623K and 773K (350°C to 500°C) and lower bainite below ~623K (350°C).

6.2 GROWTH

Growth of upper as well as lower bainite is controlled by the growth of ferritic (bainitic) plates. Bainitic plates grow in the same manner as Widmanstätten ferrite plates and their growth may be represented by the same equations as developed earlier for the growth of Widmanstätten plates.

To calculate the growth rates of bainitic plates by using Eq. (1.29), the metastable $\gamma/(\alpha + \gamma)$ and $\alpha/(\alpha + \gamma)$ phase boundaries must be known far below their stable

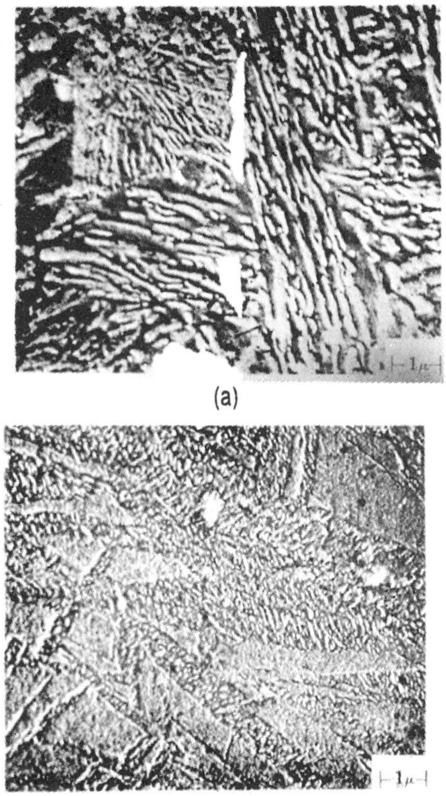

Fig. 1.24. Microstructure of (a) upper bainite, and (b) lower bainite.

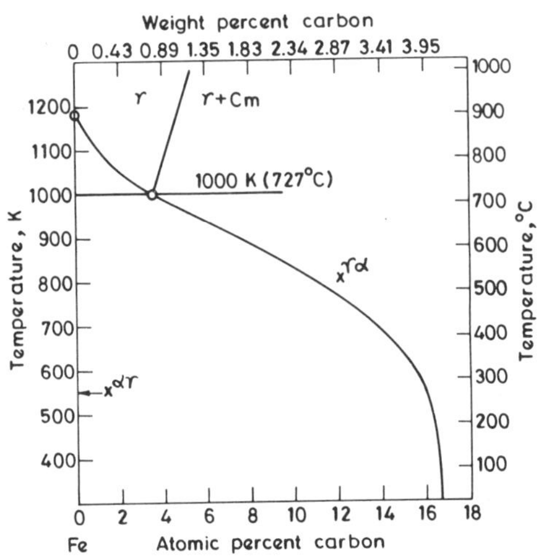

Fig. 1.25. Calculated metastable extensions of $\gamma/(\alpha+\gamma)$ and $\alpha/(\alpha+\gamma)$ phase boundaries in the Fe–C system (from Kaufman, Radcliffe and Cohen in Ref. 1).

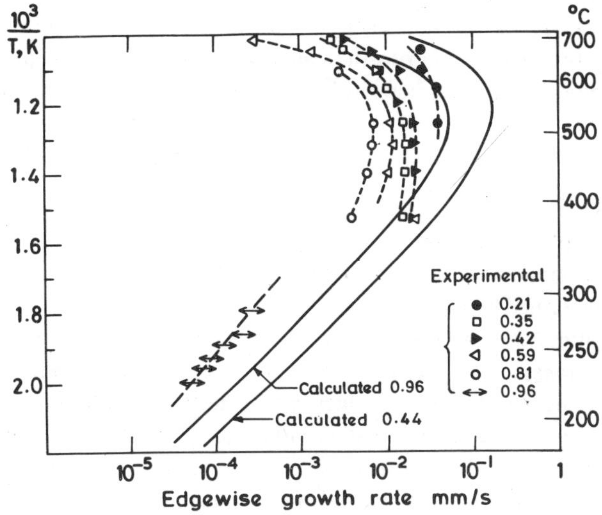

Fig. 1.26. Comparison between the experimental and calculated growth rates of bainite and Widmanstätten plates in Fe–C alloys of different carbon-contents.

range. Number of calculations of these boundaries, based on thermodynamic modelling of the α and γ phases and phase equilibria calculations, exist in literature. The results of one such calculation are shown in Fig. 1.25 (Ref. 1, p. 330). While calculating the growth rate of bainite, using Eq. (1.29), the variation of diffusion coefficient of carbon with concentration (Sec. 4.3) must also be taken into account. The growth rates of bainitic plates calculated from the above considerations are compared with the experimental results in Fig. 1.26. Also shown in this figure are some results of the growth rates of Widmanstätten plates at higher temperatures. The agreement, in general, may be considered to be good, keeping in view the uncertainties in the calculations. It also testifies that the growth mechanism of Widmanstätten plates and that of bainitic plates (lower as well as upper) is essentially the same.

7 MARTENSITE TRANSFORMATION

7.1 INTRODUCTION

When a steel is rapidly cooled (quenched) from austenitic range to room temperature; at a cooling rate sufficient to suppress its decomposition by diffusional processes to ferrite, cementite, pearlite and/or bainite; then it transforms athermally to a hard and brittle phase called martensite. Rapid cooling is normally achieved by directly quenching the austenitized steel to room temperature in water, oil or some other suitable quenching medium. The martensite, thus formed, has the same composition as the austenite from which it forms. The martensitic transformation is sometimes also called diffusionless transformation, as no redistribution of carbon or other alloying elements occurs during the transformation.

The martensite phase in steels has a body centred tetragonal (bct) structure, whose c/a ratio varies with the carbon content of martensite. Crystal structure of martensite is relatively closer to that of ferrite, the stable phase in iron at room temperature, than to that of austenite. The bct structure of c/a ratio equal to one is same as bcc structure and the c/a ratio of martensite varies form ~1.0 for very low carbon steels to ~1.1 for high carbon steels. Therefore, martensite is also generally designated as α'.

For a steel of given composition, the martensitic transformation starts at a specific temperature called martensite start temperature, M_s, and is completed at some specific lower temperature called martensite finish temperature, M_f. The fraction of austenite transformed to martensite is generally a function of temperature only and it increases continuously from zero at M_s to unity (or completion) at M_f. The time taken for the transformation to occur at a given temperature is negligible, i.e. the transformation occurs at very rapid rates, almost instantly. If the cooling is stopped between M_s and M_f, the transformation is halted and it proceeds only on further cooling. This is unlike the diffusional transformations, discussed earlier, which occur at rates characteristic of transformation temperatures. For this reason, the martensite transformation is also called athermal transformation. Such a transformation must occur without any thermally activated movements of atoms. Hence, during martensite transformation, the relative changes in atomic positions must normally be less than interatomic distances and the atoms must move in a coordinated manner. Martensite also has a definite crystallographic orientation relationship with the lattice of austenite in which it forms.

Martensitic transformation has been a subject of intensive investigations. The mathematical and crystallographic theories of martensite transformation are complex and beyond the scope of this book. Therefore, only general features of martensite transformation in Fe–C alloys are discussed here.

7.2 CRYSTAL GEOMETRY OF $\gamma \rightarrow \alpha'$ TRANSFORMATION

The transformation of face centred cubic (fcc) structuure of austenite to the body centred tetragonal (bct) structure of martensite, involving atomic movements smaller than interactomic distrances that occur during martensite transformation, can be geometrically understood by what is called Bain transformation, shown in Fig. 1.27. Fig. 1.27(i) shows two adjacent unit cells of fcc lattice of austenite. A body centred tetragonal unit cell of c/a ratio equal to $\sqrt{2}$ can be formed within these two fcc unit cells as shown in Fig. 1.27(i). In this figure, for the sake of clarity, only atomic positions that form the bct cell are marked as (o). By similar consideration of other fcc unit cells, the fcc lattice may be completely filled by such bct unit cells. Hence, it may be said that the fcc structure is equivalent to a bct structure of c/a ratio equal to $\sqrt{2}$. The unit cell of such a bct structure is separately shown in Fig. 1.27(ii). The c/a ratio of martensite is much less than $\sqrt{2}$ and is also a function of the carbon content of martensite, as shown in Fig. 1.28. The transformation of fcc lattice (austenite) to a bct lattice of c/a ratio less than $\sqrt{2}$ (martensite) may, then, be achieved by compressing the tetragonal unit cell in Fig. 1.27(ii) along the c-axis with simultaneous expansion along the a-axis to obtain the bct unit cell of martensite, shown in

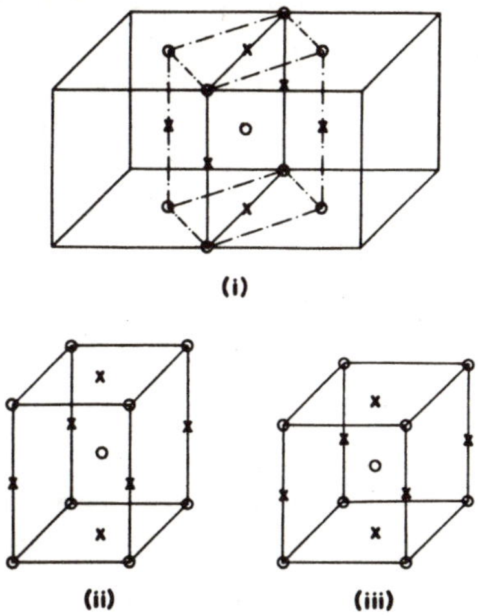

Fig. 1.27. Bain transformation; transformation of fcc structure of austenite to bct structure of martensite.

Fig. 1.27(iii). Such a geometrical transformation of fcc to bct is known as Bain transformation, and is achieved by atomic movements smaller than interatomic distances that do not require any thermal activation.

The *c/a* ratio of martensite is a function of its carbon content as shown in Fig. 1.28. Carbon forms an interstitital solution in iron. Carbon atoms in solution in the fcc

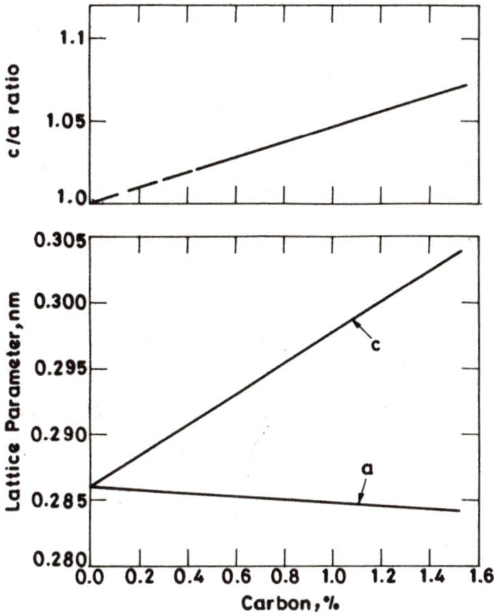

Fig. 1.28. Lattics parameters and c/a ratio of martensite in Fe–C alloys as a function of carbon concentration [after C.S. Roberts, Trans AIME **197** (1953) p. 203].

lattice of austenite randomly occupy octahedral interstitial sites. These sites exist at the centres of all edges of fcc unit cells as well as at the centres of these cells. Random occupation of these sites by carbon atoms uniformly dilates the fcc lattice. In Fig. 1.27 some of these sites, relevant to the consideration of fcc to bct transformation, are marked at (x). When fcc lattice is considered as a bct lattice of *c/a* ratio of $\sqrt{2}$, the octahedral interstitial sites (that carbon atoms occupy) are not any more uniformly distributed in all the lattice directions of bct, but exist only at the centres of cell edges along the *c*-axis and at the centres of top and bottom faces of the bct cell, positions equivalent to the centres of edges along the *c*-axis, as seen in Fig. 1.27. The presence of carbon atoms selectively along the *c*-axis of bct cells prevents the Bain transformation from converting the fcc austenite lattice to a bcc lattice of α-iron by resisting the compression along the *c*-axis. Thermodynamically stable phase in iron at these temperatures is bcc iron and the bcc lattice is equivalent to a bct lattice of *c/a* ratio of 1.0. Hence, the degree of tetragonality of martensite, i.e. its *c/a* ratio, decreases with decrease in carbon content (Fig. 1.28) and it approaches 1.0 as the carbon content approaches zero. The Bain transformation, discussed above, clearly demonstrates the possibility of $\gamma \rightarrow \alpha'$ transformation with atomic movements much smaller than the interatomic distances.

7.3 THERMODYNAMICS OF MARTENSITE TRANSFORMATION

Thermodynamically, the $\gamma \rightarrow \alpha'$ transformation may be considered as a transformation of austenite to ferrite of the same composition. This is a reasonable assumption as the structure of martensite is very close to that of ferrite and ferrite (α-Fe) is the stable phase in iron at these temperatures. Furthermore, the *c/a* ratio of bct structure of α′ is much closer to 1.0, which corresponds to bcc lattice, than to $\sqrt{2}$, which corresponds to the fcc lattice, as discussed in the previous section. Hence, martensite (α′) may be considered as supersaturated solution of carbon in α-iron and the $\gamma \rightarrow \alpha'$ transformation as a transformation of austenite to ferrite of the same composition. In the Fe–C phase diagram, a phase boundary, T_0, can be defined where the α and γ phases of the same compositon are in metastable thermodynamic equilibrium. Such a phase boundary may be obtained from the Gibbs energy functions of α and γ phases. Figure 1.29 schematically shows Gibbs energy vs composition curves for ferrite and austenite phases at some temperature *T*, below 1185K (912°C). The usual common tangent construction gives the stable two-phase $(\alpha + \gamma)$ equilibrium compositions, $C^{\gamma\alpha}$ and $C^{\alpha\gamma}$, whereas at the intersection of Gibbs energy curves of α and γ phases at composition C_0, α and γ phases of the same composition are in metastable equilibrium. At compositions lower than C_0, α phase is stable as compared to γ phase of the same composition, as the Gibbs energy of α is lower than that of γ, whereas, the reverse would be true at compositions higher than C_0. The locus of C_0 as a function of temperature, then defines the phase boundary T_0 for metastable equilibrium between α and γ phases of the same composition and can be obtained from thermodynamic calculations. The result of one such calculation of T_0 boundary in Fe–C system is shown in Fig. 1.30 (Ref. 1, p. 330). Transformation of γ to α phase of the same composition (i.e. the martensite transformation) is, then, thermodynamically feasible below T_0. Figure 1.30 also shows experimental marten-

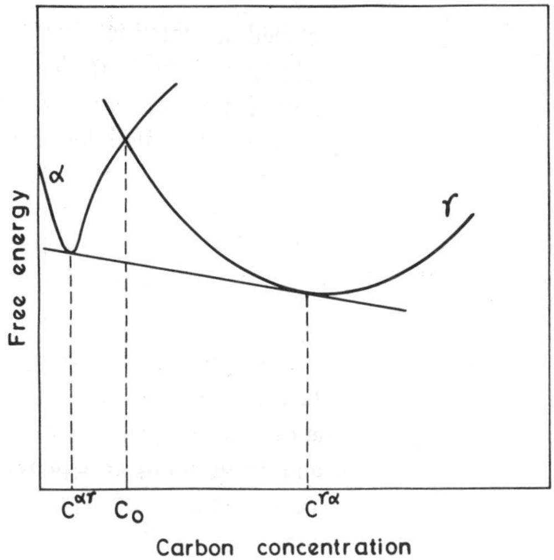

Fig. 1.29. Gibbs energy-composition diagram for α and γ phases at a temperature T, lower than 1185K.

site start temperature, M_s, in Fe–C alloys as a function of composition. The M_s line is lower than T_0 and is approximately parallel to it. The $\gamma \rightarrow \alpha'$ transformation in steels is accompanied by a ~4% volume expansion. The transformation, therefore, would be energetically possible only when the magnitude of chemical driving force of transformation, ΔG_V, becomes larger than the strain energy introduced due to

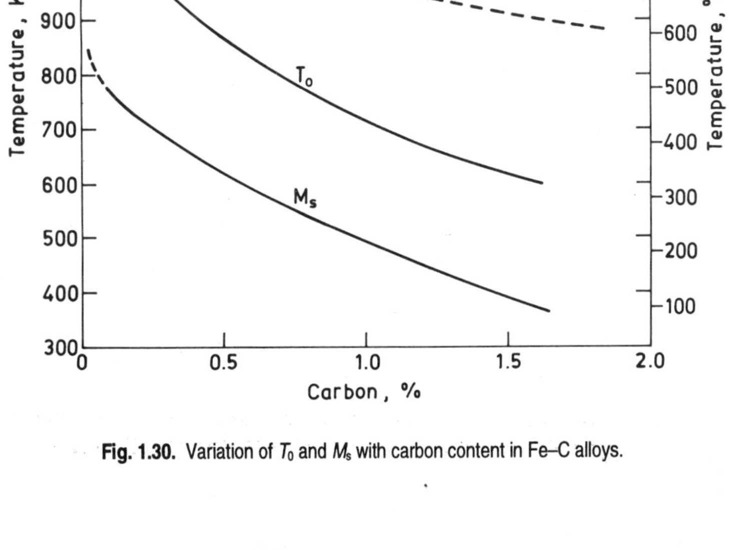

Fig. 1.30. Variation of T_0 and M_s with carbon content in Fe–C alloys.

volume change, so that the transformation is accompanied by a net decrease in Gibbs energy of the system. The Gibbs energy change per unit volume for $\gamma \rightarrow \alpha'$ transformation, ΔG_V, is negative below T_0 and its magnitude increases approximately linearly with undercooling ΔT ($\Delta T = T_0 - T$); whereas, the strain energy due to volume change is positive and approximately independent of temperature. Hence, the $\gamma \rightarrow \alpha'$ transformation becomes energeticaly feasible only below certain temperature lower than T_0 where ΔG_V becomes equal in magnitude to the strain energy per unit volume. Hence, M_s is lower than T_0.due to the strain energy involved during martensite transformation.

In Fe–C alloys, martensite transformation occurs athermally as mentioned earlier. The amount of martensite formed is a function of temperature only and it increases continuously with decreasing temperature between M_s and M_f, as schematically shown in Fig. 1.31. Figure 1.32 gives the variation of M_s and M_f temperatures for

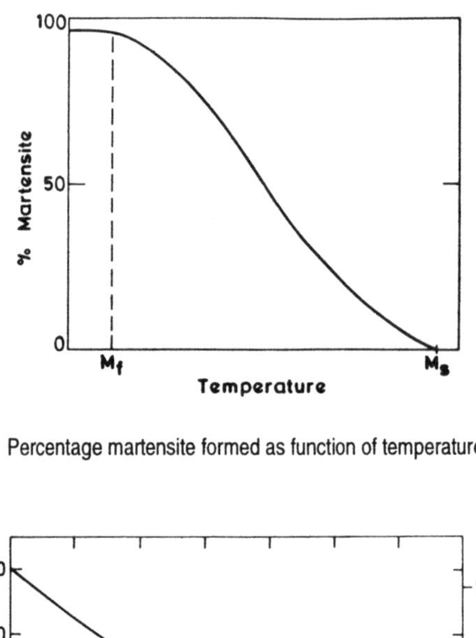

Fig. 1.31. Percentage martensite formed as function of temperature (schematic).

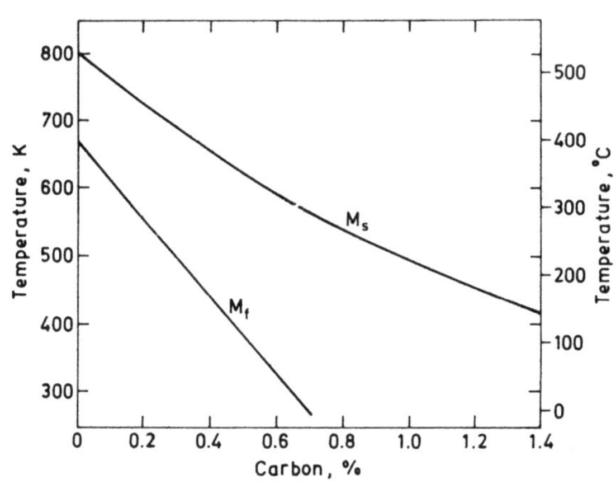

Fig. 1.32. Variation of M_s and M_f temperatures in Fe–C alloys as a function of carbon content [after A.R. Troiano & A.B. Greninger, Metal Progress, **50** (1946) p. 303].

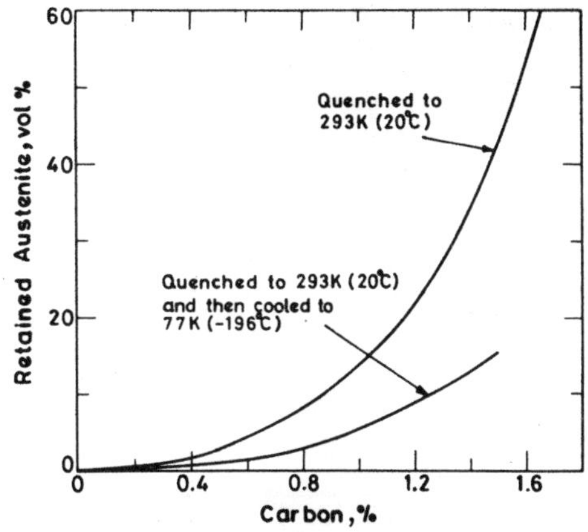

Fig. 1.33. Retained austenite as a function of carbon content in Fe–C alloys on quenching to room temperature and on further cooling to liquid nitrogen temperature. [after C.S. Roberts, Trans AIME **197** (1953) p. 203].

Fe–C alloys as a function of carbon content. The M_f temperature for high carbon alloys is below room temperature and a certain amount of untransformed austenite (called retained austenite) will be present on quenching these alloys to room temperature. This may be reduced by further cooling to temperatures below room temperature. Figure 1.33 shows the variation of retained austenite in Fe–C alloys as a function of carbon content on quenching to room temperature and on further cooling to liquid nitrogen temperature.

7.4 MORPHOLOGY OF MARTENSITE

Microstructurally, martensite exists in two principal morphologies, lath martensite and accicular martensite. The typical lath and accicular martensite structures formed in Fe–C alloys are shown in Fig. 1.34. Lath martensite is the common morphology in low and medium carbon steels. In lath martensite, martensite crystals are in the form of thin plates extending in one direction. A number of these crystals, essentially parallel to each other, together form dense packets. The adjacent crystals within a packet are separated by low angle boundaries. The width of crystals within a packet is roughly the same and it varies from ~0.1 to a few μm. The lath martensite crystals generally contain high density of dislocations, of the order of $10^{11} - 10^{12}$ cm^{-2}.

Accicular martensite is more typical of high carbon steels. Here, the martensite crystals have the form of thin lenticular plates. This shape of martensite platelets corresponds to the minimization of their elastic energy. In accicular martensite, the plates are not parallel to each other. The plate which form first (close to M_s) penetrate the whole austenite grain, essentially dividing it into two. The subsequent plates (formed on further lowering the temperature) form in the remaining parts of the austenite grains. The martensite plates cannot grow past grain boundaries or already formed martensite plates, and hence, their maximum size is limited by the

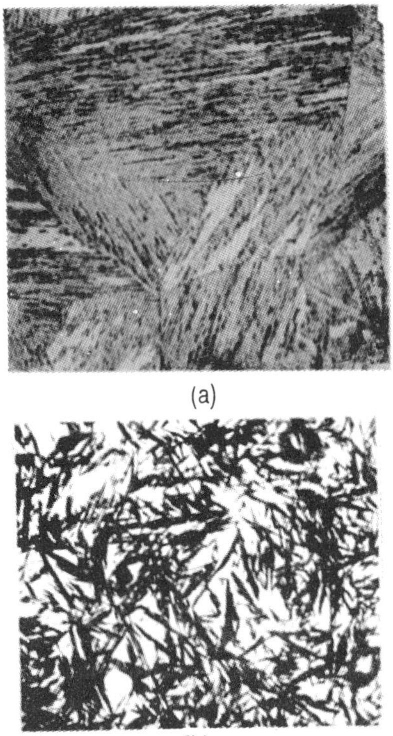

(a)

(b)

Fig. 1.34. Microstructure of martensite
(a) lath martensite (× 100), (b) accicular martensite (× 1000).

prior austenite grain size. The martensite plates in high carbon accicular martensite are, in general, highly twinned.

7.5 MECHANISM OF MARTENSITE TRANSFORMATION

Martensite transformation occurs with extremely high growth rates at relatively low temperatures. The growth rate of martensitic plates is essentially independent of temperature. This implies that no thermally activated atomic movements take place during the transformation. It has been shown earlier (Sec.7.2) that the crystal transformation from γ to α' can be obtained by atomic movements much smaller than interatomic distances. Furthermore, for the $\gamma \rightarrow \alpha'$ transformation to occur in this manner, atoms must move in a coordinated manner and the interface between γ and α', therefore, must be coherent or at the most semi-coherent. The mechanism of lattice rearrangement during martensite transformation has been described as follows:

> ''The martensitic transformation occurs by regular rearrangement of the lattice in which atoms do not change places, but are merely displaced relative to one another over distances not exceeding the interatomic distances''.

By the very nature of martensitic transformation, the crystal lattices of γ and α' must have certain orientation relationships to one another. In iron alloys, three main orientation relationships are known. Kurdjumov-Sach's orientation relationship, given by:

$$(111)_A \parallel (101)_M$$

and

$$[1\bar{1}0]_A \parallel [11\bar{1}]_M$$

is found in carbon steels in the range 0.05 – 1.4% C. In the austenite fcc lattice there are four $\{111\}$ planes, each containing three $\langle 110 \rangle$ directions. Hence, there are twelve possible orientations of martensite crystals in a given austenite grain. Nishiyami's orientation relationship, given by:

$$(111)_A \parallel (101)_M$$

and

$$[1\bar{2}1]_A \parallel [10\bar{1}]_M$$

is found in Fe–Ni alloys contained 27–34% Ni. The third orientation relationship, found in some martensites in iron alloys, called Greninger–Troiano relationship, is intermediate to the two relationships discussed above.

Apart from a specific orientation relationship, formation of martensite is accompanied by surface relief effects and there exists an invariant habit plane, which neither distorts nor deforms during the transformation. This habit plane is the boundary plane between austenite and martensite crystals. The various habit planes which have been observed in Fe-alloys are: $(225)_A$, $(259)_A$, $(3, 10, 15)_A$ and $(111)_A$; where subscript A refers to the austenite lattice. $(111)_A$ habit planes are found in low-carbon steels, $(225)_A$ in Fe–C alloys containing 0.5 – 1.4% C, $(259)_A$ in iron alloys with 1.5 – 1.8% C and $(3, 10, 15)_A$ in some Fe–Ni alloys. The presence of a specific invariant habit plane and the observed orientation relationships between austenite and martensite crystals cannot be obtained by simple Bain transformation, discussed earlier. These can be obtained only if the Bain transformation is accompanied by rotation of the martensite crystals.

Actual martensite transformation consists of three components: (*i*) shear parallel to the habit plane, (*ii*) dilation perpendicular to the habit plane, and (*iii*) an atomic shuffle within the unit cell. Furthermore, martensite transformation occurs by nucleation and growth. The nucleation of martensite at these temperatures cannot be explained by hetero-phase thermal fluctuations. It is envisaged that the martensite nuclei are formed by dislocation interactions in the parent phase near the grain boundaries, at inclusion interfaces or some other defects. Different combinations of dislocation interactions can give rise to martensite embryos of different potencies. An embryo of certain potency, pre-existing in the austenite matrix, becomes activated at certain supersaturation, and then, spontaneously grows. The interface between martensite nucleus and austenite consists of glissile dislocations. Once nucleated, the martensite crystals grow by outward motion of interface dislocations and the nucleation of new dislocations at the tips of growing plates. The interface growth rates are, then, determined by the velocity of these dislocations and are of the order of 10^6 mm/s. The strains produced during the transformation are partly accommodated by either slip or twinning, which leads, respectively, to either high dislocation density or high twin density in martensite.

8 ISOTHERMAL TRANSFORMATION (IT) DIAGRAMS

8.1 INTRODUCTION

Isothermal Transformation (IT) diagram of a steel is a representation of the overall kinetics of isothermal transformation of austenite to low temperature products, i.e. ferrite, pearlite, bainite and martensite, at different temperatures. It is assumed that the austenite is instantly cooled to the IT temperature, and then, the progress of transformations is monitored as fraction of austenite transformed as a function of time. As both the nucleation and growth rates go through a maximum with increasing undercooling, the overall austenite transformation rate also goes through a maximum. The time required to attain a given fractional decomposition of austenite is then inversely proportional to the overall transformation rate. In an IT diagram, the time required to achieve a given fractional or percentage transformation of austenite is plotted on a temperture (T) vs time (log(t)) plot. Normally, curves for the beginning and end of the transformation are only plotted. The curves for other fractional transformations of austenite, of course, can also be plotted on the same diagram. A typical IT diagram for a hypo-eutectoid steel is schematically shown in Figure 1.35. Experimentally, it is difficult to measure the time corresponding to the beginning of the transformation. Therefore, the beginning curve usually corresponds to 0.1% or 1% austenite decomposition. Similarly, the end curve may represent 99% decomposition. Fig.1.35 also shows M_s and M_f temperatures. The M_s and M_f lines are horizontal, as martensite transformation in steels is athermal.

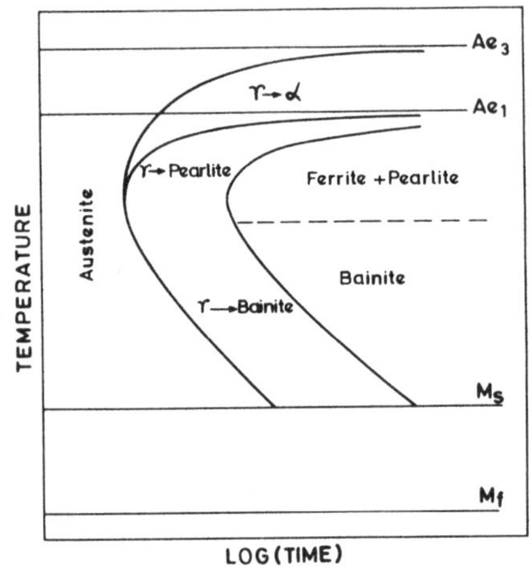

Fig. 1.35. IT diagram of a hypo-eutectoid steel (schematic).

The nose of IT diagram, i.e. the minimum time required for the beginning of austenite decomposition, at any temperature, occurs at a temperature where the rates of nucleation and growth are normally the highest. To obtain 100% martensite transformation on quenching, cooling rates from the austenite range should be such that any decomposition of austenite at temperatures higher than M_s is completely prevented. The minimum cooling rate to obtain 100% martensite transformation would depend on the position of the nose of IT start curve to a large extent. Hence, it is an important parameter.

8.2 EFFECT OF CARBON CONTENT

With increase in the carbon content of a steel, the Ae_3 temperature is lowered. Consequently, the temperature range in which $\gamma \rightarrow \alpha$ transformation takes place

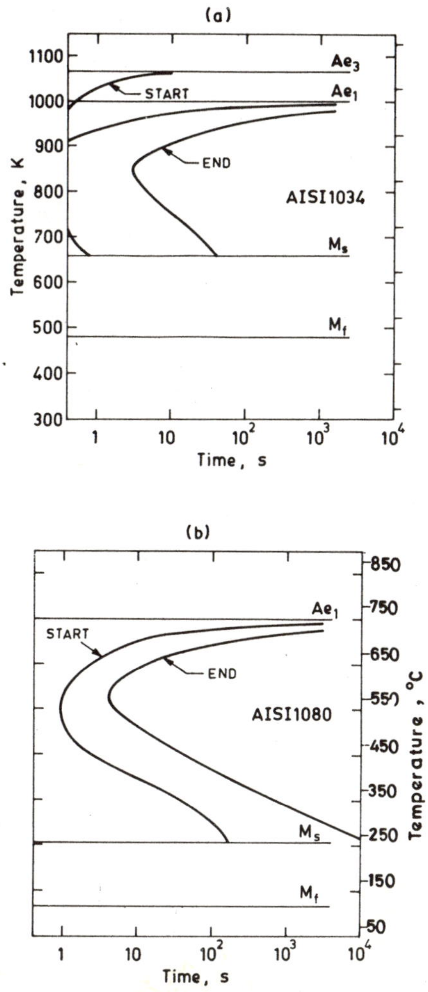

Fig. 1.36. IT diagram of (a) AISI-1034, and (b) AISI-1080 steels.

(Fig. 1.35) diminishes. In a steel of eutectoid composition, no $\gamma \rightarrow \alpha$ transformation occurs and austenite transforms fully to either pearlite or bainite, depending upon the temperature of transformation. As the carbon content increases beyond eutectoid composition, the $\gamma \rightarrow$ cm transformation occurs below A_{cm} and the pearlite and bainite transformations at lower temperatures. Furthermore, the nucleation and growth rates of ferrite at a given temperature decrease with increasing carbon content (see sec. 4), and hence, the nose of IT diagram would shift to longer times as the carbon content of a steel is increased. Figure 1.36 shows IT diagrams for AISI-1034 and AISI-1080 steels, containing 0.34% and 0.8% carbon, respectively, clearly demonstrating the above mentioned effects of carbon content on IT diagrams.

8.3 EFFECT OF GRAIN SIZE

All austenite decomposition products in steels heterogeneously nucleate at the grain boundaries of austenite. It is, therefore, expected that the prior austenite grain size would have a substantial effect on the overall kinetics of austenite decomposition. The total grain boundary area in austenite decreases as the average grain size increases. Hence, with increase in austenite grain size, the grain boundary area available for the nucleation of austenite decomposition products decreases. Therefore, to obtain the same fractional decomposition of austenite, longer time would be required in a coarse grained steel as compared to a fine grained steel of the same composition. This has the effect of shifting the start as well as the end curves of IT diagrams to longer times with increasing grain size, as schematically shown in Fig. 1.37.

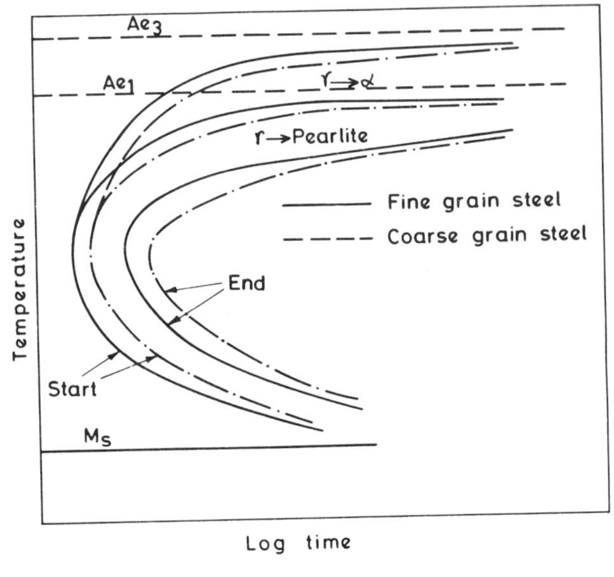

Fig. 1.37. Effect of grain size on the IT diagram of a steel (schematic).

REFERENCES

1. V.F. Zackay and H.I. Aaronson (Eds.), *Decomposition of Austenite by Diffusional Processes*, Inter Science Publishers, New York, 1962.
2. E.C. Bain and H.W. Paxton, *Alloying Elements in Steels,* 2nd Edition, American Society for Metals, Metals Park, Ohio, USA, 1962.
3. I. Novikov, *Theory of Heat Treatment of Metals*, Mir Publishers, Moscow, 1978.
4. *Phase Transformation*, Seminar Proceedings, American Society for Metals, Metals Park, Ohio, USA, 1970.

CHAPTER 2

Alloying Elements in Steels—I

(*Effect on Phase Equilibria*)

1 CLASSIFICATION

To understand the effect of alloying elements on various phase transformations in steels, and thereby on the heat treatment response of these steels, the knowledge of phase equilibria in multicomponent steels is essential. More specifically, the effect of alloying elements on the stability range of austenite, the equilibrium transformation temperatures, Ae_3, Ae_1 and A_{cm}, and the appearance of alloy carbides, if any, are of specific interest. In this chapter, phase equilibria in ternary Fe–C–M systems (where M stands for an alloying element) are considered in some detail. A limited discussion on multicomponent systems is also included. Furthermore, the discussion is limited to phase equilibria in iron-rich alloys only, mainly to the effect of alloying elements on the stabilities of austenite, ferrite and cementite phases, and the appearance of alloy carbides, if any.

Apart from carbon, the common alloying elements used in steels are: Mn, Ni, Si, Cr, Mo, Cu, W, Nb, V, Ti, etc. Based on their effect on the relative stabilities of austenite and ferrite in iron, the alloying elements in steels may be divided into: (*i*) austenite stabilizers and (*ii*) ferrite stabilizers. In binary Fe–M systems, austenite stabilizers increase the stability range of austenite by lowering the Ae_3 [i.e. $\gamma/(\alpha+\gamma)$ equilibrium] temperature and raising the Ae_4 [i.e. $\gamma/(\gamma+\delta)$ equilibrium] temperature. Carbon as an alloying element in iron is, then, an austenite stabilizing element. Other austenite stabilizing elements include: N, Mn, Ni and Cu. In the $(\alpha+\gamma)$ two phase equilibrium in ternary Fe–C–M systems, these elements, in general, preferentially segregate to the austenite phase. Figure 2.1 schematically shows the effect of a typical austenite stabilizing element M on $(\alpha+\gamma)$ equilibrium in a Fe–C–M system at some temperature T_1, below 1185K (912°C). Note that, the addition of an austenite stabilizing element in Fe–C alloys increases the stability range of austenite and decreases the Ae_3 temperature. Furthermore, orientation of the tie lines in $(\alpha+\gamma)$ region is such that, the γ phase has higher concentration of M than the α phase in equilibrium with it.

The ferrite stabilizers, on the contrary, decrease the austenite stability range of rion by raising the Ae_3 temperature and lowering the Ae_4 temperature. Elements like Si, Mo, W, V, Nb. Ti, etc., fall in this category. In the $(\alpha+\gamma)$ two-phase equilibrium in

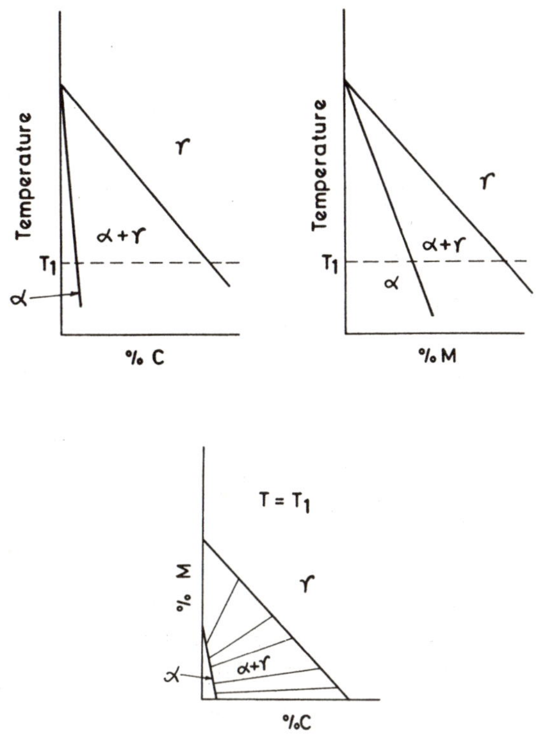

Fig. 2.1. $(\alpha + \gamma)$ equilibrium (isothermal section) in a Fe–C–M system when M is a austenite stabilizing element (schematic).

ternary Fe–C–M systems, where M stands for a ferrite stabilizing element, these elements generally segregate to ferrite in preference to austenite. Figure 2.2 schematically shows the effect of a typical ferrite stabilizing element, M, on the $(\alpha + \gamma)$ equilibrium in a Fe–C–M system. Here, with the addition of a ferrite stablizing element to Fe–C alloys, the austenite stability range is decreased and the Ae_3 temperature is increased. Cr as an alloying element in iron does not fall into any of the above categories, as they are defined. In the binary Fe–Cr system, Cr lowers the Ae_3 temperature at low concentrations while raising it at higher concentrations, whereas the Ae_4 temperature continuously decreases with increase in Cr content at all concentrations. However, the total stability range of austenite in iron is continuously decreased with increasing Cr content at all concentrations. It is, therefore, generally classified as ferrite stabilizer.

Another way, in which the alloying elements in steels may be classified, is based on their effect on the stability of cementite and their interaction with carbon, i.e. whether or not they form any alloy carbides in Fe–C–M systems. Accordingly, the alloying elements are classified as: (*i*) carbide-forming elements, and (*ii*) non-carbide-forming elements. A carbide-forming element has attractive interaction with carbon in iron and it generally increases the thermodynamic stability of cementite.

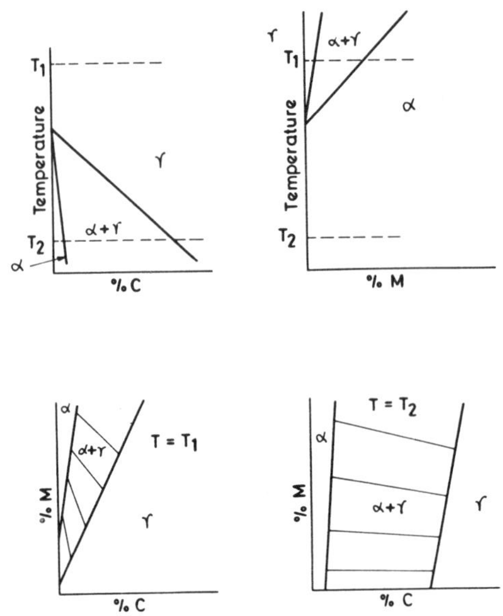

Fig. 2.2. ($\alpha + \gamma$) equilibrium (isothermal section) in a Fe–C–M system when M is a ferrite stabilizing element (schematic).

In the (γ + cm) and (α + cm) two-phase equilibria in ternary Fe–C–M systems, the carbide-forming elements segregate to cementite in preference to γ and α phases, respectively. Furthermore, at higher concentrations of a carbide-forming element, the alloy carbides may be formed. Figure 2.3 schematically shows (γ + cm) and possible (γ + alloy-carbide) equilibria in a Fe–C–M system, where M is a carbide-

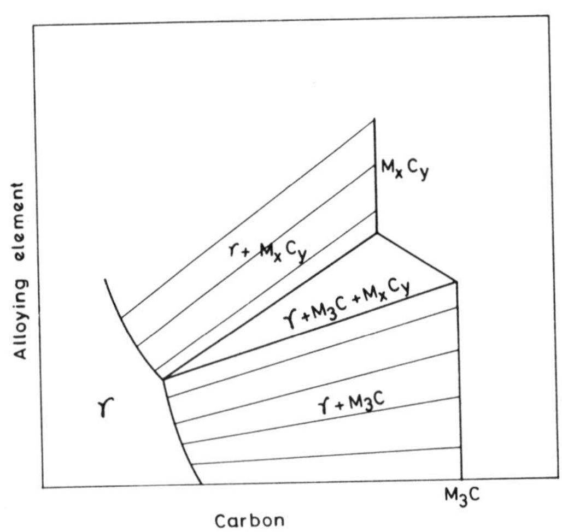

Fig. 2.3. (γ + carbide) equilibria (isothermal section) in a Fe–C–M system when M is a strong carbide-forming element and an alloy carbide M_xC_y is formed in the system (schematic).

forming element. On the other hand, non-carbide-forming elements generally have repulsive interaction with carbon in iron, and decrease the thermodynamic stability of cementite and generally segregate to γ and α phases, respectively, in (γ + cm) and (α + cm) equilibria in ternary Fe–C–M systems, where M stands for a non-carbide-forming element. No alloy carbides are formed in these systems. Figure 2.4 schematically shows the effect of a non-carbide-forming element on (γ + cm) two-phase equilibrium in a ternary Fe–C–M system. Mn, Cr, Mo, W, V, Nb, Ti, etc, are carbide-forming elements, whereas Si, Ni and Cu are non-carbide-forming. Table 2.1 summarizes the classification of alloying elements in steels, as discussed above.

Phase equilibria in important Fe–C–M systems are considered in brief in the following sections. The discussion is limited to phase equilibria in Fe-rich alloys with respect to austenite, ferrite and carbide phases only.

Table 2.1. *Classification of the Alloying Elements in Steels*

Element	*Austenite/Ferrite Stabilizer*	*Whether Carbide forming*	*Alloy Carbides formed*[a]
Mn	Austenite	Yes	$M_{15}C_4$, $M_{23}C_6$, M_7C_3
Ni	Austenite	No	None
Cu	Austenite	No	None
Si	Ferrite	No	None
Cr	Ferrite	Yes	M_7C_3, $M_{23}C_6$
Ti	Ferrite	Yes	TiC
Nb	Ferrite	Yes	NbC
V	Ferrite	Yes	V_4C_3
W	Ferrite	Yes	WC, M_6C
Mo	Ferrite	Yes	M_6C, $M_{23}C_6$, (ξ-M_3C), Mo_2C

[a]In formulae for alloy carbides, M stands for random mixing of Fe and alloying element on the metal sublattice.

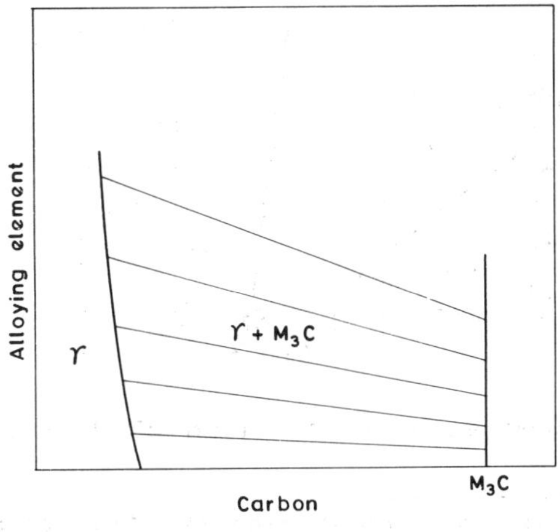

Fig. 2.4. (γ + cm) equilibrium (isothermal section) in a Fe–C–M system when M is a non-carbide-forming element (schematic).

2 Fe–C–M SYSTEMS

2.1 Fe–C–Mn SYSTEM

Mn is an austenite stabilizing and a carbide-forming element. It segregates to austenite in ($\alpha + \gamma$) equilibrium and to cementite in (γ + cm) and (α + cm) equilibria. The alloy carbides in the Fe–C–Mn system appear at relatively higher concentrations of Mn and are generally not found in steels. Figure 2.5 shows isothermal sections* of the Fe–C–Mn phase diagram at 1023 K (750°C) and 973K (700°C); and Fig. 2.6 gives the stability range of austenite in the Fe–C–Mn system. Addition of Mn to Fe–C alloys decreases both the Ae_3 and Ae_1 temperatures as well as the eutectoid carbon content, as seen in Figs. 2.5 and 2.6.

2.2 Fe–C–Ni SYSTEM

Ni is an austenite stabilizing and non-carbide-forming element. Under equilibrium conditions, it segregates to γ phase in (α + γ) and (γ + cm) equilibria and to the α phase in (α + cm) equilibrium. Figure 2.7 gives isothermal sections of the Fe–C–Ni

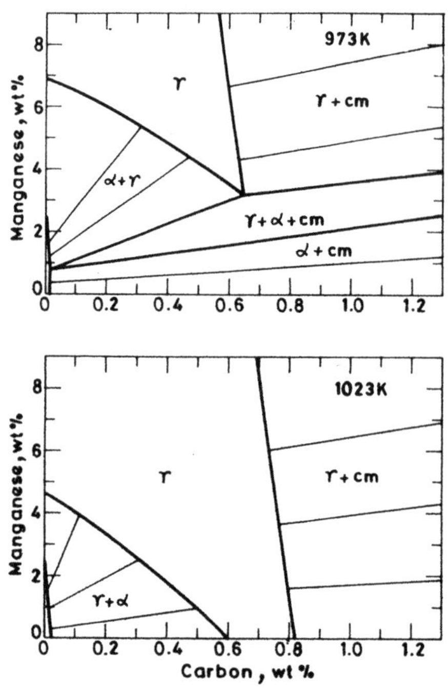

Fig. 2.5. Isothermal sections of Fe–C–Mn phase diagram at 1023K (750°C) and 973K (700°C).

* Most of the ternary phase diagrams shown in this chapter are calculated phase diagrams based on the thermodynamic modelling and optimized model parameters given by Uhrenius (Ref. 1).

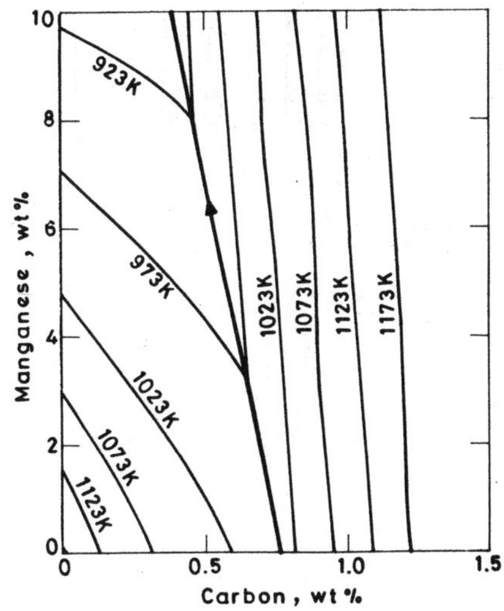

Fig. 2.6. Extension of the austenite phase field in Fe–C–Mn system below 1123K (850°C).

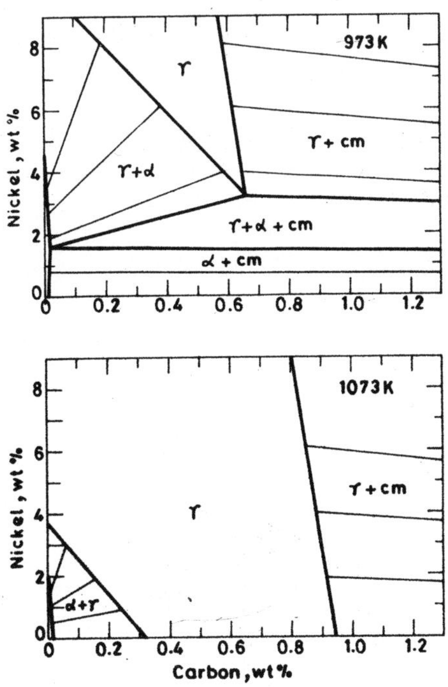

Fig. 2.7. Isothermal sections of Fe–C–Ni phase diagram at 1073K (800°C) and 973K (700°C).

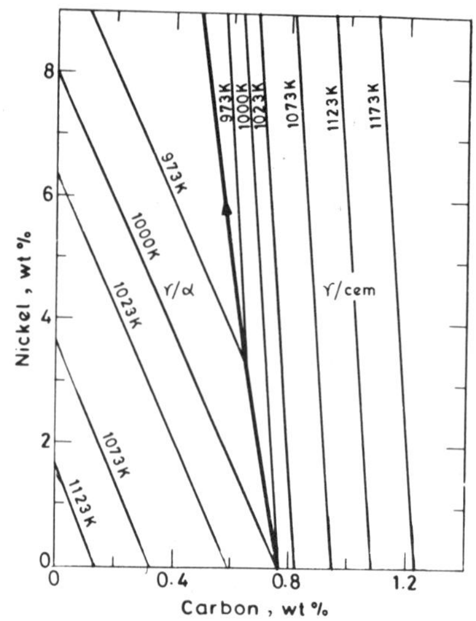

Fig. 2.8. Extension of the austenite phase field in Fe–C–Ni system below 1173K (900°C).

phase diagram at 1073 K (800°C) and 973K (700°C) and Fig. 2.8 shows the stability range of austenite in the Fe–C–Ni system. Addition of Ni to Fe–C alloys lowers the Ae_3 and Ae_1 temperatures as well as the eutectoid carbon content.

2.3 Fe–C–Cu SYSTEM

Like Ni, Cu is also an austenite stabilizing and a non-carbide-forming element. Solubility of Cu in the cementite phase is almost nil and its solubility in iron (α as well as γ) is also limited. Figure 2.9 shows the stability range of austenite in the

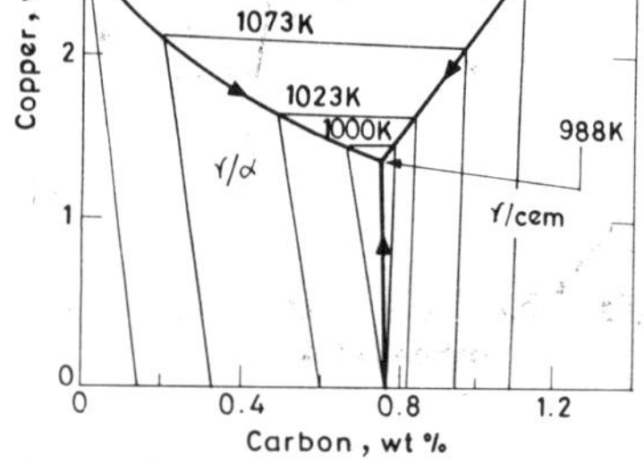

Fig. 2.9. Extension of the austenite phase field in Fe–C–Cu system below 1123K (850°C).

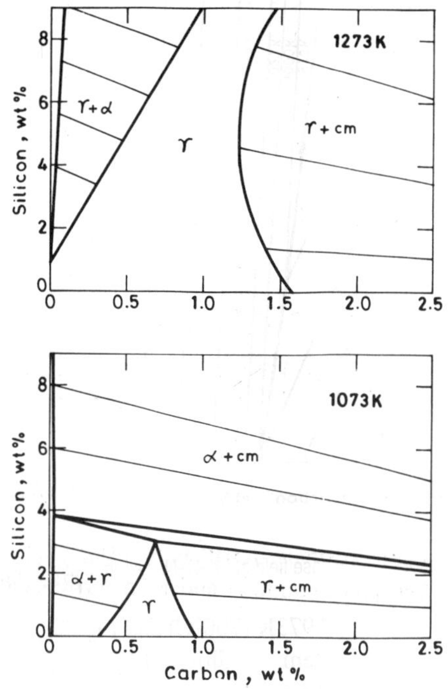

Fig. 2.10. Isothermal sections of Fe–C–Si phase diagram at 1273K (1000°C) and 1073K (800°C).

Fe–C–Cu system. A ternary eutectoid, $\gamma = \alpha + \text{cm} + \varepsilon$, appears in the Fe–C–Cu system with relatively small additions of Cu. ε is the Cu-rich fcc phase. Like Mn and Ni, Cu lowers the Ae_3 and Ae_1 temperatures as well as the eutectoid carbon content. At higher concentrations of Cu, the ε-phase appears in the system.

2.4 Fe–C–Si SYSTEM

Si is a ferrite stabilizing and non-carbide-forming element. It has very limited solubility in the cementite phase. Figure 2.10 gives isothermal sections of the Fe–C–Si phase diagram at 1273K (1000°C) and 1073K (800°C), and Fig. 2.11 shows the stability range of austenite in the system. Si segregates to α phase in $(\alpha + \gamma)$ equilibrium and to the γ and α phases, respectively, in $(\gamma + \text{cm})$ and $(\alpha + \text{cm})$ equilibria. With the addition of Si to the Fe–C alloys, both the Ae_3 and Ae_1 temperatures are increased and the eutectoid carbon content is decreased.

2.5 Fe–C–Cr SYSTEM

In binary Fe–Cr system, with the addition of Cr in Fe, the Ae_3 temperature initially decreases at low concentrations of Cr, and then, increases at higher concentrations. The Ae_4 temperature continuously decreases with increasing Cr concentration. However, the overall stability range of austenite continuously decreases with increasing Cr concentration and therefore, Cr is normally classified as a ferrite-stabiliz-

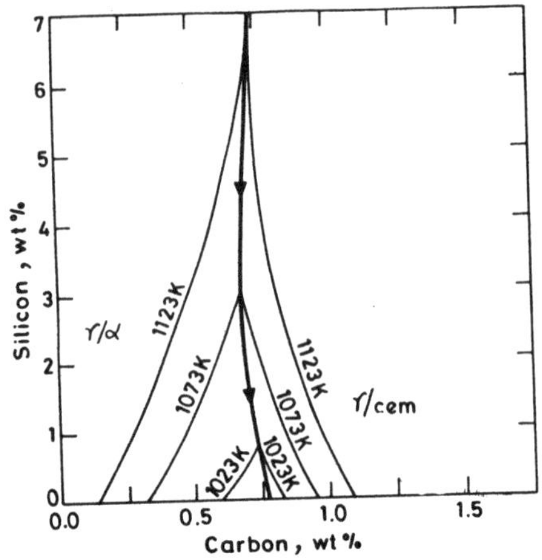

Fig. 2.11. Extension of the austenite phase field in Fe–C–Si system below 1123K (850°C).

ing element. With respect to austenite-ferrite equilibrium, Cr acts as an austenite-stabilizing element at low concentrations and as a ferrite-stabilizing element at

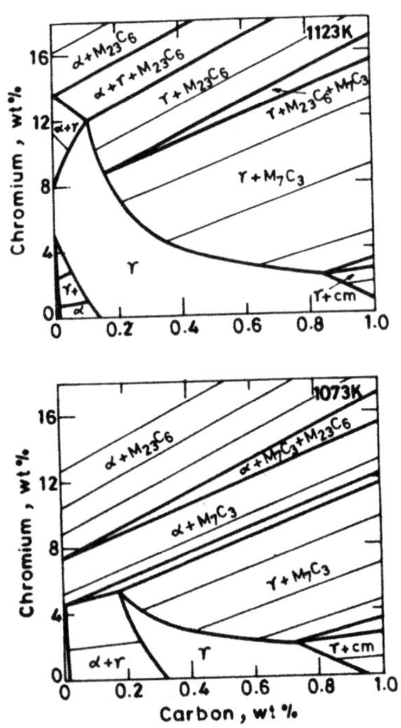

Fig. 2.12. Isothermal sections of Fe–C–Cr phase diagram at 1123K (850°C) and 1073K (800°C)

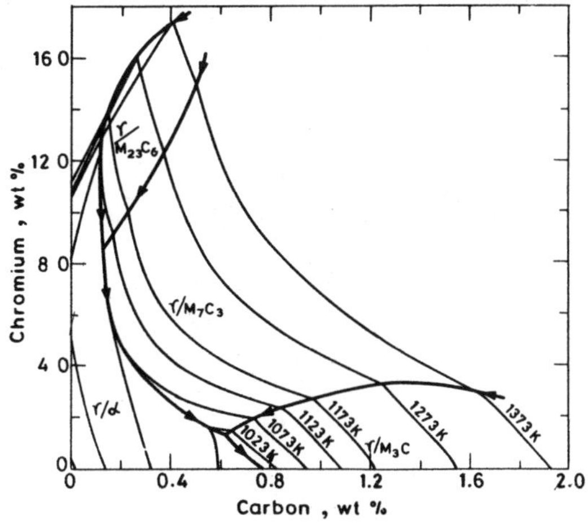

Fig. 2.13. Extension of the austenite phase field in Fe–C–Cr system below 1373K (1100°C).

higher concentrations. Cr is also a carbide-forming element. Apart from cementite (M_3C), two alloy carbide phases, M_7C_3 and $M_{23}C_6$, are formed in the Fe–C–Cr system. Cr preferentially segregates to the carbide phases in equilibrium with austenite (or ferrite). Figure 2.12 shows isothermal sections of the Fe–C–Cr phase diagram at 1123K (850°C) and 1073K (800°C), and Fig.2.13 shows the stability range of austenite in the Fe–C–Cr system. In the ($\alpha + \gamma$) two phase region, Cr segregates to γ phase at low concentrations and to the α phase at high concentrations, as seen in Fig. 2.12. The Ae_3 temperature in Fe–C–Cr alloys decreases with small additions of chromium, whereas, Ae_1 temperature increases at all concentrations. The eutectoid carbon content decreases with increasing chromium content. Furthermore, as seen in Figs. 2.12 and 2.13, in Fe–C–Cr alloys containing higher that ~2% Cr, the equilibrium carbide phase at the eutectoid point is M_7C_3 rather than cementite. Fig. 2.14 shows the isothermal section of the Fe–C–Cr phase diagram at 973K (700°C).

2.6 Fe–C–Mo SYSTEM

Mo is a ferrite-stabilizing and a strong carbide-forming element. Apart from M_3C (cementite), alloy carbides ξ-M_3C, $M_{23}C_6$, Mo_2C and M_6C are formed in the Fe–C–Mo system. Figure 2.15 gives isothermal sections of the Fe–C–Mo phase diagram at 1273K (1000°C) and 1073K (800°C). The austenite stability range in the Fe–C–Mo system is shown in Fig. 2.16. Mo segregates to α phase in ($\alpha + \gamma$) equilibrium and to the carbide phases in (γ + carbide) and (α + carbide) equilibria. With the addition of Mo to Fe–C alloys, the Ae_3 and Ae_1 temperatures are increased and the eutectoid carbon content is decreased. Cementite ceases to be the equilibrium carbide phase at the eutectoid point with relatively small additions of Mo, less than ~0.5% Mo

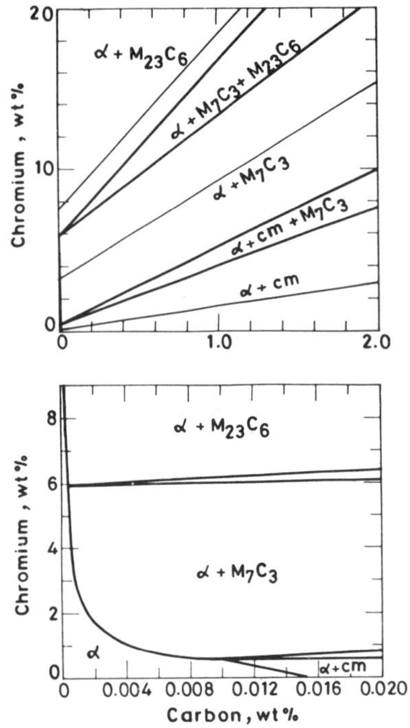

Fig. 2.14. Isothermal section of Fe–C–Cr phase diagram at 973K (700°C).

(Fig. 2.16). Fig. 2.17 gives isothermal section of the Fe–C–Mo phase diagram at 973K (700°C).

2.7 Fe–C–W SYSTEM

W is a ferrite-stabilizing and a strong carbide-forming element. Apart from cementite, M_6C and WC carbides are formed in the Fe–C–W system. Fe does not substitute for W in WC. Figure 2.18 gives isothermal sections of the Fe–C–W phase diagram at 1273K (1000°C) and 1073K (800°C), and the austenite phase field in the Fe–C–W system is given in Fig. 2.19. W segregates to the α phase in ($\alpha + \gamma$) equilibrium and to the carbide phases in (γ + carbide) and (α + carbide) equilibria. Alloy carbides appear in the system with relatively small additions of W, as seen in Figs. 2.18 and 2.19. Stability range of the γ phase is severely restricted because of the high thermodynamic stabilities, and consequently low solubilities, of alloy carbides in austenite. Figure 2.20 shows the 973K (700°C) isotherm of the Fe–C–W phase diagram.

2.8 Fe–C–V SYSTEM

Like W, V is also a ferrite-stabilizing and a strong carbide-forming element. Apart from cementite, V_4C_3 alloy carbide is formed in the Fe–C–V system. V_4C_3 has no

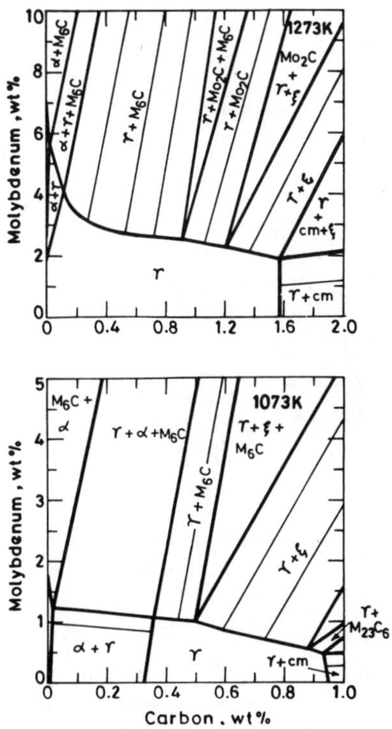

Fig. 2.15. Isothermal section of Fe–C–Mo phase diagram at 1273K (1000°C) and 1073K (800°C).

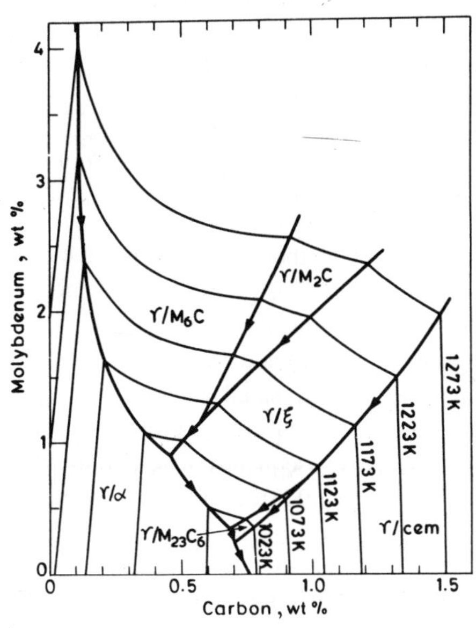

Fig. 2.16. Extension of the austenite phase field in Fe–C–Mo system below 1273K (1000°C).

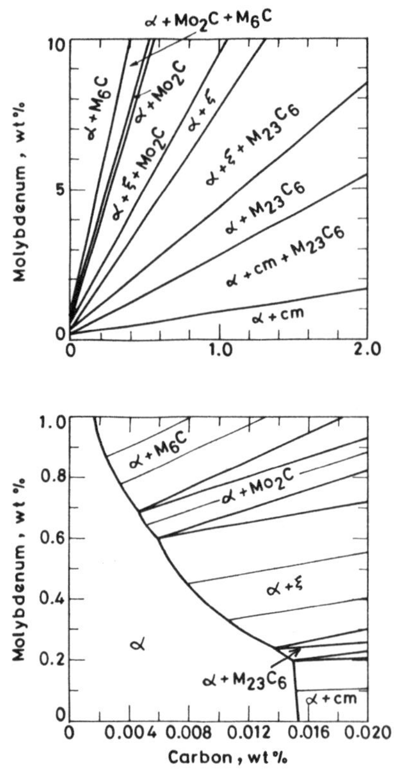

Fig. 2.17. Isothermal section of Fe–C–Mo phase diagram at 973K (700°C).

solubility for Fe and is a very stable carbide with limited solubility in the α and γ phases. Figure 2.21 shows the stability range of austenite in the Fe–C–V system. Notice, the severely restricted austenite phase field due to low solubility of V_4C_3 in the γ phase.

2.9 Fe–C–Nb AND Fe–C–Ti SYSTEMS

Nb and Ti are also ferrite stabilizing and very strong carbide-forming elements. The alloy carbides formed in the Fe–C–Nb and Fe–C–Ti systems are pure NbC and TiC, respectively, with no solubility of iron in these carbides. Due to very high stability of the alloy carbides, the solubility of Nb and Ti in cementite is negligible and alloy carbides appear with additions of very small amounts of these elements to Fe–C alloys. NbC and TiC have only limited solubilities in the austenite and ferrite phases.

In the Fe–C–Nb system, niobium carbide is a non-stoichiometric compound and may be represented as NbC_x, where x varies from 0.75 to 0.98. The average composition of NbC_x precipitates in steels, in the composition range of interest in steels,

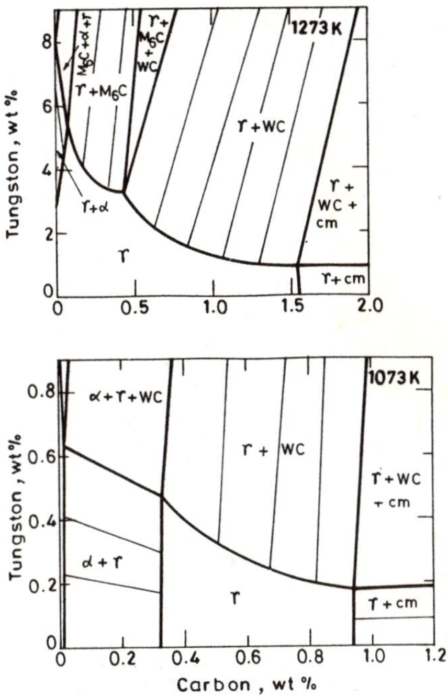

Fig. 2.18. Isothermal sections of Fe–C–W phase diagram at 1273K (1000°C) and 1073K (800°C).

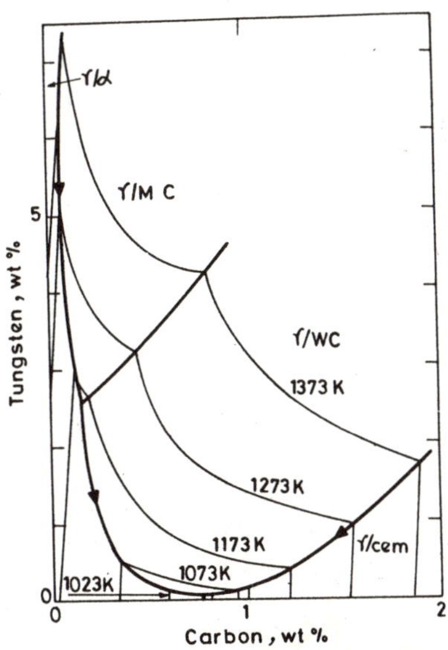

Fig. 2.19. Extension of the austenite phase field in Fe–C–W system below 1373 K (1100°C).

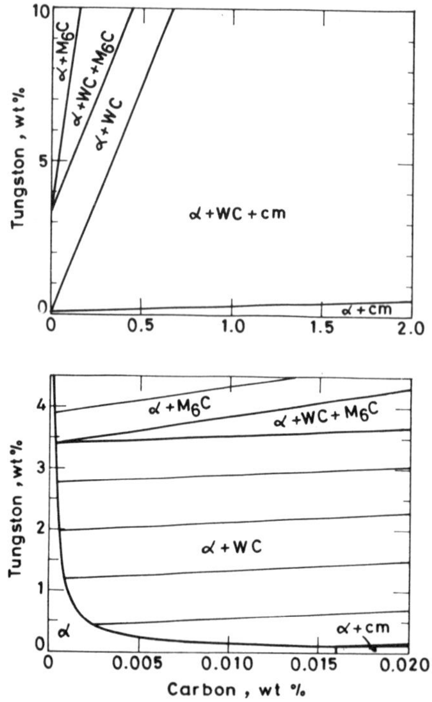

Fig. 2.20. Isothermal section of Fe–C–W phase diagram at 973K (700°C).

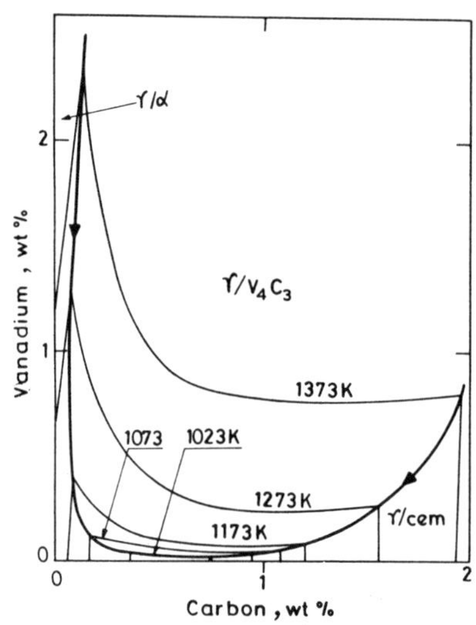

Fig. 2.21. Extension of the austenite phase field in Fe–C–V system below 1373K (1100°C).

corresponds to $x \cong 0.87$. The solubility product of $NbC_{0.87}$ in austenite is given by (Ref. 3):

$$\log_{10} [\%Nb] [\%C]^{0.87} \cong - \frac{7020}{T} + 2.81 \qquad (2.1)$$

where T is temperature in degrees Kelvin.

In the Fe–C–Ti system, TiC is a stoichiometric compound and its solubility in austenite is given by (Ref. 3):

$$\log_{10} [\%Ti] [\%C] \cong - \frac{7000}{T} + 2.75 \qquad (2.2)$$

Only small amounts of Nb and Ti are normally added to steels. The stability range of austenite in steels containing Nb and Ti is essentially determined by the solubilities of NbC_x and TiC, respectively, in austenite.

3 MULTICOMPONENT STEELS

3.1 INTRODUCTION

Commercial steels normally contain more than one alloying elements in addition to carbon. Phase diagrams of multicomponent steels are relatively more complex and very few phase equilibria determinations and/or calculations exist for such systems. However, some general features of phase equilibria in multicomponent systems, like, relative distribution of different alloying elements in various phases in equilibrium, types of alloy carbides formed, and variations of Ae_3 and Ae_1 temperatures, may be inferred from the effects of individual alloying elements on various phase equilibria in ternary Fe–C–M systems. For heat treatable low and medium carbon steels, the Ae_3 and Ae_1 temperatures, which correspond to the onset of ferrite and pearlite transformations, respectively, upon equilibrium cooling from austenite, are important parameters. The variation of these equilibrium transformation temperatures in multicomponent steels as a function of alloy composition is briefly discussed in what follows.

3.2 THE Ae_3 TEMPERATURE

Ae_3 temperature of a steel is the temperature below which the austenite to ferrite transformation becomes thermodynamically feasible on cooling from austenite. It corresponds to a temperature at which the steel composition lies on the $\gamma/(\alpha + \gamma)$ phase boundary. Ae_3 temperatures for a large number of low and medium carbon steels have been experimentally determined. These data have been used to develop empirical correlations between Ae_3 temperature and composition. These relationships may, in turn, be used to estimate the Ae_3 temperature of a steel of given composition.

Andrews (Ref. 4) has developed a correlation formula for Ae_3 temperature, consistent with the binary phase diagrams and calibrated with 19 experimental results, valid for compositions upto 0.7% C, 3.0% Mn, 0.8% Si and 5.0% Ni, and is given as:

$$\begin{aligned}Ae_3(K) = 1186 - \Delta T - 25(\%Mn) - 11(\%Cr) - 20(\%Cu) + 60(\%Si)\\ + 60(\%Mo) + 40(\%W) + 100(\%V) + 700(\%P)\end{aligned} \quad (2.3)$$

where, ΔT accounts for the effect of C and Ni as given in Table 2.2.

Table 2.2. *ΔT for C and Ni to be used in Eq. (2.3)*

%C + 0.1(%Ni)	ΔT	%C + 0.1(%Ni)	ΔT	%C + 0.1(%Ni)	ΔT
0.05	24	0.25	93	0.45	137
0.10	48	0.30	106	0.50	145
0.15	64	0.35	117	0.60	160
0.20	80	0.40	128	0.70	176

Grange (Ref. 5) derived a different expression for the variation of Ae_3 temperature with composition, by regression analysis, from the same set of experimental data as used by Andrews (Ref. 4) for developing Eq. (2.3), to give:

$$\begin{aligned}Ae_3(K) = 1127 - 179(\%C) - 14(\%Mn) - 15(\%Ni)\\ + 22(\%Si) - 23(\%Cr)\end{aligned} \quad (2.4)$$

Eq. (2.4) is not consistent with the binary Fe–C and Fe–M phase diagrams. For example, in the binary Fe–C system, Ae_3 temperature does not vary linearly with carbon concentration, as in Eq. (2.4). Equation (2.4) is, then, valid only for multicomponent steels in the limited composition range of steels whose data have been used in the regression analyses. Furthermore, the discrepancies in the coefficients for other elements between Eqs. (2.3) and (2.4), in general, suggest that the use of linear equations in these correlations is probably not justified.

Kirkaldy and Baganis (Ref. 6) have developed a method, based on principles of phase equilibria and using Wagners' formalism for thermodynamics of dilute solutions to describe the activities of carbon and other alloying elements in austenite and ferrite, to calculate Ae_3 temperatures of multicomponent steels. Their predictions agrees well with the experimental data for a wide range of low and medium carbon steels. The actual formalism is not discussed here. The numerical results of their calculations of Ae_3 temperatures for multicomponent steels can be represented as follows (Ref. 7).

Ae_3 temperature of binary Fe–C alloys up to 0.765% C, the eutectoid composition, are fitted empirically to give:

$$Ae_3(K)\ [Fe\text{–}C] = 1115.0 - 150.3(\%C) + 216.0(0.765 - \%C)^{4.26} \quad (2.5)$$

The effect of alloying elements on Ae_3 temperature of a steel of given carbon content is, then, given as the initial partial slopes of Ae_3 temperature with respect to composition of different alloying elements. These partial slopes at different carbon contents are given in Table 2.3 (calculated by Baganis (Ref. 7). The partial slopes are calculated by assuming the concentration of other alloying elements as zero, i.e. they are based on the calculations of Ae_3 temperatures in the respective ternary Fe–C–M systems. A close look at Table 2.3 clearly shows that a single linear regression formula for Ae_3 temperatures, of the type given in Eq. (2.3) or (2.4), for a wide range of compositions can not be valid. A reasonably good estimate of the Ae_3 temperature of a steel may, however, be obtained by using Eq. (2.5) to calculate the effect of carbon and formulating a suitable linear equation for the effect of other alloying elements with the help of Table 2.3. In principle, the coefficients in such a linear equation are valid only at small concentrations and in absence of other alloying elements. However, the results obtained by using this method agree quite well with the experimental data for a wide variety of low and medium carbon steels. More accurate values may be obtained by using the detailed calculation procedure given by Kirkaldy and Baganis (Ref. 6).

Table 2.3. *Initial Partial Slopes of Ae_3 Temperature for Different Alloying Elements (M) at Various Carbon Contents for Fe–C–M alloys*

M \ %C	0.0	0.1	0.2	0.3	0.4	0.5	0.6	0.7	0.76
Mn	–49.6	–29.2	–25.7	–21.9	–18.8	–15.6	–14.0	–12.9	–12.3
Si	51.3	32.8	21.7	19.8	15.9	13.8	11.7	11.4	11.2
Ni	–36.0	–23.3	–20.9	–18.3	–15.7	–13.6	–12.5	–11.9	–11.7
Cr	–22.9	–12.3	–9.1	–7.6	–5.7	–4.0	–3.0	–2.1	–1.6
Mo	31.2	18.5	11.6	10.3	7.6	6.0	4.6	4.0	3.6
Cu	–27.3	–18.6	–15.4	–14.3	–13.8	–12.0	–11.4	–10.8	–10.8

3.3 THE Ae_1 TEMPERATURE

Figure 2.22 shows the effect of different alloying elements on the eutectoid point; the eutectoid temperature (Ae_1) as well as eutectoid composition. The dotted lines are from Bain and Paxton (Ref. 2) and the solid lines are based on the calculated phase equilibria by Uhrenius (Ref. 1). The calculated data in this case are probably more

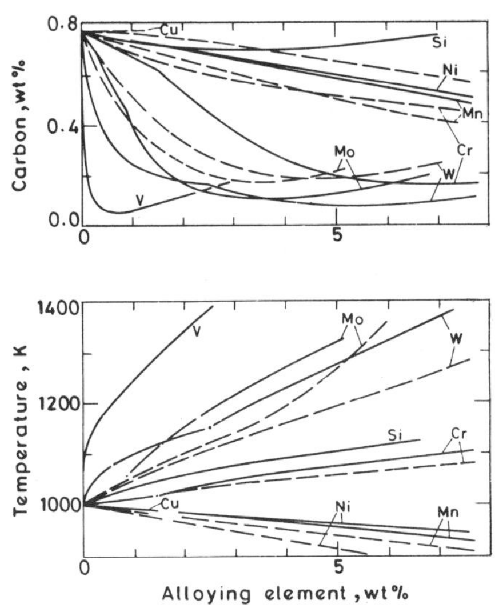

Fig. 2.22. Effect of alloying element on the eutectoid temperature and composition in Fe–C–M systems. (- - - -) Bain and Paxton; (———) calculated (Ref. 1).

accurate. The data summarized by Bain and Paxton (Ref. 2) are based on relatively old experimental phase diagrams, whereas the calculations of Uhrenius fit fairly well with the recent experimental information for a number of Fe–C–M systems. Note that, in the case of strong carbide-forming elements, the rate of change of Ae_1 temperature with composition discontinuously changes at certain compositions (Fig. 2.22). These points correspond to change over from $\gamma = \alpha + cm$ eutectoid equilibrium to $\gamma = \alpha +$ alloy-carbide eutectoid equilibrium. The Ae_1 temperature of a multicomponent steel, to a first approximation, may be obtained by linearly adding the effect of individual alloying elements.

REFERENCES

1. B. Uhrenius, in *Hardenability Concepts with Application to Steel*, (Eds. D. V. Doane and J.S. Kirkaldy). The Metallurgical Society of AIME, Warrendale, Pa, 1978.
2. E.C. Bain and H.W. Paxton, *Alloying Elements in Steel*, 2nd Edition, American Society for Metals, Metals Park, Ohio, 1962.
3. E.T. Turkdogan, *Iron & Steel Maker*, **16** (1989) 61.
4. K.W. Andrews, *J. Iron Steel Inst.* **203** (1965) 721.
5. R.A. Grange, *Metal Prog.*, **79** (1961) 73.
6. J.S. Kirkaldy and E.A. Baganis, *Metall. Trans. A*, **9A** (1978) 495.
7. E.A. Baganis, *M. Engg. Thesis*, McMaster University, Hamilton, Canada, 1976.

CHAPTER 3

Alloying Elements in Steels—II

(*Effect on Phase Transformations*)

1 INTRODUCTION

Alloying elements affect the heat treatment response of steels through their effect on the kinetics of various solid state transformations that occur in steels. Thermodynamics and kinetics of these transformations in plain carbon steels, i.e. in Fe–C alloys, have already been discussed in Chapter 1, in some detail. Except for martensite transformation, all other transformations from austenite in Fe–C alloys, i.e. ferrite, cementite, bainite and pearlite transformations, involve redistribution of carbon. The kinetics of these transformations is controlled and affected by the diffusional processes. In alloy steels, an alloying element affects the overall kinetics of a given transformation by its effect on the thermodynamic driving force for the transformation as well as on the diffusional and other kinetic processes.

The thermodynamic driving force for a transformation, i.e. the volume Gibbs energy change, ΔG_V, depends on the relative stabilities of different phases involved in the transformation. ΔG_V for ferrite/bainite or pearlite transformation at a given temperature T, ΔT below the equilibrium transformation temperature, is to a first approximation proportional to undercooling ΔT, where ΔT is equal to $(Ae_3 - T)$ for ferrite transformation and $(Ae_1 - T)$ for pearlite transformation. Therefore, for transformations occuring at a given temperature T, the addition of an alloying element to a Fe–C alloy would decrease ΔG_V (in magnitude) for ferrite/bainite transformation when it decreases the Ae_3 temperature, and that for pearlite transformation when it decreases the Ae_1 temperature. It would, then, normally be expected that at this temperature, the rates of nucleation and growth of these transformations in the presence of such an alloying element would be lower than in Fe–C alloy of the same carbon content. Similarly, when the Ae_3 and Ae_1 temperatures are raised by the addition of an alloying element, the respective transformations would be expected to be accelerated. However, this simplistic view does not explain the total effect of various alloying elements on these transformations in steels. For example, addition of Cr to Fe–C eutectoid steel increases the Ae_1 temperature, still at temperatures lower than the binary Fe–C eutectoid temperature, the pearlite transformation rates are lower in the Fe–C–Cr alloys than in Fe–C eutectoid steel. Similar discrepancies occur in number of other cases for ferrite as well as pearlite transformations.

Effect of individual alloying elements on various transformations in steels are discussed in this chapter in some detail. The discussion is limited mainly to ferrite and pearlite transformations in low alloy ternary Fe–C–M systems. The IT diagrams of multicomponent low alloy steels are, then, briefly discussed.

2 FERRITE AND BAINITE TRANSFORMATIONS

2.1 INTRODUCTION

For the purpose of present discussion, ferrite and bainite transformations are considered together, as both of them are primarily $\gamma \rightarrow \alpha$ transformations, as discussed in Chapter 1. Furthermore, only growth kinetics of the grain boundary allotriomorphs will be considered in detail to elucidate the effect of alloying elements on the growth mechanisms and growth kinetics. The growth of Widmanstätten and bainitic plates is affected in a similar manner, except that the effect of curvature at the plate tip must be taken into consideration. Effect of alloying elements on the nucleation of ferrite is not discussed, as it is easily explained (qualitatively) in most cases by thermodynamic considerations alone, i.e. by the effect of alloying elements on the volume Gibbs energy change, ΔG_V.

2.2 GROWTH KINETICS

Let us consider that a ternary Fe–C–M alloy of composition #1, where M is an austenite-stabilizing element, is instantly cooled from austenite state at some higher temperature to temperature T, below Ae_3, where it falls in the $(\alpha + \gamma)$ two-phase region, as schematically shown in Fig. 3.1, and is held there isothermally. At this

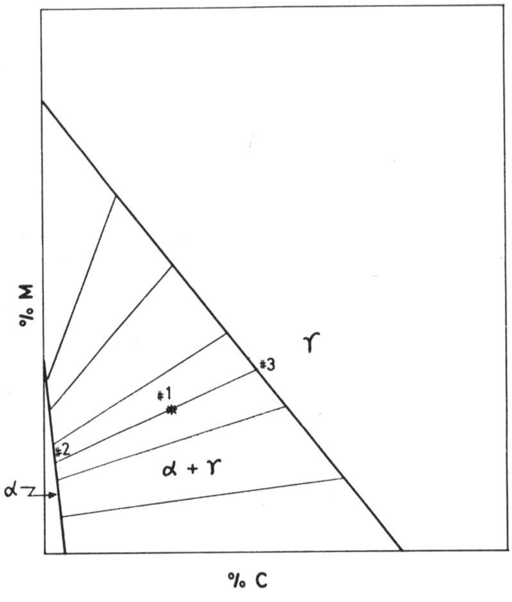

Fig. 3.1. An isothermal section of a Fe–C–M phase diagram, showing the $(\alpha + \gamma)$ two-phase region at some temperature T < 1185K, where M is an austenite-stabilizing element (schematic).

temperature, austenite would eventually decompose to equilibrium phases, i.e. ferrite of composition #2 and austenite of composition #3 in Fig. 3.1. The decomposition to equilibrium phases would occur by partial transformation of austenite to ferrite. As in binary Fe–C-alloys (see Chapter 1), ferrite in ternary Fe–C–M alloys also nucleates heterogeneously at the austenite grain boundaries and covers them early during the transformation, before any substantial thickening of the grain boundary allotriomorphs occurs. The ferrite growth, then, may be considered as a one-dimensional plane front growth. During ferrite transformation in ternary Fe–C–M systems, the composition of ferrite, that is initially formed, is generally not the same as final equilibrium composition given by the phase diagram. During the plane front ferrite growth of grain boundary allotriomorphs in Fe–C–M systems, the growth velocity, v, at any instant, must be consistent with the following mass balance equations at the α/γ interface:

$$v\,(C_C^{\gamma\alpha} - C_C^{\alpha\gamma}) = -D_C^{\gamma}\left[\frac{dC_C}{dx}\right]_{x=x_0} \tag{3.1}$$

and

$$v\,(C_M^{\gamma\alpha} - C_M^{\alpha\gamma}) = -D_M^{\gamma}\left[\frac{dC_M}{dx}\right]_{x=x_0} \tag{3.2}$$

where, D_C^{γ} and D_M^{γ} are diffusion coefficients of carbon and alloying element M respectively, in austenite at the α/γ interface; C_C and C_M refer to concentrations of carbon and alloying element M respectively, in austenite; x is distance from the prior austenite grain boundary; x_0 is the distance to which the ferrite has grown; $C_C^{\gamma\alpha}$ and $C_M^{\gamma\alpha}$ are concentrations of carbon and alloying element M respectively, in austenite at $x = x_0$, i.e. at the α/γ interface; and $C_C^{\alpha\gamma}$ and $C_M^{\alpha\gamma}$ are carbon and alloying element concentrations respectively, in ferrite at the α/γ interface.

Now, if it is assumed that the incoherent α/γ interface is in local equilibrium, then, $(C_C^{\gamma\alpha}, C_M^{\gamma\alpha})$ and $(C_C^{\alpha\gamma}, C_M^{\alpha\gamma})$ must represent, respectively, the austenite end and ferrite end of the same tie line in the $(\alpha + \gamma)$ two-phase region. For Eqs. (3.1) and (3.2) to be simultaneously satisfied, this tie is uniquely determined and, in general, will not be the tie line that passes through the original composition #1 in Fig. 3.1 (Ref. 1). The tie line passing through the alloy composition represents the local equilibrium concentrations at the α/γ interface only when $D_C^{\gamma} = D_M^{\gamma}$. In Fe–C–M alloys, in general, D_M^{γ} is orders of magnitude smaller than D_C^{γ}. Under these conditions, the $(\alpha + \gamma)$ two phase region may be divided into two sub-regions, such that the ferrite growth rate is essentially controlled by carbon diffusion in one sub-region and by alloying element diffusion in the other; and in either case, Eqs. (3.1) and (3.2) are simultaneously satisfied (Ref. 1).

Let us, therefore, consider a particular tie line *ab* in the $(\alpha + \gamma)$ two-phase region as shown in Fig. 3.2, and then, consider the ferrite growth mechanism for all the alloys for which this tie line would represent the local equilibrium concentrations at the α/γ interface. When the growth of ferrite is essentially controlled by carbon diffusion in accordance with Eq. (3.1), the alloying element M, having a diffusion

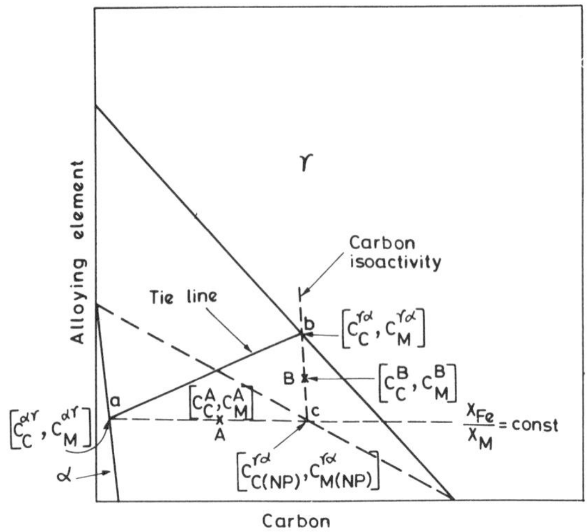

Fig. 3.2. Local equilibrium condition at the α/γ interface during plane front ferrite growth.

coefficient orders of magnitude smaller than that of carbon, will essentially remain unpartitioned between α and γ phases, except for a very slight depletion of M in ferrite and build-up of a sharp concentration spike of M at the interface in austenite, just enough to satisfy Eq. (3.2), as schematically shown in Fig. 3.3 for an alloy of composition *A* in Fig. 3.2. Under these conditions, the atomic ratio of iron to alloying element in ferrite is essentially the same as in parent austenite. Therefore, the composition of alloy *A* is such that the atomic ratio of iron to alloying element M in alloy *A* is the same as that of point *a* of the tie line *ab*. The total amount of alloying element in the concentration spike at the interface in austenite is negligible. Similarly, any alloy whose composition is on the line *ac* in Fig. 3.2, will transform by carbon diffusion control with the tie line *ab* representing the local equilibrium concentrations at the α/γ interface. Along the line *ac*, the atomic ratio of iron to alloying element, M, remains unchanged and point *c* is the intersection of carbon isoactivity line in austenite, passing through *b*, with the line *ac*. Let us now consider the growth kinetics of ferrite grain boundary allotriomorphs in alloy *A* in Fig. 3.2. Figure 3.3 schematically gives the carbon and alloying element concentration profiles during the early stages of transformation, before the overlap of carbon concentration profiles from opposite sides of the grain boundaries. An approximate analysis, similar to the plane front ferrite growth in Fe–C alloys, Chapter 1, Sec. 4.3, gives the ferrite growth velocity, *v*, as:

$$v = \left(\frac{\alpha}{2}\right)\frac{1}{\sqrt{t}} \tag{3.3}$$

where α is the ferrite growth rate parameter, given by:

$$\alpha = \left[\frac{(C_{C(NP)}^{\gamma\alpha} - C_C^A)^2 \, D_C^\gamma}{(C_{C(NP)}^{\gamma\alpha} - C_C^{\alpha\gamma})\,(C_C^A - C_C^{\alpha\gamma})}\right]^{1/2} \tag{3.4}$$

where, t is time : D_C^{γ} is diffusion coefficient of carbon in austenite; and the concentration terms are as defined in Figs. 3.2 and 3.3. Note that, the ferrite growth in Fe–C–M alloys, occurring by above mechanism, is given by the same equations as in binary Fe–C alloys. The presence of alloying element only affects the driving force for carbon diffusion, $(C_{C(NP)}^{\gamma\alpha} - C_C^A)$.

According to Eq. (3.4), ferrite growth rate in an alloy of composition c in Fig. 3.2 will be zero. Furthermore, any alloy lying beyond c along the line ac, but still within the $(\alpha + \gamma)$ two-phase region, will have negative driving force for ferrite growth by this mechanism, and therefore, cannot transform by this mechanism. In such alloys, the alloying element must partition between ferrite and austenite, and the growth is, then, controlled by the diffusion of alloying element.

Now, let us consider the alloys where ferrite growth is primarily controlled by alloying element diffusion in accordance with Eq. (3.2), with tie line ab in Fig. 3.2 still representing the local equilibrium concentrations at the α/γ interface. As $D_C^{\gamma} >> D_M^{\gamma}$, carbon will diffuse much faster than the alloying element and the carbon diffusion distances at any time will be orders of magnitude larger than thickness of the growing ferrite grain boundary allotriomorphs (controlled by diffusion of M). Carbon would, then, maintain essentially uniform activity throughout the austenite phase. Therefore, during the early stages of ferrite transformation, carbon at the interface in austenite would have same activity as the original alloy. In Fig. 3.2,

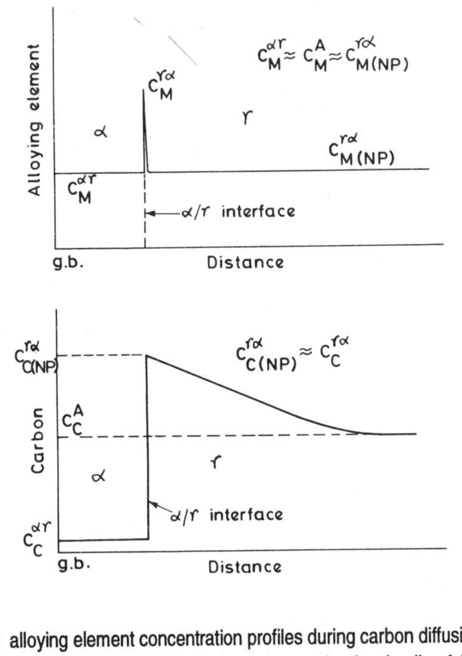

Fig. 3.3. Carbon and alloying element concentration profiles during carbon diffusion controlled plane front ferrite growth by local-equilibrium no-partition mechanism in alloy A in Fig. 3.2.

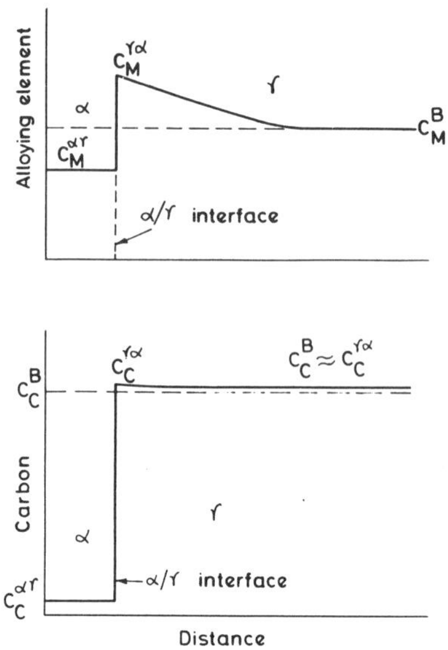

Fig. 3.4. Carbon and alloying element concentration profiles during alloying element diffusion controlled plane front ferrite growth in alloy B in Fig. 3.2.

then, any alloy of composition along the isoactivity line of carbon from point *b* to point *c* will transform by alloying element diffusion control, with tie line *ab* representing the local equilibrium concentrations at the α/γ interface. Let us consider the ferrite growth kinetics in an alloy *B* in Fig. 3.2, lying on the isoactivity line *bc*. Figure 3.4 schematically shows concentration profiles of carbon and alloying element, M, that would be obtained during the plane front ferrite growth. An approximate analysis of the growth kinetics, then, gives ferrite growth velocity, *v*, as:

$$v = \left(\frac{\alpha}{2}\right)\frac{1}{\sqrt{t}} \tag{3.5}$$

with

$$\alpha = \left[\frac{(C_M^{\gamma\alpha} - C_M^{B})^2\, D_M^{\gamma}}{(C_M^{\gamma\alpha} - C_M^{\alpha\gamma})\,(C_M^{B} - C_M^{\alpha\gamma})}\right]^{1/2} \tag{3.6}$$

where, α is ferrite growth rate parameter; D_M^{γ} is diffusion coefficient of the alloying element in austenite; and all the concentration terms are as defined in Figs. 3.2 and 3.4.

Now referring back to Fig. 3.2, according to the mechanisms discussed above, ferrite growth would occur by carbon diffusion control in alloys lying along *ac* and by alloying element diffusion control in alloys lying along *bc*; with tie line *ab* representing the local equilibrium at the α/γ interface in all cases. When different tie lines in the $(\alpha + \gamma)$ two-phase region are considered, the locus of point *c* will divide the $(\alpha+\gamma)$ region into two parts. Note that, point *c* is the intersection of constant (x_M/x_{Fe}) line from the ferrite end of a tie line with the isoactivity line of carbon in austenite from the austenite end of the same tie line, where x_M and x_{Fe} are mole fractions of alloying element and iron respectively. Locus of point *c*, shown as dotted line in Fig. 3.2, is called local-equilibrium no-partition (LENP) line.

According to the mechanisms discussed above, within the $(\alpha+\gamma)$ two-phase region, alloys below the LENP line will transform with carbon diffusion control [Eqs. (3.3) and (3.4)] and essentially no partitioning of the alloying element between ferrite and austenite would occur, whereas, alloys above this line will transform with alloying element diffusion control [Eqs. (3.5) and (3.6)] and ferrite would have different (lower) concentration of the alloying element than parent austenite. Since $D_C^\gamma >> D_M^\gamma$, alloys that transform by carbon diffusion control will transform at rates comparable to binary Fe–C alloys, whereas, the alloys transforming by alloying element diffusion control will have orders of magnitude lower growth rates.

There is another mechanism by which carbon diffusion controlled $\gamma \rightarrow \alpha$ transformation can occur in Fe–C–M alloys without any partitioning of the alloying element, known as para-equilibrium mechanism. Here again, the ratio of alloying element to iron (x_M/x_{Fe}) in ferrite remains the same as in parent austenite, same as in LENP mechanism. However, in this case, the α/γ interface is assumed to be in local equilibrium only with respect to carbon and the (x_M/x_{Fe}) ratio remains the same throughout, including at the interface and its vicinity, i.e. there is no build-up of alloying element concentration spike at the interface to give complete local equilibrium at the interface. The para-equilibrium $(\alpha+\gamma)$ phase boundaries can be calculated from the Gibbs energy functions of the ferrite (α) and austenite (γ) phases. Complete $(\alpha+\gamma)$ two-phase equilibrium in a ternary Fe–C–M system is given by:

$$\overline{G_i^\alpha} = \overline{G_i^\gamma} \qquad (i = \text{Fe, C, M}) \tag{3.7a,b,c}$$

where $\overline{G_i^\alpha}$ and $\overline{G_i^\gamma}$ are partial molar Gibbs energies of component *i* in ferrite and austenite respectively. These three equations can be simultaneously solved to calculate the tie lines and phase boundaries of the $(\alpha+\gamma)$ two-phase region. For a given tie line, there are four compositional unknowns and Eqs. (3.7a) to (3.7c) can be solved for a tie line by fixing one of the compositions and solving for the other three. A similar calculation of other tie lines would, then, give the whole $(\alpha+\gamma)$ two-phase region. The para-equilibrium $(\alpha+\gamma)$ two-phase region, where (x_M/x_{Fe}) remains constant throughout and equilibrium exists only with respect to carbon, is given by the following thermodynamic equations (Ref. 2):

$$\overline{G_C^\alpha} = \overline{G_C^\gamma} \tag{3.8a}$$

$$\overline{G_{Fe}^\alpha} + \left(\frac{x_M^\alpha}{x_{Fe}^\alpha}\right)\overline{G_M^\alpha} = \overline{G_{Fe}^\gamma} + \left(\frac{x_M^\gamma}{x_{Fe}^\gamma}\right)\overline{G_M^\gamma} \tag{3.8b}$$

and

$$\left(\frac{x_M^\alpha}{x_{Fe}^\alpha}\right) = \left(\frac{x_M^\gamma}{x_{Fe}^\gamma}\right) = \left(\frac{x_M}{x_{Fe}}\right) \tag{3.8c}$$

These equations can now be solved for different (x_M/x_{Fe}) ratios to calculate the $(\alpha + \gamma)$ para-equilibrium phase boundaries. The relative positions of $(\alpha + \gamma)$ para-equilibrium and $(\alpha + \gamma)$ equilibrium two-phase regions that would generally be obtained are schematically shown in Fig. 3.5. Note that, the para-equilibrium boundaries would always lie within the stable $(\alpha + \gamma)$ two-phase region. If, the ferrite transformation in a Fe–C–M alloy, say *D* in Fig. 3.5, lying within the para-equilibrium region, were to occur by para-equilibrium mechanism, then, the concentration profiles during the plane front ferrite growth would be as shown Fig. 3.6 and the ferrite growth rate, *v*, would be given by:

$$v = \left(\frac{\alpha}{2}\right)\frac{1}{\sqrt{t}} \tag{3.9}$$

with

$$\alpha = \left[\frac{(C_{C(P)}^{\gamma\alpha} - C_C^D)^2\, D_C^\gamma}{(C_{C(P)}^{\gamma\alpha} - C_{C(P)}^{\alpha\gamma})\,(C_C^D - C_{C(P)}^{\alpha\gamma})}\right]^{1/2} \tag{3.10}$$

where α is ferrite growth rate parameter; *t* is time, D_C^γ is diffusion coefficient of carbon in γ, and all the concentration terms are as defined in Figs. 3.5 and 3.6. Here again, the ferrite growth rates are given by the same equations as in binary Fe–C alloys. The presence of an alloying element only affects the driving force for carbon diffusion, $(C_{C(P)}^{\gamma\alpha} - C_C^D)$.

Figure 3.7 shows the $(\alpha + \gamma)$ two-phase region in a Fe–C–M system, where M is an austenite-stabilizing element, alongwith the para-equilibrium (PE) phase boundaries and the local-equilibrium no-partition (LENP) line, as discussed above. The $(\alpha + \gamma)$ region has been divided into three distinct regions marked, *A*, *B* and *C* in Fig

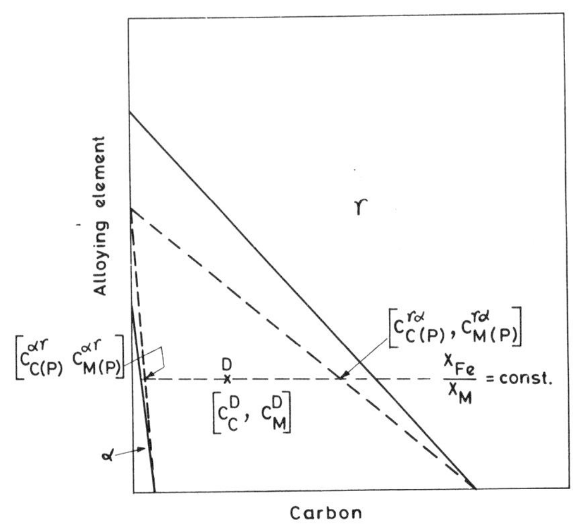

Fig. 3.5. $(\alpha + \gamma)$ Equilibrium and para-equilibrium phase boundaries in a Fe–C–M system, where M is austenite stabilizing element (schematic).

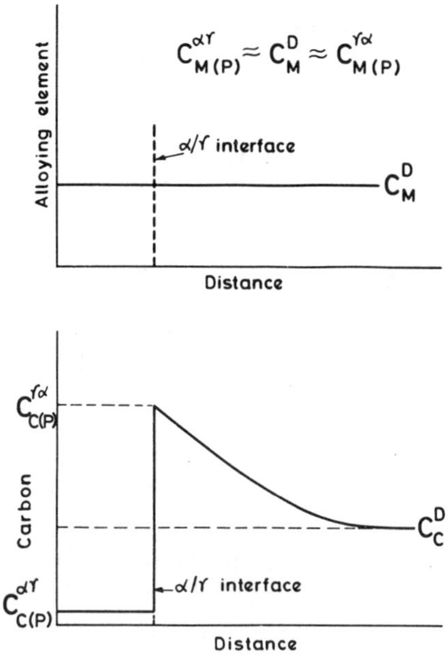

Fig. 3.6. Carbon and alloying element concentration profiles during carbon diffusion controlled plane front ferrite growth by para-equlibrium mechanism in alloy D in Fig. 3.5.

3.7. In region *A*, the ferrite transformation is always controlled by alloying element diffusion and partitioning of the alloying element between ferrite and austenite must occur. In region *B*, the transformation is possible with carbon diffusion control (and no partitioning of M) in accordance with the para-equilibrium (PE) mechanism, however, if complete local equilibrium is obtained at the interface, then, in this region also, the transformation would be controlled by alloying element diffusion, as in region *A*. In region *C*, the transformation is possible with carbon diffusion control, without any partitioning of the alloying element, either by para-equilibrium (PE) mechanism or by local-equilibrium no-partition (LENP) mechanism.

In the discussion presented so far, the alloying element M has been considered to be an austenite-stabilizing element. The same arguments, in general, would also be valid when M is a ferrite-stabilizing element. Figure 3.8 schematically shows para-equilibrium (PE) and local-equilibrium no-partition (LENP) boundaries within the equilibrium $(\bar{\alpha} + \gamma)$ two-phase region that would be obtained in a Fe–C–M system, when M is a ferrite-stabilizing element.

Now, referring to Figs. 3.7 and 3.8, for a given Fe–C–M alloy, three different "equilibrium" transformation temperatures for the $\gamma \rightarrow \alpha$ transformation can be defined: (*i*) equilibrium transformation temperature, Ae_3, corresponding to the equilibrium $\gamma/(\alpha + \gamma)$ phase boundary. (*ii*) para-equilibrium transformation tempera-

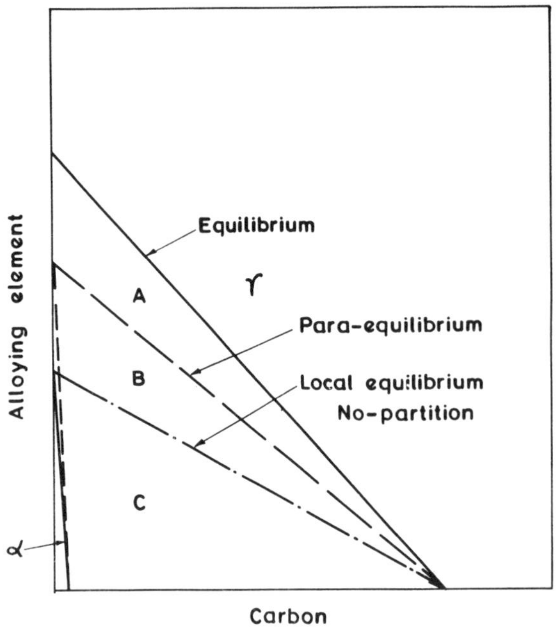

Fig. 3.7. Equilibrium, para-equilibrium and local-equilibrium no-partition boundaries in the ($\alpha + \gamma$) two-phase region in a Fe–C–M alloy, where M is austenite-stabilizing element.

ture, Ae_3(PE), corresponding to the para-equilibrium $\gamma/(\alpha + \gamma)$ phase boundary, and (*iii*) local-equilibrium no-partition transformation temperature, Ae_3(LENP), corresponding to the LENP line. For an alloy of given composition, Ae_3(LENP) < Ae_3(PE) < Ae_3. The experimental evidence suggests that no-partitioning reaction, essentially controlled by carbon diffusion, generally occurs only below Ae_3(LENP), whereas, between Ae_3 and Ae_3(LENP), i.e. in regions *A* and *B* in Figs. 3.7 and 3.8, the transformation is alloying element diffusion controlled and is accompanied by partitioning of the alloying elements between ferrite and austenite. This is consistent with local equilibrium no-partition mechanism. Transformation in accordance with para-equilibrium may, however, occur at very high supersaturations, further below Ae_3(LENP), where the alloying element may not be able to maintain local equilibrium at the α/γ interface due to relatively higher ferrite growth rates and lower alloying element mobility. Note that for a given alloy the ferrite growth rate increases up to a point and the alloying element mobility exponetially decreases with increasing supersaturation, i.e. decreasing temperature.

In general, the alloying element diffusion controlled reaction (partitioning reaction), that occurs above Ae_3(LENP), is extremely slow as compared to the carbon diffusion controlled reaction occurring below Ae_3(LENP), as $D_C^\gamma >> D_M^\gamma$. Therefore, Ae_3(LENP) may be considered as the effective "Ae_3" temperature for the $\gamma \rightarrow \alpha$ transformation in Fe–C–M alloys. The transformation, then, practically occurs only below Ae_3(LENP), with carbon diffusion control and without any effective partitioning of the alloying element.

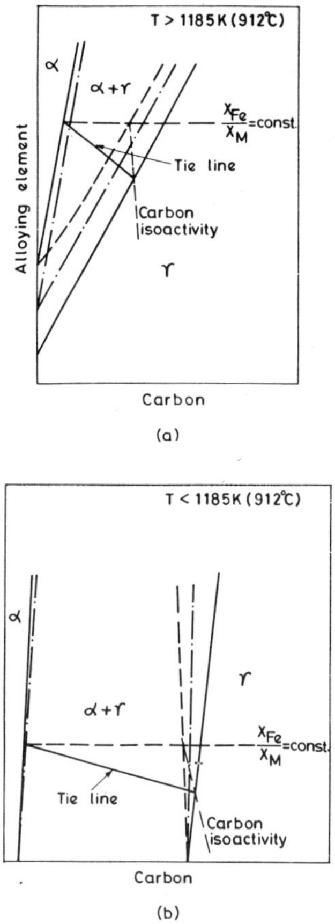

Fig. 3.8. Equilibrium (———), para-equilibrium (—•—) and local-equilibrium no-partition (— — —) boundaries in the (α + γ) two-phase region in a Fe–C–M alloy, where M is a ferrite-stabilizing element.

Let us now qualitatively consider the effect of different alloying elements on the kinetics of ferrite transformation in steels. The austenite-stabilizing elements, like Mn, Ni, and Cu, lower the equilibrium Ae_3 temperature (see Chapter 2) and the effective "Ae_3" temperature for the $\gamma \rightarrow \alpha$ transformation, i.e. the Ae_3(LENP) temperature, would be still lower. Hence, these elements would substantially retard the ferrite transformation. Note that the ferrite growth rate parameter, α, at a given temperature is, to a first approximation, proportional to the concentration difference ($C_{C(NP)}^{\gamma\alpha} - C_C^A$) in Eq. (3.4) (also see Figs. 3.2 and 3.3), or to the undercooling ΔT below Ae_3(LENP); $\Delta T = [Ae_3(LENP) - T]$. The ferrite-stabilizing elements, like Si, Mo, etc., on the other hand, raise the quilibrium Ae_3 temperature. The Ae_3(LENP) temperature in the presence of a ferrite-stabilizing element (which is always lower than equilibrium Ae_3) may be higher or lower than that of the binary Fe–C alloy of the same carbon content, depending upon the concentration of the alloying element and thermodynamics of the system. When it is lower, the $\gamma \rightarrow \alpha$ transformation is retarded and when it is higher, the transformation is accelerated. Experimentally, it

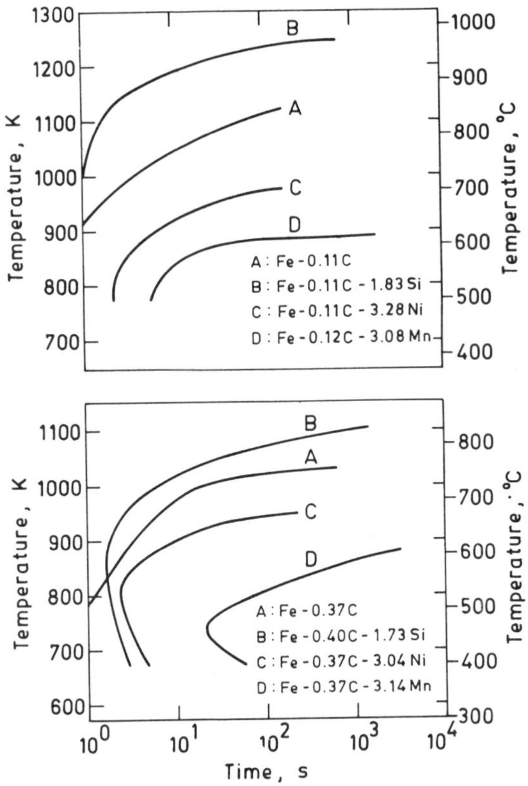

Fig. 3.9. Effect of Si, Mn and Ni on the start curves of IT diagrams of low and medium carbon steels (Ref. 3).

is observed that all alloying elements in steels, with the possible exception of Co, retard the ferrite transformation at temperatures close to the nose of IT diagrams. Figure 3.9 shows the effect of Si, Mn and Ni on the start curves of IT diagrams of low and medium carbon steels, reflecting the effect of these elements on the kinetics of $\gamma \rightarrow \alpha$ transformation. Mn and Ni, being austenite-stabilizing elements, substantially retard the $\gamma \rightarrow \alpha$ transformation, as discussed above, whereas Si, a ferrite-stabilizing element, accelerates the ferrite transformation at higher temperatures, as expected, but around the nose of the IT diagram, the transformation is little slower than in Si-free Fe–C alloys, reflecting the effect of thermodynamics of the system on the effective driving force for carbon diffusion during the transformation. The experimental results shown in Fig. 3.9, then, qualitatively agree with the expected effect of these alloying elements on ferrite transformation as discussed in this section.

2.3 EFFECT OF STRONG CARBIDE-FORMING ELEMENTS

Based on the discussion in the previous section, elements like Mo, Cr, etc., which are ferrite stabilizers (as well as strong carbide-forming elements), would be expected to accelerate or at the most only moderately slow down the ferrite transformation.

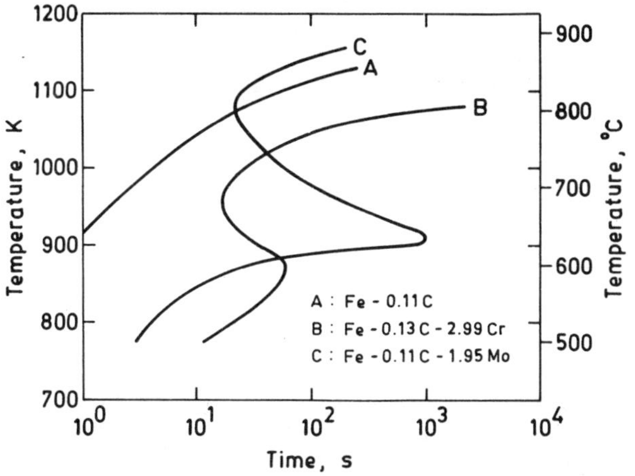

Fig. 3.10. Effect of Cr and Mo on the start curves of IT diagrams of low carbon steels (Ref.3–4).

However, they do not behave in this expected manner. Fig. 3.10 gives experimental IT start curves for Fe–C, Fe–C–Mo and Fe–C–Cr steels of approximately same carbon contents, reflecting the effect of Mo and Cr on the kinetics of ferrite transformation. The transformation rates in Fe-C-Mo and Fe-C-Cr alloys are generally as expected up to certain temperature below Ae_3 temperatures, and then, slow down considerably, forming a deep bay in the IT diagrams, and again become faster at still lower temperatures. The transformation rates in the low temperature bainite range are also more or less in the expected range. Hence, the ferrite transformation is unexpectedly, and strongly, retarded by the presence of these elements in the intermediate temperature range. These elements are also strong carbide forming elements. The strong retardation effect of these alloying elements on ferrite transformation in the intermediate temperature range is thought to be related to the strong carbide-forming tendencies of these elements and/or the strong attractive interaction between carbon and alloying elements in these alloys. The exact mechanism for the formation of "bay" (i.e. the retardation of ferrite transformation in the intermediate temperature range) in the presence of strong carbide-forming elements is not quite well understood. Earlier, it was speculated that the alloying elements partition between ferrite and austenite above the "bay" and the transformation is controlled by alloying element diffusion, whereas carbon diffusion controlled transformation (without partitioning) occurs in the low temperature bainitic range. However, recent experimental evidence completely disapproves this explanation.

Formation of the "bay" in the presence of strong carbide-forming elements is still to be completely satisfactorily explained. Two alternative hypotheses for its occurence have been offered. In the first hypothesis (Ref. 5), it is envisaged that due to strong attractive interaction between these alloying elements and carbon, "alloying element-carbon" clusters are formed in austenite ahead of the advancing α/γ interface and the interaction between these clusters and the interface greatly reduces the

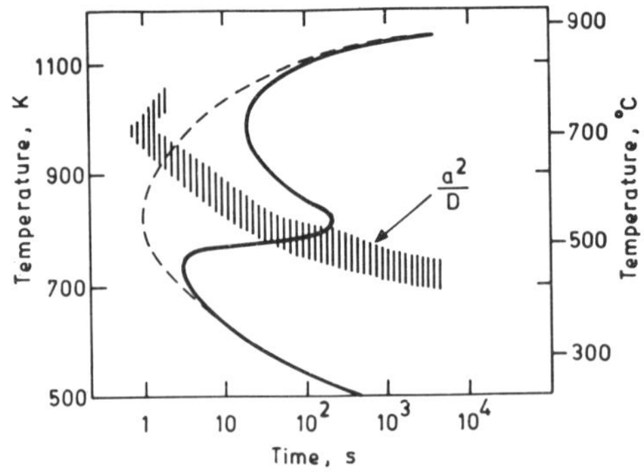

Fig. 3.11. (////) Time for the "alloying element-carbon" clusters' growth to ~2 nm diameter estimated as a^2/D, where a is cluster radius and D is alloying element diffusivity, (———) IT diagram of a steel containing Mo and/or Cr, (- - - - -) the expected IT diagram in the absence of a retardation effect (Ref. 5).

mobility of the interface. The formation of these clusters would be controlled by the diffusion of alloying element atoms, the slower diffusing species in the clusters. Figure 3.11 semi-qualitatively shows the relationship between the time required to form ~2 nm size clusters and the IT diagram of one such steel. It is clear that the retardation effect due to these clusters would be maximum in the intermediate temperature range, where the "bay" is formed.

In the other hypothesis (Ref. 4), formation of the "bay" is ascribed to "impurity drag effect". It is postulated that, because of its strong affinity for carbon, the alloying element segregates to the α/γ interface, where the carbon concentration in austenite is highest. Mobility of the interface is retarded in a manner similar to the "impurity drag effect" on grain boundary motion during recrystallization and grain growth. Here again, the drag effect is expected to be maximum in the intermediate temperature range. At higher temperatures, the "impurity atmosphere" moves with the interface, offering little resistance, as the alloying element diffusivity is relatively higher and the interface velocity is lower. At low temperatures, where driving force for ferrite transformation is relatively large, the interface breaks away from the "impurity atmosphere" and is not affected by it. In some intermediate temperature range, maximum resistance to interface motion is offered by the "impurity atmosphere", strongly retarding the ferrite transformation. Whether one or the other of these mechanisms operates during the actual transformation is a matter of conjecture and no judgement will be offered here. However, it is clear that strong attractive interaction between carbon and alloying elements in austenite is in some way responsible for the formation of "bay" in the IT diagrams of these steels.

3 PEARLITE TRANSFORMATION

As in the case of ferrite transformation and for reason discussed therein, the effect of alloying elements only on the growth kinetics of pearlite will be discussed. During the austenite to pearlite transformation in a Fe–C–M alloy, the alloying element, M, may partition between α and cm phases with overall composition in pearlite remaining same as in austenite, or, the transformation may occur without any partitioning of the alloying element. Effect of alloying elements on the eutectoid temperature and composition has already been discussed in Chapter 2. The no-partition Ae_1 temperature for pearlite transformation may be defined in a similar manner as no-partition Ae_3 temperatures for ferrite transformation. For pearlite transformation, only the local-equilibrium no-partition (LENP) mechanism will be considered. The para-equilibrium mechanism, which may be operative during the ferrite/bainite transformation at relatively high supersaturations, as discussed in the previous section, is most likely not operative during pearlite transformation (Refs. 6–7).

During pearlite transformation, austenite transforms simultaneously to a lamellar mixture of ferrite and cementite. The local-equilibrium no-partition (LENP) phase boundary for $\gamma \rightarrow \alpha$ transformation has already been defined in the previous section. LENP boundary for the $\gamma \rightarrow$ cm transformation, within the (γ + cm) two-phase region, may be obtained in the same manner, as schematically shown in Fig. 3.12. Figures 3.13 and 3.14 schematically show the equilibrium and LENP phase boundaries for the $\gamma \rightarrow \alpha$ and $\gamma \rightarrow$ cm transformations in the pearlite transformation range, their intersections defining the respective eutectoid points, for typical Fe–C–M systems containing an austenite stabilizing element and a ferrite stabilizing element, respectively. Note that, the LENP eutectoid temperature, Ae_1(LENP), is lower than the equilibrium Ae_1 temperature in both cases. The pearlite transformation, then, must occur with partitioning of the alloying element between equilibrium Ae_1 and Ae_1(LENP) temperatures, and may occur without partitioning below Ae_1(LENP). Detailed thermodynamic calculations show that, in general, the addition of an austenite stabilizing element to Fe–C alloys lowers the equilibrium Ae_1 temperature and the Ae_1(LENP) temperature would be still lower, whereas the addition of a ferrite stabilizing element increases the equilibrium Ae_1 temperature and the Ae_1(LENP) temperature is not only lower than equilibrium Ae_1 temperature, but is also lower than the binary Fe–C eutectoid temperature (Ref. 7).

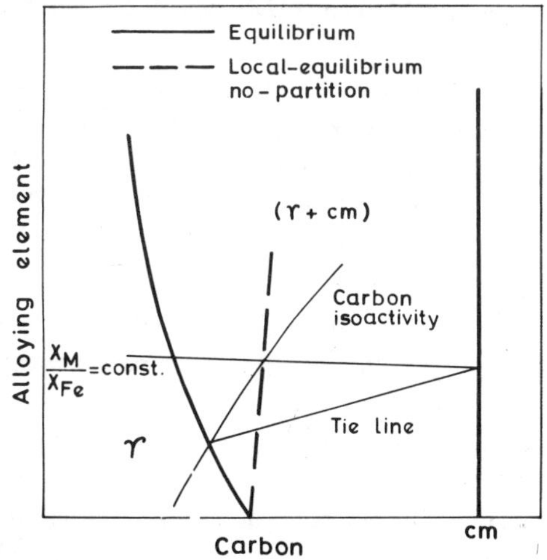

Fig. 3.12. Local equilibrium no-patition (LENP) boundary for $\gamma \rightarrow$ cm transformation (schematic).

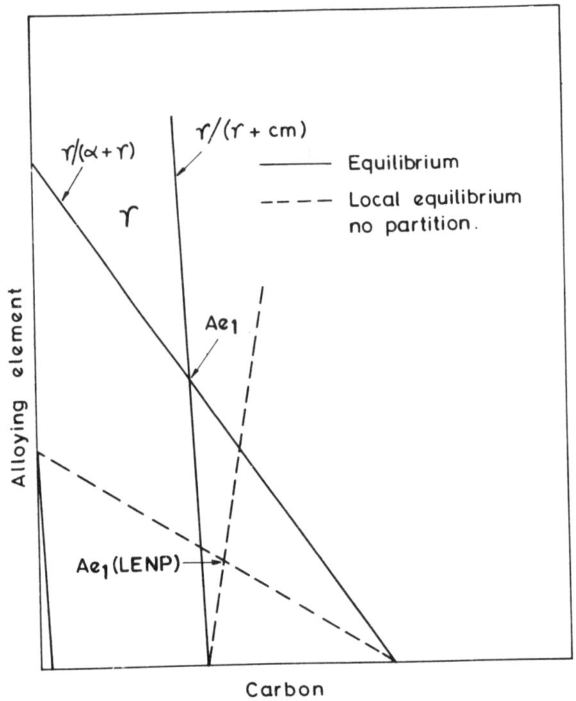

Fig. 3.13. Equilibrium and LENP boundaries in the pearlite transformation range in a Fe–C–M system, when M is a austenite-stabilizing element (schematic).

During the γ to pearlite transformation, the redistribution of carbon as well as that of the alloying elements between ferrite and cementite is possible either by volume diffusion (i.e. by diffusion through the austenite matrix ahead of the γ/pearlite interface) or by interface boundary diffusion (i.e., by diffusion through the γ/pearlite interfaces), as schematically shown in Fig. 3.15. The actual diffusion path depends on the relative magnitudes of (δD^b) and (SD^γ), where, δ is interface boundary thickness, S is interlamellar spacing, and D^b and D^γ are interface boundary and volume diffusivities, respectively. When $\delta D^b >> SD^\gamma$, redistribution of the element predominantly occurs by interface boundary diffusion, and when $SD^\gamma >> \delta D^b$, it occurs mainly by volume diffusion. During pearlite transformation in Fe–C–M alloys, whenever the alloying element partitions between ferrite and cementite, it diffuses essentially through the interface boundary, whereas carbon is generally redistributed by volume diffusion.

As discussed above, partitioning of the alloying elements must occur during pearlite transformation between Ae_1 and Ae_1(LENP) temperatures. Assuming that local equilibrium is maintained at the γ/pearlite interface and partitioning of the alloying elements sufficiently slows down the pearlite growth rates for the faster diffusing carbon to essentially attain uniform activity in austenite ahead of the γ/pearlite interface; the interface local equilibrium concentrations (ignoring the capillarity effect) would be as schematically shown in Fig. 3.16 when alloying element segregates to

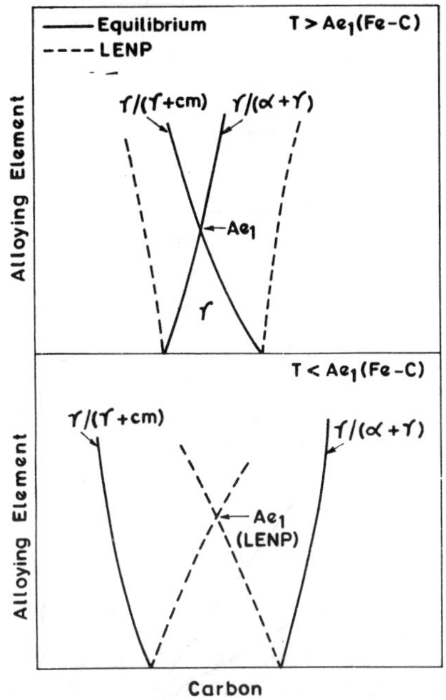

Fig. 3.14. Equilibrium and LENP boundaries in the pearlite transformation range in a Fe–C–M system, when M is a ferrite-stabilizing element (schematic).

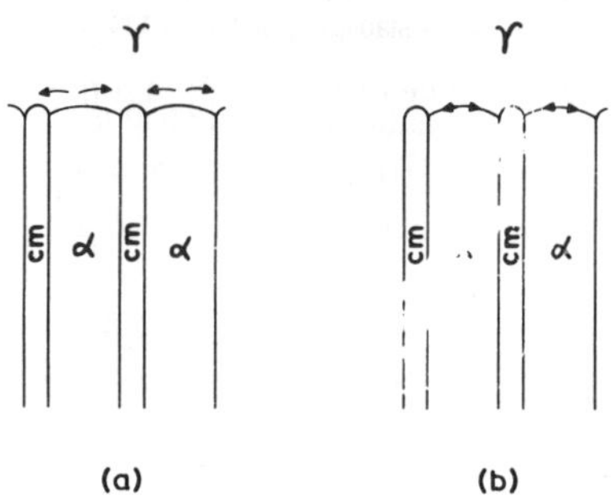

Fig. 3.15. Possible diffusion paths for the redistribution of elements between ferrite and cementite during pearlite transformation, (a) volume diffusion, (b) interface boundary diffusion.

cementite, and as in Fig. 3.17 when it segregates to ferrite. In Figs. 3.16 and 3.17, *ab* is carbon isoactivity line in austenite, and *cb* and *ad* are tie lines in the $(\alpha + \gamma)$ and $(\gamma + \text{cm})$ equilibrium regions respectively. Points *c* and *d* give concentrations of ferrite and cementite respectively, in pearlite behind the growing γ/pearlite interface, and the difference in concentration of the alloying element between points *a* and *b* is the driving force for alloying element diffusion. The pearlite growth rate *v*, with the alloying element diffusing through the interface boundary, is then given by (Refs. 6–8):

$$v = 12\,(K\delta D_M^b)\left(\frac{S^2}{S_\alpha\, S_{cm}}\right)\left(\frac{|C_M^{\gamma\alpha} - C_M^{\gamma cm}|}{C_M}\right)\frac{1}{S^2}\left(1 - \frac{S_0}{S}\right) \tag{3.11}$$

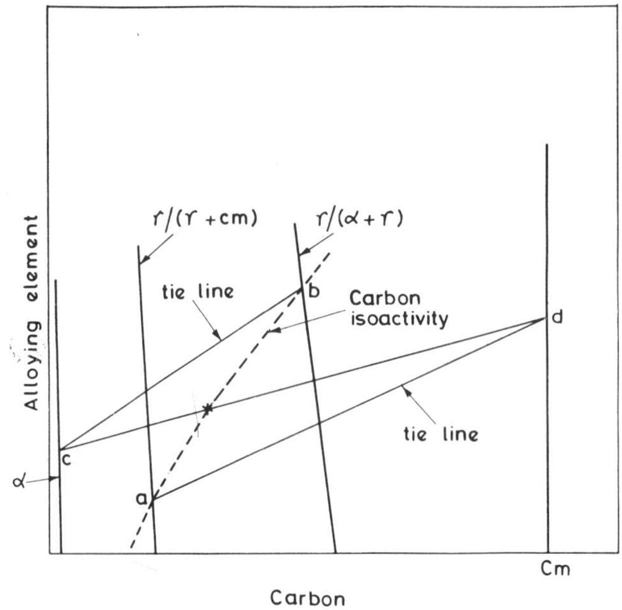

Fig. 3.16. Local-equilibrium condition during pearlite growth, when alloying element partitions and segregates to cementite.

where, S_α, S_{cm}, S_0 and S are ferrite lamellar thickness, cementite lamellar thickness, critical inter-lamellar spacing and inter-lamellar spacing, respectively, $\overline{C}_M$ is the average concentration of alloying element in pearlite; $(K\delta D_M^b)$ is boundary diffusivity term; and $C_M^{\gamma\alpha}$ and $C_M^{\gamma cm}$ are alloying element concentrations corresponding to points

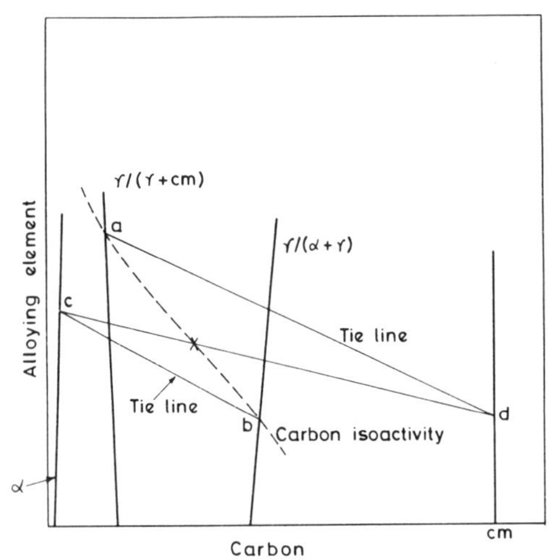

Fig. 3.17. Local-equilibrium condition during pearlite growth, when alloying element partitions and segregates to ferrite.

b and a, respectively, in Fig. 3.16, or 3.17. Taking $(S_\alpha/S) \cong (7/8)$; $(S_{cm}/S) \cong (1/8)$ and $S = 2S_0$ (according to the maximum entropy production rate criterion (Ref. 6), Eq. (3.11) becomes:

$$v = 55\,(K\delta D_M^b)\left(\frac{|C_M^{\gamma\alpha} - C_M^{\gamma cm}|}{\bar{C}_M}\right)\frac{1}{S^2} \tag{3.12}$$

In Eq. (3.12), in the boundary diffusivity term, $(K\delta D_M^b)$, it is difficult to separately obtain K (segregation coefficient), δ (boundary thickness) and D_M^b (bounary diffusion coefficient). Furthermore, experimental data on interface boundary diffusivity are not available. However, limited data for grain boundary diffusivities of iron and some other alloying elements in austenite and ferrite exist and can be summarized as:

$$(K\delta D_M^b) = 5.4 \times 10^{-8} \exp\left(\frac{-154,\ 800J}{RT}\right) \tag{3.13}$$

In the absence of interface diffusivity data, Eq. (3.13) may be used for the interface diffusivity term in Eq. (3.12). Equation (3.12), then, gives pearlite growth rates between Ae_1 and Ae_1(LENP) temperature, where alloying elements partition between ferrite and cementite during the pearlite transformation.

Below Ae_1(LENP), alloying elements normally do not partition between ferrite and cementite, the pearlite growth is controlled by carbon volume diffusion, and the growth rates are given by the same equations as in binary Fe–C alloys (see Chapter 1), i.e.:

$$v = \frac{kD_C^\gamma}{S}\frac{(C_C^{\gamma\alpha} - C_C^{\gamma cm})}{(C_C^{cm} - C_C^{\alpha})} \tag{3.14}$$

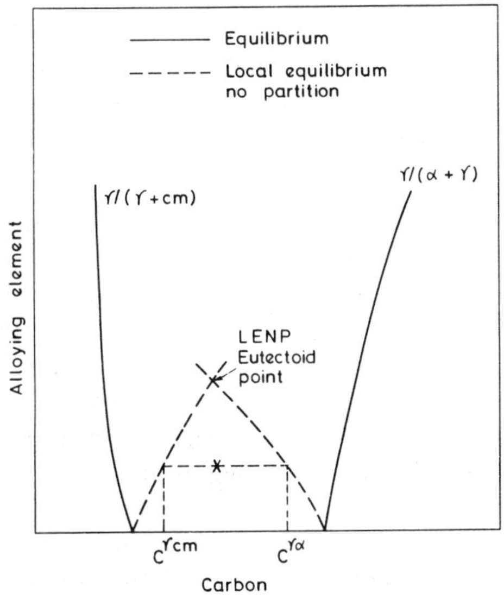

Fig. 3.18. Driving force for carbon diffusion during pearlite growth without partitioning of the alloying element.

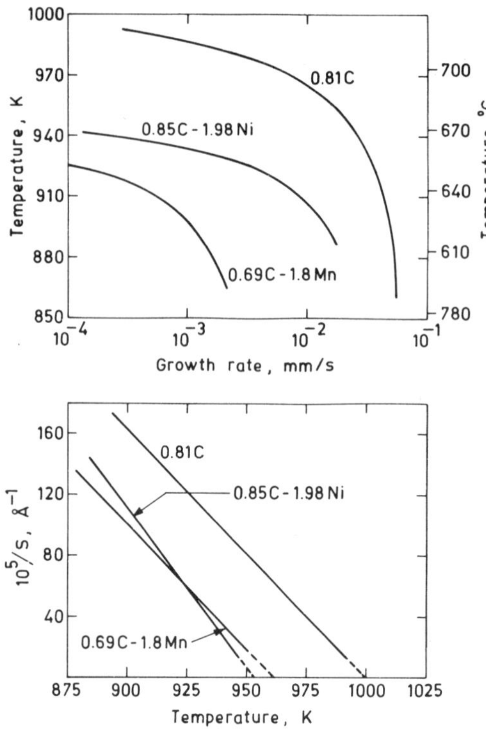

Fig. 3.19. Effect of Mn and Ni on the pearlite growth rates and inter-lamellar spacings (Ref. 9).

where, C_C^{cm} and C_C^{α} are, respectively, the carbon concentrations of cementite and ferrite in pearlite; D_C^{γ} is carbon diffusion coefficient in austenite; k is a constant; and $C_C^{\gamma\alpha}$ and $C_C^{\gamma cm}$ are, respectively, the local equilibrium carbon concentrations in austenite given by the LENP boundaries, as shown in Fig. 3.18. Note that the driving force for pearlite transformation, measured as ($C_C^{\gamma\alpha}$ – $C_C^{\gamma cm}$), is lower than for binary Fe–C eutectoid alloy.

Experimental data on pearlite growth rates, inter-lamellar spacings and alloying element partitioning in number of ternary Fe–C–M alloys, containing different alloying elements, are satisfactorily explained (semi-quantitatively) by above discussed mechanisms of pearlite growth (Ref. 7). To summarize, between Ae_1 and Ae_1(LENP) temperatures, pearlite growth is accompanied by partitioning of the alloying elements between ferrite and cementite and the growth rates are essentially controlled by alloying element interface boundary diffusion; below Ae_1(LENP), pearlite growth occurs without any partitioning of the alloying elements and the growth rates are essentially controlled by carbon volume diffusion. Figure 3.19 shows the effect of austenite stabilizing elements, Mn and Ni, on the pearlite growth rates and interlamellar spacings in Fe–C–M alloys. Being austenite-stabilizing elements, both Mn and Ni lower the equilibrium Ae_1 temperature and the Ae_1(LENP)

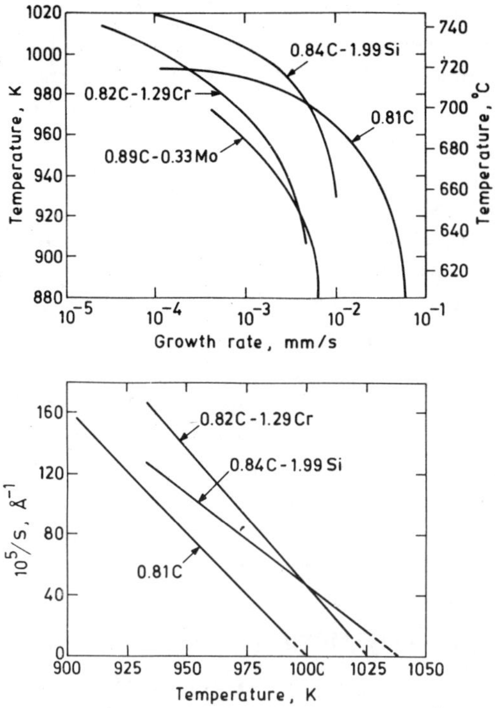

Fig. 3.20. Effect of Si, Cr and Mo on the pearlite growth rates and inter-lamellar spacings (Ref. 9).

temperatures are still lower. Hence, the pearlite growth rates are substantially retarded with the addition of Mn and Ni to Fe–C alloys. This is in general agreement with the mechanisms discussed above. Figure 3.20 compares the pearlite growth rates and inter-lamellar spacings in Fe–C–Si, Fe–C–Mo and Fe–C–Cr alloys with that of binary Fe–C eutectoid alloy. Si, Mo and Cr, the ferrite stabilizing elements, increase the Ae_1 temperature. Hence, the pearlite transformation starts at temperatures higher than the binary Fe–C alloy. The $1/S$ vs T plots intercept the temperature

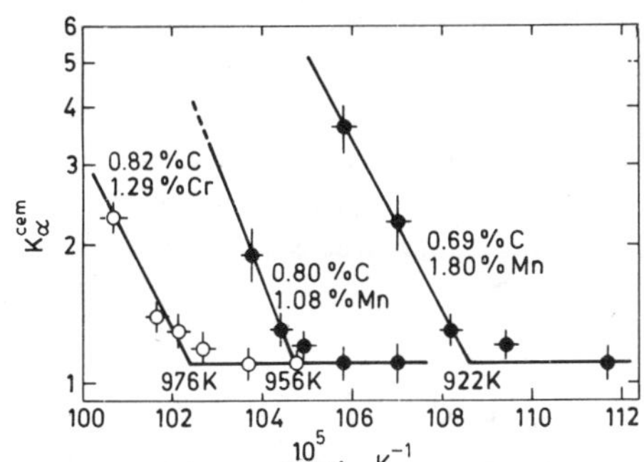

Fig. 3.21. Partitioning of alloying elements during pearlite growth in Fe–C–Mn and Fe–C–Cr alloys (Ref. 9).

axis at equilibrium Ae_1 temperatures and the pearlite growth rate curves are asymptotic to equilibrium Ae_1 temperatures. The Ae_1(LENP) temperatures in these alloys are, however, lower than the binary Fe–C eutectoid temperature (Ref. 7). Therefore, at temperatures lower than Ae_1(LENP), where carbon volume diffusion controlled transformation occurs, the pearlite growth rates are lower than in the binary Fe–C alloy. Between Ae_1 and Ae_1(LENP) also, the pearlite growth rates are relatively slower due to alloying element diffusion (boundary diffusion) control. Note that, in the partitioning range, the pearlite transformation is not as exceptionally slow as ferrite transformation, because the alloying element partitioning during pearlite transformation occurs by interface boundary diffusion as opposed to austenite matrix diffusion during ferrite transformation. Hence, in these alloys, though the pearlite transformation starts at temperatures higher than the binary Fe–C eutectoid temperature, the growth rates at lower temperatures are slower than in binary Fe–C alloy (Fig. 3.20). Partitioning of the alloying elements between ferrite and cementite, during pearlite transformation, has been experimentally measured in a number of Fe–C–M alloys. Results for some Fe-C-Mn and Fe-C-Cr alloys are shown Fig. 3.21. It is seen that partitioning occurs down to a certain temperature, characteristic of the specific alloying element and its concentration, as expected from the theory of pearlite growth discussed in this section.

4 MARTENSITE TRANSFORMATION

In low alloy steels, martensite transformation occurs essentially in the same manner as in binary Fe–C alloys. The alloying elements only affect the M_s and M_f temperatures. Andrews (Ref. 11) has developed empirical formulae for the variation of M_s temperature with composition in low-alloy multicomponent steels, as:

$$\begin{aligned} M_s(\mathrm{K}) = {} & 812 - 423(\%\mathrm{C}) - 30.4(\%\mathrm{Mn}) - 12.1(\%\mathrm{Cr}) \\ & - 17.7(\%\mathrm{Ni}) - 7.5(\%\mathrm{Mo}) \end{aligned} \tag{3.15}$$

and

$$\begin{aligned} M_s(\mathrm{K}) = {} & 785 - 453(\%\mathrm{C}) - 16.9(\%\mathrm{Ni}) + 15(\%\mathrm{Cr}) \\ & - 9.5(\%\mathrm{Mo}) + 217(\%\mathrm{C})^2 - 71.5(\%\mathrm{C})(\%\mathrm{Mn}) \\ & - 67.6(\%\mathrm{C})(\%\mathrm{Cr}) \end{aligned} \tag{3.16}$$

Equations (3.15) and (3.16) are valid for alloys containing up to 0.6% C, 4.9% Mn, 5% Cr, 5% Ni and 5.4% Mo. Elements like Si, S and P did not show significant correlation. The non-linear formula in Eq. (3.16) has slightly better correlation than the linear formula in Eq. (3.15). As seen in Eqs. (3.15) and (3.16), all alloying elements decrease the M_s temperature. Only Co is known to slightly raise the M_s temperature. As a consequence of lowering of M_s temperature with the addition of alloying elements, retained austenite in alloy steels on quenching to room temperature is increased, as the M_f temperature is also correspondingly lowered.

5 ISOTHERMAL TRANSFORMATION DIAGRAMS

Effect of alloying elements on the kinetics of various transformations from austenite is reflected in their isothermal transformation (IT) diagrams. Figures 3.22 to 3.26

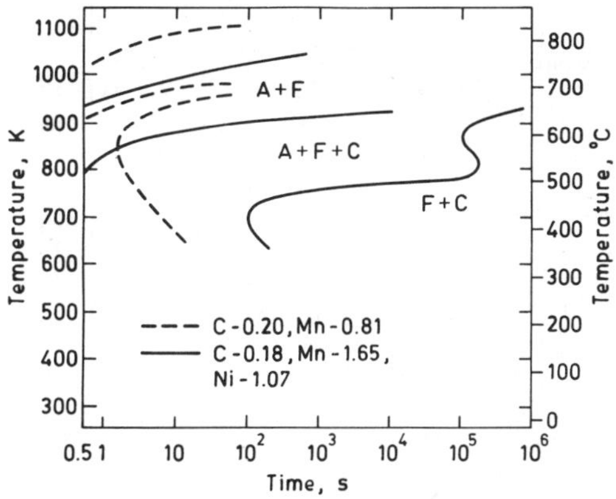

Fig. 3.22. IT diagrams for (AISI-1021) (- - - - -) and (AISI-1021)+ 1%Ni + 1%Mn steels (———) (A austenite, F: ferrite, C: carbides).

give IT diagrams of a number of low-alloy steels, reflecting the effect of different alloying elements on the kinetics of austenite decomposition products. Based on the discussions in this chapter, the effect of different alloying elements on phase transformations in low-alloy steels and their isothermal transformation diagrams can be qualitatively summarized as follows:

(*i*) The austenite-stabilizing elements, like Mn, Ni and Cu, lower the equilibrium Ae_3 and Ae_1 temperatures. The no-partition Ae_3(LENP) and Ae_1(LENP) temperatures for the carbon diffusion controlled transformations are still lower. Hence, these elements substantially slow down the ferrite and pearlite transformations and shift the IT curves to lower temperatures

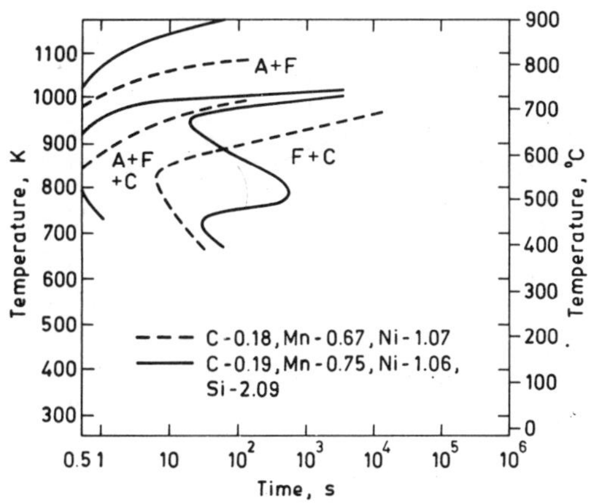

Fig. 3.23. IT diagrams for (AISI-1021) + 1%Ni (- - - -) and (AISI-1021) + 1% Ni + 2% Si steels. (———) (A: austenite, F: ferrite, C: carbides).

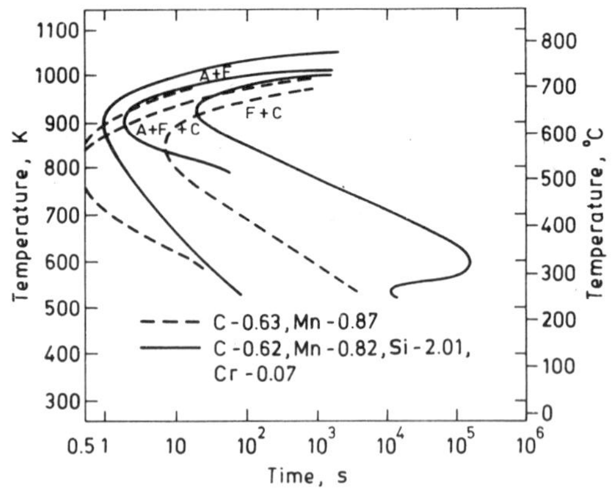

Fig. 3.24. IT diagrams for AISI-1060 (- - - -) and AISI-9260 steels (———) (A: austenite, F: ferrite, C: carbides).

and longer times, as seen in Fig. 3.22. For the same addition of alloying elements, Mn has a higher effect as compared to Ni or Cu.

(*ii*) Si, a ferrite-stabilizing element, raises the equilibrium Ae_3 and Ae_1 temperature. Hence, the transformations start at higher temperatures than in the corresponding Si-free Fe–C alloys. At lower temperatures, Si has a slight retardation effect on the ferrite transformation, as discussed earlier. However, the pearlite transformation is considerably slowed down with the addition of Si, as Si has almost no solubility in cementite and it partitions during the pearlite transformation till very low temperatures. Therefore, in low-carbon steels, where ferrite is the main austenite decomposition product, Si does not significantly affect the IT diagrams (see Fig. 3.23), whereas in medium- and high-carbon steels, where pearlite is the main austenite decom-

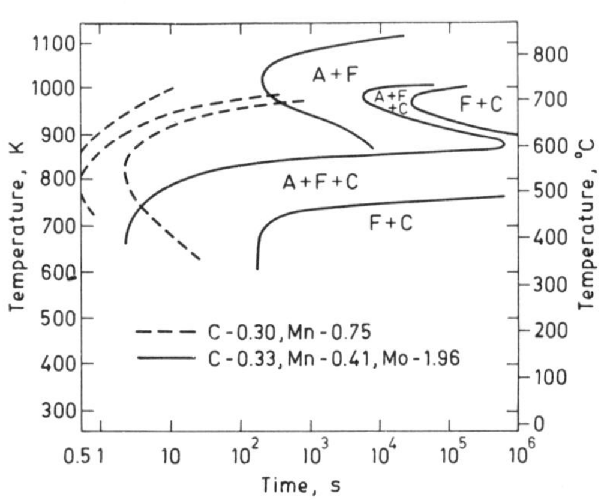

Fig. 3.25. IT diagrams for AISI-1030 (- - - -) and (AISI-1030) + 2%Mo steels. (———) (A austenite, F: ferrite, C: carbides).

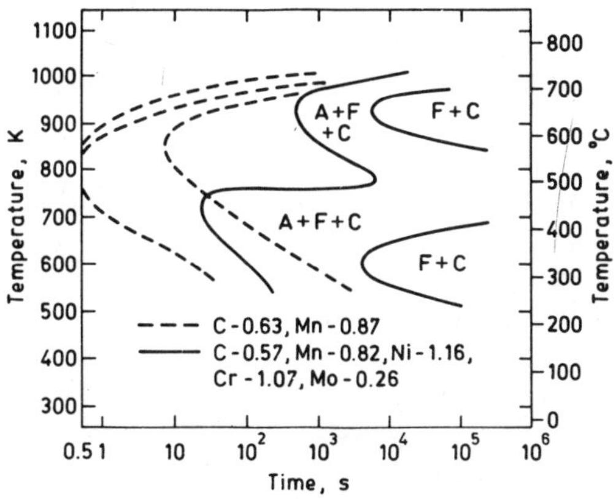

Fig. 3.26. IT diagrams for AISI-1060 (- - - -) and AISI-9860 steels. (————)
(A austenite, F: ferrite, C: carbides).

position product, the IT curves are shifted to longer times, as seen in Fig. 3.24.

(*iii*) Strong carbide-forming elements, like Cr and Mo; preferentially retard the ferrite transformation at intermediate temperatures, for reasons not completely well understood. With respect to pearlite transformation, Cr and Mo increase the equilibrium Ae_1 temperature, however, the no-partition Ae_1(LENP) temperatures are lower than the binary Fe–C eutectoid temperature and the difference between Ae_1 (Fe–C) and Ae_1(LENP) in Fe–C–M alloys (M: Cr, Mo, etc.) increases with increasing concentration of the alloying element (Ref. 7). Hence, though the pearlite transformation starts at temperatures higher than the binary Fe–C eutectoid temperature, at lower temperatures, the transformation rates are slower than in the binary Fe–C alloy. The retardation effect of Cr and Mo on ferrite and pearlite transformations is relatively stronger than on the bainite transformation, which most likely occurs by para-equilibrium mechanism at still lower temperatures. This gives rise to a deep bay (double C-curve) in the IT diagrams of steels containing Cr and Mo. In these steels, the upper nose of the IT diagrams, due to ferrite and/or pearlite transformations, is at higher temperatures and longer times in relation to the IT diagrams of corresponding plain carbon steels of the same carbon contents. Effect of Cr and Mo on the IT diagrams can be seen in Figs. 3.25 and 3.26.

REFERENCES

1. D.E. Coates, *Metall. Trans.*, **3** (1972) p. 1203 and **4** (1973) p. 2313.
2. J.B. Glimour, G.R. Purdy and J.S. Kirkaldy, *Metall. Trans.*, **3** (1972) p. 1455.
3. H.I. Aaronson and H.A. Domian, *Trans TMS-AIME*, **236** (1966) p. 781.

4. K.R. Kinsman and H.I. Aaronson, in *Transformations and Hardenability in Steels*, Climax Molybdenum Company of Michigan, 1967.
5. R.C. Sharma and G.R. Purdy, *Metall. Trans.*, **5** (1974) p. 939.
6. R.C. Sharma, G.R. Purdy and J.S. Kirkaldy, *Metall. Trans A.*, **10A** (1979) p. 1129.
7. S.K. Tewari and R.C. Sharma, *Metall. Trans. A.*, **16A** (1985) p. 597.
8. M. Hillert, *Jernk. Ann.,* **141** (1957) p. 757.
9. N. Ridley, 'Pearlite Transformation' in *Heat Treatment* **76**, The Metals Society, London, 1976.
10. N. Ridley, ''Pearlite Transformation'' in *Phase Transformations in Ferrous Alloys* (Eds. A.R. Marder, J.I. Goldstein), TMS-AIME Publication, 1984.
11. K.W. Andrews, *JISI*, **203** (1965) pp. 721–27.
12. *Atlas of Isothermal Transformation Diagrams*, American Society for Metals, Metals Park, Ohio, 1977.

CHAPTER 4

Structure-Property Relationships

1 INTRODUCTION

Mechanical properties of a steel, or any metal/alloy for that matter, strongly depend on its microstructural features and may be changed to a large extent by manipulating the microstructure. The purpose of any heat treatment of a steel component is to achieve the desired combination of mechanical properties by subjecting it to an appropriate temperature-time cycle, designed to obtain specific microstructural features. A comprehensive discussion on the structure-property relationships in metals and alloys is beyond the scope of this book. However, an elementary understanding of the relations between mechanical properties and microstructures of steels is essential to fully appreciate the different heat treatment processes to which the steel components are normally subjected. A brief discussion on strength, toughness and ductility of carbon and low-alloy steels as a function of their composition and microstructural features is, therefore, included in this chapter.

2 FERRITE–PEARLITE STEELS

2.1 GENERAL FEATURES

A major portion of steel production is low and medium carbon steels, sold as hot rolled products. These steels are essentially cooled in air from rolling (austenite) temperatures and their room temperature microstructure is duplex ferrite-pearlite structure. The amount of pearlite in these steels is mainly a function of their carbon content, varying from zero to 100% as the carbon content is increased from zero to around eutectoid composition (0.77%C in plain carbon steels). Beyond eutectoid composition, the structure is cementite plus pearlite.

Ferrite is a relatively soft and ductile phase having a tensile strength of approx. 275 MPa (~40,000 psi) and ~40% elongation in a 50 mm tensile test specimen. Cementite is hard and brittle with a probable strength of ~35 MPa (~5000 psi). Pearlite, which is a lamellar mixture of ferrite and cementite, has a much higher strength than any of its constituent phases. Pearlite has a tensile strength of the order of 800 MPa (~150,000 psi) and an elongation of ~10% in a 50 mm tensile test specimen. Figure 4.1 shows general variation in mechanical properties of hot-rolled plain carbon steels as a function of carbon content. The yield and tensile strengths increase with carbon content up to ~0.9%C and then level off; however, the Brinell hardness continues to increase as the content of hard cementite phase keeps increasing. The ductility decreases with increasing carbon content and is practically nil beyond ~1.3%C. A relation similar to ductility holds true for the impact strength also. These relations are however only approximate. The mechanical properties of ferrite-pearlite steels greatly vary with the grain size of ferrite, pearlite inter-lamellar spacing, and the amount and type of alloying elements present in steels, as discussed in the following sections.

2.2 TENSILE STRENGTH

The relationship between the strength of a ferrite-pearlite steel and its carbon content as shown in Fig. 4.1 is only approximate. More accurately, the strength of ferrite is a function of its grain size and that of pearlite of its inter-lamellar spacing. Furthermore, any alloying element present in the steel contributes to solid solution strengthening of ferrite. The strong carbide/nitride forming elements, like Nb, V, Ti, etc., whose carbides and nitrides have very limited solubilities in ferrite and austenite, normally precipitate out as fine dispersion of carbides, nitrides and/or carbonitrides, and contribute to strength due to precipitation hardening. The yield strength of ferrite, σ_y, in low alloy steels may be expressed as a function of the above mentioned factors as:

$$\sigma_y = \sigma_o + \sigma_s + \sigma_p + k_y d^{-1/2} \quad (4.1)$$

where σ_o is apparent friction stress; σ_s and σ_p are contributions to σ_y due to solid solution strengthening and precipitation strengthening, respectively; k_y is a constant; and d is average ferrite grain diameter. The term $k_y d^{-1/2}$ is the effect of grain size on

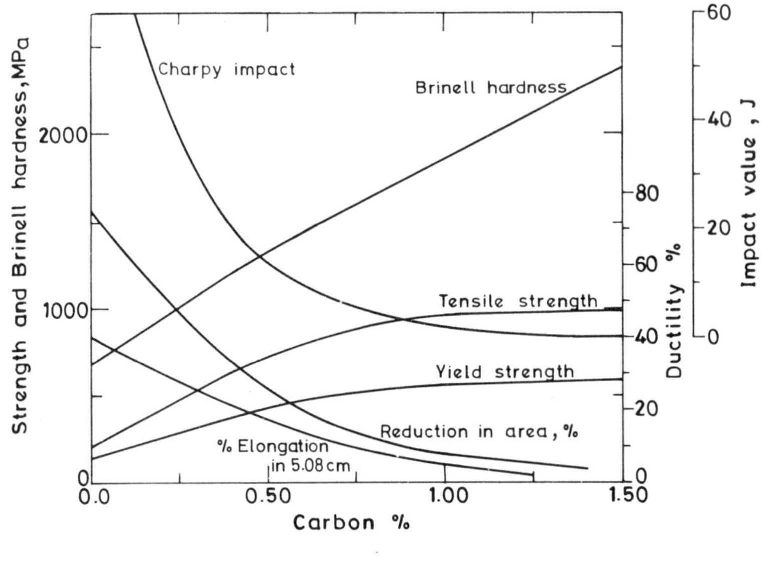

Fig. 4.1. Variation of mechanical properties of ferrite-pearlite carbon steels with carbon content.

the yield stength of ferrite according to the Hall–Petch relationship. For ferrite in slowly cooled steels, σ_o is ~70–90 MPa. The solid solution hardening effect, σ_s, is theoretically proportional to the square root of concentration; however, at low concentrations a lineaer dependence may be used, i.e.:

$$\sigma_s = A \times (\% \text{ Alloying Element in Solution}) \tag{4.2}$$

The constant A in Eq. (4.2) for a number of alloying elements in steels is given in Table 4.1 (Ref. 5). The precipitation strengthening contribution, σ_p, to the yield strength of ferrite is a function of the volume fraction of the precipitates and their average size. The Ashby–Orowan model gives strengthening due to precipitation as:

$$\sigma_p \text{ (MPa)} = \left(\frac{5.9\sqrt{f}}{\overline{X}}\right) \ln\left(\frac{\overline{X}}{2.5 \times 10^{-4}}\right) \tag{4.3}$$

where, f is volume fraction of the precipitates and $\overline{X}$ is their mean planar intercept diameter in μm. Here again, for the sake of simiplicity, the precipitation strengthening effect, σ_p, may be assumed to be proportional to the amount of alloying element present (Ref. 5), i.e.:

$$\sigma_p = B \times (\% \text{ Alloying Element in Steel}) \tag{4.4}$$

where the constant B for different alloying elements that contribute to precipitation strengthening in low-alloy steels is given in Table 4.2. B_{max} corresponds to the maximum strengthening effect that may be obtained, whereas B_{avg} corresponds to the average effect normally obtained. Finally, for the grain size strengthening effect, the parameter k_y in Eq. (4.1) is ~15–17 when strength is expressed in MPa and the average grain diameter, d, in mm.

Table 4.1. *Constant A (MPa / %M) for Use in Eq. (4.2) for Different Alloying Elements (Ref. 5)*

M	*A*	M	*A*	M	*A*
Mn	37	Cu	38	Sn	120
Si	83	Mo	11	P	680
Ni	33	Cr	–30	C and N	5000

Table 4.2. *Constant B (MPa/%M) for use in Eq. (4.4), (Ref. 5)*

M	Precipitate	B_{max}	B_{avg}	Alloy range (wt%)
V	V_4C_3	1000	500	0–0.15
V	VN	3000	1500	0–0.06
Nb	Nb(CN)	3000	1500	0–0.05
Ti	TiC	3000	1500	0.03–0.18

The strength of low-carbon (predominantly ferritic) steels may now be correlated to different strengthening mechanisms in terms of Eq. (4.1). Pearlite in small volume fractions does not contribute much to the yield strength of ferrite-pearlite steels. For example, the yield strength of essentially ferritic silicon-killed C-Mn steels containing up to ~0.25% C has been expressed as (Ref. 2):

$$\sigma_y\ (\pm 30\text{MPa}) = 88 + 37(\%\text{Mn}) + 83(\%\text{Si}) + 2918(\%\text{N}_f) + 15.1\, d^{-1/2} \tag{4.5}$$

where (% alloying element) refers to wt % of the alloying element in steel and N_f stands for free nitrogen in solution. The contribution of pearlite to the yield stength of low-carbon steels is relatively small and therefore does not appear in Eq. (4.5). Fig. 4.2 graphically shows the relative contributions of different stengthening mechanisms to the yield strength of a low-carbon C-Mn steel as a function of grain size of ferrite, according to Eq. (4.5).

The yield strength of pearlite, σ_{Pe}, is a function of its inter-lamellar spacing, S, and it also follows the Hall–Petch relationship:

$$\sigma_{Pe} = \sigma_i + k\, S^{-1/2} \tag{4.6}$$

where, σ_i is apparent friction stress and k is a constant.

The yield strength of ferrite–pearlite duplex steels is a function of the yield strengths of ferrite and pearlite, and their relative volume fractions. A relationship of the following type has been found to be most suitable to describe the yield strength of ferrite–pearlite steels (Ref. 6).

$$\sigma_y = f_\alpha^n\, \sigma_\alpha + (1 - f_\alpha^n)\, \sigma_{Pe} \tag{4.7}$$

where, f_α is volume fraction of the ferrite phase; and σ_y, σ_α and σ_{Pe} are yield stengths of the ferrite–pearlite aggregate, ferrite and pearlite, respectively. The coefficient n allows a non-linear variation of yield strength with the volume fraction of

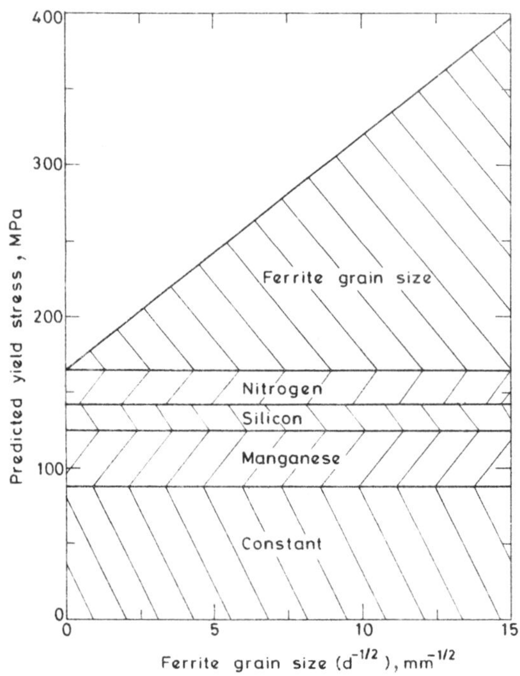

Fig. 4.2. Effect of grain size on the yield strength of normalized Fe–0.2C–1.0Mn–0.25Si–0.01N steel.

ferrite and has been found to be ~1/3. A typical relationship for the yield strength of ferrite-pearlite steels has been found as (Ref. 6):

$$\sigma_y\ (\pm\ 45\text{MPa}) = f_\alpha^{1/3}\ [35 + 58\ (\%\text{Mn}) + 17.4\ d^{-1/2}] + (1 - f_\alpha^{1/3})\ [178 + 3.8S^{-1/2}] + 63(\%\text{Si}) + 425\ (\sqrt{\%\text{N}_f}) \qquad (4.8)$$

where N_f refers to free nitrogen in solution. Figure 4.3 shows the contributions of different factors to the yield stength of ferrite-pearlite steels according to Eq. (4.8). Note that the contribution of pearlite to the yield strength becomes significant only at relatively higher volume fractions of pearlite, i.e. at carbon concentrations approaching eutectoid value.

The tensile strength of ferrite-pearlite steels follows relationships very similar to yield stength and has been expressed as (Ref. 6):

$$\sigma_T\ (\text{MPa}) = f_\alpha^{1/3}\ [246 + 1140\ (\sqrt{\%\text{N}_f}) + 18.2d^{-1/2}] + (1 - f_\alpha^{1/3})\ [720 + 3.5S^{-1/2}] + 97\ (\%\text{Si}) \qquad (4.9)$$

where, σ_T is tensile strength and other terms are as defined earlier.

The specific relationships discussed above are based on empirical regression analysis of the data for large number of steels and give the general effect of different microstructural and compositional variables on the yield and tensile stength of air cooled ferrite–pearlite steels. For a steel of given composition, some of the microstructural features can be manipulated to some extent by controlling the transformations from austenite. For example, if austenite is transformed at lower temperatures, i.e. at higher undercoolings, then, the ferrite grain size and the pearlite inter-lamellar spacing are smaller and the volume fraction of pearlite is somewhat higher. During continuous cooling of steels, the transformations occur at lower

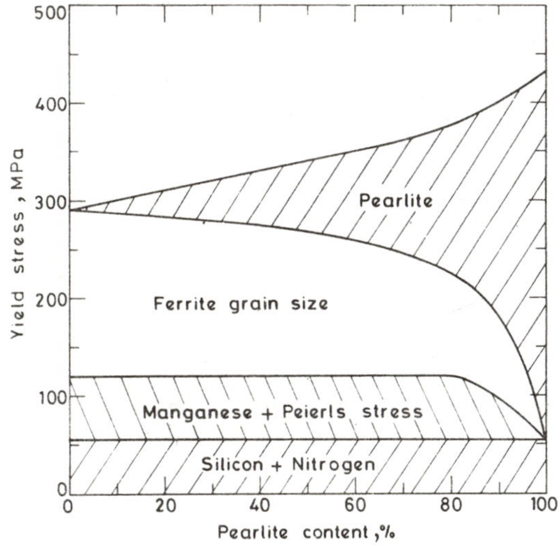

Fig. 4.3. Contributions of different strengthing mechanisms to the yield strength of ferrite-pearlite steels as a function of pearlite content.

temperatures at faster cooling rates. (This will be discussed in more detail in Chapters 6 and 7). Furthermore, the grain size of ferrite also depends on prior austenite grain size, which is a function of the parameters of high temperature austenite treatment prior to cooling, like, hot deformation, time and temperature of holding, etc. The nature of austenite treatment and the cooling rates from austenite also affect the extent of precipitation and the precipitate sizes in steels containing strong carbide/nitride forming elements. Hence, to an extent, the stength of a ferrite–pearlite low alloy steel of given composition can be manipulated/altered by controlling the processing parameters.

2.3 DUCTILITY

Ductility is a more complex property and is defined in a number of ways. The variation of ductility with microstructure and composition is also more complex. In general, all factors except grain size, which increase the strength would decrease ductility. Also, ductility is severely affected by the presence of inclusions in steels and varies with the type of inclusions as well as their size, shape and volume fraction. Most extensive work on the ductility of steels has been done on low-carbon formable steels. Two most important ductility parameters during a tensile test, the uniform strain prior the plastic instability, ε_u, and the total strain at fracture, ε_T, have been related to various compositional and microstructural parameters in these steels and the following type of correlations have been obtained (Ref.7):

$$\varepsilon_u = 0.27 - 0.016(\%\text{pearlite}) - 0.025(\%\text{Mn}) - 0.044(\%\text{Si}) - 0.039(\%\text{Sn}) - 1.2(\%\text{N}_f) \quad (4.10)$$

and

$$\varepsilon_T = 1.3 - 0.020(\%\ \text{pearlite}) - 0.3(\%\text{Mn}) - 0.2(\%\text{Si}) - 3.4(\%\text{S}) - 4.4(\%\text{P}) - 0.29(\%\text{Sn}) + 0.015d^{-1/2} \quad (4.11)$$

As can be seen from the above equations, all parameters that increase the strength of a steel, except grain size, decrease the ductility, though not by similar relative factors. The decrease in grain size increases strength as well as total ductility, ε_T, and has negligible effect on uniform strain, ε_u. The presence of pearlite in small volume fractions has essentially no effect on strength, as discussed earlier; however, it adversely affects ductility. The uniform elongation, ε_u, and more so the total ductility, ε_T, are also severely affected by the presence of inclusions in steels. The sulphur term in Eq. (4.11) is essentially due to sulphide inclusions. Inclusions act as stress raisers and cracks easily initiate at these inclusions, either due to cracking of inclusions or decohesion of inclusion/matrix interfaces. Elements which preferentially segregate at the grain boundaries, like P and Sn, also decrease total ductility.

The decrease in total ductility due to inclusions essentially depends on the volume fraction of the inclusions rather than on the type of inclusions and is not quite linear with volume fraction, as implied in Eq. (4.11). Figure 4.4 shows the variation of total ductility, ε_T, with the volume fraction of various types of inclusions. The ductility is also affected by shape of the inclusions. Spherical inclusions, in general, are less detrimental than elongated inclusions with sharp corners/edges, as the stress

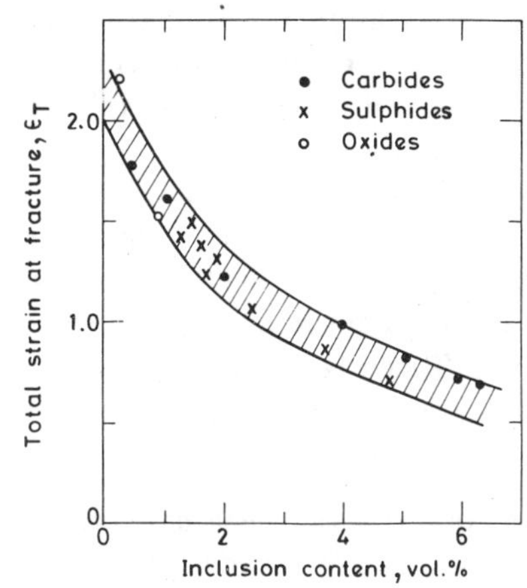

Fig. 4.4. Effect of inclusions on the total ductility of a low carbon steel. (from Ref.7).

concentration is essentially a function of the radius of curvature of inclusion/matrix interfaces. Some inclusions, like MnS, may deform during hot rolling or other high temperature deformation processes and become elongated in the direction of deformation. This leads to anisotropy in ductility as shown in Fig. 4.5. The radius of curvature at the tips of the elongated inclusions is considerably decreased, leading to a decreased ductility in the direction transverse to the rolling/deformation direction.

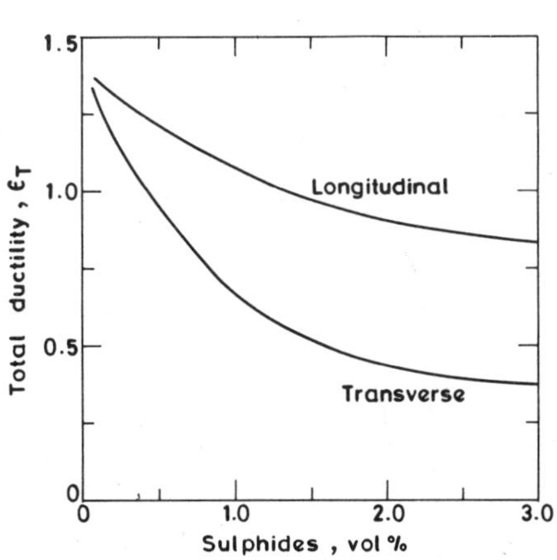

Fig. 4.5. Total ductility as a function of volume fraction of sulphide inclusions in a hot-rolled steel in longitudinal and transverse directions. (from Ref. 3).

2.4 TOUGHNESS

Toughness of steels is generally characterized by two parameters; the Charpy Shelf Energy (CSE) and the Impact Transition Temperature (ITT). Charpy shelf energy is the total energy that is absorbed during the Charpy impact test and is a measure of the toughness of a material. When the toughness of a steel is measured as a function of temperature, the Charpy shelf energy (CSE) suddenly drops to very low values below a certain temperature, where it also fractures in a characteristic brittle manner. The temperature at which such a ductile to brittle transition occurs in a steel is called impact transition temperature (ITT). At temperatures lower than ITT, steels behave like typical brittle materials, whereas at higher temperatures they behave like ductile materials. Figure 4.6 shows the impact strength of plain carbon steels of different carbon concentrations as a function of temperature. As the carbon content of a steel is increased, CSE falls and ITT increases. Hence, with increase in carbon content, though the strength of steels is increased, their ductility and impact strength (toughness) are decreased.

The toughness properties of low carbon steels have been extensively studied and correlated to compositional and microstructural parameters. The typical relationships are given as (Refs. 1–2).

$$(CSE)_{max}(J) = 112 - 2.8d^{-1/2} - 0.18\sigma_p - 832(\%S) - 43(\%Al) - 0.76\,(\%Pearlite) + 107(\%Zr) \quad (4.11)$$

and

$$ITT(K) = 254 + 44(\%Si) + 700(\sqrt{\%N_f}) + 2.2\,(\%Pearlite) - 11.5\,d^{-1/2} \quad (4.12)$$

where, σ_p is precipitation stengthening contribution to the strength of a steel, if any; d is average grain diameter in mm; and other terms are as defined earlier. From Eqs. (4.11) and (4.12), it is clear that, in general, the factors that improve total ductility also improve toughness properties, i.e. increase CSE and decrease ITT. The pearlite

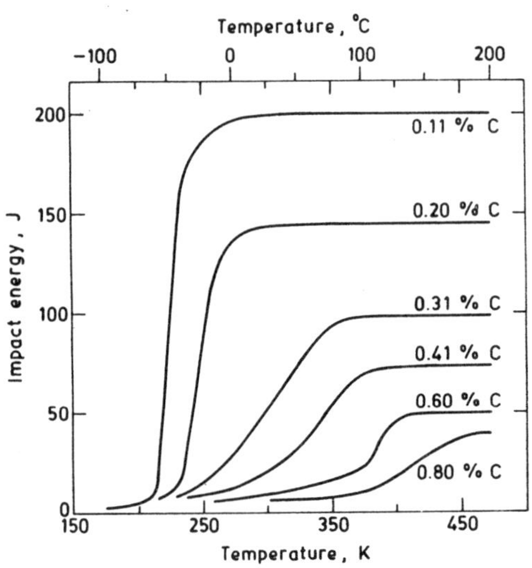

Fig. 4.6. Effect of carbon (pearlite) content on the impact strength of normalized carbon steels. (from K.W. Burns and F.B. Pickering, JISI, 202 (1964) p. 899.)

constituent, solid solution strengthening and precipitation hardening are detrimental to toughness. The inclusions, in general, have little effect on ITT; however, they adversely affect CSE, without any increase in strength. The sulphur term in Eq. (4.11) reflects the effect of inclusions on $(CSE)_{max}$, as almost all of sulphur in steels is normally present as sulphide inclusions. The large positive effect of Zr on $(CSE)_{max}$ in Eq. (4.11) is due to the inclusion modifying characteristics of Zr. In the presence of Zr, the ductile deformable MnS inclusions are replaced by more stable, non-deformable, hard and spherical ZrS inclusions. This leads to substantial improvement in ductility and toughness. As far as the trade off between strength and toughness is concerned, the grain size is one factor which is beneficial for both. With decrease in grain size, the strength and $(CSE)_{max}$ are increased and ITT is decreased. In low carbon steels, $(CSE)_{max}$, in general, is proportional to total ductility, ε_T, as all factors that improve ductility also increase toughness. Figure 4.7 shows the relationship between ε_T and $(CSE)_{max}$.

In steels containing higher percentages of pearlite, toughness also depends on the details of the pearlite structure, apart from its volume fraction. For steels containing higher volume fractions of pearlite, the following correlation for ITT has been derived (Ref. 1):

$$\begin{aligned} \text{ITT(K)} &= f_\alpha \; [227 - 11.5d^{-1/2}] + (1 - f_\alpha) \\ &\quad \times [-62 + 5.6S^{-1/2} - 13.3p^{-1/2} + 3.48 \times 10^6\, t] \\ &\quad + 48.7(\%\text{Si}) + 762\, (\sqrt{\%\text{N}_f}) \end{aligned} \tag{4.13}$$

where, d is ferrite grain size; S is pearlite inter-lamellar spacing; p is average pearlite colony size; and t is cementite lamellar thickness; all in mm; and f_α is volume fraction of ferrite. In pearlitic steels, ITT decreases with decreasing pearlite colony size and decreasing thickness of cementite lamellae, whereas it increases with decreasing inter-lamellar spacing. It should be noted that as the temperature of transformation to pearlite is decreased, the pearlite colony size, inter-lamellar spacing and cementite

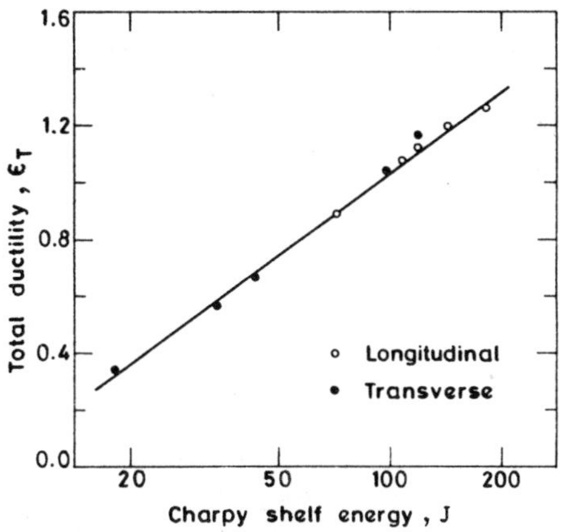

Fig. 4.7. Relationship between Charpy shelf energy and total ductility at fracture (from Ref. 3).

lamellar thickness, all decrease. Furthermore, relative changes in cementite lamellar thickness may be obtained by changing the overall carbon content of pearlite to some extent.

3 BAINITIC STEELS

3.1 INTRODUCTION

When austenite is transformed at temperatures lower than ~823K (550°C) and down to ~573K (300°C), it transforms to bainite irrespective of its carbon content. Bainite structure may, therefore, be obtained by isothermally transforming the steels in 573–823K (300–550°C) temperature range. The bainite structure may also be obtained on continuous cooling from austenite in steels containing Mo or Mo–B. Additions of Mo (or Mo–B) to a steel preferentially retard the ferrite-pearlite transformations and give a double 'C' isothermal transformation diagram, as schematically shown in Fig. 4.8. On continuous cooling, these steels normally transform to bainitic structure below B_s temperature. The B_s temperature to some extent can be controlled by the addition of other alloying elements. Almost all alloying elements depress B_s temperature.

The main microstructural features of bainitic steels that affect their mechanical properties are: (*i*) fine bainitic ferrite grain, or lath, size, (*ii*) high dislocation density in bainite accompanying the bainite transformation, (*iii*) carbide dispersion, and (*iv*) carbon in solid solution. Apart from these, some high-carbon/high-alloy steels may contain some retained austenite and/or martensite.

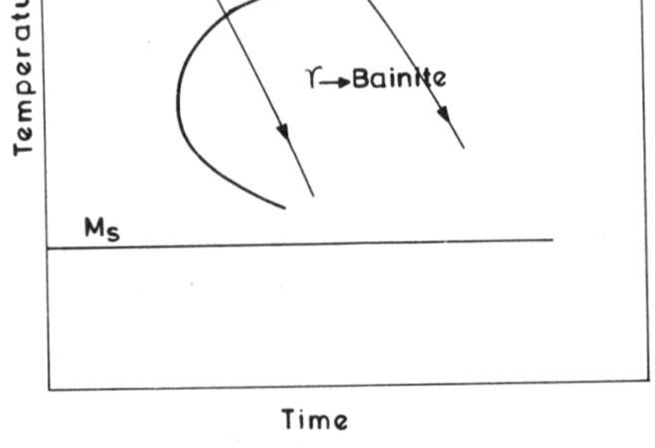

Fig. 4.8. Typical IT diagram of Mo–B bainitic steel (schematic). (B_s: bainite start temperature, M_s: martensite start temperature).

With decreasing temperature of transformation to bainite, the grain (or lath) size of bainite decreases, dislocation density increases and more carbon is retained in solid solution in bainitic ferrite. In upper bainite, cementite is formed as thin films between ferrite laths. However, in lower bainite, formed below ~623–673K (350–400°C), a fine dispersion of cementite or ε-carbide is obtained within the ferrite plates, contributing to precipitation (dispersion) strengthening of bainitic steels.

3.2 TENSILE STRENGTH

For the strength of low carbon bainitic steels, with very little retained austenite or martensite, an analysis similar to the one used for low carbon ferrite–pearlite steels can be used. Accordingly, the yield strength, σ_y, of low carbon bainitic steels has been expressed as (Ref. 2):

$$\sigma_y \text{ (MPa)} = 88 + 37(\%\text{Mn}) + 83(\%\text{Si}) + 2900(\%\text{N}_f) + 15.1 d_L^{-1/2} + \sigma_d + \sigma_p \quad (4.14)$$

where d_L is bainite lath/plate size in mm; σ_d and σ_p are dislocation and precipitation strengthening contributions respectively; N_f refers to free nitrogen in solution; and other terms are as defined earlier. The dislocation strengthening term is a function of dislocation density and is approximately given as (Ref. 8):

$$\sigma_d \text{ (MPa)} = 1.2 \times 10^{-3} \sqrt{\rho} \quad (4.25)$$

where ρ is dislocation density per cm^2. Precipitation strengthening in bainite is a function of the volume fraction and average size of the carbide precipitates. No precipitation strengthening occurs in upper bainite, where cementite precipitates are in the form of thin films, or relatively large particles, at the lath boundaries. However, the carbide precipitates (cementite or ε-carbide) in lower bainite are formed as finely dispersed particles within the ferrite plates and contribute substantially to the strength of bainite. Carbide dispersion strenghening contribution in bainite can be obtained by using Orowan analysis (Ref. 8), as:

$$\sigma_p \text{ (MPs)} = 600 + \frac{1.25\, Gb}{\lambda} \quad (4.16)$$

where, G is shear modulus; b is Burgers vector of slip dislocations; and λ is average inter-particle spacing. Figure 4.9 shows the relative contributions of different strenghening mechanisms to the hardness (strength) of bainite as a function of its carbon content.

From the above discussion, it is clear that the strength of bainite is a function of composition as well as the temperature at which the bainite is formed. As bainite transformation temperature is lowered, in general, ferrite lath size decreases, carbide dispersion becomes finer, and dislocation density and carbon in solution increase. All these factors contribute to increase in the strength of bainite. Figure 4.10 gives the strength of bainite in low carbon steels as a function of the temperature of transformation. It also shows the relative contributions of different strengthening mechanisms to total strength.

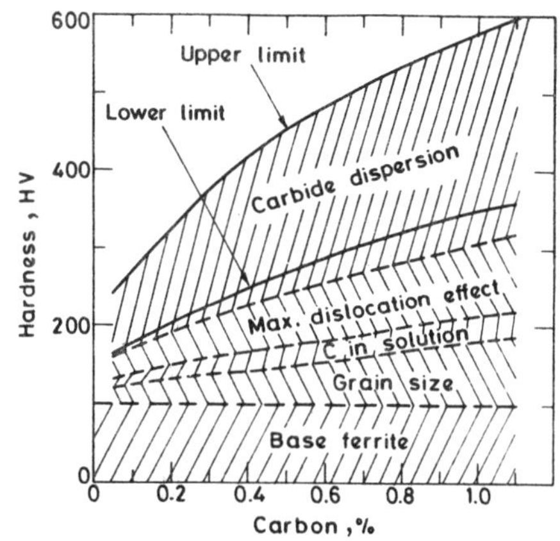

Fig. 4.9. Possible contributions of various mechanisms to the strength of bainite (from Ref. 1).

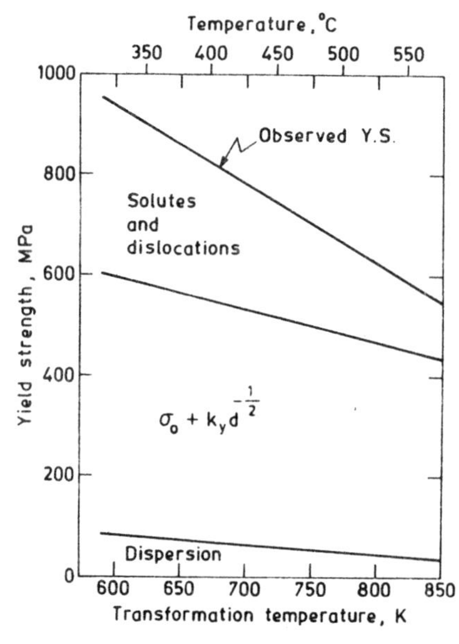

Fig. 4.10. Effect of transformation temperature on the contributions of various strengthening mechanisms to yield strength of low carbon (0.1–0.15%C) bainites (from Ref. 1).

3.3 TOUGHNESS

The toughness of bainite is less understood in terms of quantitative relationship with microstructural features than strength. The toughness of bainite, in general, decreases as its strength increases. The presence of dislocations and precipitate carbides raise the impact transition temperature, (ITT), and lower the Charpy Shelf energy (CSE), whereas, the decrease in grain size (not the lath size) has a beneficial effect, in that it decreases ITT. The impact strength of upper bainite is further

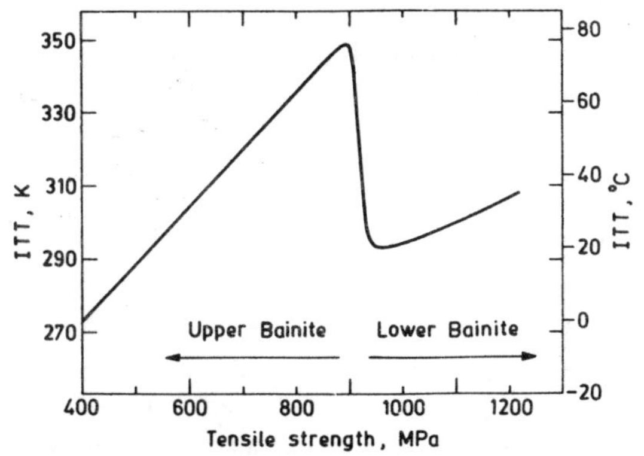

Fig. 4.11. Impact transition temperature of bainitic steels as a function of their tensile strength (from Ref. 9).

adversely affected by the presence of cementite as thin film or coarse particles at the lath boundaries of bainite, which does not contribute to strength but lowers the toughness. Figure 4.11 shows the variation of ITT as a function of tensile strength in low carbon bainitic steels, clearly showing the adverse effect of carbides at the lath boundaries in upper bainite.

4 MARTENSITE

Martensite is hardest of all the phases that are formed in steels. Following factors contribute to the hardness (strength) of martensite:

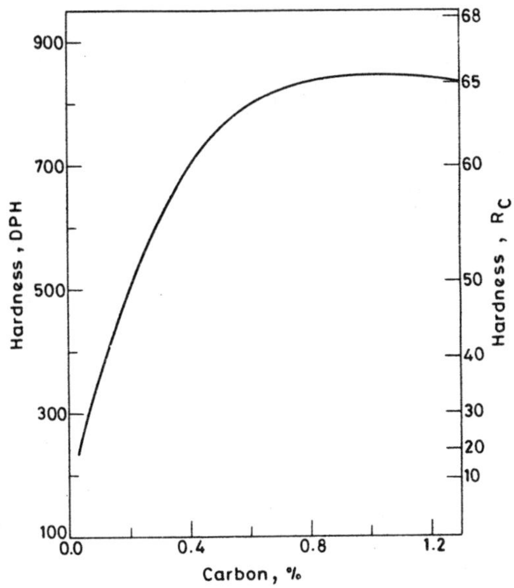

Fig. 4.12. Hardness of martensite as a function of its carbon content.

(*i*) carbon in solid solution,

(*ii*) fine martensite plate or lath size,

(*iii*) high dislocation density, of the order of $10^{10} - 10^{12}$ cm^{-2}, in low carbon lath martensites, and high density of twins in high carbon accicular martensites,

(*iv*) clustering of carbon, and

(*v*) interaction between dislocations and interstitially dissolved carbon.

The yield and tensile strengths of martensite are difficult to measure because of its brittleness, particularly at carbon contents higher than ~0.3% C. The most available data are on the hardness of martensite. In low alloy steels, the alloying elements do not seem to contribute much to the hardness of martensite and it which is essentially a function of its carbon content. Hardness of martensite increases with increase in carbon content. The rate of increase in hardness with carbon decreases with increasing carbon content and the hardness levels off at around 0.8% C, as seen in Fig. 4.12.

Martensitic steels are usually very brittle and structurally unstable. They are invariably tempered before use. Tempering of steels and mechanical properties of tempered steels are discussed separately in Chapter 5.

REFERENCES

1. F.B. Pickering, in *Hardenabiliy Concepts with Applications to Steel*, (Eds. D.V. Doane and J.S. Kirkaldy). The Metallurgical Society of AIME, Warrendate, Pa, 1978, p. 179.
2. T. Gladman, D. Dullieu and I.D. Mclvor, in ''Micro-alloying' 75'', *Proc. Int. Conf. HSLA Steels*, Union Carbide Corp., New York, 1977, p. 32.
3. F.B. Pickering, *ibid*, p. 9.
4. F.B. Pickering, *Physical Metallurgy and the Design of Steels*', Applied Science Publishers, London, 1980.
5. W.B. Morrison, *Controlled Processing of Steels*, British Steel Corporation Conference, York 1976, paper 1.
6. T. Gladman, I.D. Mclvor and F.B. Pickering *J. Iron Steel Inst.*, **210** (1972) p. 916.
7. T.Gladman, B.Holmes and F.B. Pickering, *J. Iron Steel Inst.*, **208** (1970) p. 172.
8. M.E. Bush and P.M. Kelly, *Acta, Metall.*, **19** (1971) p. 1363.
9. F.B. Pickering, in *Transformation and Hardenability in Steels*, Climax Moly. Company of Michigan, 1967, p. 109.

CHAPTER 5

Tempering of Martensite

1 INTRODUCTION

Steel components are frequently quenched to martensite to increase their hardness. Martensite is hardest of all the phases that are formed in a steel. However, it is also generally brittle and microstructurally unstable. Therefore, quenched steels are normally tempered to improve their impact properties and to increase their microstructural stability. Tempering is done by heating the quenched steels between room temperature and lower critical point (Ae_1). Final properties of tempered martensite, apart from its composition, depend on the temperature and time of tempering.

Martensite is a metastable phase. On tempering above room temperature, it decomposes to ferrite plus carbides, the more stable phases at these temperatures. On tempering, the hardness (strength) of martensite falls, whereas its ductility and impact strength are generally improved.

There are three important features of quenched steels which affect the processes occurring during the decomposition of martensite upon tempering. These are: (*i*) an extremely high supersaturation of carbon in solid solution, (*ii*) high density of lattice defects, i.e. dislocations, subgrain boundaries and/or twins, and (*iii*) the presence of retained austenite, if any. Depending mainly on temperature, different processes occur during the tempering of martensite. In this chapter, the structural changes that occur during tempering and the mechanical properties of tempered steels are discussed.

2 SEGREGATION OF CARBON

On tempering, the first structural change that occurs in martensite is the segregation of carbon. Martensite has a high density of crystal lattice defects, which provide energetically more favourable sites for carbon atoms than the normal sites these atoms occupy in martensite structure. Dislocations and dislocation arrays (low angle boundaries) are particularly favoured sites for the segregation of carbon. Low-carbon lath martensites may contain up to $\sim 10^{12}$ dislocations per cm^2, and the high-carbon accicular martensites contain high density of twins. Segregation of carbon atoms to dislocations can occur even at room temperature, as only few atomic jumps are required for the segregation to take place. When martensite start temperature, M_s, is relatively high, some carbon segregation may also occur between M_s and room (quenching) temperature in martensite formed close to M_s during quenching itself.

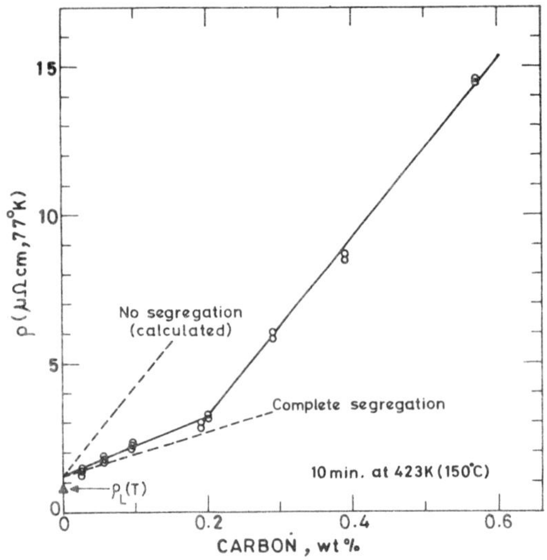

Fig. 5.1. Carbon segregation on quenching of Fe–C steels as defected by electrical resistivity (ρ) measurements [from G.R. Speich, *Trans TMS-AIME*, **245** (1969) p.2553].

Apart from segregating at dislocations, carbon atoms in martensite form clusters along [100] planes in lath martensite and along [112] twinning planes in accicular martensite. On heating above room temperature, further segregation occurs, till equilibrium amount of segregation has been achieved. In lath martensite, equivalent of approx. 0.2% carbon in iron is sufficient to saturate all sites to which the carbon atoms may segregate. Figure 5.1 shows carbon segregation in iron–carbon martensites, as detected by electrical resistivity measurements. In steels containing up to ~0.2% C, about 90% of the total carbon present segregates to dislocations and other imperfections in martensite. In higher carbon steels, equivalent of about 0.2% C in iron segregates to various sites and only the excess is in normal interstitial sites.

On tempering above room temperature, martensite also starts decomposing to more stable phases. The nature of processes occurring during the tempering of martensite essentially depend on tempering temperature and may be divided into three distinct stages. These are separately discussed in the following sections.

3 FIRST STAGE OF TEMPERING

In the first stage of tempering, martensite containing more than ~0.2% C decomposes to low-carbon martensite, containing ~0.2% C, and ε-carbide. This occurs on tempering up to ~473K (200°C). In low-carbon martensites, containing less than ~0.2% C, precipitation of ε-carbide is inhibited as most of the carbon is locked up by the dislocations. Carbon segregated at dislocations is relatively more stable and does not precipitate out as ε-carbide.

ε-carbide, which precipitates during the first stage of tempering, has a hexagonal structure and its composition corresponds to $Fe_{2.4}C$. ε-carbide is metastable with respect to cementite (Fe_3C). However, precipitation of ε-carbide cannot be considered as a first step in the formation of more stable cementite phase. It (ε-carbide) is an entirely different phase, which under the conditions existing during the first stage of tempering, nucleates and grows more rapidly than cementite.

It has been generally reported that the tempering reaction during the first stage does not consist of progressive rejection of carbon from martensite to ε-carbide particles, but rather, the high carbon martensite decomposes, by nucleation and growth, to a two-phase mixture of ε-carbide and low-carbon martensite. For this reason, it has also been designated as a two-phase reaction. Carbon content of this low-carbon martensite is independent of the original martensite carbon content and is approximately 0.2%.

ε-carbide has a hexagonal crystal structure with the lattice parameters:

$$c = 0.433 \text{ nm}; \quad a = 0.273 \text{ nm}; \quad \text{and} \quad c/a = 1.58$$

The ε-carbide particles nucleate with a specific orientation relationship with the martensite matrix, i.e.:

$$(0001)_\varepsilon \parallel (011)_M$$

The lattice matching at the interface between ε-carbide and martensite is very good. This leads to a lower activation energy for the nucleation of ε-carbide as compared to that of cementite. Hence, even though cementite is the more stable phase, ε-carbide precipitates first at these temperatures. The ε-carbide precipitates, which form on tempering up to ~473K (200°C), are extremely small in size (of the order of 0.015 to 0.02 μm), as expected considering the low temperatures at which they are formed. They form as platelets or needles at the subgrain boundaries of martensitic plates. The subgrain size in martensite is about 0.1 to 1 μm. The ε-carbide particles in tempered steels have been observed and identified by electron microscopy.

First stage of tempering is accompanied by a decrease in the specific volume of martensite. It is, therefore, possible to follow the kinetics of tempering by using a dilatometer. Figure 5.2 shows the change in length of 0.68% carbon martensite samples tempered at 293K (20°C) and 366K (93°C). It is clear from Fig. 5.2, that tempering occurs even at room temperature, though at a very slow rate. The tempering rate at 366K (93°C) is appreciably higher. The change in dilation at this temperature asymptotically approaches a value of $\sim 1.2 \times 10^{-3}$, which corresponds to the end of reactions taking place during the first stage of tempering. The structure obtained after the first stage of tempering is generally referred to as tempered martensite.

4 SECOND STAGE OF TEMPERING

The second stage of tempering occurs in the temperature range 423–573K (150–300°C), where, the retained austenite, if present, transforms to bainite. This does not deal with the tempering of martensite as such. However, since all quenched steels contain varying amounts of retained austenite, depending on the composition of steel

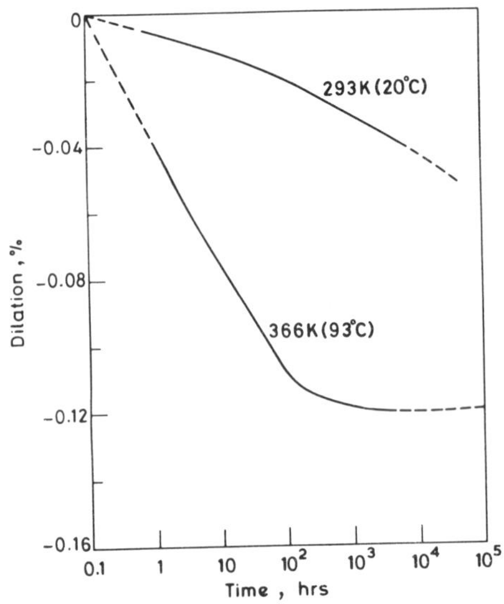

Fig. 5.2. Increase in length as a function of time during the first stage of tempering (from C.S. Roberts, B.L. Averbach and M. Cohen, *Trans. ASM*, **45** (1953) p.576).

and the temperature to which it is quenched, it is an important factor during the tempering of quenched steels.

Kinetics of bainite reaction has already been discussed in the previous chapters. The temperature range in which bainite is formed during tempering, is generally low,

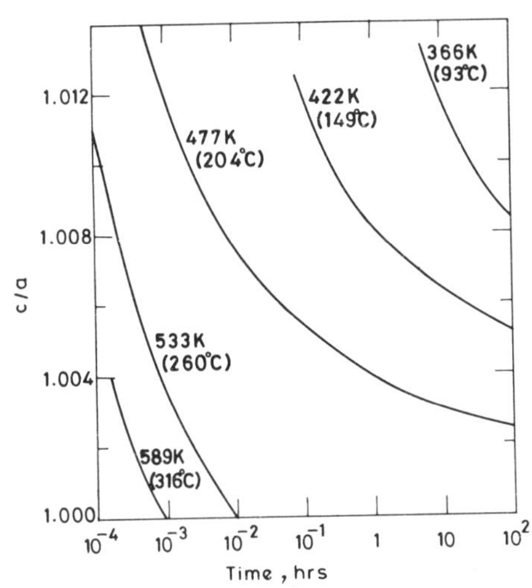

Fig. 5.3. Change in c/a ratio of martensite as a function of time at different tempering temperatures [from F.E. Werner, B.L. Averbach and M. Cohen, *Trans. ASM*, 49 (1957) p.823].

and hence, normally lower bainite is formed. Furthermore, more often than not, the carbide precipitating in bainitic ferrite is ε-carbide rather than cementite. The overall kinetics of this stage of tempering may also be followed by measuring the changes in length of a specimen, as austenite to bainite transformation is accompanied by an increase in specific volume.

5 THIRD STAGE OF TEMPERING

5.1 GENERAL

When martensite is tempered at temperatures higher than ~473K (200°C), the cementite precipitates form and grow with time, with simultaneous dissolution of ε-carbide precipitates, if present. With the growth of cementite precipitates, the carbon content of martensite continuously decreases, till it reaches the solubility limit of carbon in ferrite. Simultaneously, martensite loses its tetragonality and the c/a ratio of bct lattice of martensite reaches unity, i.e. it becomes bcc, or completely ferritic. On further tempering, spheroidization and coarsening of cementite particles takes place. In the initial stages, the extent of cementite precipitation can be followed by determining the change in c/a ratio of martensite. Figure 5.3 shows the change in c/a ratio of martensite as a function of time for different tempering temperatures. At temperatures higher than ~523K (250°C), it takes relatively short time for the equilibrium amount of cementite to precipitate. The cementite particles, during their precipitation from martensite, form as platelets or rod shaped particles at the boundaries of martensite plates as well as globules and platelets inside the martensite plates. On further tempering at higher temperatures and/or for longer times, the cementite particles spheroidize and coarsen. Figure 5.4 shows the microstructures of martensite tempered at different temperatures, in plain carbon steels. In steels containing strong carbide-forming elements, like V, Mo, W, Cr, etc., the more stable alloy carbides form at the expense of cementite at temperatures higher than ~773K (500°C). This leads to the phenomenon of secondary hardening, discussed separately later in this chapter.

5.2 SPHEROIDIZATION AND COARSENING OF CEMENTITE

On tempering at higher temperatures, equilibrium amount of cementite precipitates in a relatively short period, as discussed above. On continued tempering at these temperatures, spheroidization and coarsening of cementite precipitates occurs. When tempering is done at relatively high temperatures, 923–973K (650–700°C), a structure consisting of cementite spheroids embedded in soft ferrite matrix is readily obtained and the cementite particles are large enough to be visible under light microscope, as seen in Fig. 5.4(f).

The thermodynamic driving force for spheroidization and coarsening of cemenitite particles is the minimization of total interfacial energy of α/cm interfaces in the system. In the early stages, cementite particles that precipitate as platelets or rods are partly semi-coherent with the martensite matrix. As these particles grow, coherency at the interface is lost and the interfaces become completely incoherent.

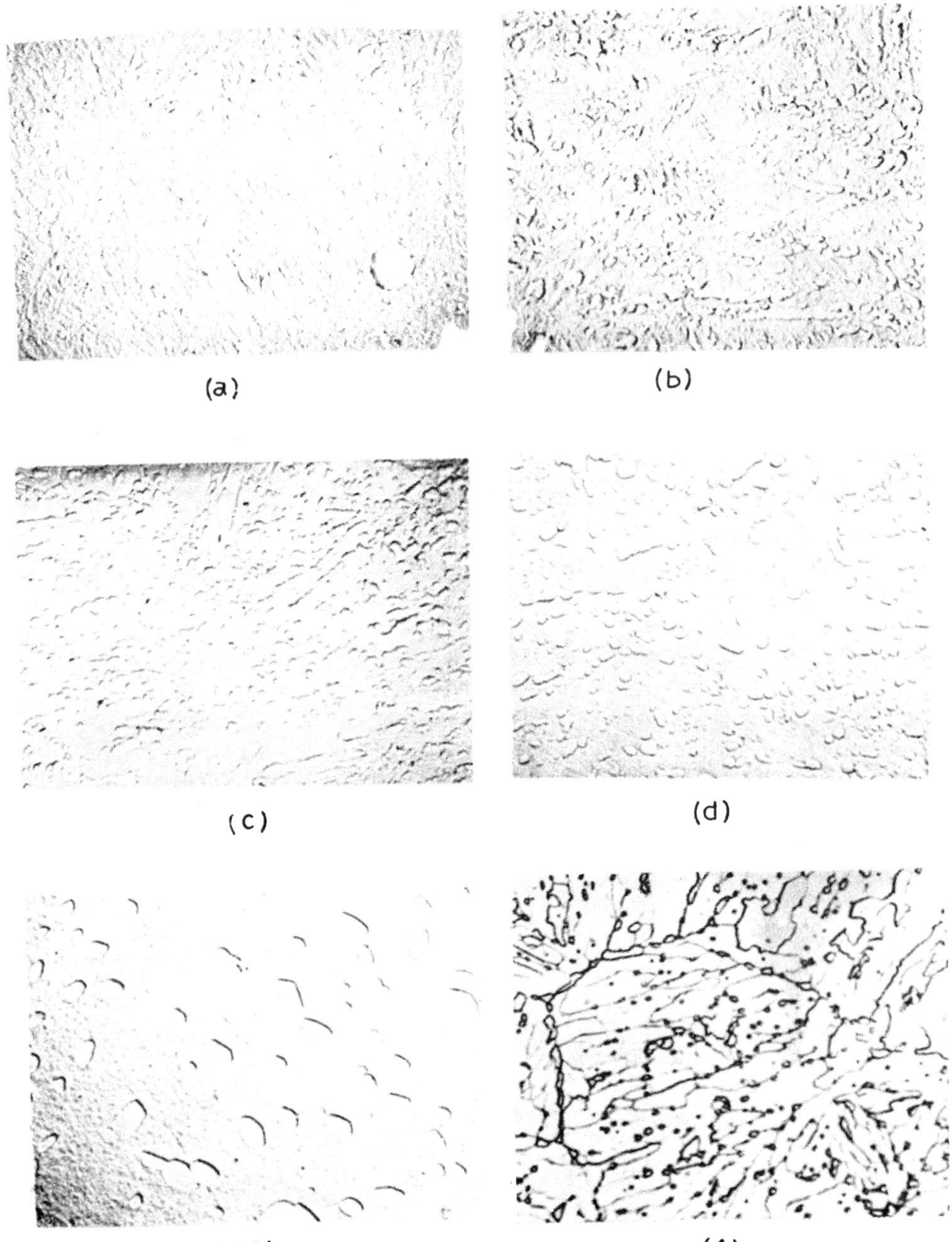

Fig. 5.4. Microstructures of tempered martensite: (*a*) to (*e*) electron micrograph (carbon replica) of Fe–0.56C–1.36Mn alloy quenched and tempered for 1 hour at 477K (204°C), 588K (315°C) 699K (426°C), 866K (593°C) and 948K (675°C), respectively: (*f*) 0.4C steel quenched and tempered at 973K (700°C) for 1 h (optical micrograph).

The cementite particles then tend to spheroidize to minimize their interfacial energy. Spherical particles have minimum surface to volume ratio. Simultaneously, the coarsening process occurs, whereby, larger particles grow at the expense of smaller ones, some of which eventually vanish, decreasing the total number of particles and increasing the average particle size. Both, spheroidization and coarsening lead to a decrease in the total α/cm interfacial area, and thereby, to a decrease in total energy of the system. The process of spheroidization and coarsening of irregularly shaped particles is theoretically a more difficult problem. However, generally the spheroidization of particles with incoherent interfaces occurs early and is over much faster, whereas, the coarsening process continues as long as annealing (tempering) is continued. Therefore, the overall problem may be dealt as coarening of spherical precipitates. The theory of coarsening of spherical precipitates, with specific reference to coarsening of cementite particles in ferrite, is briefly discussed here.

The solubility of a spherical cementite particle in ferrite is a function of its radius (due to Gibbs-Thompson effect) and may be written as:

$$C_r = C_o \left(1 + \frac{2\sigma V}{RTr}\right) \tag{5.1}$$

where, C_r and C_o are carbon concentrations in ferrite in equilibrium with particles of radii r and infinity (flat interface), respectively; σ is α/cm interfacial energy; V is molar volume of cementite; R is gas constant; and T is temperature in degrees kelvin. C_o corresponds to the solubility of cementite in ferrite as given by the Fe–C phase diagram. According to Eq. (5.1), in a two-particle system, smaller particle would have higher solubility in ferrite as compared to the larger one. This would, then, set up a carbon concentration gradient in ferrite, such that carbon would diffusion from the smaller to larger particle. Assuming that local equilibrium is maintained at the (incoherent) α/cm interfaces, the larger particle would then grow and the smaller one would dissolve.

In a system consisting of large number of cementite particles of varying radii, particles with different radii would have different solubilities in ferrite, all greater than C_o. The ferrite matrix at any instant would, then, have an average carbon concentration, $\bar{C}$, higher that C_o. Since, the solubility of cementite in ferrite is very small, it may be safely assumed that total volume fraction of the cementite precipitates during the coarsening process essentially remains constant. Under these conditions, it can be easily shown that the average composition of the ferrite matrix, $\bar{C}$, at any instant corresponds to the solubility of the average sized particle of radius r_a, where, $r_a = (1/n)\,\Sigma\, r_i$. Hence, the coarsening process may be considered as growth (or dissolution) of cementite particles of different radii in the ferrite matrix of average composition $\bar{C}$. During coarsening, both r_a and $\bar{C}$ would change with time.

Now, let us consider a cementite particle of radius r in the ferrite matrix of average composition $\bar{C}$. Assuming the particle to be in local equilibrium with the matrix, mass balance at the particle/matrix interface gives:

$$(C_{cm} - C_r)\,\frac{dr}{dt} = D_C \left(\frac{\bar{C} - C_r}{r}\right) \tag{5.2}$$

where, C_{cm} is carbon concentration of cementite; C_r and $\overline{C}$ are carbon concentrations in ferrite next to the particle and far away from it respectively; and D_C is diffusivity of carbon in ferrite. $(\overline{C} - C_r)/r$ is carbon concentration gradient in ferrite at the interface and dr/dt is the instant rate of change of radius (growth rate) of the particle. Figure 5.5 schematically shows carbon concentration profiles during the growth/dissolution of cementite particles during the coarsening process. Substituting for C_r and $\overline{C}$ using Eq. (5.1) and assuming $(C_{cm} - C_r) \cong (C_{cm} - C_o)$, we get:

$$\frac{dr}{dt} = \left(\frac{2\sigma V C_o D_C}{RT\,(C_{cm} - C_o)}\right)\frac{1}{r}\left(\frac{1}{r_a} - \frac{1}{r}\right) \tag{5.3}$$

The growth rate of a particle according to Eq. (5.3) is a function of its radius, as schematically shown in Fig. 5.6. Particles of radius less than r_a have a negative growth rate, and hence, will dissolve with time, whereas, particles greater than r_a, have positive growth rate and would grow with time. The growth rate of particles larger than r_a goes through a maximum at $r = 2r_a$. Hence, the smaller particles will shrink with time and eventually vanish, whereas, the larger ones would grow. The number of particles would, then, decrease and the average size of particles increase.

An interesting feature of Eq. (5.3) is that, if all the particles were to be of the same size, no particle coarsening would take place. However, any small deviation from equality will lead to an instability and the size distribution will broaden with time and the average size would increase. Another feature of Eq. (5.3) of interest is the maximum in the growth rate of particles at $r = 2r_a$. Since, within the particles of radii greater than r_a, the larger particles grow at a slower rate than the smaller ones, the particle size distribution after some time reaches a pseudo-steady state, i.e. the frac-

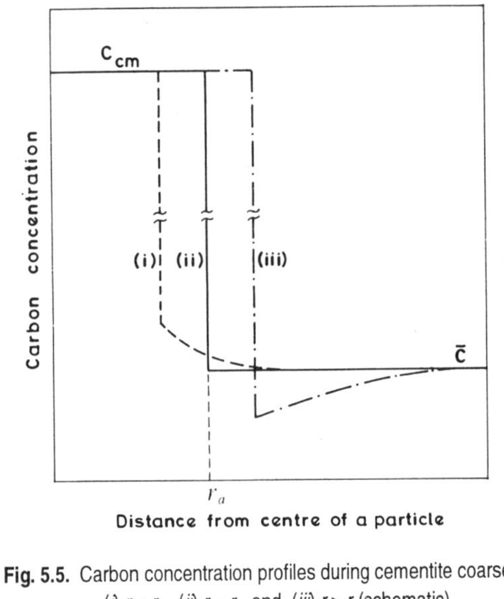

Fig. 5.5. Carbon concentration profiles during cementite coarsening, (*i*) $r < r_a$, (*ii*) $r = r_a$, and (*iii*) $r > r_a$ (schematic).

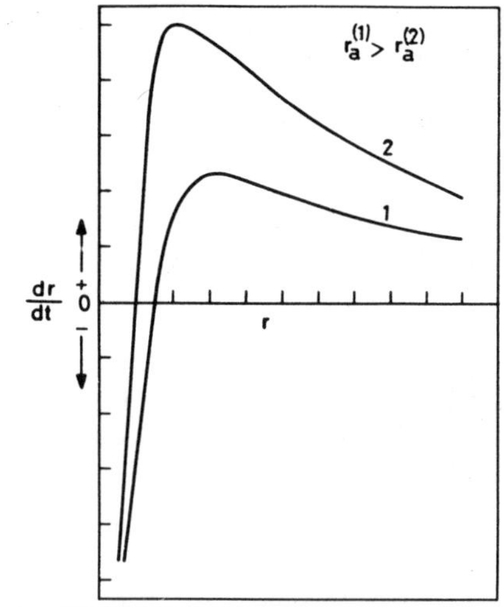

Fig. 5.6. Variation of growth rate, (dr/dt), with radius, r, as per Eq. (5.3), for two different values of r_a, (schematic).

tion of particles of any relative size (r/r_a) is essentially the same at all times, and an upper limit of ~$2r_a$ in the size distribution of particles is established. Figure 5.7 shows some experimental results on the size distribution of cementite particles during coarsening.

To obtain average particle size as a function of time during particle coarsening, one would require initial particle size distribution and an averaging procedure, using Eq. (5.3). However, to a first approximation, the rate of coarsening can be obtained by assuming that the average size of particles, r_a, increases at a rate equal to one half of the maximum rate of growth. The maximum rate of growth, from Eq. (5.3), is given by:

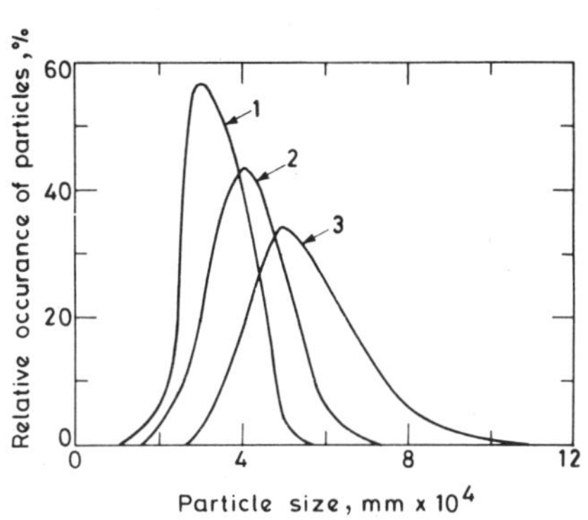

Fig. 5.7. Size distribution of cementite particles in 0.4%C steel tempered at 903K (630°C) for (1) 10 min, (2) 1 h, and (3) 25 h.

$$\left(\frac{dr}{dt}\right)_{max} = \left(\frac{dr}{dt}\right)_{r=2r_a} = \frac{1}{2}\left(\frac{\sigma V C_o D_C}{RT\,(C_{cm} - C_o)}\right)\frac{1}{r_a^2} \tag{5.4}$$

The rate of change of average size, r_a is, then:

$$\left(\frac{dr_a}{dt}\right) = \frac{1}{2}\left(\frac{dr}{dt}\right)_{max} = \frac{1}{4}\left(\frac{\sigma V C_o D_C}{RT\,(C_{cm} - C_o)}\right)\frac{1}{r_a^2} \tag{5.5}$$

and by integrating Eq. (5.5), we get:

$$r_a^3 - r_o^3 = \frac{3}{4}\left(\frac{\sigma V C_o D_C}{RT\,(C_{cm} - C_o)}\right) t \tag{5.6}$$

where, r_o is initial average size at $t = 0$. The experimental results on the coarsening of cementite particles generally follow Eq. (5.6).

5.3 RECOVERY AND RECRYSTALLIZATION

Apart from precipitation and coarsening of cementite particles, recovery and recrysallization of ferrite occurs on tempering at higher temperatures. As mentioned previously, martensite contains high concentration of lattice defects, i.e. dislocations and/or twins, almost equivalent to that of heavily cold-worked metals. Annealing of these defects takes place during the third stage of tempering. In the early stage, annealing of dislocations and any movement of subgrain or grain boundaries is retarded due to the presence of fine cementite precipitates. Substantial recovery and recrystallization processes, therefore, start taking place only above ~673K (400°C). At the very initial stages of tempering, cementite precipitates are scarce and thus cannot be very effective barriers to dislocation movement. A certain amount of recovery takes place during this period. Then, upon the precipitation of large number of cementite particles, the dislocations and sub-grain boundaries are pinned down by these precipitates and the structure of the matrix stabilizes. The extensions of laths of α'-iron are retained up to relatively high temperatures of tempering, as seen in Fig. 5.4.

After a sufficiently long period of tempering at higher temperatures, when the boundary locking by the precipitates weakens due to coaresening of cementite particles, grains coarsen by movement of high angle boundaries. The microstructure loses the typical morphological features of martensite and equiaxed ferrite grain structure is obtained. In high-carbon steels, the growth of ferrite grains is even more retarded because of the high concentration of carbide particles and the accicular structure may be retained up to ~923K (650°C). Unlike in heavily cold-worked metals, primary recrystallization by nucleation and growth is not observed during tempering of martensites, notwithstanding the very high concentration of lattice defects in quenched steels.

6 MECHANICAL PROPERTIES OF TEMPERED STRUCTURES

6.1 PLAIN CARBON STEELS

On tempering, the hardness (strength) of a quenched steel decreases, whereas its ductility and impact strength are generally improved. Figure 5.8 to 5.10 show hardness of binary iron–carbon alloys, quenched and tempered for 1 hr at various temperatures from 373K (100°C) to 973K (700°C). Fig. 5.8 gives hardness as a function of carbon content at different tempering temperatures, whereas Figs. 5.9 and 5.10 give hardness as a function of tempering temperature at various carbon levels. Figure 5.9 also shows the various processes occurring during the tempering of martensite.

On tempering, the martensite decomposes by precipitation of carbides from supersaturated α' phase. The usual precipitation hardening effect is, however, normally not observed during tempering. On tempering, the hardness of martensite continuously decreases with increasing temperature of tempering, only slighly up to ~473K (200°C) and at an accelerated rate at higher temperatures. Any contribution to the hardness of tempered martensites due to precipitation hardening effect of fine carbides at lower tempering temperatures is overcompensated by the loss of hardness due to depletion of carbon in solid solution, except in high-carbon steels, where a slight increase in hardness is observed at lower tempering temperatures (Fig. 5.10). In these steels, the volume fraction of carbide precipitates is relatively high, giving a small net overall hardening effect. In high carbon steels, a small hardening effect is also sometimes observed on tempering in the range of 473–573K (200–300°C), where retained austenite transforms to bainite. High carbon steels normally have more retained austenite on quenching. On tempering at still higher temperatures, the hardness falls off rapidly as cementite precipitation occurs and martensite loses all

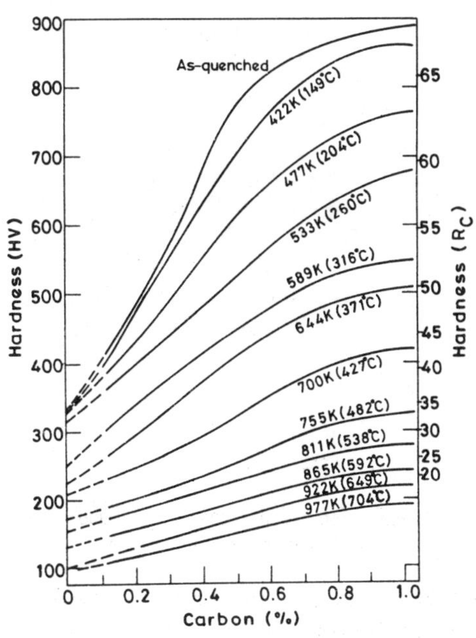

Fig. 5.8. Hardness of tempered Fe–C martensites as a function of carbon content, tempered at different temperatures for 1 h [from R.A. Grange, C.R. Hribal and L.F. Porter, *Metall. Trans. A*, 8A (1977) p.1775].

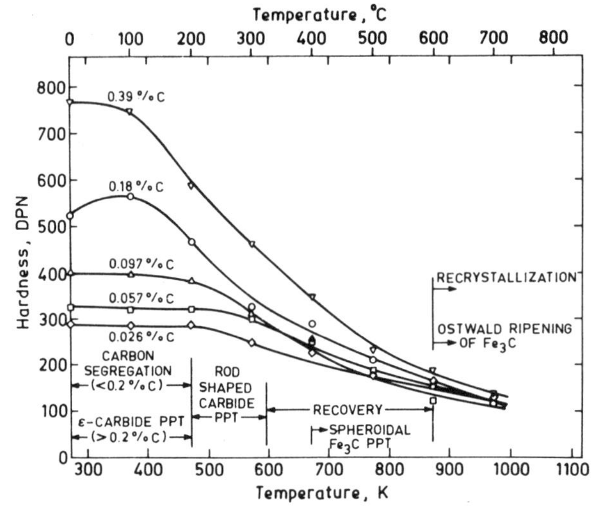

Fig. 5.9. Hardness of iron–carbon martensites tempered for 1 hr at 373K (100°C) to 973K (700°C) for various carbon levels. The figure also shows the various processes occurring during tempering. [from G.R. Speich, *Trans TMS-AIME*, 245 (1969) p.2553].

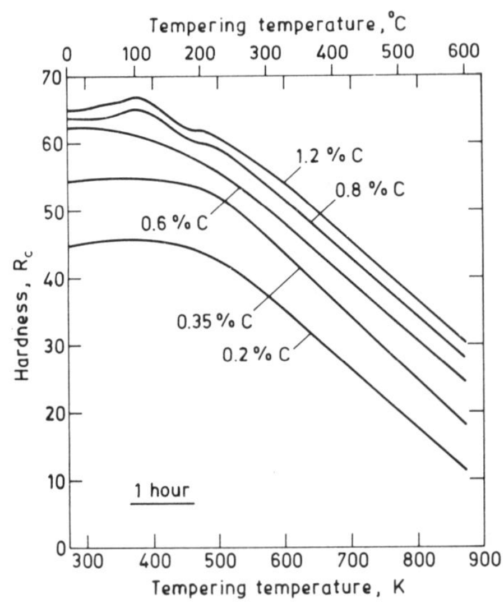

Fig. 5.10. Hardness of iron–carbon martensites tempered for 1 hour at 373K (100°C) to 973K (700°C) for various carbon levels.

its carbon. On further tempering, cementite particles coarsen and the recovery and recrystallization of ferrite matrix occurs, both leading to further softening of the steel. The decrease in hardness (strength) on tempering is generally accompanied by an increase in ductility and impact strength. Figure 5.11 shows various mechanical properties of tempered 0.45%C plain carbon steel as a function of tempering temperature. Note the improvement in ductility and fall in strength with increasing temperature of tempering.

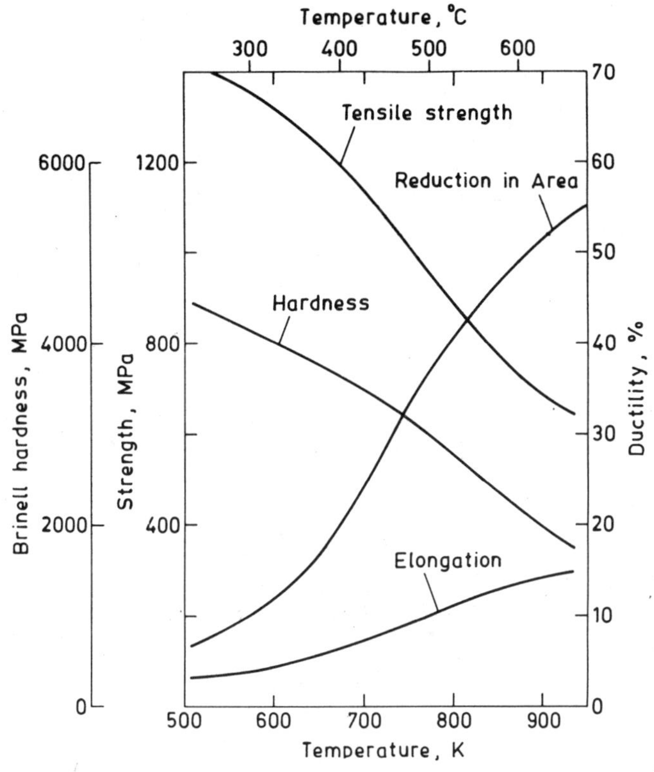

Fig. 5.11. Effect of tempering temperature on the mechanical properties of a quenched and tempered 0.45C steel.

Figures 5.8 to 5.10 give the hardness of tempered steels for a tempering time of one hour. To estimate the hardness of tempered steels for any other tempering time, the so called ''tempering parameter'', developed by Hollomon and Jeff, may be used. It relates the hardness upon tempering to tempering temperature and time. For any thermally activated process like tempering, the time and temperature are related by the rate equation:

$$\frac{1}{t} = A \exp\left(-\frac{Q_1}{RT}\right) \tag{5.7}$$

where t is the time required to reach a given hardness level and Q_1 is empirical ''activation energy'' for the process. For a complicated process like tempering, the activation energy, in general, is not constant but changes with hardness. It is, therefore, assumed that hardness would be a function of time and temperature in the following manner:

$$H = f\left[t \exp\left(-\frac{Q_1}{RT}\right)\right] \tag{5.8}$$

It has been found that the term $[t \exp\{-Q_1/(RT)\}]$ is constant, say t_o. Equating the activation energies in Eqs. (5.7) and (5.8) and converting to the logarithmic form, we get:

$$Q_1 = T[\ln(t) - \ln(t_o)] = f(H)$$

or

$$H = f[T(C + \log t)] \tag{5.9}$$

The quantity {T (C+log t)} is called "tempering parameter". Figure 5.12 shows the relation between tempering parameter and the temperature and time of tempering. The combinations of tempering temperature and time having the same value of tempering parameter will produce the same hardness.

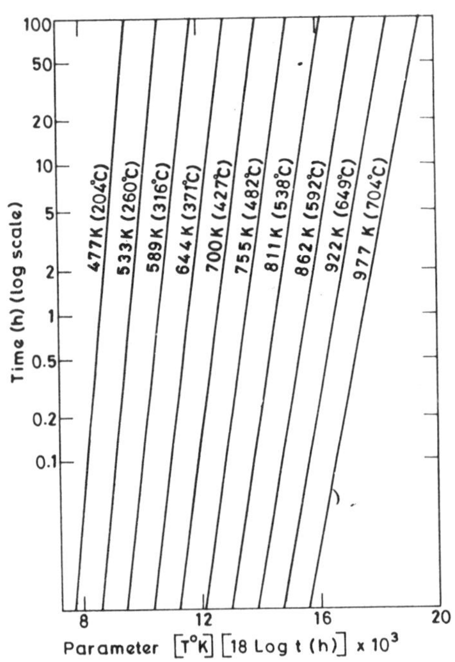

Fig. 5.12. Chart showing the relationship of tempering parameter to tempering temperature and time.

6.2 EFFECT OF ALLOYING

Tempering of alloy steels differs from that of plain carbon steels mainly in the following respects. Quenched alloy steels, in general, contain more retained austenite, as all alloying elements decrease the M_s and M_f temperatures. Therefore, decomposition of retained austenite during tempering may play a more significant role on the properties of quenched and tempered alloy steels, particularly, in steels containing higher carbon and alloy contents. Furthermore, the strong carbide forming elements, like, Cr, Mo, Ti, V, Nb, W, etc., precipitate out as alloy carbides on tempering at temperatures higher than ~773K (500°C). These precipitates, when finely dispersed, contribute substantially to the hardness of these steels. This is called secondary hardening and is discussed separately in the next section.

Notwithstanding the above mentioned differences, the basic reactions occuring during tempering of low alloy steels are essentially the same as in plain carbon steels, except the precipitation of alloy carbides. At lower tempering temperatures and in the early stages of tempering at higher temperatures, the alloy content of the precipitating carbides (cementite or ε-carbide) is same as that of original martensite and only carbon actively participates in the tempering reactions. However, the alloying elements do affect the activity and diffusivity of carbon as well as the stability of these carbides. Most alloying elements, in general, slow down the softening of martensite on tempering.

Grange *et al.* (Ref. 6) have systematically studied the effect of small additions of Mn, P, Si, Ni, Cr, Mo and V on the hardness of tempered low to medium carbon steels, tempered for 1 hr at 473K (200°C) to 973K (700°C). The effect of carbon has been previously shown in Fig. 5.8. Contribution of alloying elements to the hardness of tempered martensites, over and above that of carbon (Fig. 5.8), is shown in Fig. 5.13 for some tempering temperatures. Effect of P and Ni on the hardness of tempered martensite is essentially same at all tempering temperatures and is mainly due to solid solution hardening of ferrite by these elements. Si has a much greater effect on the hardness of tempered martensite at around 573K (300°C) than at any other temperature. Silicon enhances the stability of ε-carbide vis-a-vis cementite, and hence, delays the precipitation of cementite at the expense of ε-carbide, a change that occurs around 573K (300°C). At other tempering temperatures, the silicon effect is also essentially due to solid solution hardening. The carbide forming elements, like, Mn, Cr, Mo, V, etc., which segregate to the cementite phase, in general retard the coarsening of cementite particles, and hence, give enhanced hardening effect over and above solid solution hardening. Furthermore, the strong carbide-forming elements, like, Mo, V, Ti, Nb, etc. precipitate out as finely dispersed alloy carbides above ~773K (500°C), giving rise to secondary hardening. The effect of Mo and V in this temperature range in Fig. 5.13 reflects their secondary hardening effect.

7 SECONDARY HARDENING

In alloy steels containing strong carbide-forming elements, like, Cr, Mo, Ti, V, Nb, W, etc., the hardness of martensite on tempering initially decreases as the tempering temperature is increased, then, starts increasing again and goes through a maximum somewhere between 773K (500°C) and 973K (700°C). This phenomenon is called secondary hardening. In this temperature range, the coarse cementite particles are replaced by a fine dispersion of more stable alloy carbide precipitates. This gives

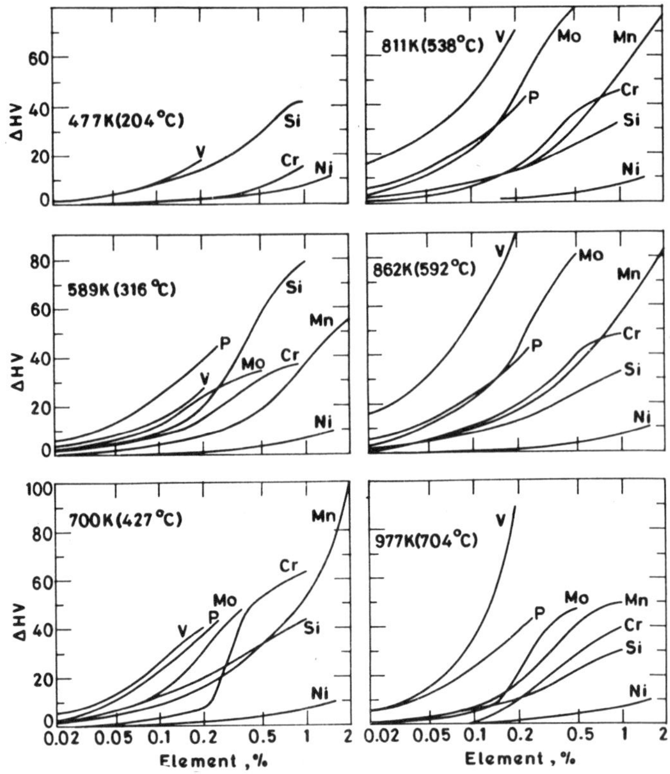

Fig. 5.13. Effect of alloying elements on the hardness of martensite tempered at different temperatures [from R.A. Grange, C.R. Hribal and L.F. Porter, *Metall. Trans. A*, 8A (1977) p.1775].

rise to increase in the hardness due to precipitation hardening. Figure 5.14 shows the secondary hardening effect in 0.1% to 0.5% carbon steels containing, Mo, Ti, V, and Cr. Cr does not have a significant secondary hardening effect, as M_7C_3 carbide precipitates formed in Fe–C–Cr alloys coarsen readily and form as relatively massive particles. On the other hand, steels containing Mo, Ti, and V show substantial secondary hardening effect due to fine precipitation of Mo_2C , TiC, and V_4C_3 carbides, respectively, in these steels. For secondary hardening effect to be observed, the alloy carbides must precipitate as fine particles, dispersed uniformly throughout the ferrite matrix. Any alloy carbide which forms as massive particles on the grain boundaries (or inside the grains) will not contribute to secondary hardening. Figure 5.15 shows an electron micrograph (carbon extraction replica) of a 0.2%C – 3.6%Mo – 0.2%Ta steel, quenched and tempered at 865K (592°C) for 100 hr. The fine accicular particles are Mo_2C precipitates that contribute to secondary hardening, whereas, the massive particles, M_6C carbides, do not contribute to any hardening. The steel is already tempered past the secondary hardness peak.

The alloy carbides that contribute to secondary hardening contain much higher concentrations of carbide forming alloying elements than the average concentration of these elements in the steel. Hence, the precipitation of alloy carbides requires long range diffusion of these elements. As the mobility (diffusivity) of the alloying

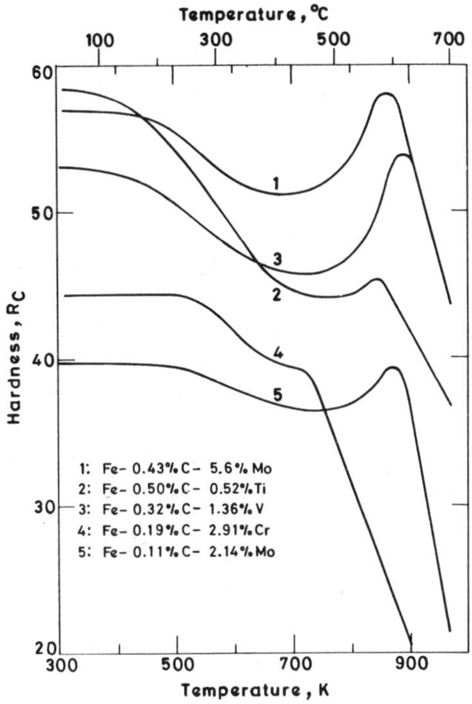

Fig. 5.14. Secondary hardening in 0.1 to 0.5 %C steels containing Mo, Ti, V and Cr [from K. Kuo, *J. Iron Steel Inst.*, 184 (1956) p. 258].

Fig. 5.15. Electron micrograph (carbon extraction replica) of 0.2C – 3.6Mo – 0.2Ta steel, quenched and tempered at 865K (592°C) for 100 h (× 12,000).

elements at lower tempering temperatures is almost negligible, no alloy carbides are formed. As tempering temperature is increased, the mobility of these elements increases and is sufficient at temperatures higher than about 773K (500°C) for the alloy carbides to precipitate out within a reasonable time during tempering at these temperatures. On tempering at higher temperature and/or for longer times, the alloy carbide precipitates eventually spheroidize and coarsen and the precipitation hardening effect falls off.

The increase in hardness due to secondary hardening is directly proportional to the volume fraction of alloy carbides contributing to secondary hardening, and hence, to the concentration of strong carbide-forming elements present in the steel, as seen in Fig. 5.16. Furthermore, in a thermally activated process like precipitation, the time and temperature required to obtain the same extent of precipitation, and hence hardness, are related.in a manner given by Eq. (5.7). Therefore, the time for peak hardness during secondary hardening decreases as the tempering temperature is increased, as seen in Fig. 5.17. Finally, it must be mentioned that in secondary hardening steels, the alloy carbides are relatively more stable and must be completely dissolved during the austenitizing treatment prior to quenching to obtain maximum secondary hardening response on tempering. The undissolved alloy carbides are relatively coarse and do not contribute to precipitation hardening. In addition, if

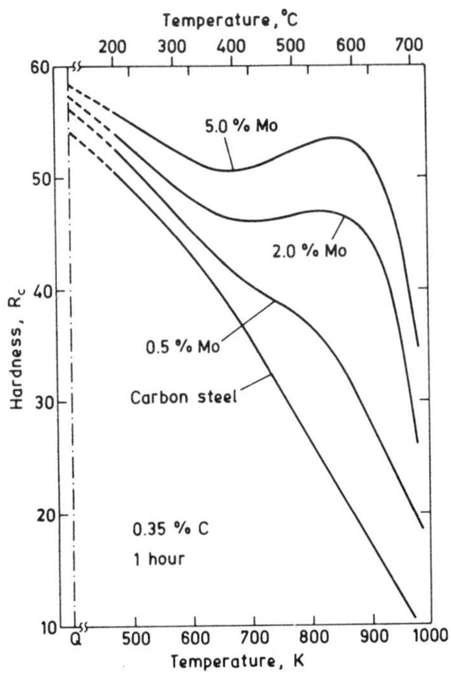

Fig. 5.16. Secondary hardening in steels containing 0.35%C and different percentages of Mo; tempering time 1 h (from Ref. 1).

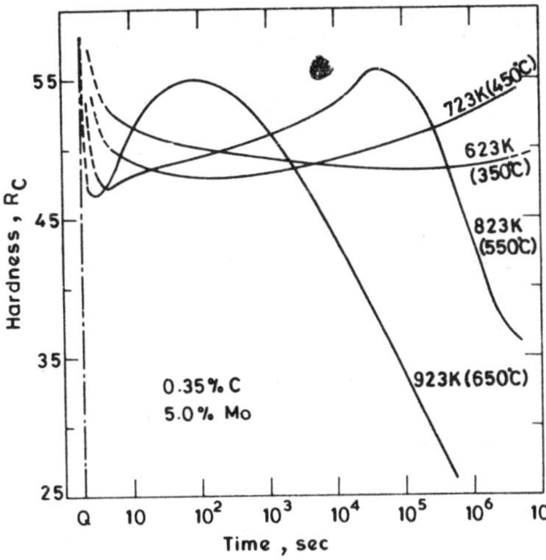

Fig. 5.17. Variation of hardness with time of tempering in quenched and tempered 0.35%C – 5%Mo steel tempered at various temperatures (from Ref. 1).

alloy carbides are not completely dissolved during austenitization, then, not only the secondary hardness peak is lower, but the initial hardness of quenched martensite is also lower due to lower amount of carbon in solid solution in austenite, and hence also in martensite, as some of the carbon is tied up in the undissolved carbides.

8 TEMPER EMBRITTLEMENT

8.1 INTRODUCTION

As the strength of a quenched steel decreases and its ductility, in general, improves on tempering, one would expect a steady increase in its impact strength with increasing tempering temperature. However, this is not always true. On tempering in certain ranges of temperature, there is an unexpected fall in the impact strength of quenched and tempered steels. This phenomenon is known as temper embrittlement and it occurs to some extent in all commercial alloy steels. Some steels are more prone to temper embrittlement than others. For example, Ni–Cr and Mn–Cr alloy steels are more prone to temper embrittlement than plain carbon steels, whereas the presence of small amounts of Mo in these steels usually decreases temper embrittlement. Temper embrittlement is also very sensitive to the presence of certain impurities, like, Sb, P, As, Sn, etc., in steels.

Many alloy steels have two tempering temperature zones of temper embrittlement. Figure 5.18 schematically shows the impact strength of a quenched and tempered alloy steel, which is highly prone to temper embrittlement, as a function of tempering temperature. Temper embrittlement occurs on tempering in the 523–673K (250–400°C) and again in the 723K (450°C) to 873K (600°C) temperature regions. Temper embrittlement that occurs in the low temperature range, 523–673K (250–

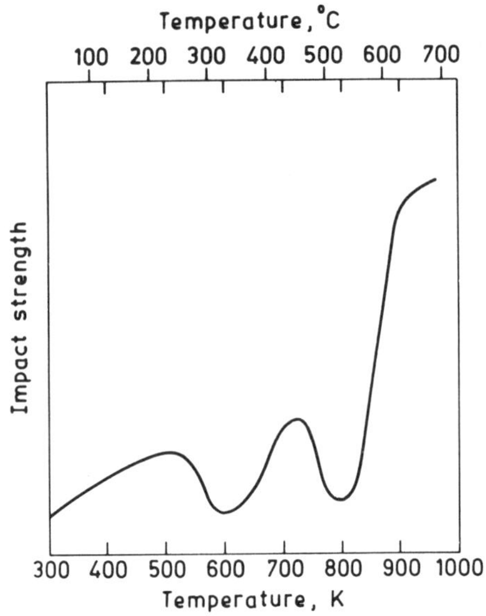

Fig. 5.18. Variation of impact strength as a function of tempering temperature of a steel highly prone to temper embrittlement (schematic).

400°C), is irreversible, whereas that in the intermediate temperature range, 723–873K (450–600°C), is reversible.

8.2 LOW TEMPERATURE RANGE EMBRITTLEMENT

Figure 5.19 shows room temperature notch toughness of several quenched and tempered alloy steels as a function of tempering temperature, tempered up to ~723K (450°C). Toughness initially increases as the tempering temperature is increased, but falls off after about 523K (250°C) and on tempering at ~573K (300°C) is scarcely greater than that of untempered steels. However, it starts increasing again as the tempering temperature is increased beyond ~623K (350°C). Once a steel has been tempered to a tougher state at a higher temperature, the embrittlement is not restored on holding the steel again in the embrittlement range of 523–673K (250–400°C), ie. the embrittlement is irreversible. All steels, including plain carbon steels, are prone to irreversible temper embrittlement to varying extent. A steel tempered in the irreversible temper embrittlement range fractures by bright inter-crystalline fracture along the former austenite grain boundaries. Generally, the tempering range of 523–673K (250–400°C) is avoided in all steels. Temper embrittlement in this range is caused by the formation of cementite in the form of thin plates, or films, at prior austenite grain boundaries. On further tempering at higher temperatures, above ~673K (400°C), with the spheroidization and coarsening of cementite, the embrittlement disappears. Therefore, once martensite has been tempered at temperatures higher than ~673K (400°C), this type of temper embrittlement does not occur again on heating the steel in this temperature range (523–673 K).

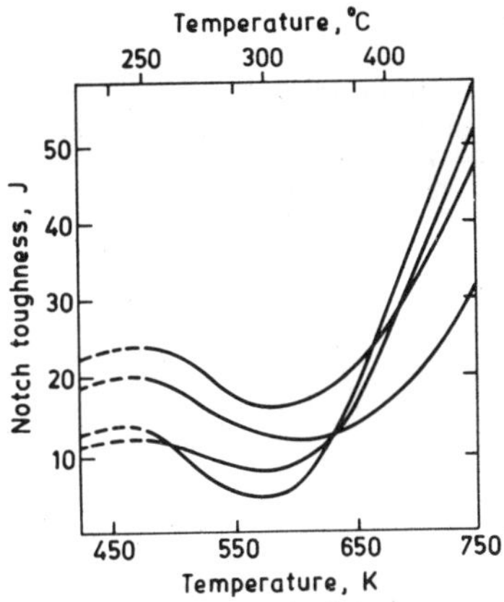

Fig. 5.19. Room temperature notch toughness of several quenched and tempered alloy steels as a function of tempering temperature.

8.3 INTERMEDIATE TEMPERATURE RANGE EMBRITTLEMENT

Temper embrittlement in the intermediate temperature range, 723–873K (450–600°C), is reversible. It can occur either on tempering in this temperature range, or, on tempering at a temperature higher than 873K (600°C) and then cooling it slowly through 873–723K (600–450°C) temperature range. However, when the steel is cooled rapidly after tempering at a higher temperature, higher than ~873K (600°C), the embrittlement does not appear. However, it becomes embrittled again if reheated in the 723–873K (450–600°C) temperature range. Hence, it is called reversible temper embrittlement. Steels prone to this type of embrittlement become embrittled whenever heated in the embrittling temperature range (723–873K). Figure 5.20 schematically shows the effect of tempering in the embrittlement and non-embrittlement temperature regions on the impact properties of a steel highly prone to this type of temper embrittlement. By tempering in the embrittlement range, the impact transition temperature (ITT) of the steel is greatly reduced.

Plain carbon steels containing less than ~0.5%Mn are not prone to reversible temper embrittlement. This phenomenon occurs only in alloy steels. Furthermore, alloy steels made from very high purity elements are also not susceptible to this type of temper embrittlement. It occurs only in commercial steels that normally contain small amounts of impurities, like, P, As, Sb, Sn, S, etc. In addition, different alloying elements have varying effect on the proneness of a steel to reversible temper embrittlement in the presence of these impurities. Elements like Ni, Cr and Mn enhance temper embrittlement, whereas small additions of Mo (0.2–0.3%) diminish it, while higher additions again enhance it. The highest embrittlement effect is normally observed in Ni–Cr and Mn–Cr steels.

Temper embrittlement in commercial steels is caused by the presence of various impurities in them, particularly phosphorus, antimony, tin and arsenic. Embrittlement in these steels is caused by segregation of these impurities at the grain boundaries. The effect of alloying elements on temper embrittlement is through their effect on the grain boundary segregation of these impurities. For a given concentra-

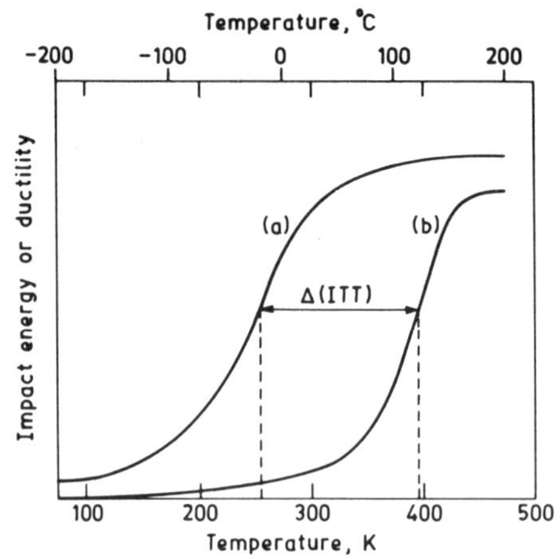

Fig. 5.20. Variation in fracture energy of a steel (experimental) with testing temperature (*a*) after non-embrittling treatment, and (*b*) after embrittling treatment. [after H. Jolivet and G. Vidal, *Rev. Met.*, 41 (1944) p.387].

tion of impurity in solution in a steel of given composition, there exists an equilibrium value at a given temperature for its maximum possible segregation at the grain boundaries. This equilibrium segregation decreases as the temperature is increased. Steels quenched from high (austenite) temperatures have very little impurity segregation at the grain boundaries. On tempering, the extent of segregation of an impurity at the grain boundaries is a function of impurity concentration in solution, temperature and time of tempering, and the concentration of various alloying elements in the steel. At higher temperatures, > ~873K (600°C), the maximum possible (equilibrium) segregation is generally low and is not enough to cause embrittlement. On the other hand, at lower temperatures, diffusivities of the impurities are too low to cause sufficient segregation during normally employed tempering times. Hence, this type of embrittlement is normally observed in the temperature range of 723–873K (450–600°C), where sufficient impurity segregation occurs during tempering.

Figure 5.21 shows tempering times at different temperatures that give the same impact transition temperature (ITT), a measure of toughness, in a Ni–Cr steel. The fastest embrittlement is observed at ~823K (550°C). The change in ITT in steels prone to embrittlement has been experimentally related to the extent of impurity segregation at the grain boundaries. Segregation of impurities at the grain boundaries may be experimentally measured by Auger electron spectroscopy.

Segregation of impurities at the grain boundaries changes the impact transition temperature (ITT) of a steel by lowering the grain boundary cohesive energy, and hence, its fracture strength. Figure 5.22 schematically shows how ITT is increased with decrease in grain boundary fracture strength. The effect of different impurities on grain boundary cohesion is approximately proportional to the difference by which the atomic size of an impurity in the grain boundary is greater than that of iron. Thus,

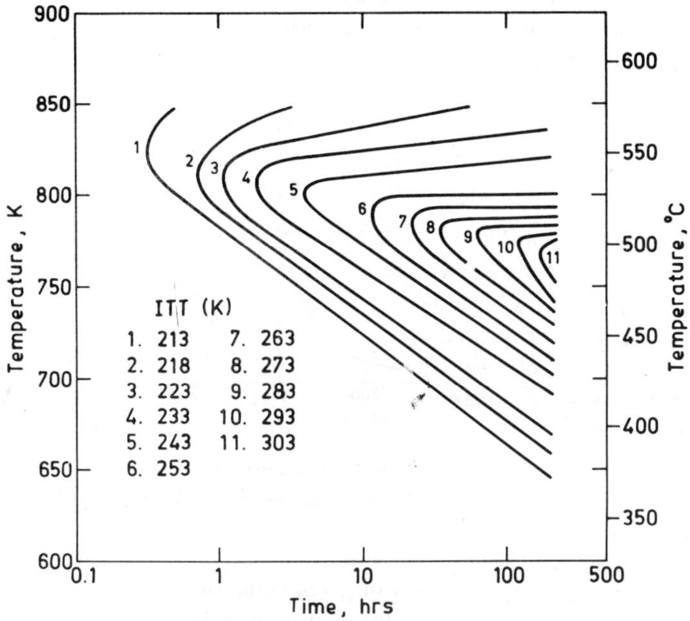

Fig. 5.21. Experimental time temperature curves for constant impact transition temperature (ITT) for tempering of a Ni–Cr steel [L.D. Jafee and D.C. Buffum, *Trans. ASM*, 42 (1952) p.604].

for the same extent of segregation, Sb has the largest embrittling effect followed by Sn, As and P.

As mentioned earlier, plain carbon steels do not show reversible temper embrittlement even when the embrittlement-causing impurities are present in the steel. The

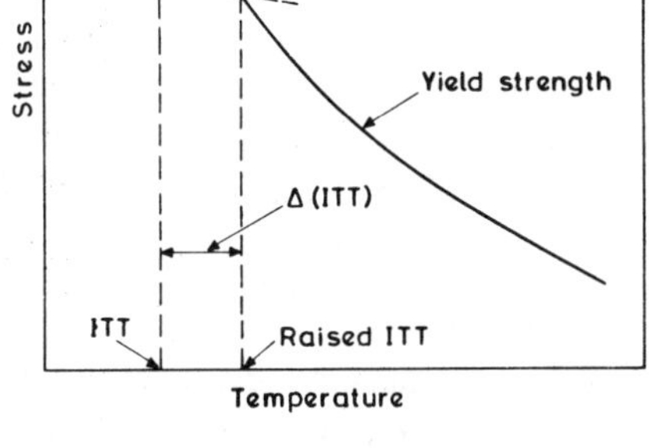

Fig. 5.22. Effect of temperature on the tensile properties of a steel (schematic).

equilibrium grain boundary segregation of these impurities in plain carbon steels is relatively low and is not enough to cause severe embrittlement. Another factor which would affect the change in ITT upon impurity segregation is the rate at which yield stress of the steel increases with decreasing temperature (see Fig. 5.22). If it rises sharply with decreasing temperature, the effect on ITT would be smaller for the same decrease in grain boundary cohesive energy. This is generally true for plain carbon steels and may partly explain their immunity to temper embrittlement.

In alloy steels, elements like Ni, Cr and Mn promote segregation of P, Sb, Sn and As impurities at the grain boundaries. Increase in impurity segregation in the presence of these elements is substantial. In the process, these elements themselves segregate at the grain boundaries also. This mutual promotion of segregation of impurities and alloying elements at the grain boundaries is due to strong attractive interaction between the impurity and alloying element atoms. An additional segregation of impurities occurs in some cases when two alloying elements are present simultaneously, besides their individual effects on segregation. For example, the amount of segregation of Sb in Ni–Cr steels is higher than what would be expected by simply adding the effects of Ni and Cr, when present separately. Hence, in alloy steels, impurity segregation at the grain boundaries is generally higher, making these steels highly prone to temper embrittlement. The alloying elements may also decrease the rate at which the yield strength of the steel increases with decreasing temperature, thereby further enhancing the embrittlement effect (see Fig. 5.22). For a given steel, the maximum embrittlement effect is proportional to the concentration of impurities in solution. For example, in 0.32%C – 3.0%Ni – 0.75%Cr steel, the embrittlement, expressed as shift in ITT, has been expressed as [Ref. 8]:

$$\Delta(\text{ITT}) = 0.9(\text{P}) + 16(\text{Sb}) + 0.08(\text{As}) + 0.34(\text{Sn}) + 0.013(\text{Mn}) \quad [\text{in K}] \tag{5.10}$$

where, (P) refers to concentration of P in ppm by weight, and so on. Addition of Mo in small concentrations reduces the embrittlement effect of the impurities. For example, in the steel discussed above, with the addition of 0.52%Mo, the embrittlement is reduced to:

$$\Delta(\text{ITT}) = 0.2(\text{P}) + 1.1(\text{Sb}) + 0.02(\text{As}) + 0.09(\text{Sn}) + 0.001(\text{Mn}) \quad [\text{in K}] \tag{5.11}$$

However, with higher additions of Mo, the embrittlement is again restored.

In some alloy steels, temper embrittlement is a serious problem. In practice, the following measures are generally taken to minimize temper embrittlement: (*a*) keeping the impurities as low as possible, (*b*) alloying with Mo, and (*c*) quenching after tempering at higher temperatures, i.e. higher than ~873K (600°C).

9 TEMPERING OF OTHER STRUCTURES

The tempering operation to improve ductility and toughness is usually applied to quenched (martensitic) steels. However, sometimes bainite and pearlite structures are also tempered, either intentionally, or, unavoidably with the tempering of martensite, when partly present in quenched steels along with martensite. On tempering, bainite and pearlite also soften. In bainite the coalescence and growth of carbides takes place. In pearlite, the lamellar structure spheroidizes on tempering for a long period at higher temperatures. On tempering at higher temperatures, after an initial short period of tempering, the hardness of all three structures becomes similar, and then, they soften slowly with the coarsening of cementite particles.

REFERENCES

1. E.C. Bain and H.W. Paxton, *Alloying Elements in Steel*, American Society for Metals, Metals Park, Ohio, 1962.
2. I. Novikov, *Theory of Heat Treatment of Metals*, Mir Publishers, Moscow, 1978.
3. W.C. Leslie, *The Physical Metallurgy of Steels*, McGraw-Hill Book Company, New York, 1981.
4. *The Mechanisms of Phase Transformations in Crystalline Solids*, Institute of Metals, London, Monograph No. 33, 1969.
5. R.E. Read-Hill, *Physical Metallurgy Principles*, D. Van Nostrand Company Inc. New York, 1964.
6. R.A. Grange, C.R. Hribal and L.F. Porter, *Metall. Trans. A.*, **8A** (1977) p. 1775.
7. G.R. Speich, *Trans. TMS-AIME*, **245** (1969) p. 2553.
8. M.P. Seah, *Surf. Sci.*, **53** (1975) p. 168.

CHAPTER 6

Continuous Cooling Transformation (CCT) Diagrams

1 INTRODUCTION

Continuous Cooling Transformation (CCT) diagrams of steels represent the progress of transformations from austenite during continuous cooling from austenitic temperatures. In Chapters 1 and 3, various transformations from austenite under isothermal conditions and Isothermal Transformation (IT) diagrams of steels were discussed. In most practical heat treatment processes, isothermal conditions rarely exist and, more often than not, steel components are continuously cooled. Under such conditions, it would be desirable to know the progress of transformations from austenite during continuous cooling. Mathematical analysis of the nucleation and growth processes of various transformations under non-isothermal conditions does not yield analytical solutions. Furthermore, for a given steel, a single IT diagram is obtained, whereas, in principle, the progress of transformations during continuous cooling would also depend on the nature of cooling. An IT diagram can be easily determined, needing only a simple metallographic equipment and few furnaces. For these reasons, though usefulness of CCT diagrams was realised, most of the early work on transformations in steels has been done on IT diagrams. Most books extensively cover IT diagrams, whereas only a passing reference is made to CCT diagrams.

In recent years, a large amount of work has been done on CCT diagrams. Now, more efficient methods for determining CCT diagrams exist, where metallography is only used as an auxiliary tool. In this chapter, methods for experimental determination and presentation of CCT diagrams as well as their relationship with IT diagrams are discussed.

2 EXPERIMENTAL PROCEDURES

Progress of transformations from austenite may be continuously monitored by measuring the change in some physical property that changes appreciably during these transformations. This can be done either for isothermal holding or during continuous cooling. The physical property being measured should change considerably during the transformations and should be easily measurable. Specific volume and magnetic permeability are two physical properties which satisfy these criteria for transformations in steels. Measurements of changes in specific volume by using dilatometers has become a common method for monitoring phase transformations in solids and is being widely used for determination of transformation diagrams in steels. Though, some IT and CCT diagrams in steels have been determined by magnetic permeability measurements, majority of work has been done by measuring the changes in specific volume by using dilatometric method. The principle of determination of IT and CCT diagrams by dilatometric method is briefly given in the following.

Figure 6.1 schematically shows the main features of a dilatometric equipment. The temperature and dilation of the sample are simultaneously monitored as a function of time. With the latest sophisticated equipments, length changes of the order of 10^{-4} mm can be easily measured. The dilatometric method is always used in conjunction with metallography to cross check the microstructures after transformation. Figure 6.2 schematically shows dilatometer plots that are typically obtained when austenite is isothermally transformed fully to either, a single products (curve "a"), or, to a mixture of two products (curve "b"). The type of microstructural products, though easily inferred from the composition of steel and the temperatures of transformation, are normally metallographically cross-checked. After austenitizing at a suitable temperature, the sample is quenched to desired temperature and held there isothermally, and the change in length as a function of time is recorded. When austenite fully transforms to a single product, the percentage transformation at any instant is directly proportional to the relative change in length, as shown in Fig. 6.2. For a mixture of products, the percentage of austenite transformed may not be strictly proportional to change in length, however, it is a reasonable assumption and is generally used. For a given steel, plots of the type shown in Fig. 6.2 are obtained at different temperatures and its IT diagram is easily constructed from these plots.

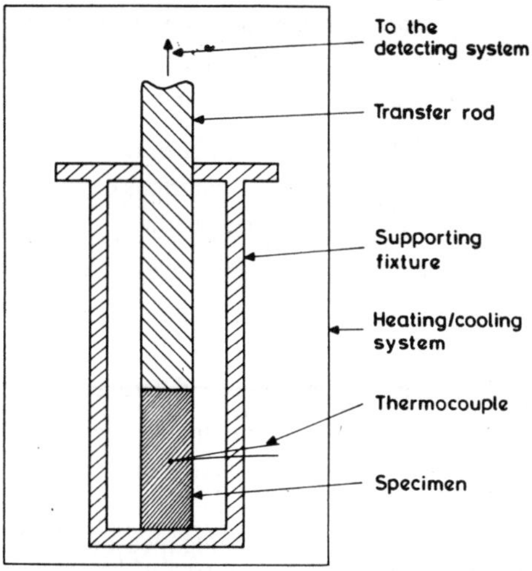

Fig. 6.1. Schematic illustration of a dilatometer set-up for determining transformation diagrams.

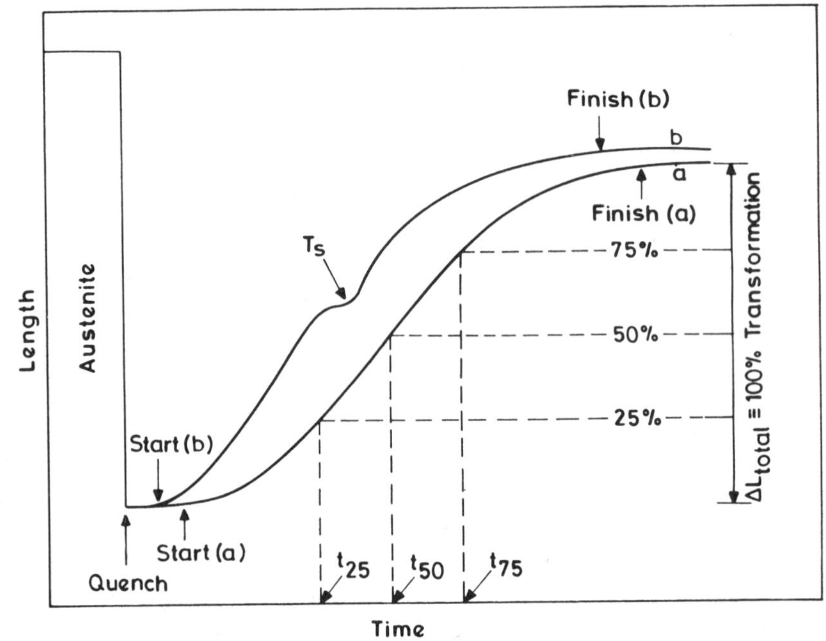

Fig. 6.2. Typical dilatometer plots during isothermal transformation to (a) single product, (b) two products (schematic).

To determine a CCT diagram by dilatometric method, the sample is continuously cooled and the changes in length and temperature are simultaneously recorded as a function of time. The cooling rate imposed on the sample may be by natural cooling (Newtonian) or a programmed linear/non-linear cooling. To obtain higher cooling rates the samples may be gas quenched, and natural Newtonian type cooling occurs, whereas, for low cooling rates furnaces are easily programmed for linear cooling. During the determination of a CCT diagram, the highest cooling rate should be able to produce 100% martensite structure and the slowest cooling rate should give 100% coarse ferrite–pearlite structure.

Figure 6.3 schematically shows the type of dilatometer plots that are obtained during continuous cooling of a steel at various cooling rates, also given in the figure. The steel transforms to 100% martensite at cooling rate "a" and to 100% ferrite–pearlite mixture at cooling rate "e". Mixtures of microstructures are obtained at intermediate cooling rates. Figure 6.4 gives the CCT diagram which is constructed from the data in Fig. 6.3. The cooling curves and hardness values obtained at the end of cooling are also normally shown in CCT diagrams, as seen in Fig. 6.4.

In actual determination of CCT diagram of a steel, the dilatometer plots may not as sharply delineate the start and end of different transformations as in Fig. 6.3, and a considerable judgement on the part of the investigator may be required to estimate the start and end temperatures of different transformations and their relative proportions. The dilatometry experiments are invariably supplemented by metallography

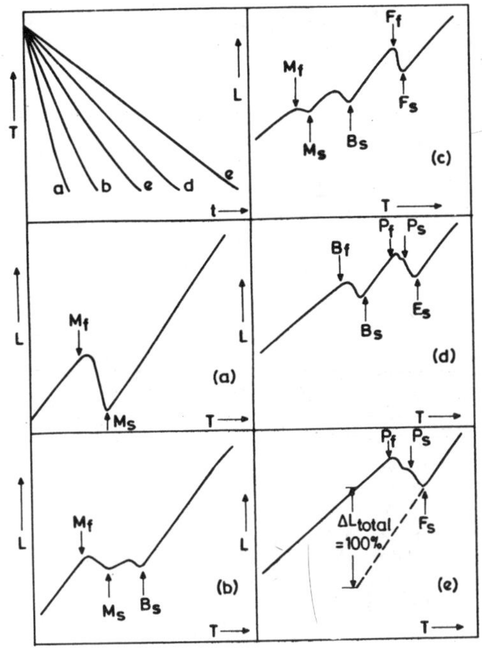

Fig. 6.3. Dilatometer plots during transformations on continuous cooling at different cooling rates (schematic). F, P, B and M stand for ferrite, pearlite, Bainite and martensite, respectively, and subscripts s and f for start and finish of transformation to these products.

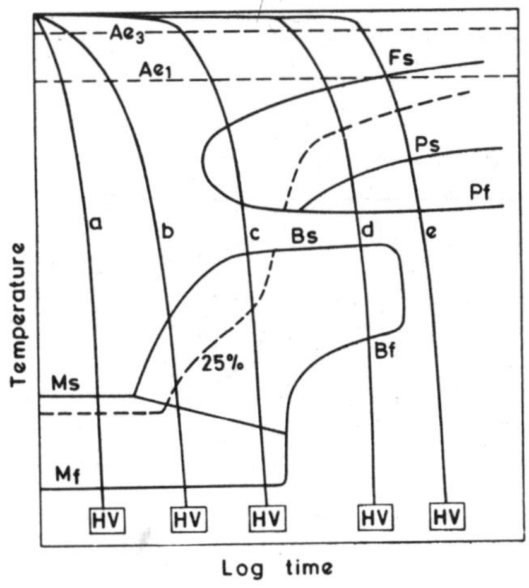

Fig. 6.4. CCT diagram constructed from data in Fig. 6.3 (schematic). F, P, B and M stand for ferrite, pearlite, Bainite and martensite, respectively, and subscripts s and f for start and finish of transformation to these products. Dotted line is for 25% total transformation.

and hardness measurements on the transformed samples. An experienced investigator, having a basic understanding of kinetics of various transformations in steels and the relative effect of different alloying elements on these transformations, weighing all the evidence, can arrive at reasonably accurate CCT diagrams. The progress of transformations during continuous cooling is also a function of the nature of cooling curves to some extent, i.e. of the relative time spent in different temperature regions. The CCT diagram plots, therefore, invariably contain cooling curves superimposed on them, as schematically shown by lines a to e in Fig. 6.4. Figures 6.5 and 6.6 show CCT diagrams of two different commercial steels determined by

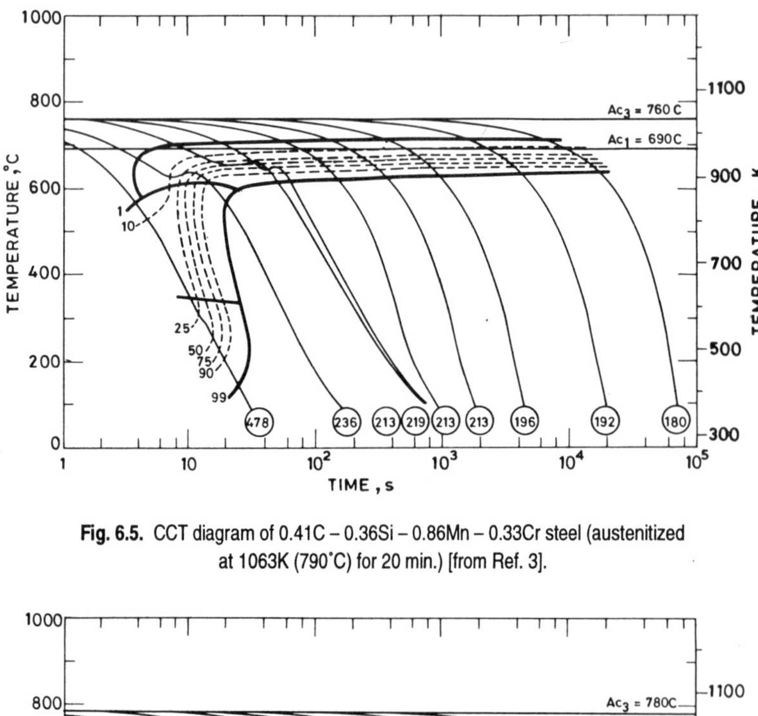

Fig. 6.5. CCT diagram of 0.41C – 0.36Si – 0.86Mn – 0.33Cr steel (austenitized at 1063K (790°C) for 20 min.) [from Ref. 3].

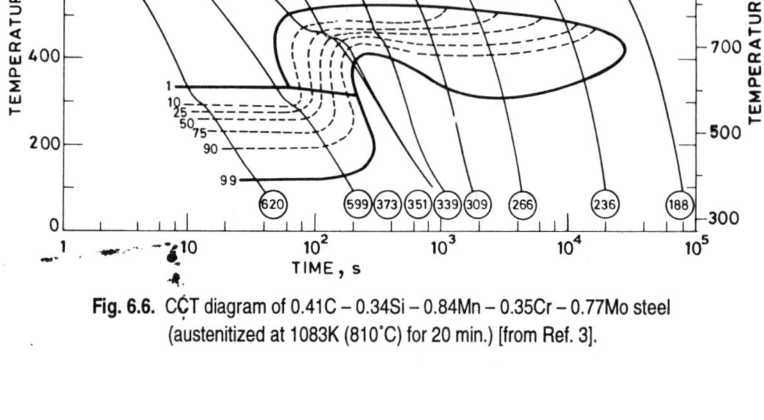

Fig. 6.6. CCT diagram of 0.41C – 0.34Si – 0.84Mn – 0.35Cr – 0.77Mo steel (austenitized at 1083K (810°C) for 20 min.) [from Ref. 3].

dilatometric method (Ref. 3). Numbers at the end of cooling curves are room temperature hardness (VHN) of steel at the end of cooling. Note that, in Fig. 6.6, the ferrite–pearlite transformation is shifted to right (longer times) in relation to the bainite transformation. This steel contains Mo and Cr, the elements which promote the formation of 'bay' in IT diagrams of steels (Chapter 3), i.e. they preferentially retard ferrite/pearlite transformations.

3 PRESENTATION OF CCT DIAGRAMS

CCT diagram of a steel is uniquely determined only for a given set of cooling curves used for its determination. Hence, CCT diagrams of the same steel determined by using different cooling procedures would, in principle, be different. A CCT diagram of a steel would predict the progress of transformations and the final microstructure and hardness at the end of cooling, only if the time–temperature relationships (cooling curves) are similar to the ones used in its determination. Of course, it would be desirable to have a single CCT diagram for a given steel and be able to predict the transformation products and hardness under different cooling conditions by using this diagram. For example, CCT diagram of a steel may have been determined by using Newtonian cooling at higher cooling rates and controlled linear cooling at slower cooling rates. Now, if a component of complex shape made from the same steel is quenched from austenite, say in water or oil, the time–temperature relationships (cooling curves) at different points in the component will not exactly match the cooling curves used for determining the CCT diagram. The question therefore is, can this CCT diagram, determined by using a set of cooling curves, be used to predict the microstructure and hardness at a given point in the component when the cooling curves do not exactly match the ones used for its determination? The answer to this question is a qualified yes.

A number of methods have been used to overcome the above mentioned problem, all based on the concept of equivalent cooling curves. Two different cooling curves may be considered equivalent, if the microstructure and hardness obtained at the end of cooling are essentially the same. In practice, the following criteria for the equivalence of two different cooling curves are generally used. Two cooling curves are considered equivalent, if, either.

(*i*) the times to cool from Ae_3 to 773K (500°C) are the same; or

(*ii*) the times to cool from Ae_3 to $(Ae_3 + 298K)/2$, a temperature half way between Ae_3 and room temperature 298K (25°C), are the same; or

(*iii*) the cooling rates, defined as $v(K/hr) = (1073K–773K)/t$, where t is the time to cool from 1073K (800°C) to 773K (500°C), are the same; or

(*iv*) the instant cooling rates at 973K (700°C) are the same.

All these criteria give similar and satisfactory results as along as the cooling is "natural", i.e. continuous cooling from Ae_3 to ambient temperatures at a rate controlled by, either heat transfer to the cooling medium, or thermal conductivity of the cooling medium, or some combination of these two limiting conditions. Though, the different methods for determining the equivalence of cooling curves seem different and somewhat arbitrary, they essentially give similar and satisfactory results, as they are all based on the estimation of time spent in the temperature range where high temperature non-martensitic transformations from austenite mostly occur.

Based on different criteria for equivalent cooling curves, different methods for plotting of CCT diagrams have also been suggested, as shown in Figs. 6.7 and 6.8. In Fig. 6.7, CCT diagram of a steel is plotted as a temperature vs time of cooling from 1073K (800°C) to 773K (500°C). The individual cooling curves no longer need to be shown and the diagram is read vertically for a desired 1073K (800°C) to 773K (500°C) cooling time. Hardness values at the end of cooling as a function of cooling rate are also plotted in the same diagram. In another method of representation of CCT diagrams, shown in Fig. 6.8, relative proportions of different microstructural constituents at the end of cooling are plotted as a function of cooling velocity, defined as, either v(K/hr) = (1073K–773K)/t or instant cooling velocity (K/hr) at 973K (700°C). This diagram is also read vertically and the relative proportions of different microstructural constituents at the end of cooling can be read directly from the diagram. Hardness at the end cooling as a function of cooling rate is given in the accompanying plot (see Fig. 6.8). As mentioned earlier, these diagrams may be used to predict the transformation behaviour of steels only when the cooling is "natural". For any heat treatment in which an artificial cooling programme is imposed on the component, these diagrams are not directly useful. However, CCT and IT diagrams may still be useful, if used judiciously.

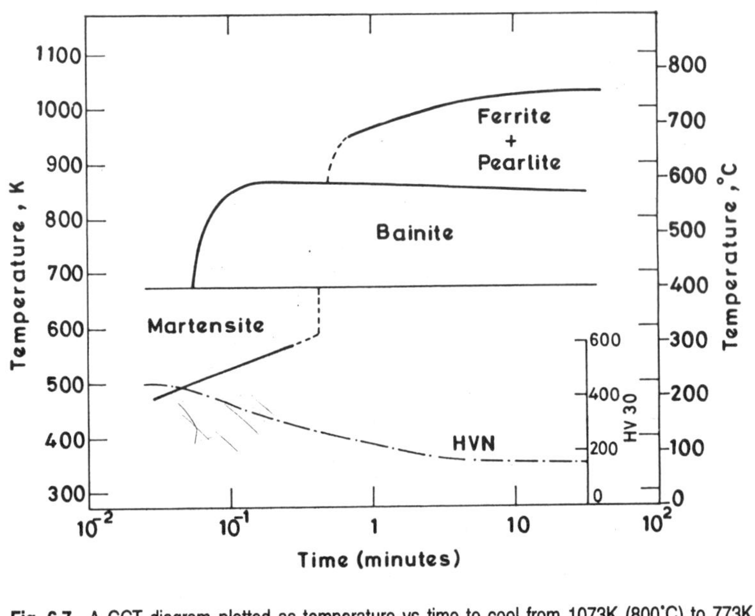

Fig. 6.7. A CCT diagram plotted as temperature vs time to cool from 1073K (800°C) to 773K (500°C). Only start curves are shown. [from M. Economopoulos, N.Lambert and L. Habraken, Diagrammes de transformation des aciers fabriques dans ie Benelux, Centre National de Recherches Metallurgiques, Brussels, 1967].

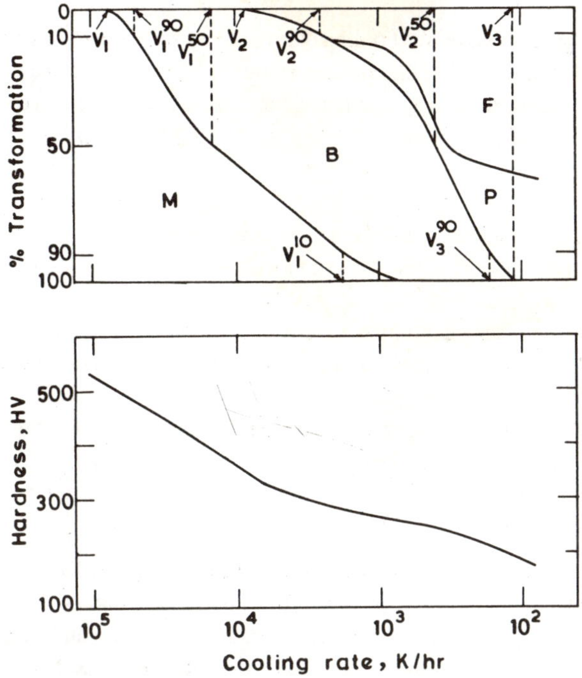

Fig. 6.8. A CCT diagram plotted as % microstructural constituents vs cooling rate [from Ref.2].

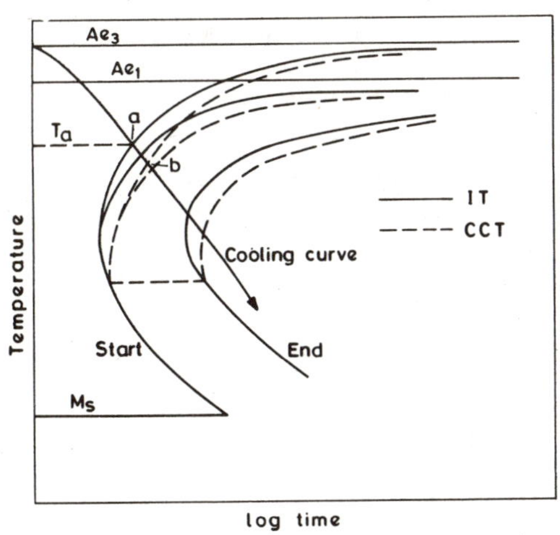

Fig. 6.9. Relationship between IT and CCT diagrams of a plain carbon steel (schematic).

4 RELATION BETWEEN IT AND CCT DIAGRAMS

Figure 6.9 schematically shows the relative positions of IT and CCT diagrams of a plain carbon steel, plotted on the same graph. The CCT diagram is generally shifted to longer times with respect to the IT diagram. This shift can be understood by considering a given continuous cooling curve, shown in Fig. 6.9. This cooling curve meets the start curve of IT diagram at a point "a", which represents the time for 0.1% transformation when the sample is quenched to T_a and held there isothermally. However, on continuously cooling to point "a" along this cooling curve, the sample has spent most of the time at temperatures higher than T_a, where the nucleation and growth rates are, in general, slower. Therefore, on continuous cooling to point "a", the amount of transformation would be less than 0.1%. Hence, on continuous cooling, 0.1% transformation would be attained at some point beyond "a" along the cooling curve; i.e. at point "b" in Fig. 6.9. By extending the same argument to other cooling curves, we can qualitatively see how the relative positions of IT and CCT diagrams of the same steel would be as shown in Fig. 6.9. Below the nose of the IT diagram, transformation rates are again slowed down and the CCT curve becomes closer to the IT curve, meeting it at some temperature below the nose. The point at which IT and CCT start curves meet, below the nose of IT diagram, is on the critical cooling curve. At cooling rates higher than this, no non-martensitic transformation would occur in the steel.

The above analysis of the relative positions of the IT and CCT diagrams of a given steel also suggests possibilities of converting the IT diagram of a steel to its CCT diagram and vice versa. Two different methods for converting an IT diagram to CCT diagram exist. The first method, due to Grange and Kiefer (Ref. 4), is a graphical method, and is shown in Fig. 6.10. According to this method, during continuous cooling along a given cooling curve which intercepts the IT start curve at temperature T_1, the transformation will start at temperature T_2, such that the time of cooling between T_1 and T_2 is equal to the time for the start of transformation during isothermal holding at temperature $(T_1 + T_2)/2$. The construction is schematically shown in

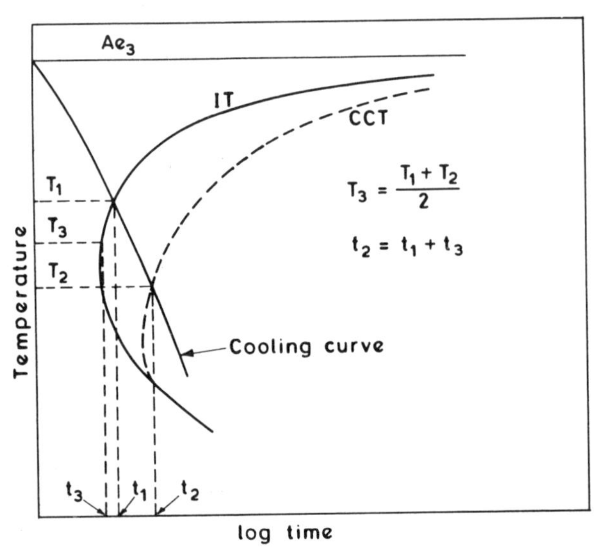

Fig. 6.10. Illustration of the graphic method of converting an IT diagram to CCT diagram [after Grange and Kiefer, Ref. 4].

Fig. 6.10. A similar construction for different cooling rates will, then, produce the CCT start curve. The same procedure may be adopted for the IT end curve, or any other curve corresponding to a given amount of transformation. Thus, an IT diagram may be completely converted to CCT diagram. The assumptions involved in this method are not strictly valid; however, it gives reasonable results, particularly for the transformation start curves in ferrite-pearlite transformation range.

The other method of converting an IT diagram to CCT diagram is known as Avrami rule and may be arrived at as follows. Let $\tau(T)$ be the time required to obtain a given percentage transformation, X, at temperature T during isothermal transformation. Then the time required to obtain the same percentage transformation, X, on continuous cooling is given by the condition:

$$X = \int_{Ae_3}^{T_{CCT}} dX = \int_{Ae_3}^{T_{CCT}} \frac{dX}{dt}\, dt = \int_{Ae_3}^{T_{CCT}} \bar{g} dt \qquad (6.1)$$

where T_{CCT} is temperature along the cooling curve where X per cent transformation is obtained and $\bar{g}$ is time average transformation rate at any temperature, T. $\bar{g}$ is given by:

$$\bar{g} = X/\tau(T) \qquad (6.2)$$

Substituting for $\bar{g}$ from Eq. (6.2) in Eq. (6.1), we get:

$$\int_{Ae_3}^{T_{CCT}} \frac{dt}{\tau(T)} = 1 \qquad (6.3)$$

Equation (6.3), called the Avrami integral, is integrated along the given cooling curve. Equation (6.3) can also be written as:

$$\int_{Ae_3}^{T_{CCT}} \frac{dT}{\tau(T)\dfrac{dT}{dt}} = 1 \qquad (6.4)$$

Integrals (6.3) and (6.4) are equivalent and either one may be used to convert an IT diagram to CCT diagram. The integral (6.3) or (6.4) is to be evaluated for each cooling curve.

As more and more CCT diagrams are being directly generated, it is also desirable to have a procedure for converting a CCT diagram to IT diagram. Such a procedure has been recently suggested by Kirkaldy and Sharma (Ref. 5) and is briefly discussed here. Let $\tau_{CCT}(T_{CCT})$ be the time for a given percentage transformation in the CCT diagram. If it is assumed that, the CCT Diagram is determined by using constant cooling rates (linear cooling), then:

$$\frac{dT}{dt} = -\frac{(Ae_3 - T_{CCT})}{\tau_{CCT}(T_{CCT})} \qquad (6.5)$$

Substituting from Eq. (6.5) in Eq. (6.4), cross-multiplying and differentiating with respect T_{CCT} gives:

$$\tau_{IT}(T_{CCT}) = \frac{1}{\dfrac{d}{dT_{CCT}}\left[\dfrac{Ae_3 - T_{CCT}}{\tau_{CCT}\,(T_{CCT})}\right]} \tag{6.6}$$

where τ_{IT} is time for the given percentage transformation, when carried out isothermally at T_{CCT}.

Next, consider a case when the cooling rates are not constant, but can be expressed either analytically or empirically as;

$$\frac{dT}{dt} = f_1\,(x)\; f_2\,(\,T\,) = f_1\,(T_{CCT})\; f_2\,(\,T\,) \tag{6.7}$$

where x is distance from the surface of a continuously cooled sample. Substituting from Eq. (6.7) in Eq. (6.4), cross-multiplying and differentiating, gives:

$$\tau_{IT}\,(T_{CCT}) = \frac{1}{f_2\,(T_{CCT})\,\dfrac{df_1}{dT_{CCT}}} \tag{6.8}$$

The conversion of a CCT diagram to IT Diagram is, then, achieved via Eq. (6.6), when the cooling rates are given by Eq. (6.5), and via Eq. (6.8), when the cooling rates can be expressed by Eq. (6.7). Figure 6.11 shows the conversion of a calculated IT diagram of an eutectoid steel to CCT diagram using Eq. (6.4) for Jominy cooling curves and its convertion back to IT diagram by using Eq. (6.8), demonstrating the salutary and expected agreement (Ref. 5). The Jominy cooling curves as a function of Jominy distance were expressed in the form of Eq. (6.7).

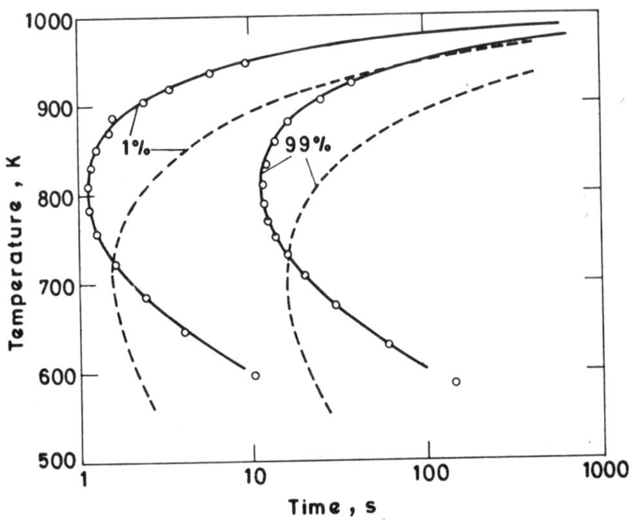

Fig. 6.11. Results of IT→ CCTand CCT→IT conversions using Eqs. (6.4) and (6.8), respectively, and Jominy cooling curves. (——) original IT diagram ,(- - - -) converted CCT diagram using Eq. (6.4), (o) reconverted IT diagram points using Eq. (6.8) [from Ref. 5].

REFERENCES

1. George T. Eldis, in *Hardenability Concepts with Applications to Steels*, (Eds. D.V. Doane and J.S. Kirkaldy). The Metallurgical Society of AIME, Warrendale, Pa., 1978; p.126.
2. Ph. Maynier, J. Dollet and P. Bastien, Ref. 1, p.163.
3. W.W. Cias, *Phase Transformation Kinetics and Hardenability of Medium Carbon Steels,* Climax Moly. Company, Greenwich, Connecticut, 1972.
4. R. Grange and J. Kiefer, *Trans Am. Soc. Metals*, **29** (1941) p.85.
5. J.S. Kirkaldy and R.C. Sharma, *Script Met.*, **16** (1982) p.1193.

CHAPTER 7

Formation of Austenite

1 INTRODUCTION

After other manufacturing processes prior to heat treatment, most steel components have ferrite–pearlite, pearlite or cementite–pearlite structure. The first step in most heat treatment processes of steels is austenitizing, i.e. to obtain homogeneous austenite at appropriate temperature in the austenite stability range. To attain total transformation to austenite and homogeneity in composition, steel must be heated in the austenite temperature range for a sufficiently long period. Another variable which affects most heat treatment processes and the final properties after heat treatment is prior austenite grain size. In any ferrite–pearlite steel, the final ferritic grain size to a large extent depends on the prior austenite grain size. Austenite grain size also has a significant effect on the IT and CCT diagrams, and hence, on the ability of a steel to be quench hardened to martensite. The austenite grain size to a large extent depends on the temperature and time of austenitization and to a lesser extent also on the composition of steel. In this chapter, different aspects of austenitizing treatment of steels are discussed.

2 KINETICS OF AUSTENITE FORMATION

The structure of most steel components prior to heat treatment is ferrite–carbide mixture, normally in the form of ferrite–pearlite, pearlite, or cementite–pearlite structure, depending upon the carbon content of steel. Alloy carbides may also be present in some alloy steels. On heating a ferrite–pearlite steel, pearlite transforms to austenite first, as temperature is raised above Ae_1. Once all the pearlite has transformed to austenite, the austenite further grows by consuming the remaining ferrite, either partially (according to the lever rule) when the temperature is between Ae_1 and Ae_3, or completely if it is above Ae_3. Similarly, in cementite–pearlite steels, pearlite transforms to austenite first, followed by the dissolution of pro-eutectoid cementite. Alloy carbides, if present, normally dissolve last. Kinetics of formation of austenite from these structures is qualitatively discussed in this section.

Let us first consider the austenitization of a hypo-eutectoid plain carbon steel of composition C_0 at temperature T, between Ae_3 and 1185K (912°C), as shown in Fig. 7.1 This steel will normally have a ferrite–pearlite structure at room temperature, which at temperature T is metastable with respect of homogeneous austenite of composition C_0. Within the ferrite–pearlite structure, ferrite is essentially pure bcc

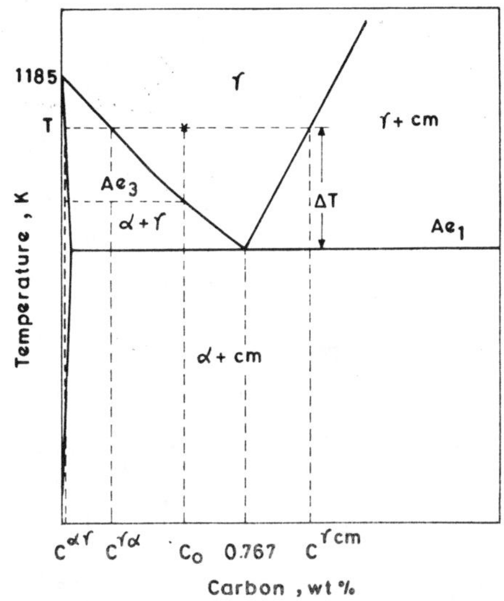

Fig. 7.1. Local equilibrium concentrations during austenitization of plain carbon ferrite–pearlite steel of composition C_0 at temperature T.

iron, as it dissolves very little carbon. Hence, at temperature T, which is lower than the equilibrium α/γ transformation temperature in pure iron (1185K), the ferrite is more stable than austenite. The pearlite, of approximately average eutectoid composition (0.767% C in Fe–C alloys), is metastable with respect to homogeneous austenite of the same composition. Therefore, on heating at temperature T, pearlite transforms to austenite first. Pearlite is a two-phase lamellar mixture of ferrite and cementite. During pearlite to austenite transformation, a two-phase mixture (α + cm) transforms to a single phase, γ. Within pearlite, ferrite is essentially pure bcc iron and by itself would transform to austenite only above ~1185K (912°C), whereas, cementite by itself is stable up to its melting point. Therefore, at temperature T, none of the constituent phases of pearlite are individually metastable with respect to austenite, but the overall structure is, as schematically shown in Fig. 7.2 Hence, nucleation of austenite completely within any of the constituent phases of pearlite is thermodynamically impossible. However, austenite nucleation can, and does, occur at ferrite/cementite interfaces. Some possible nucleation geometries of austenite formation from (α + cm) structures are shown in Fig. 7.3. Nucleation of austenite at α/cm interfaces occurs by heterophase fluctuations. Factors which determine the energetics and kinetics of austenite nucleation are the same as in any solid state transformation, i.e. (*a*) volume Gibbs energy change for the transformation (schematically shown in Fig.7.2), (*b*) increase in Gibbs energy due to creation/replacement of interfaces, and (*c*) strain energy due to volume change, if any.

Once nucleated at α/cm interfaces within the pearlite structure, austenite grows by consuming both the constituent phases of pearlite, i.e. α as well as cm. Figure 7.4 schematically shows carbon concentration profiles during the growth of austenite

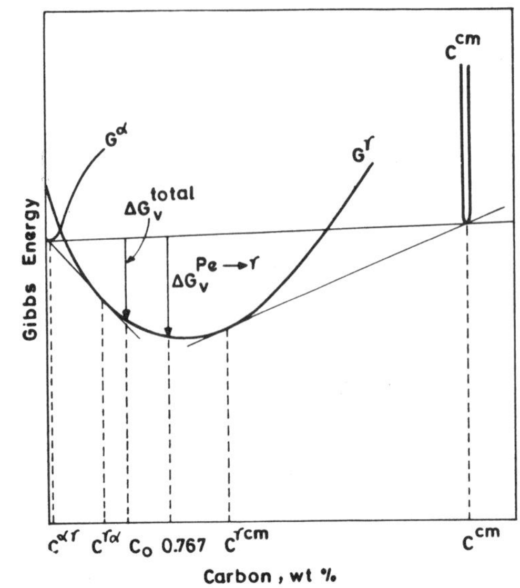

Fig. 7.2. Volume Gibbs energy change during pearlite to austenite transformation.

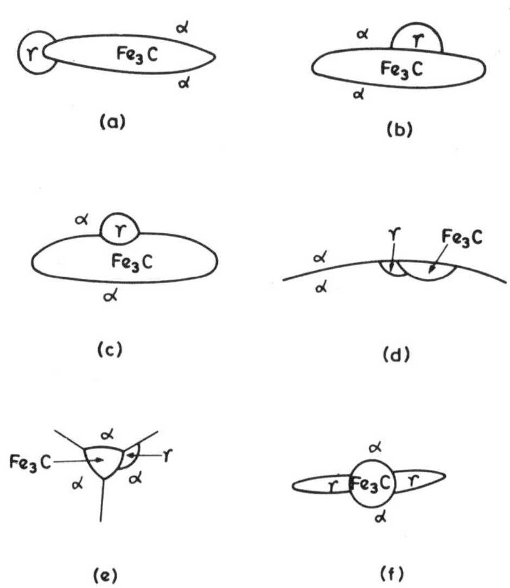

Fig. 7.3. Possible austenite nucleation geometries at α/cm interfaces (schematic).

within pearlite, assuming local equilibrium at γ/cm and γ/α interfaces, in the hypo-eutectoid Fe–C alloy of composition C_o transformed at temperature T between Ae_3 and 1185K (912°C) (also see Fig. 7.1). The austenite growth rate under these conditions is essentially determined by carbon diffusion through austenite. The carbon concentration difference, ($C^{\gamma cm}$ – $C^{\gamma\alpha}$), between points *b* and *a* in Fig.7.4 is the driving force for carbon diffusion in austenite and, to a first approximation, is proportional to superheating, ΔT, above Ae_1; ($\Delta T = T - Ae_1$). Furthermore, the rate of growth of austenite into ferrite and cementite lamellae is inversely proportional to the magnitude of concentration difference across the γ/α and γ/cm interfaces, respectively. The concentration difference across the γ/cm interface, (C^{cm} – $C^{\gamma cm}$), is an order of magnitude larger than across the γ/α interface, ($C^{\gamma\alpha}$ – $C^{\alpha\gamma}$), as seen in Figs. 7.1 and 7.4. Hence, the austenite boundary moves much faster into the α phase, completely consuming it, before cementite is completely dissolved. Then on, the remaining cementite dissolves in austenite to complete the transformation of peralite to austenite. On the completion of pearlite dissolution, the carbon concentration in austenite is not uniform. It is highest at the centres of prior cementite lamellae, where cementite dissolves last, given by $C^{\gamma cm}$ in Fig. 7.1, and lowest at the centres of former α lamallae, approximately given by $C^{\gamma\alpha}$ in Fig. 7.1. Therefore, additional time is required to obtain homogeneous austenite.

Completely homogeneous austenite in prior pearlite regions is obtained in relatively short times due to small inter-lamellar spacings in pearlite. At a given temperature, the time required for complete pearlite dissolution and homogenization of austenite within the pearlite regions decreases with decreasing inter-lamellar spacing. Hence, the austenite formation is faster when the starting structure is finer pearlite. With increasing austenitization temperature, the diffusion coefficient of carbon increases exponentially with temperature and the driving force for diffusion, ($C^{\gamma cm}$ – $C^{\gamma\alpha}$), increases approximately linearly and is proportional to superhearting ΔT. Hence, the rate of austenite formation increases continuously, and rapidly, with increasing temperature.

In the ferrite–pearlite steel of composition C_o (Fig. 7.1) under consideration, containing pro-eutectoid ferrite in addition to pearlite, austenite grows into pro-eutectoid

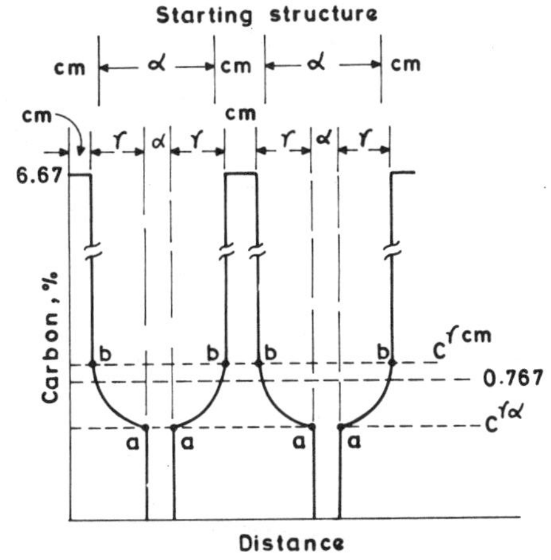

Fig. 7.4. Carbon concentration profiles during pearlite to austenite transformation (schematic).

ferrite essentially after pearlite has completely transformed into homogeneous austenite. This is due to the relatively short time required for complete pearlite dissolution. Austenite growth into pro-eutectoid ferrite is also controlled by carbon diffusion in austenite. Assuming local equilibrium at the γ/α interfaces, the carbon concentration profiles during the growth of austenite into pro-eutectoid ferrite grains at various stages of transformation, for an alloy of composition C_o at temperature T in Fig. 7.1, would be as schematically shown in Fig.7.5. Initially, austenite in the prior pearlite regions has approximately uniform carbon concentration given by the average carbon concentration of pearlite, C^{Pe}, and the carbon concentration of ferrite, $C^{\alpha\gamma}$, is very small, as schematically shown in Fig. 7.5(a). The driving force for carbon diffusion in austenite during ferrite dissolution is ($C^{Pe} - C^{\gamma\alpha}$). In plain carbon steels, $C^{Pe} \cong 0.767$, the eutectoid composition in the Fe–C system. It is clear from Fig. 7.5(a) that carbon diffusion would occur in a manner such that in time the ferrite would completely dissolve. It can also be seen that complete dissolution of ferrite would occur only at temperatures higher than Ae$_3$, i.e. when $C_o > C^{\gamma\alpha}$. Figure 7.5(b) shows the carbon concentration profiles at an intermediate stage during the dissolution of ferrite.

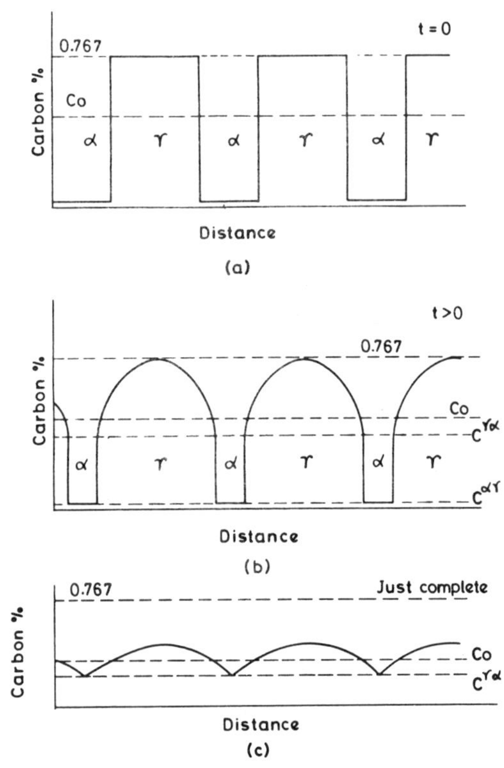

Fig. 7.5. Carbon concentration profiles during the dissolution of pro-eutectoid ferrite (schematic), (a) just after pearlite dissolution is complete, (b) at an intermediate stage, and (c) when the ferrite dissolution is just complete.

When ferrite dissolution is just complete, the austenite is still inhomogeneous in carbon concentration, with lowest concentration, $C^{\gamma\alpha}$, at points where ferrite has dissolved last, as seen in Fig. 7.5(c). Additional time required to obtain homogeneous austenite depends on the scale of ferrite–pearlite structure, i.e., on the average grain size. Less time would be required for ferrite dissolution as well as homogenization when the prior structure is fine grained. The rate of dissolution of pro-eutectoid ferrite also increases rapidly with increasing austenitization temperature, as both, (C^{Pe} – $C^{\gamma\alpha}$), the driving force for carbon diffusion (or for ferrite dissolution) and carbon diffusivity increase with increasing temperature.

When a hypo-eutectoid steel is transformed to austenite at temperatures higher than 1185K (912°C), the equilibrium α/γ transformation temperature in iron, the situation is a little different. Now, ferrite (pro-eutectoid as well as within pearlite) can transform by itself to austenite of the same composition. This transformation does not require any long range diffusion of carbon, and therefore, occurs very rapidly. The remaining cementite, in prior pearlite, then dissolves in austenite. At the end of cementite dissolution, the austenite is very inhomogeneous in carbon. Homogenization first occurs within the prior pearlite regions in a relatively short time, due to small diffusion distances involved in the process. At this stage, the austenite is still very inhomogeneous in carbon, with former pro-eutectoid ferrite regions with almost zero carbon and former pearlite region with approximately eutectoid carbon content. Then on, homogenization throughout the austenite occurs by diffusion of carbon.

In hyper-eutectoid steels also, austenitization occurs essentially in the same manner as in hypo-eutectoid steels. Below 1185K (912°C), the pearlite transforms to homogeneous austenite first, and then, pro-eutectoid cementite dissolves in austenite in a manner similar to the dissolution of pro-eutectoid ferrite in hypo-eutectoid steels. At temperatures higher than 1185K (912°C), the ferrite, within the pearlite regions, instantly transforms to austenite, followed by, first the dissolution of pearlitic cementite and homogenization within the pearlitic regions and then the dissolution of pro-eutectoid cementite. At the end of complete dissolution of cementite, austenite is still inhomogeneous and additional time is required to obtain completely homogeneous austenite. Here again, the rate of formation of austenite rapidly increases with increasing austenitization temperature, as both, the driving force for the formation of austenite and carbon diffusivity increase with increasing temperature.

The overall kinetics of austenite formation can be represented by isothermal transformation diagrams, as schematically shown in Fig.7.6 for a hypo-eutectoid steel and in Fig. 7.7 for a hyper-eutectoid steel. Similar diagrams can also be constructed for the formation of austenite during continuous heating. Figure 7.8 gives transformation diagrams for austenite formation of 1%C – 1.5%Cr steel on isothermal as well as continuous heating.

During austenitization in any heat treatment process, it is normally important to have complete transformation to austenite and to attain homogeneity in composition in austenite. In plain carbon steels, this is easily obtained in a few minutes to half an

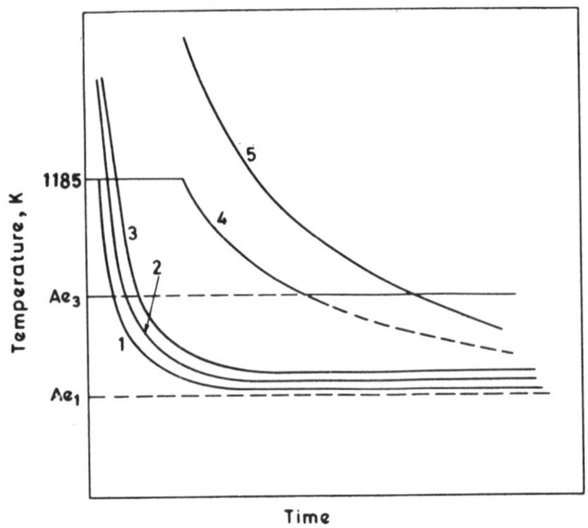

Fig. 7.6. Schematic IT diagram for austenite formation in a hypo-eutectoid steel; 1. dissolution of ferrite within pearlite, 2. cementite dissolution in pearlite regions, 3. homogeneous austenite in pearlite regions, 4. dissolution of pro-eutectoid ferrite, and 5. completely homogeneous austenite.

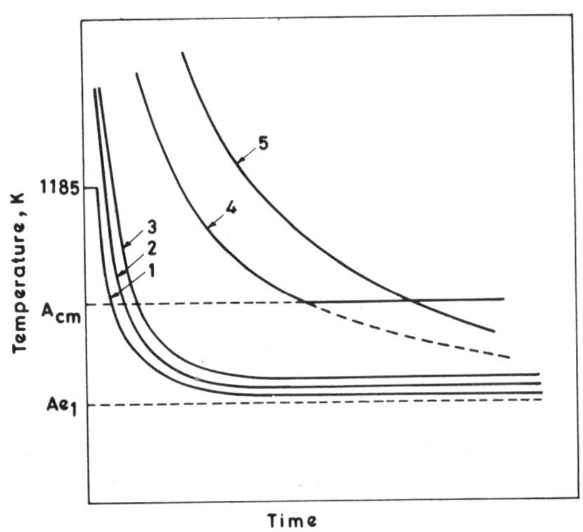

Fig. 7.7. Schematic IT diagram for austenite formation in a hyper-eutectoid steel, 1. dissolution of ferrite within pearlite, 2. cementite dissolution in pearlite regions, 3. homogeneous austenite in pearlite regions, 4. dissolution of pro-eutectoid cementite, and 5. completely homogeneous austenite.

hour, depending upon the morpholoy of prior structure and temperature of austenitization. At a given austenitizing temperature, shorter times are required to obtain homogeneous austenite if the structure is relatively uniform, as in pearlite, as compared to duplex structures like ferrite–pearlite, or cementite–pearlite. Further-

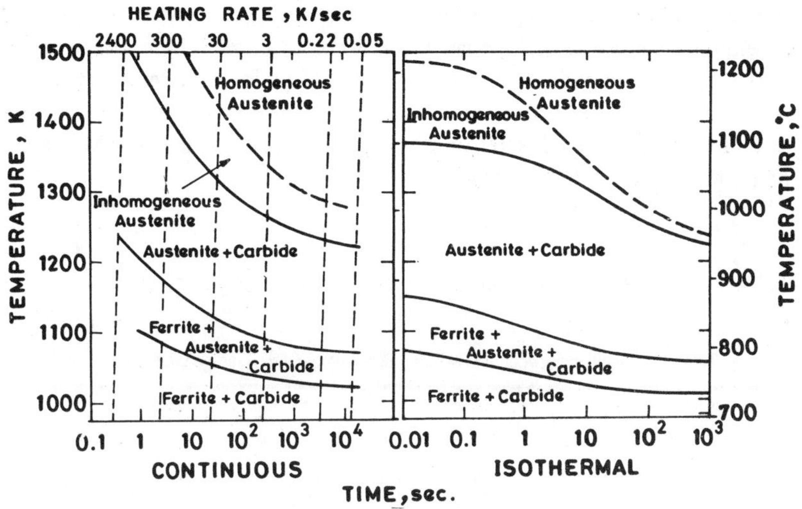

Fig. 7.8. Kinetics of austenite formation in a 1%C–1.5%Cr steel on continuous heating, and isothermal holding [from J.orlich, Harterei-Technische Mitteilungen, 29 (4) (1974) p.23].

more, austenitization of fine grained ferrite–pearlite and cementite–pearlite structures is faster as compared to that of coarse structures. Any spheroidized cementite particles generally take longer time to dissolve.

In alloy steels, the austenitization kinetics also depends on the nature of alloying elements and their distribution in the starting structure. First, the alloying elements affect the stability range of austenite, as discussed in Chapter 2. Therefore, appropriate austenitizing temperatures must be used. Apart from this, an alloying element may have segregated to cementite or ferrite, depending upon whether it is a carbide-forming element or not. During austenitizing, the transformation to austenite may be complete and carbon may establish uniform activity in a relatively short time, but the austenite may still be inhomogeneous with respect to the alloying elements. Diffusion of alloying elements in austenite is, in general, orders of magnitude slower than that of carbon. In such cases, sufficient time must be given for austenite to homogenize with respect to the alloying elements also. If alloy carbides are present in the steel, then, generally higher austenitizing temperatures and/or longer times are required to dissolve these carbides and obtain homogeneous austenite. The stability of alloy carbides is generally higher than that of cementite and they also contain higher concentrations of alloying elements. Some very stable carbides, like, TiC, V_4C_3, NbC, etc., do not dissolve in austenite until very high temperatures. In steels containing alloy carbides, the temperature and time for complete austenitization essentially depend on the nature and distribution of alloy carbides and are normally determined experimentally.

3 AUSTENITE GRAIN SIZE

The mechanical properties and the heat treatment response of a steel vary considerably with prior austenite grain, apart from its composition. Grain size is normally specified by average grain diameter, or, by ASTM grain size number. The ASTM grain size number is defined as follows. If there are n number of grains per square inch at a magnification of ×100 on a planar section, then, the ASTM grain size number, N, is given by the relation:

$$n = 2^{N-1} \tag{7.1}$$

Table 7.1 gives the relation between n, N and average grain diameter.

Table 7.1. Relation between ASTM Grain Size Number and Average Grain Diameter

ASTM grain size no. N	Grains/in^2 at (× 100) n	Average grain diameter in (× 10^{-3})	Average grain diameter mm
–1	0.25	20.0	0.508
0	0.5	14.1	0.359
1	1	10.0	0.254
2	2	7.07	0.180
3	4	5.0	0.127
4	8	3.54	0.0898
5	16	2.50	0.064
6	32	1.77	0.045
7	64	1.25	0.032
8	128	0.884	0.0224
9	256	0.625	0.0159
10	512	0.442	0.0112
11	1024	0.313	0.00794
12	2048	0.221	0.00561
13	4096	0.156	0.00397
14	8192	0.111	0.00281

During austenitizing, new austenite grains nucleate at a number of sites and grow from these points. After the transformation to austenite is complete, the average austenite grain size keeps increasing by the process of grain growth. During grain growth, larger austenite grains grow at the expense of smaller ones, some of which eventually vanish, thus, reducing the number of grains and increasing the average grain size. Hence, the austenite grain size obtained after austenitizing would depends on the temperature and time of austenitizing as well as the grain size and distribution of phases in the starting structure. However, the final austenite grain size is primarily determined by the grain growth processes occuring during heating at high (austenitizing) temperatures. The driving force for grain growth is the reduction in total grain boundary area in austenite. Grain growth kinetics in austenite is also affected by the presence of inclusions, if any.

On the basis of their grain growth behaviour, steels can be divided into two categories; (*i*) gradually coarsening steels, and (*ii*) abruptly coarsening steels. The gradually coarsening steels do not contain any significant dispersion of inclusions, i.e. not enough to affect the grain growth processes in these steels. Grain growth occurs according to the parabolic law and the grain size increases gradually with temperature and time of austenitizing, as:

$$D^2 - D_o^2 = Kt \tag{7.2}$$

where D is average grain diameter at any time t and D_o is average initial grain diameter at $t = 0$. K is a constant at a given temperature and as a function of temperature it varies as:

$$K = K_o \exp[-Q_o/(RT)] \tag{7.3}$$

where K_o is a constant and Q_o is activation energy for grain growth. Q_o is approximately equal to the activiation energy for an atomic jump across the grain boundary. Since, K in Eq. (7.2) increases exponentially with temperature, final austenite grain size strongly depends on austenitizing temperature. Figure 7.9 shows the grain growth behaviour of two gradually coarsening steels.

The abruptly coarsening steels contain large number of finely dispersed inclusions. These inclusions pin down the grain boundaries and do not permit them to grow until very high austenitizing temperatures, where enough thermal energy exists to overcome the pinning effect of these inclusions or, the inclusions partly (or com-

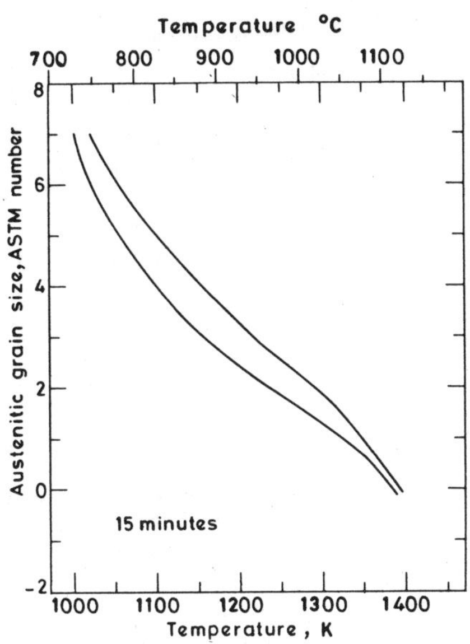

Fig. 7.9. Austenite grain size as a function of austenitizing temperature for two gradually coarsening steels for same austenitizing times.

pletely) dissolve in austenite. These inclusions are generally AlN precipitates in aluminium-treated steels, or highly stable undissolved carbides and nitrides of Ti, Zr, Nb, etc. When an inclusion is present at a grain boundary, additional thermal energy must be supplied to the grain boundary for it to move away from the inclusion. This is due to the additional grain boundary area created during the process, as schematically shown in Fig. 7.10. Hence, in the presence of inclusions, there is a considerable resistance to grain growth. However, if the austenitizing temperature is high enough to overcome this resistance, or, where inclusions partly (or completely) dissolve in austenite, the austenite grain size abruptly increases, essentially to that characteristic of the gradually coarsening steels at these temperatures. Figure 7.11 shows the grain growth behaviour of a typical abruptly coarsening steel as a function of temperature.

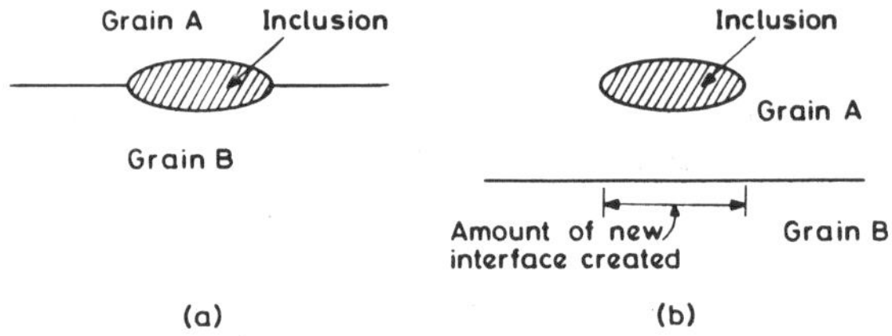

Fig. 7.10. Schematic representation of a grain boundary leaving an inclusion and creating a new grain boundary area, (a) inclusion at the grain boundary, (b) after grain boundary has moved.

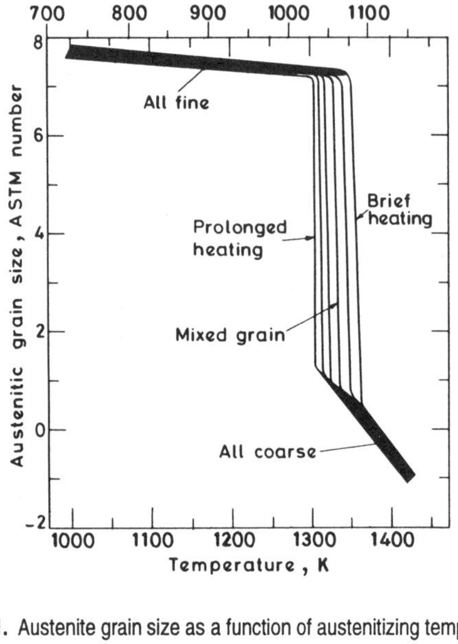

Fig. 7.11. Austenite grain size as a function of austenitizing temperature for a typical abruptly coarsening steel.

4 SUMMARY

When steels are heated for austenitizing during any heat treatment, the following factors, in general, must be kept in mind:

(*a*) The austenitizing temperature should be high enough to dissolve all alloy carbides, but not too high to give a coarse austenite grain size. In abruptly coarsening steels, the temperatures above which abrupt coarsening occurs should normally be avoided.

(*b*) At a given austenitizing temperature, the time should be sufficient to attain homogeneous austenite, but not too long to allow much grain coarsening. Time to attain homogeneous austenite would, in general, be longer for alloy steels, due to slow diffusivities of the alloying elements. It would also depend on the distribution of alloying elements in the prior structure.

Guidelines for austenitizing temperatures and times for plain carbon and low-alloy steels exist and can be found in handbooks on heat treatment. Recommended austenitizing temperatures for some steels for different heat treatment processes are given in Appendix VI. For steels containing higher amounts of alloying elements, particularly strong carbide-forming elements, the austenitizing temperatures and times under given conditions often have to be experimentally determined.

REFERENCES

1. H.W. Paxton, in *Transformation and Hardenability in steel*, Symposium proceedings, Climax Molybdenum Company of Michigan, published by Climax Moly. 1967.
2. E.C. Bain and H.W. Paxton, *Alloying Elements in Steels,* 2nd Edition, American Society of Metals, Metals Park, Ohio, 1962.
3. I. Novikov, *Theory of Heat Treatment of Metals,* Mir Publishers, Moscow, 1978.

CHAPTER 8

Annealing and Normalizing

1 INTRODUCTION

Annealing of metals and alloys normally refers to heating the material to a certain high temperature for a specific period of time and then cooling it slowly, either at a controlled rate or in a natural manner. The purpose of annealing and the nature of fundamental processes occuring during an annealing process could, however, be different depending upon the state of the material before annealing, temperature at which it is annealed and the type of material itself. In general, annealing may be carried out for one or more of the following purposes:

(i) homogenization of segregated structures;

(ii) softening of deformed materials by recovery and recrystallization;

(iii) softening of chilled grey cast iron by dissociation of cementite;

(iv) reducing internal stresses in cast, welded, or deformed structures; and

(v) softening and/or grain refinement of quenched, cast or deformed steels.

All these processes will not be dealt with here. Only the annealing processes that are specific to steels are discussed in this chapter.

Annealing of steels differs from the annealing of most non-ferrous materials, in that a steel on heating transforms to austenite at higher temperatures and on subsequent slow cooling to ferrite–pearlite, pearlite, or pearlite–cementite structures, i.e., unlike most non-ferrous materials, phase transformations occur during the annealing of steels. Furthermore, cooling rates from annealing temperatures play a more significant role in steels than in non-ferrous metals. Cooling rates from annealing (austenite) temperatures determine the undercoolings at which austenite transforms during cooling, and hence, the final structure and properties of annealed steels. Therefore, annealing processes in steels are classified on the basis of cooling rates from annealing (austenite) temperatures and are discussed under different headings in this chapter. Annealing of steels below Ae_1 temperatures for the purpose of stress relief and/or recrystallization is not discussed.

2 FULL AND PARTIAL ANNEALING

2.1 FULL ANNEALING

Full annealing is carried out to obtain uniform, soft ferrite–pearlite structures in hypo-eutectoid and eutectoid steels. In full annealing, a hypo-eutectoid, or eutectoid, steel is heated to a temperature 20–40K above the upper critical temperature (Ae_3) into the austenite range (see Fig. 8.1), held there for a sufficiently long time to obtain homogeneous austenite, and then, cooled slowly to room temperature, normally in the furnace itself by switching it off. In full annealing, cooling from austenite is generally very slow, and therefore, transformations from austenite occur at relatively low undercoolings, as schematically shown in Fig. 8.2. In Fig. 8.2, cooling rate during full annealing is superimposed on the CCT diagram of a hypo-eutectoid steel. It can be seen that, on full annealing the ferrite and pearlite transformations begin and end at relatively small undercoolings. This results in a relatively coarse ferrite–pearlite structure. In the presence of alloying elements, CCT diagrams of steels are generally shifted to longer times, and therefore, during full annealing of alloy steels the cooling rates in general should be still slower than in carbon steels for transformations to occur at similar undercoolings to obtain similar (coarse ferrite–pearlite) structures. The recommended cooling rates for full annealing are ~200 K/hr for carbon steels and 30–100 K/hr for alloy steels. In actual practice, the cooling rate may be controlled by opening or closing the furnace doors, controlled power input to the furnace, or by using special cooling chambers.

On full annealing of hypo-eutectoid and eutectoid steels relatively coarse ferrite-pearlite structures are obtained, as discussed above. The grain structure is refined to an extent and the steel becomes soft and ductile. Also, any internal stresses present in the steel get relieved in the process. Full annealing is resorted to for one or more of the following purposes:

(i) to soften the steel before machining:

(ii) to relieve internal stresses;

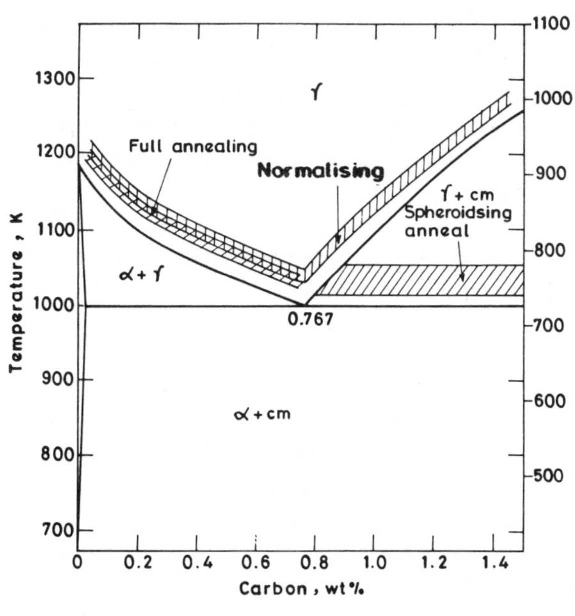

Fig. 8.1 Austenitizing temperatures for full annealing and normalizing.

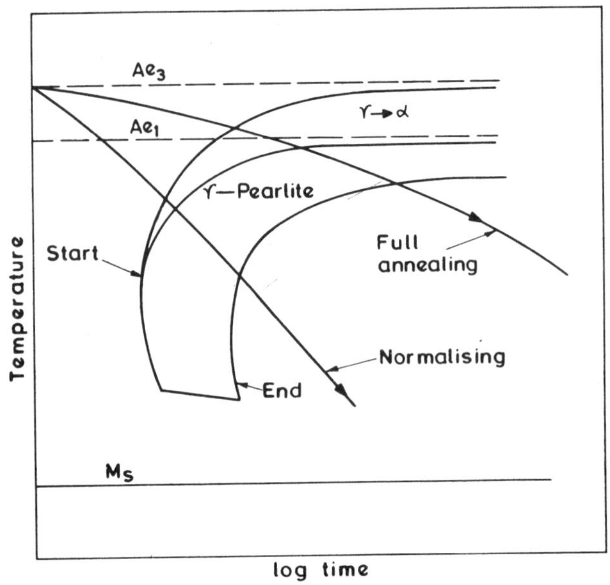

Fig. 8.2 Cooling curves during full annealing and normalizing in relation to CCT diagram of a hypo-eutectoid steel.

(iii) to grain-refine the cast or hot worked steel; and

(iv) to eliminate certain microstructural defects formed during casting, hot working, heat treatment or welding.

In cast steels, the austenite grains formed during solidification are relatively coarse, which lead to a large ferrite grain size on further cooling to room temperature. In addition, some ferrite often forms as Widmanstatten structure, primarily due to large prior austenite grain size, which adversely affects impact properties of the steel. In hot worked steels also, when finishing temperature is relatively high, austenite grains get sufficient time to grow, leading to a coarse grain structure. In welded steels, the welded seams have a structure very similar to cast structure and grain coarsening occurs in the heat affected zone next to the weld. Grain coarsening may also occur in certain heat treatment operations; for example, during homogenization anneal, which is normally carried out around 1373–1473K (1100–1200°C). Coarse austenitic grain size, on subsequent cooling to room temperature, leads to coarse ferrite grain size and also to the formation of Widmanstätten structure in some cases. Coarse ferrite grain size in general, and Widmanstätten structure in particular, adversely affect mechanical properties of steels. In order to rectify these undesirable microstructural features, steels are normally fully annealed. On heating to temperatures only 20–40K above the Ae_3 temperature, with the nucleation and growth of fresh austenite grains, the austenite grain size is refixed at a lower value, and on subsequent slow cooling, finer and homogeneous ferrite plus coarse pearlite structure is obtained. As an example, Fig. 8.3 shows the effect of full annealing on the cast structure of a hypo-eutectoid steel. The as-cast structure in Fig. 8.3(a) has a

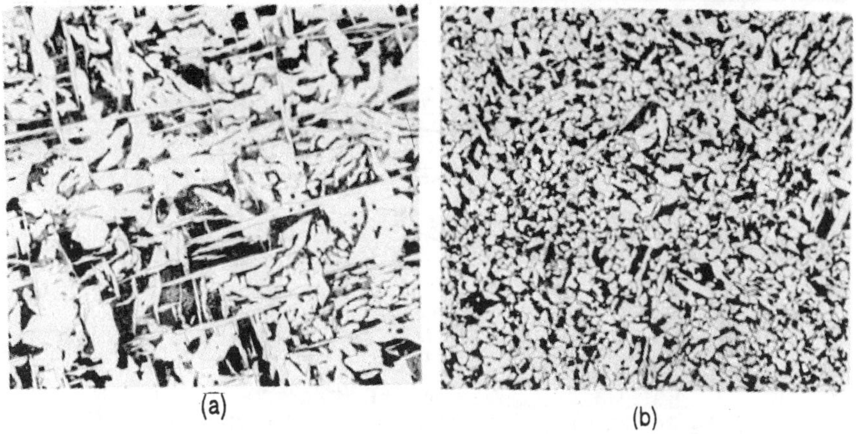

Fig. 8.3 Microstructure of (a) as-cast hypo-eutectoid steel, (b) the same steel after full annealing.

coarse ferrite grain size and some Widmanstätten plates are also seen. After full annealing, the ferrite grain size has been considerably refined and no Widmanstätten plates are formed, as seen in Fig. 8.3(b).

Sometimes, the desired refinement of structure may not be obtained in a single annealing treatment, which may have been carried out with another purpose in mind. For example, at times higher austenitizing temperatures are used to induce primary recrystallization in austenite in rolled products to get rid of any texture and to dissolve some of the elongated inclusions. Higher austenitizing temperatures are also used for the purpose of compositional homogenization. In such cases, substantial austenite grain growth occurs and the structure after annealing is still relatively coarse. In these cases double annealing is done. The first annealing operation is done at relatively high austenitizing temperatures for the reasons mentioned above and the second one at normal annealing temperatures to further refine the structure.

2.2. PARTIAL ANNEALING

Partial annealing of hypo-eutectoid steels is done by heating it to a temperature in between Ae_1 and Ae_3, followed by slow cooling. During partial annealing, pearlite is completely dissolved, but all the ferrite is not converted to austenite. A steel may sometimes be partially annealed as an intermediate step in the manufacturing process to improve machinability and/or ductility. It saves time as well as money.

3 SPHEROIDIZING ANNEAL

If a hyper-eutectoid steel is fully annealed by heating it to a temperature higher than A_{cm}, then, on subsequent slow cooling to room temperature, a coarse cementite network is formed along the prior austenite grain boundaries. The presence of hard and brittle cementite phase all along the prior austenite grain boundaries adversely affects ductility and impact properties of the steel. Therefore, hyper-eutectoid steels are normally annealed by heating in the temperature range 20–40K above Ae_1 temperature, as shown in Fig. 8.1, followed by slow cooling. This is referred to as spheroidizing anneal.

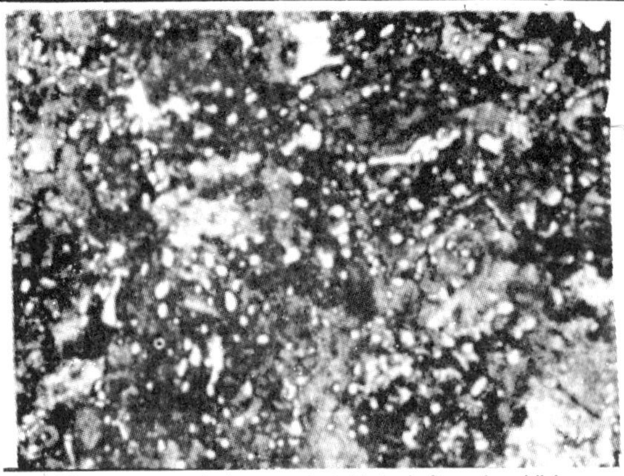

Fig. 8.4 Microstructure of a hyper-eutectoid steel after spheroidizing anneal.

At temperatures just above Ae_1, the equilibrium phases in a hyper-eutectoid steel are austenite plus cementite. As the carbon content of cementite is very high, the volume fraction of cementite is generally small. On annealing just above Ae_1, the excess cementite spheroidizes. The driving force for spheroidization of cementite is the minimization of total γ/cm interfacial energy. On subsequent cooling, these cementite spheroids act as nuclei for further precipitation of cementite up to Ae_1 and for pearlite and/or continued growth of cementite spheroids below Ae_1. The resulting structure consists of spheroidal cementite particles in pearlite matrix, as shown in Fig. 8.4. This annealing process is, therefore, called spheroidizing anneal.

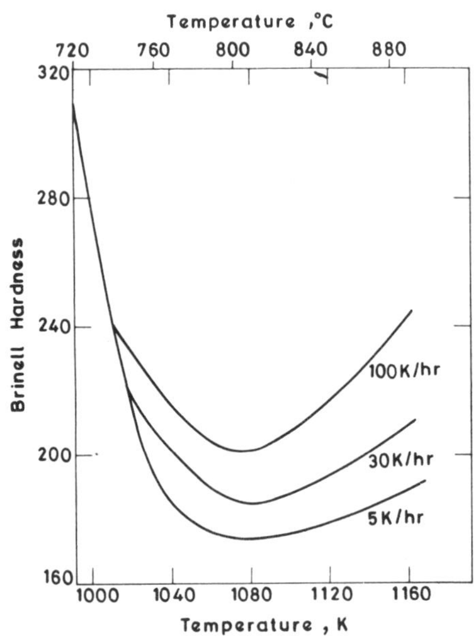

Fig. 8.5 Effect of austenitizing temperature and cooling rate on the hardness of a hyper-eutectoid steel after spheroidizing anneal.

The final hardness/strength of hyper-eutectoid steels after spheroidizing anneal is a function of annealing temperature as well as the cooling rate from annealing temperatures as shown in Fig. 8.5. When annealing temperature is close to Ae_1, hardly any additional independent cementite particles form in austentite on cooling between annealing temperature and Ae_1, which may act as nuclei for further precipitation of cementite below Ae_1. Most of the austenite is, then, transformed to pearlite below Ae_1. As annealing temperature is increased further above Ae_1, a greater number of cementite nuclei form on cooling and more carbon deposits on these nulei even below Ae_1, thus reducing the amount of pearlite and increasing the spheroidal cementite. This leads to reduced hardness/strength. However, if the annealing temperature is too high, more and more cementite is dissolved in austenite and on subsequent cooling, cementite film may form along the austenite grain boundaries and the remaining austenite transform to pearlite below Ae_1, giving a harder structure. Hardness of the final structure also depends of the cooling rate from annealing temperature. At very slow cooling rates, most of the carbon may precipitate by growth of existing cementite particles, resulting in a very soft structure, mostly consisting of cementite spheroids in predominantly ferrite matrix. As the cooling rate is increased, more and more pearlite forms and also pearlite gets finer with increasing cooling rate, thus giving a harder structure.

4 ISOTHERMAL ANNEALING

Isothermal annealing of hypo-eutectoid and eutectoid steels involves heating the steel to austenite, 20–40K above Ae_3, same as in full annealing, and then, transforming it isothermally to ferrite–pearlite structure at some lower temperature, as schematically shown in Fig. 8.6. Isothermal annealing may be carried out by trans-

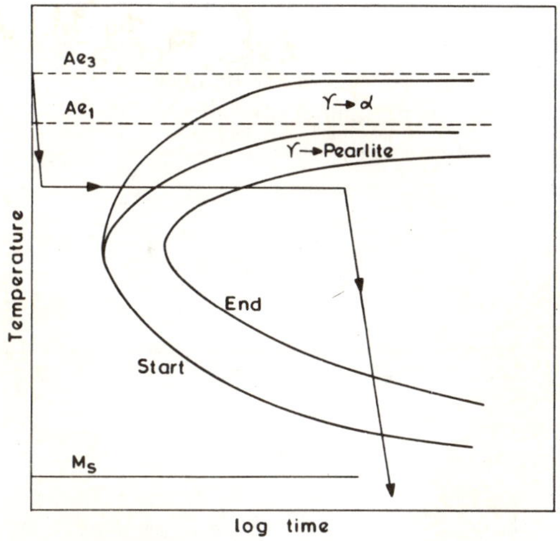

Fig. 8.6 Schematic illustration of isothermal annealing process.

ferring the austenitized steel to another furnace maintained at desired isothermal transformation temperature and keeping it at this temperature till the transformation is complete. It may subsequently be cooled in air.

The purpose of isothermal annealing is generally the same as that of full annealing. In isothermal annealing, there is a better control of undercooling at which the austenite is transformed; a more uniform pearlite is obtained, as it forms at a single temperature, and some process time may be saved by annealing only for the time in which the steel is completely transformed. The time required for complete transformation may be obtained from IT diagram of the steel. Furthermore, hardness of the steel can be better controlled by controlling the exact undercooling at which the transformations occur, i.e. by choosing an appropriate isothermal annealing temperature. Hardness of pearlite increases with descreasing temperature of transformation, i.e. with increasing undercooling. Also, for a given composition of steel, normally more pearlite is obtained at higher undercoolings than at smaller undercoolings (see Fig. 8.6). Furthermore, ferritic grain size decreases with increasing undercooling, due to higher nucleation rates. All these factors lead to higher hardness/strength with decreasing isothermal annealing temperature.

5 NORMALIZING

In normalizing, a steel is heated 30–50K above Ae_3, or A_{cm}, temperature into the austenitic range (see Fig. 8.1), held there for sufficient time to obtain homogeneous austentite, and then, cooled in air. The cooling rates during normalizing are faster than during full annealing. Therefore, the transformations from austenite occur at relatively lower temperatures, i.e. at higher undercoolings, as schematically shown in Figs. 8.2 and 8.7. After normalizing, a finer ferrite grain structure and finer

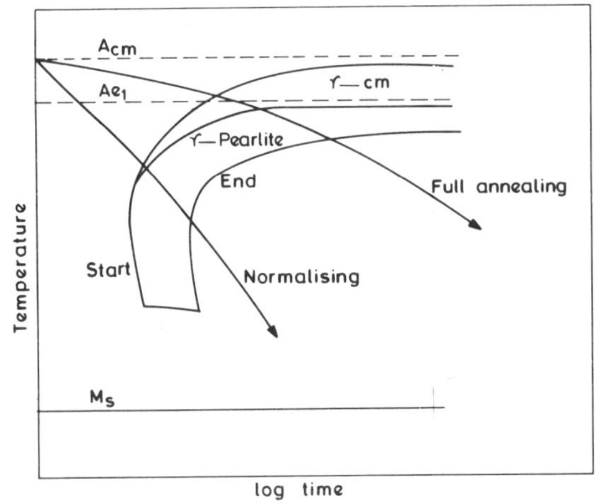

Fig. 8.7 Effect of full annealing and normalizing on the transformation range and the volume fraction of cementite in a hyper-eutectoid steel (schematic).

pearlite are obtained. In addition, the precipitation of pro-eutectoid ferrite and pro-eutectoid cementite in hypo-eutectoid and hyper-eutectoid steels respectively, is partially suppressed, as seen in Figs. 8.2 and 8.7. Thus, normalized steels have higher hardness/strength as compared to fully annealed steels.

Normalizing is often employed as an intermediate step to soften steels before machining, to eliminate microstructural defects, or, to produce general refinement in structure before austenitization for quench hardening. Thus, normalizing as an intermediate step has essentially the same purpose as full annealing. Normalizing is preferred over full annealing where both processes produce desired results, as normalizing involves less time and lower costs. However, normalizing cannot substitute for full annealing, where the steel must be softened to a large extent. In plain low-carbon steels, normalizing is widely used as a softening process instead of full annealing, as the transformation kinetics of these steels is such that, both normalizing and full annealing produce very similar results in terms of microstructures and mechanical properties. Normalizing, however, cannot replace full annealing as a softening process in high-carbon or alloy steels. Figure 8.8 schematically shows CCT diagrams of a plain low-carbon steel and an alloy steel, along with the cooling curves during full annealing and normalizing superimposed on them. In plain low-carbon steel, the transformations from austenite occur at similar undercoolings during both the processes, whereas in the alloy steel transformations occur at relatively higher undercoolings during normalizing than during full annealing. Therefore, similar results are produced by both the processes in plain low-carbon steels but

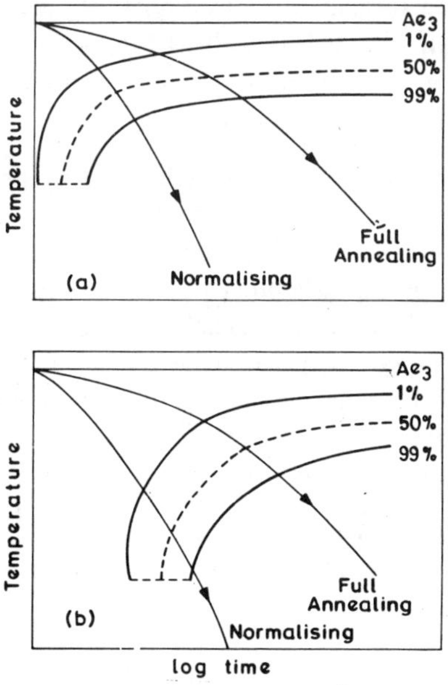

Fig. 8.8 Transformation temperature range during full annealing and normalizing in (a) low-carbon steel, (b) alloy steel.

not in high-carbon or alloy steels. Certain alloy steels, whose CCT curves are very much shifted to longer times, may actually transform to bainite, or martensite, on cooling in air. The air cooling of such steels is not called normalizing. In normalizing, austenite must fully transform to ferrite-pearlite or cementite–pearlite structure.

In hyper-eutectoid steels, normalizing eliminates, or greatly limits, the coarse cementite notwork that is formed in these steels along the prior austenite grain boundaries at slower cooling rates. On heating above A_{cm}, complete dissolution of cementite occurs. On subsequent air cooling, the cooling rate is normally high enough to substantially reduce the volume fraction of pro-eutectoid cementite, as schematically shown in Fig. 8.7. This greatly limits the cementite network along the prior austenite grain boundaries. Note that, in hyper-eutectoid steels the equilibrium volume fraction of cementite is generally small due to very high carbon content of cementite and it gets further reduced during normalising.

Normalizing is also commonly used to eliminate some microstructural irregularities and to refine the grain structure of hot worked steels. In some cases, better results are obtained by normalizing than full annealing. Particularly, in steels that are prone to microstructural banding, more uniform microstructure is obtained by normalizing than full annealing. Microstructural banding in steels is primarily due to inhomogeneity in Mn concentration in C–Mn steels, resulting from Mn segregation during ingot solidification. In these steels, on slow cooling from austenite, ferrite transformation preferentially starts in Mn depleted regions, rejecting carbon to Mn rich regions, which later transform to pearlite. This gives rise to alternate regions (bands) of ferrite and pearlite, and is known as banding. However, if such a steel is cooled at a relatively faster rate, as in normalizing, greater undercooling is obtained and ferrite transformation can start relatively more uniformly throughout the volume, i.e. in Mn depleted as well as Mn rich regions, thus, minimizing microstructural banding in these steels. Banding would of course reappear, if the steel is again austenitized and slow cooled.

Normalizing is often used for general refinement of structure prior to quench hardening treatment. If a steel has relatively coarse grain structure and pearlite is widely dispersed, then, during austenitization prior to quenching in a quench hardening treatment, homogeneous austenite may not be obtained during the normal (recommended) austenitizing cycle. Heating to higher temperatures and/or for longer times to obtain homogeneous austenite may lead to unacceptably large austenite grain size. Normalizing gives a general refinement of structure and facilitates the formation of homogeneous austenite during austenitizing, without much grain coarsening. Figure 8.9 shows the effect of normalizing treatment on the grain structure of a hot rolled steel.

Normalizing is also used as a final step in the production of some medium-carbon and high-carbon steel sections. This has the effect of moderately increasing the strength of these steels.

Finally, it must be mentioned that during air cooling in any normalizing treatment, the surface and inside of the material will cool at different rates and the rate of

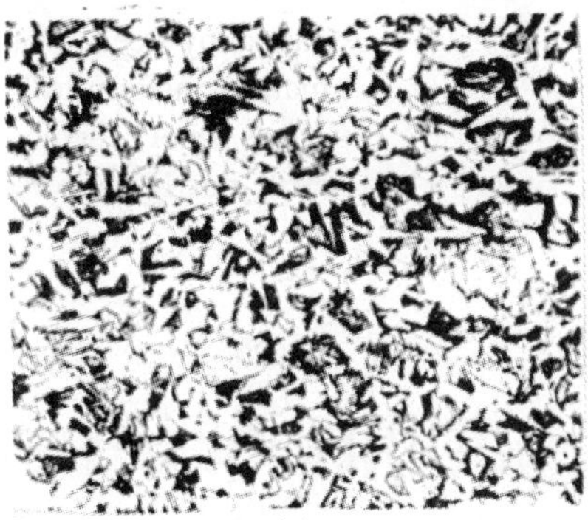

(a)

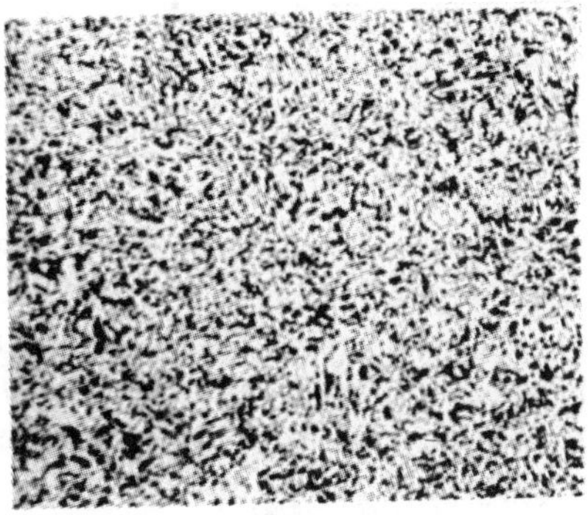

(b)

Fig. 8.9 Effect of normalizing on the grain structure in steels, (a) structure of as-hot rolled steel, (b) same steel after normalizing.

cooling also depends on the surface to volume ratio of the material. This can affect the final structure and mechanical properties of normalized steels and must be kept in mind.

REFERENCES

1. *Metals Handbook*, Vol 2, 8th Edition, American Society for Metals, Metals Park, Ohio, 1964.
2. I. Novikov, *Theory of Heat Treatment of Metals* (Translated from Russian by V. Afanasyev), Mir Publishers, Moscow, 1978.

CHAPTER 9

Hardenability of Steels — I

(*Concepts and Characterization*)

1 INTRODUCTION

Martensite is hardest of all the phases that are formed in steels. It is also most unstable as well as brittle. A large number of steel components are usually quenched to martensite and then tempered at appropriate temperatures to attain desired strength-ductility combinations. Formation and tempering of martensite have been discussed in detail in the earlier chapters. A steel transforms to 100% martensite structure when cooled rapidly from austenite at a rate greater than, or equal to, the critical cooling rate, schematically shown in Fig. 9.1. The critical cooling rate for a steel is the slowest cooling rate at which it transforms to 100% martensite. The term 100% martensite, as used in this chapter, would usually mean 100% of martensite plus retained austenite, if any, unless otherwise mentioned.

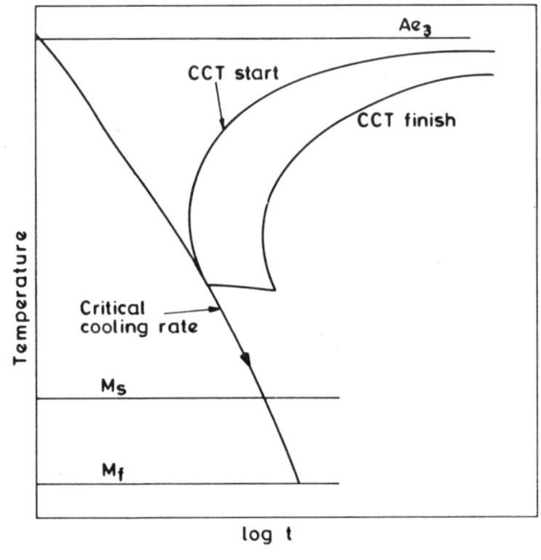

Fig. 9.1 CCT diagram of a steel and critical cooling rate for 100% martensite formation (schematic).

Normally, 100% martensite may be obtained in a small steel sample by quenching it to room temperature in water or some other suitable medium. However, when a relatively larger piece of steel is quenched, cooling rates at the surface and inside (below the surface) are different. The cooling rate is highest at the surface and would drop with distance below the surface. Hence, 100% martensite may form only upto certain depth below the surface, where the cooling rates are greater than, or equal to, the critical cooling rate. Further below the surface, where the cooling rates would be slower than the critical cooling rate, austenite would also transform, either partially or completely, depending upon the cooling rate, to softer high temperature products, like, ferrite, pearlite and/or bainite. Therefore, steel parts larger than certain size made of a given steel, cannot be hardened completely throughout its cross-section upon quenching from austenite.

The property of a steel which determines the depth to which it can be hardened on quenching is called hardenability. The depth of hardening, in general, would depend on the size and geometry of the steel part being quenched, the quenching medium and other quenching conditions, as well as the composition of steel and austenite grain size prior to quenching. The quantitative methods of defining and characterizing the hardenability of steels are discussed in this chapter. The dependence of hardenability on composition and grain size will be considered separately in the next chapter.

2 CONCEPT OF HARDENABILITY

Qualitatively, hardenability may be defined as a property of steel which corresponds to its susceptibility to hardening upon quenching. Here, hardenability must be distinguished from the intensity of hardening. Hardness of quenched (martensitic) steels is essentially a function of their carbon content and generally refers to the hardness of 100% martensite structure. Hardenability, on the other hand, deals with the depth of hardening upon quenching of finite sized samples. A steel quenched to 100% martensite may have lower hardness but higher hardenability as compared to a steel having higher hardness on quenching to 100% martensite; and vice versa.

For a steel of given composition and grain size, the depth of hardening would depend on the quenching conditions as well as on the size and geometry of the component. Let us consider a cylindrical specimen of a steel quenched in water from austenite. Let this specimen be large enough, so that 100% martensite is formed at the surface and no martensite is formed at the centre. Note that, on quenching, the cooling rate would be highest at the surface and lowest at the centre. Now, if this specimen is fractured at the middle, normal to the cylindrical axis, the fractured surface would have two distinct regions, as schematically shown in Fig. 9.2. Outer rim of the specimen, where martensite has formed (hardened region), fractures in a brittle manner, whereas, the inner core, where austenite transforms to softer products (soft core), shows ductile fracture. The two regions are easily distinguishable by visual examination. The outer hardened rim, then, defines the depth of hardening. If we polish this surface and measure hardness as a function of distance along a diagonal, a curve of the type schematically shown in Fig. 9.3 is generally obtained.

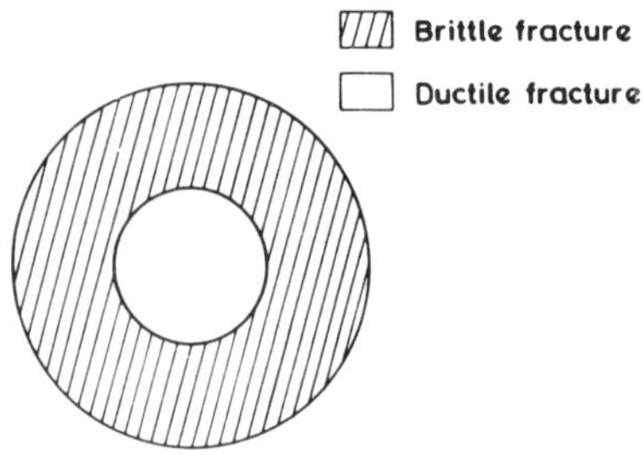

Fig. 9.2 Fracture appearance of a partially hardened cylindrical specimen (schematic).

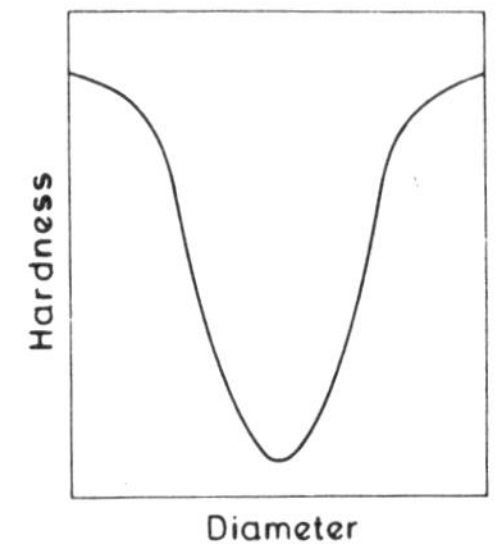

Fig. 9.3 Hardness vs. distance along the diagonal of a partially hardened cylindrical specimen (schematic).

Hardness is maximum, and essentially constant, upto a certain depth form the surface, and then, it decreases at an increasing rate, goes through an inflection point and then decreases slowly to a minimum at the centre. Region upto the inflection point of hardness vs distance curves is generally defined as the hardened region. It also corresponds to the brittle/ductile transition point in the fractured specimen, discussed above. The metallographic examination would show ~100% martensite upto certain distance, the distance to which hardness is approximately constant, and then, the martensite percentage decreases continuously to zero at the centre. The inflection point of hardness vs. distance curve, or the brittle/ductile transition point in the fractured specimen, normally corresponds to 50% martensite structure. Therefore, the hardened region may alternatively be defined as a region where 50% or more martensite is formed. The hardness of 50% martensite structure in most low alloy steels is essentially a function of their carbon content. Figure 9.4 gives the hardness of fully martensitic and 50% martensitic steels as a function of carbon content.

Fundamentally, the amount of martensite present at any point in a quenched steel sample is a function of the cooling rate at that point and may be obtained from the CCT diagram of the steel. Cooling rates at different points in the sample may be measured or calculated. The cooling rate at any point during quenching is, in general, not constant but varies with temperature. The time required to cool from austenitizing temperature to a temperature half way between austenitizing and room temperatures (called half-cooling time) has been found as a suitable measure of the cooling rate, in that, for the same half-cooling time similar microstructure and hard-

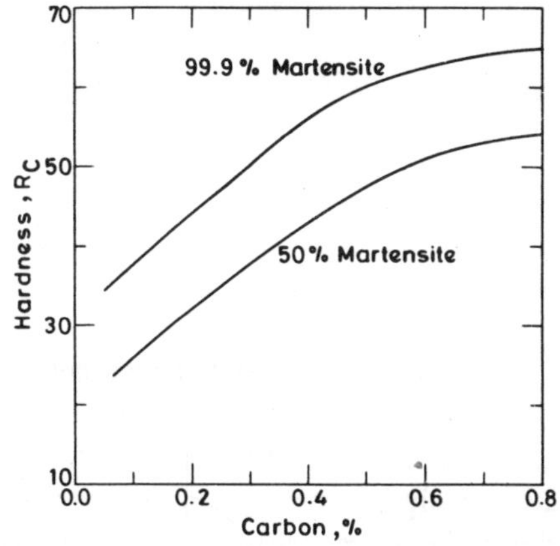

Fig. 9.4 Hardness of 100% and 50% martensitic structures as a function of carbon content in low alloy steels.

ness are obtained. Other criteria for equivalent cooling curves, given in Chapter 6, may also be used and would, in general, give similar results. Figure 9.5 shows hardness of a steel as a function of half-cooling time. Here, hardenability of the steel may be defined in terms of critical half-cooling time at which inflection in the hardness curve occurs, or, 50% martensite is formed.

In the discussion above, hardenability, or depth of hardening, of a steel has been defined in a number of ways to illustrate the different mainfestations of hardenability. Depth of hardening during any quenching experiment, in general, would depend on the following factors: (i) grain size and composition of steel, (ii) geometry and size of the sample, and (iii) nature and state of the quenching medium. For any quantitative definition of hardenability in a manner that it depends only on the composition of steel and austenite grain size, factors (ii) and (iii) must be eliminated from this definition, i.e. they must be standardized. This is essential for comparing the hardenability of different steels and for specification and design purposes.

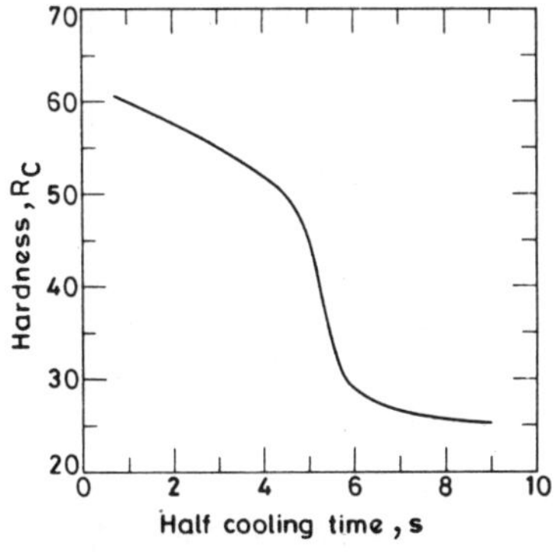

Fig. 9.5 Hardness vs half-cooling time for a steel.

3 CHARACTERIZATION OF HARDENABILITY

3.1 CRITICAL DIAMETER

Critical (hardenable) diameter of a steel, under given quenching conditions, is defined as diameter of a cylindrical specimen at the centre of which 50% martensite would form upon quenching from normal austenitizing temperature. When a series of cylindrical specimens of a steel of increasing diameter are quenched under given conditions, the centre hardness as a function of specimen diameter varies as schematically shown in Fig. 9.6. In the above experiment, size of the smallest specimen should be such that 100% martensite is formed at its centre and the largest specimen should give 100% ferrite–pearlite structure at the centre. The inflection point of centre hardness vs diameter curve in Fig. 9.6 corresponds to the critical diameter, as defined above. Critical diameter of a steel under different quenching conditions would, in general, be different, as schematically shown in Fig. 9.7. In principle, hardenability of a steel could be defined in terms of critical diameter under

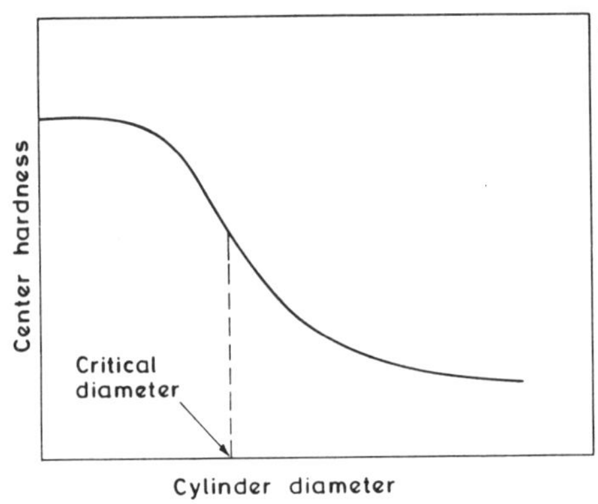

Fig. 9.6 Centre hardness vs diameter of quenched round bars of a steel (schematic).

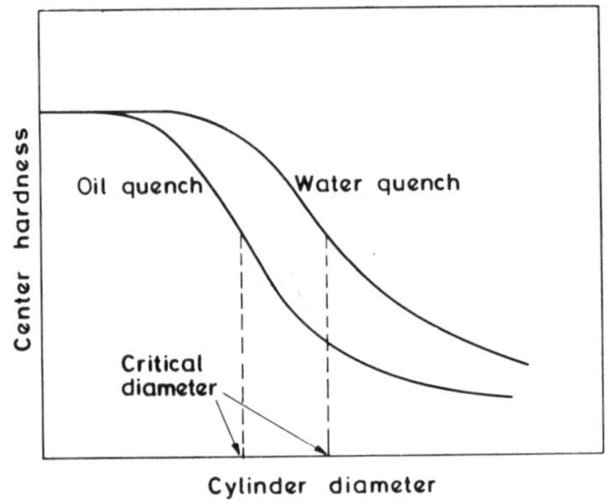

Fig. 9.7 Centre hardness vs diameter of quenched round bars of the same steel quenched in two different quenching media (schematic).

some standard quenching conditions. However, along with this, a method must exist whereby the data obtained under standard conditions may be used to predict the hardening behaviour of a steel under different quenching conditions, which may exist in a given heat treatment operation.

3.2 PHYSICS OF QUENCHING

If it is agreed that the microstructure and hardness at any point in a quenched steel part are essentially a function of the cooling rate at that point, then the data from one quenching experiment can be transferred to another by using the concept of equivalent cooling rates in terms of same half-cooling times, or, some other suitable criterion. The cooling rates can be obtained either experimentally or theoretically by heat transfer analysis. Grossmann has solved the heat flow problem during the quenching of cylindrical steel specimens by making the following assumptions:

(i) the thermal conductivity, K, and the thermal diffusivity, a, of steels are constant over the temperature range involved, and

(ii) the quenching power of the bath, H, remains constant during the entire cooling period. The quenching power, H, of a quenching medium is defined as:

$$H = \frac{f}{2K} \tag{9.1}$$

where, f is heat transfer coefficient of the metal-quenchant interface. H has the units of $(\text{length})^{-1}$. Quenching power of some commonly used quenching media is given in Table 9.1.

The assumptions made in this analysis are not strictly valid; however, it provides a workable solution to the problem of comparing the hardening response of a steel under different quenching conditions. Further assuming that the microstructure and hardness at any point in a steel sample are a function of half-cooling time only, the following has been arrived at.

Table 9.1. Quenching Power of Some Common Quenching Media

Quenching Medium	H-value	
	in.$^{-1}$	mm^{-1}
Still air	0.02	0.0008
Moderately agitated oil	0.4 to 0.5	0.015 to 0.02
Still water	1.0	0.039
High-velocity oil	1.5	0.059
Moderately agitated brine	2.0	0.079
Moderately agitated water	3.0 to 4.0	0.12 to 0.16
High velocity water or brine	5.0 and up	0.2 and up

For quenched cylindrical steel specimens, when unhardened core is defined as the central cylindrical region with 50% or less martensite, as schematically shown in Fig. 9.8, the data for quenching of steels of different hardenabilities in quenching

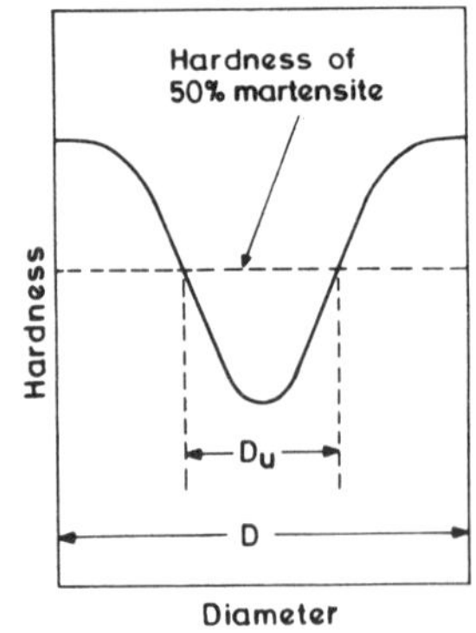

Fig. 9.8 Definition of unhardened core in a quenched cylindrical specimen.

media of different quenching powers can be summarized in a single graph given in Fig. 9.9. In Fig. 9.9, ratio of the unhardened diameter of the central region, D_u, to

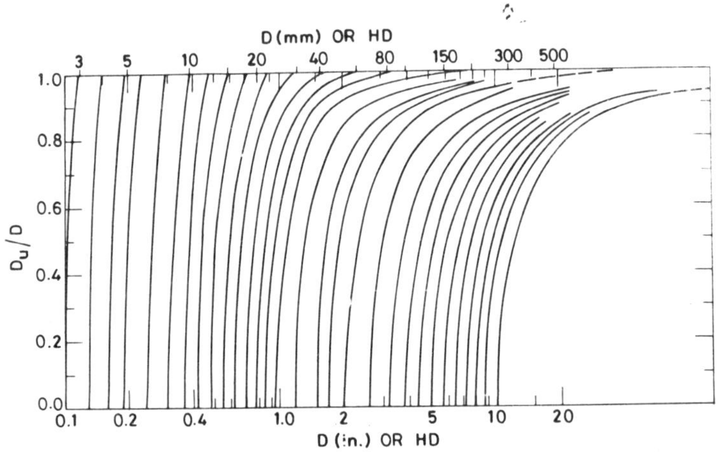

Fig. 9.9 Curves for estimating the cooling powers of quenching media.

total diameter, D, is plotted against D, or HD, and a unique set of curves are obtained. Note that, when D_u is zero, then, D corresponds to the critical diameter. This graph is of great practical utility and can be used in a number of ways, as follows.

(i) Estimating the Quenching Power

Quenching power of any quenching medium can be estimated by quenching a series of round bars of a steel in this medium and measuring the unhardened core, D_u, as a function of diameter, D. Then, D_u/D is plotted against D on a transparent graph on the same scale as in Fig. 9.9 and horizontally moved to match one of the curves in Fig. 9.9. HD is read on the horizontal axis and is divided by the D value at this point, i.e., by the critical diameter of steel, to obtain quenching power, H, of the medium in which the steel bars have been quenched.

It must be noted here that, if round specimens of a steel are quenched in two different quenching media of different quenching powers, then, according to Fig. 9.9, not only the critical diameters in the two media would be different, but the D_u/D vs D plots at higher diameters would also have different characteristics. D_u/D would increase faster in the medium of lower H value than in the medium of higher H value; as schematically shown in Fig. 9.10. This is consistent with the experimental observation that the large diameter rounds quenched in mild quenching medium do not even form a hardened rim at the surface. It also implies that two different steels of different hardenabilities may have same critical diameter in two different quenching media, but their unhardened core at all diameters higher than the critical diameter would always be different. Unhardened core would be more in the lower hardenability steel.

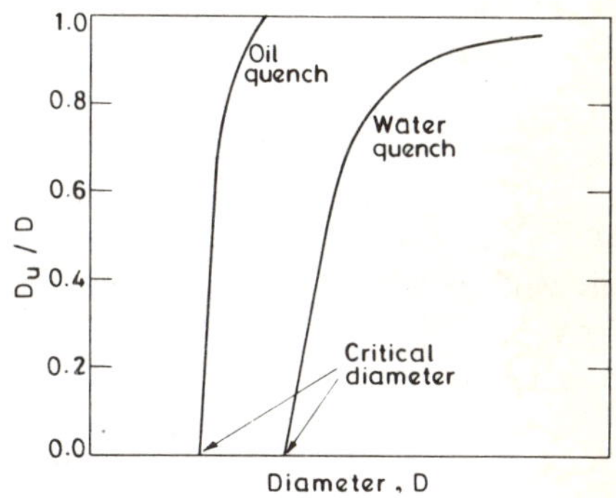

Fig. 9.10 D_u/D vs D for a given steel in two quenching media of different quenching powers (schematic).

(ii) Estimating Critical Diameter from a Single Experiment

If the quenching power of a medium is known, the critical diameter of any steel in this medium may be determined by a single quenching experiment. A relatively large sized round bar of diameter D is quenched in this medium and the unhardened

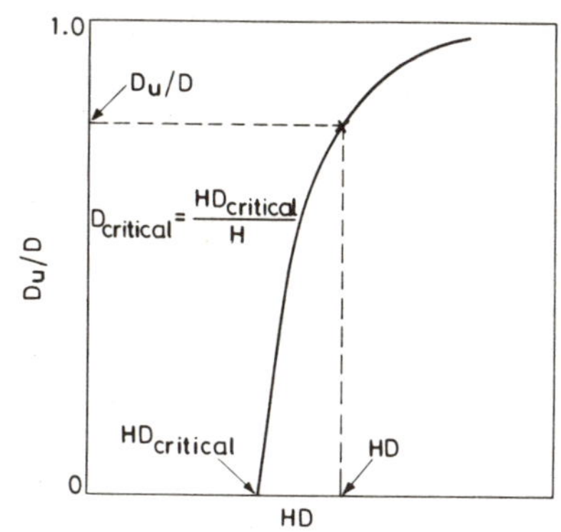

Fig. 9.11 Estimating the critical diameter of a steel by a single quenching experiment in a medium of known quenching power, H, using the graph in Fig. 9.9.

core diameter, D_u, is measured. Point (HD, D_u/D) is then located on Fig. 9.9 and the curve on which it falls is followed to $D_u/D = 0$. The value of HD on the horizontal axis, thus obtained, is divided by H value of the quenching medium to arrive at the critical diameter, as schematically shown in Fig. 9.11.

3.3 IDEAL CRITICAL DIAMETER

To define the hardenability of steels in terms of critical diameters, the critical diameters must be referred to a standard quenching medium of known quenching power. Grossmann has suggested that an "ideal quenching medium" of infinite quenching power, maintained at room temperature (298K), be used for this purpose. An ideal quench is such that, upon quenching, surface temperature of the specimen falls instantly to the temperature of quenching medium and is maintained there for the duration of quenching, i.e. the heat transfer coefficient, f, of the metal/quenchant interface is infinite. The quenching power, H, of such a medium, according to Eq. (9.1), is also infinite. Critical diameter of a steel obtained under ideal quenching conditions is called "Ideal Critical Diameter", D_I, and is normally used as a measure of its hardenability.

"Ideal Critical Diameter", D_I, of a steel is, then, the diameter of a cylindrical specimen of the steel at the centre of which 50% martensite is formed upon quenching in a medium of infinite quenching power. The critical diameter in a quenchant of any other quenching power (severity) can be obtained with the help of Fig. 9.12, which has been obtained by heat transfer analysis and the assumption that equivalent microstructures and hardness are obtained for equivalent half-cooling times. It is

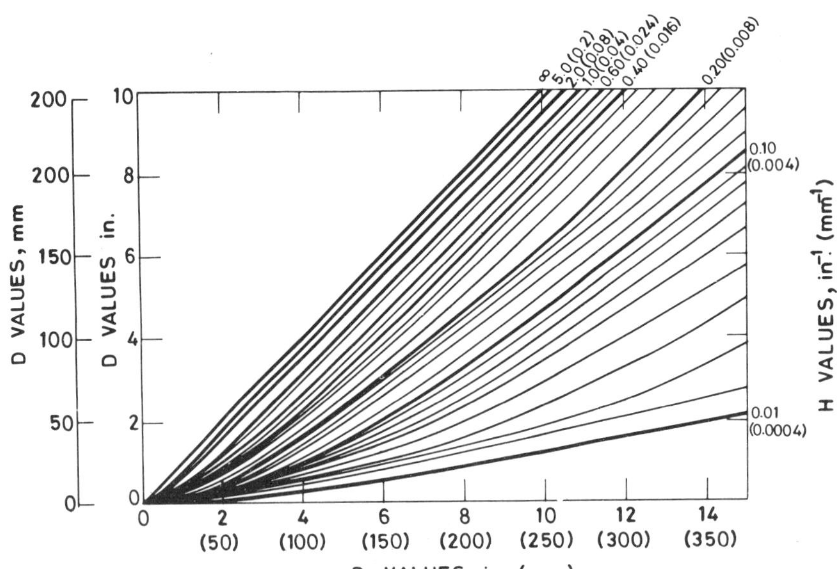

Fig. 9.12 Relation between D_I and D for different H values.

normally difficult to attain ideal quench in actual practice. Of the common quenching media, quenching in high velocity water, or brine, is closest to the ideal quenching conditions, as seen in Fig. 9.12 (also see Table 9.1).

Figs. 9.9 and 9.12 together can be used for converting the hardening behaviour of a steel in one quenching medium to its hardening behaviour in any other quenching medium, if quenching powers of the media are known.

4 HARDENABILITY TESTS

4.1 JOMINY END-QUENCH TEST

Determination of "Ideal Critical Diameter" of a steel, in general, would require: (i) quenching of series of cylindrical specimens in appropriate range of diameters in a quenching medium, preferably of known quenching power, (ii) determination of unhardened core at different diameters, and then, (iii) arriving at critical diameter and converting it to ideal critical diameter. This is a relatively long and tedious procedure. Therefore, simpler tests for measuring and specifying the hardenability of steels have been designed.

Hardenability test most widely used in practice to measure and specify the hardenability of steels is the Jominy End-Quench Test. In this test a 25.4 mm (1.0 inch) diameter and 102 mm (4.0 inches) long specimen is quenched by a water jet from one end. The test is done under standardized conditions, as shown in Fig. 9.13. The

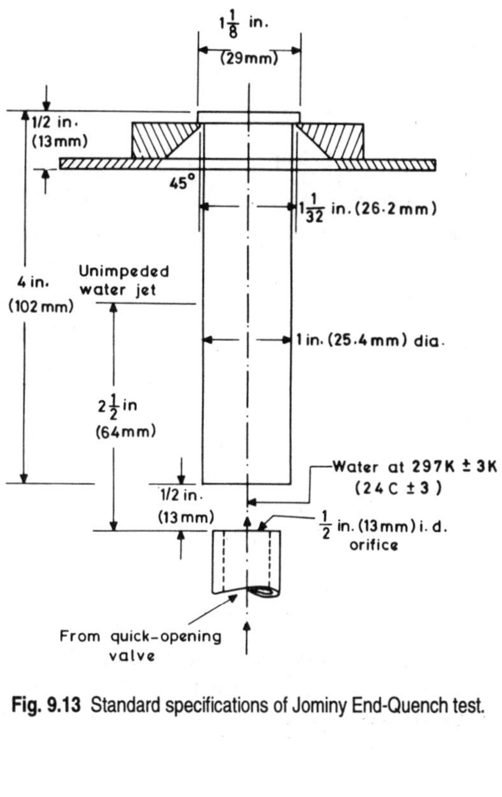

Fig. 9.13 Standard specifications of Jominy End-Quench test.

austenitized Jominy test bar is put into the fixture and the water outlet is instantly opened. Water jet hits the bottom end of the bar, instantly cooling it to the water temperature. Water does not come into contact with any other part of the bar. Cooling of the bar essentially occurs by unidirectional flow of heat to the cooled bottom end. Heat loss from other surfaces of the bar, exposed to air, is negligible in comparison. The cooling is continued till the whole bar is cooled to room temperature. The cooled bar is ground flat, 0.38 mm (0.015 inches) deep, on two diagonally opposite sides and hardness is measured as a function of distance from the quenched end. Hardness is usually measured on Rockwell-C scale at intervals of 1.6 mm (1/16th of an inch), starting from the quenched end. Figure 9.14 shows a typical hardness vs distance plot of a Jominy test, also called the Jominy curve. The inflection point of the Jominy curve usually corresponds to 50% martensite structure and may be used as a measure of hardenability.

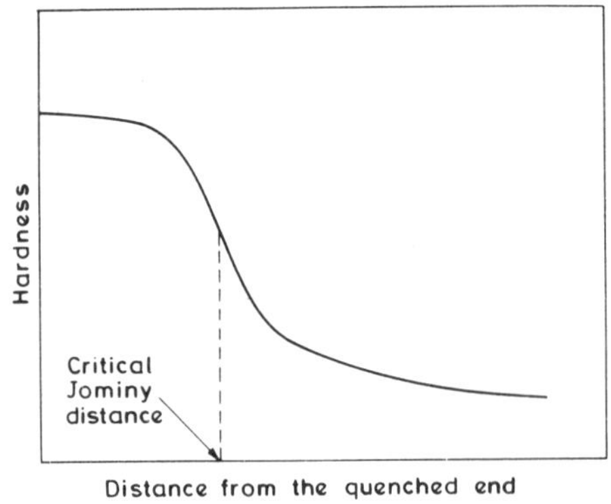

Fig. 9.14 Typical Jominy curve (schematic).

Distance from the quenched end of the Jominy bar can be related to the centre of a round bar on ideal quenching by using the concept of equivalent microstructure/hardness for equivalent half-cooling times. Figure 9.15 shows the relation between Grossmann's ideal critical diameter, D_I, and Jominy distance, J, the distance from quenched end of the Jominy bar.

For most hardenable steels, the Jominy test is quite suitable and is extensively used in practice. It is, therefore, logical to look at the reproducibility of Jominy test and the effect of deviations from standard test conditions on the results obtained. Results of Jominy tests on the samples from a single heat of AISI 4068 steel done in nine different laboratories are shown in Fig. 9.16, reflecting the reproducibility of the test. Effect of varying the standard test conditions and other factors have also been investigated extensively and can be summarized as:

(*a*) Temperature of quenching water could be varied from 277 to 333K (4 to 60°C) without significantly affecting the results.

(*b*) Free height of the after jet could be altered from 25 to 500 mm (1 to 20 in.), and diameter of the jet orifice from 10 to 16 mm (3/8 to 5/8 in.) without seriously affecting the results.

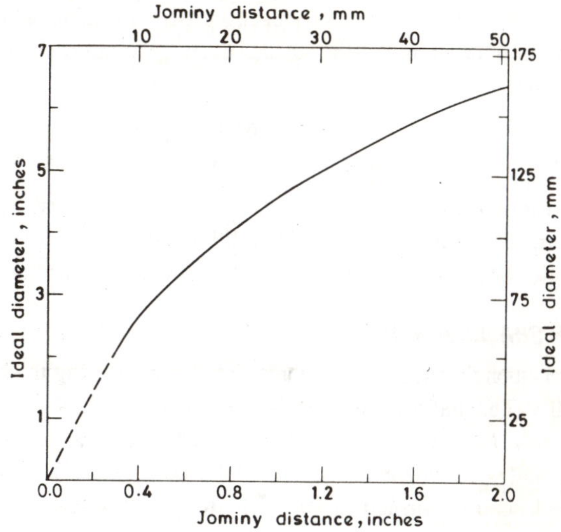

Fig. 9.15 Relation between ideal diameter (D_I) and Jominy distance.

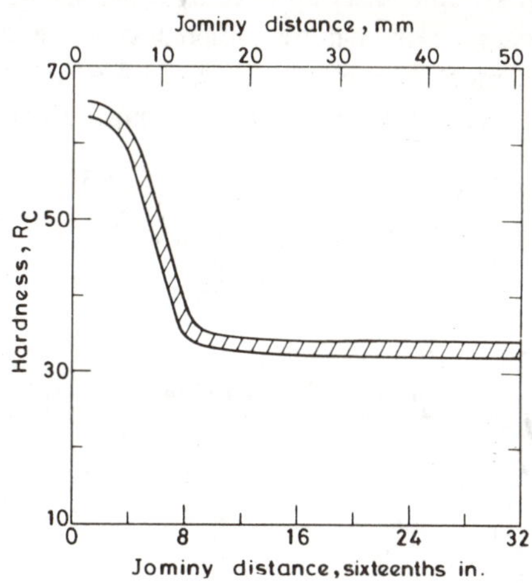

Fig. 9.16 Reproducibility of the standard Jominy test for the same steel (ASI 4068) done in nine different laboratories.

(*c*) Distance between the test bar and jet orifice could be 9 to 19 mm (1/4 to 3/4 in.).

(*d*) Length of the test specimen could be reduced considerably below the standard 102 mm (4 in.).

(*e*) Oxide film on the quenched end could seriously affect the results, and hence, the test piece must be properly protected during austenitizing.

(*f*) A delay of up to 20s in transferring the austenitized test bar from the furnace to test rig does not significantly affect the results.

(*g*) To prepare the flats for hardness testing, the depth of grinding up to 3.3 mm (0.13 in.) below the surface produced indistinguishable results. However, , burning or overheating of the surface during grinding could seriously affect the results.

(*h*) Reproducibility and accuracy of the test is generally improved by using Vicker's diamond pyramid hardness test in place of Rockwell-C.

During any Jominy test, above precautions and factors must be kept in mind. Though considerable latitude in standard conditions of the test exists, it is suggested that normally one should conform to the standard procedure and specifications.

4.2 TESTS FOR SHALLOW-HARDENING STEELS

The Jominy end-quench test is not very accurate for measuring the hardenability of low hardenability (i.e. shallow-hardening) steels of ideal critical diameter less than ~ 25 mm (1.0 in.). Figure 9.17 shows Jominy curve of a shallow-hardening steel. Hardness of a small water quenched sample of the same steel is also shown Fig. 9.17. The small sample is transformed to 100% martensite structure upon quenching in water. It is clear that, during the Jominy test even the region next to the quenched end, where first hardness indentation is made, is not fully hardened. Accuracy of the Jominy test in this range is somewhat improved by using Vickers diamond pyramid hardness tester and placing the first hardness impression closer to the quenched end and spacing the impressions at intervals shorter than 1.6 mm (1/16 in.) in the critical region close to the quenched end, where hardness changes rapidly with distance.

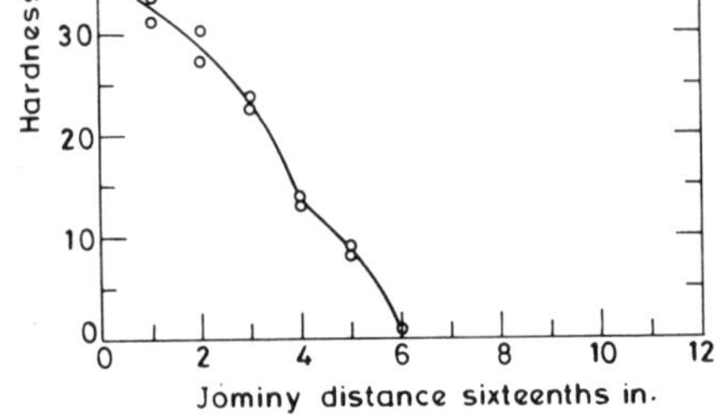

Fig. 9.17 Jominy curve of a typical shallow-hardening steel (from Ref. 5).

Post, Greene and Fenstermacher (Ref. 4) have proposed a cone test for shallow-hardening steels. The test piece dimensions are shown in Fig. 9.18. The test specimen is austenitized at appropriate temperature and then quenched in brine. The quenched test piece is split longitudinally along the centre line and hardness is

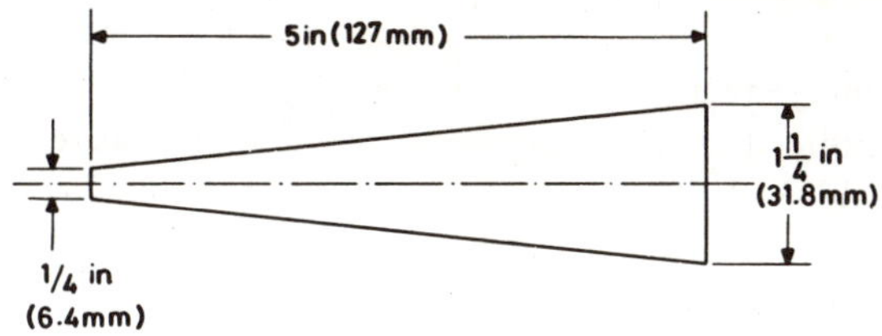

Fig. 9.18 Test specimen dimensions for cone hardenability test for shallow-hardening steels (from Ref. 4).

measured along the longitudinal axis. The depth of hardening can also be estimated by etching with acid, as shown in Fig. 9.19. The hardened region is etched dark on acid etching.

Fig. 9.19 Etched longitudinal sections of hardened cone specimens of different steels of successively greater hardenability (from Ref. 4).

Grange (Ref. 5) has proposed a hot brine test for determining the hardenability of shallow-hardening steels. The specimen dimensions and locations for hardness measurements are shown in Fig. 9.20. A series of samples are austenitised and

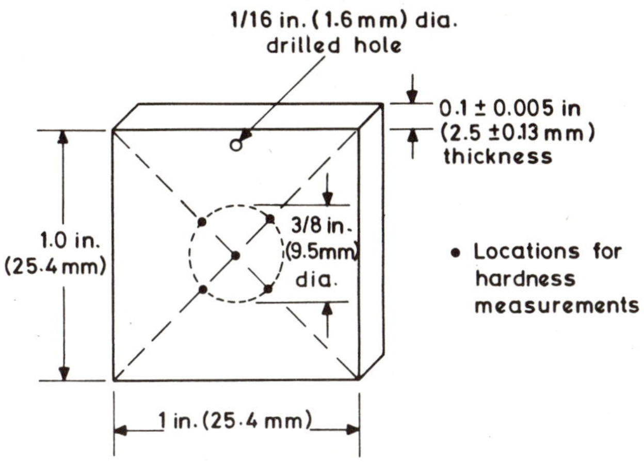

Fig. 9.20 Test specimen dimensions and hardness measurement locations for the hot brine test for shallow-hardening steels. (from Ref. 5).

quenched in brine of successively increasing temperature to vary the cooling rate during quenching. Hardness is measured at five locations, shown in Fig. 9.20, and averaged. Percentage martensite is estimated by metallographic examination. Results of the hot brine test on the same steel whose Jominy curve is given in Fig. 9.17, are shown in Fig. 9.21. Results of the hot brine test can be related to hardenable diameter of a round cylindrical specimen, quenched in water or oil, via Fig. 9.22. Figure 9.22 is experimentally established and 90% martensite, rather than 50% martensite, was used as a criterion for hardenability. In these steels 10% non-martensite product was found to be more reproducible. Hence, in Fig. 9.22, hardenable

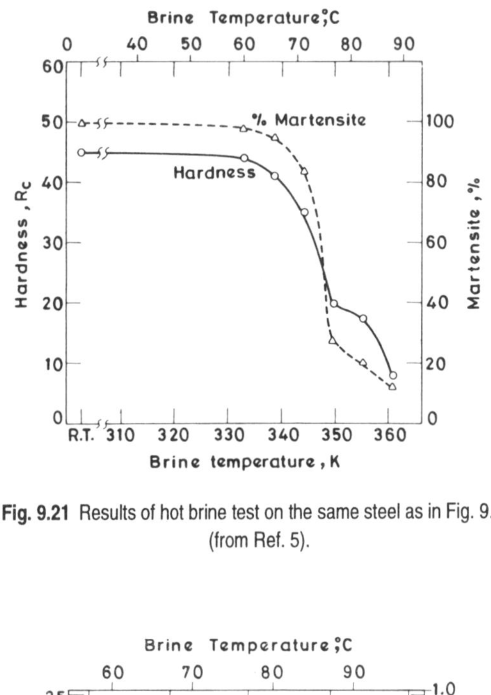

Fig. 9.21 Results of hot brine test on the same steel as in Fig. 9.17 (from Ref. 5).

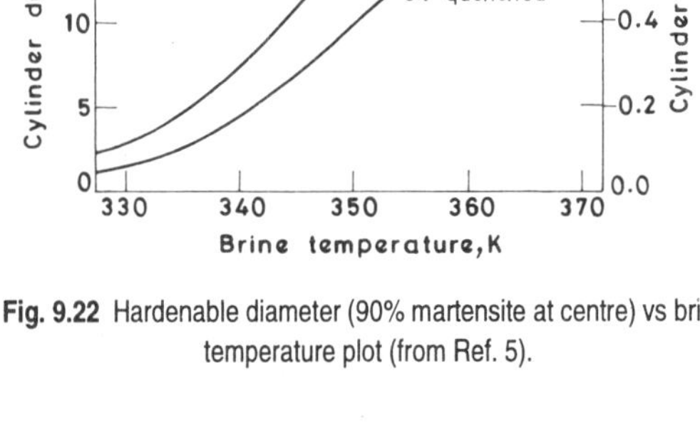

Fig. 9.22 Hardenable diameter (90% martensite at centre) vs brine temperature plot (from Ref. 5).

diameter is defined as diameter of a cylindrical specimen at the centre of which 90% martensite will form upon quenching in water, or oil.

4.3 TEST FOR DEEP-HARDENING STEEL

The Jominy hardenability test is also not very suitable for deep-hardening steels, with D_I greater than ~ 152 mm (6.0 in.). Jominy curve of a deep-hardening steel is relatively flat (see Fig. 9.23) and not much useful information can be obtained. Steels in this range are air-hardening, i.e. martensite is formed even on air cooling of small steel samples.

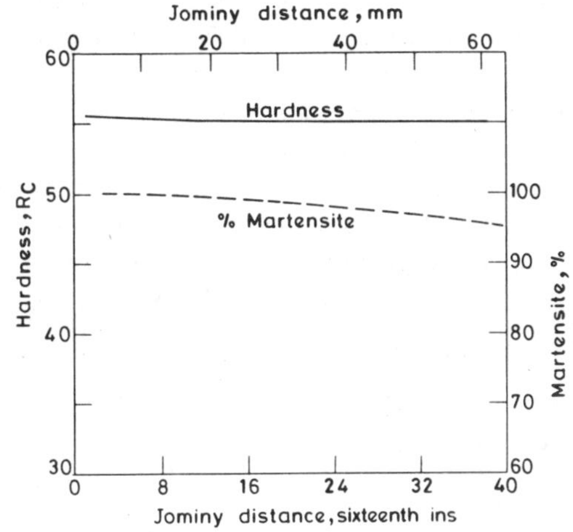

Fig. 9.23 Jominy curve of a typical deep-hardening steel (AISI 4340).

Post, Fetzer and Fenstermacher (Ref. 6) have proposed a test for air hardening steels. A 25.4 mm (1.0 in.) diameter test bar is partially inserted into a 152 mm (6 in.) diameter bar. The whole assembly is air cooled from austenitizing temperature. Portion of the test bar inside the larger bar cools at slower rates than the one exposed to air. The cooling rates are established by inserting thermocouples at appropriate positions. Hardness is measured along the length of the test piece and is correlated to the cooling rates at these positions.

5 USE OF TRANSFORMATION DIAGRAMS

Hardenability of a steel is related to the kinetics of phase transformations from austenite. In principle, one should be able to arrive at the hardenability of a steel from the kinetics of phase transformations and heat flow analysis; but, the theory of phase transformations in steels has not yet reached a stage where quantitative predictions of hardening behaviour of steels can be made. However, experimental transformation diagrams (IT and CCT) of a large number of steels have been determined and compiled, and, in principle, can be used for hardenability predictions.

Most of the early work was done on IT diagrams, which give transformation behaviour of steels during isothermal treatments only, and as such cannot be used for hardenability predictions. However, a qualitative and relative hardening behaviour can be inferred from these diagrams. Lately, a large amount of work has also been done on CCT diagrams of steels. These diagrams are directly capable of predicting the hardening behaviour of steels at different cooling rates. CCT diagrams have been discussed earlier in Chapter 6.

Use of CCT diagrams for hardenability predictions is on the increase, though it is not universally accepted in the industry yet. Use of CCT diagrams for hardenability predictions has some advantages over the Jominy test and Ideal Critical Diameter specifications. For example, CCT diagrams can easily distinguish pearlite hardenability (where the main non-martensitic product is ferrite-pearlite) from bainite hardenability (where the prodominant non-martensitic product is essentially bainite). The distinction, though very important from the point of view of properties, is not easily made in the Jominy test specifications, where hardness is the main criterion. CCT diagrams are also very useful in predicting the hardening behaviour of deep-hardening steels for which no standard test exists. Recent work on predicting the hardenability of steels by CCT diagrams will be briefly discussed in the next chapter.

REFERENCES

1. M.A. Grossmann, *Principle of Heat Treatment*, American Society for Metals, Cleveland, Ohio, 1935.
2. *Hardenability Concepts with Applications to Steels* (Eds. D.V. Doane and J.S. Kirkaldy), The Metallurgical Society of AIME, Warrendale, Pa., 1978.
3. C.A. Siebert, D.V. Doane and D.H. Breen, *The Hardenability of Steels,* American Society for Metals, Metals Park, Ohio, 1977.
4. C.B. Post, O.V. Greene and W.H. Fenstermachr, *Trans Am, Soc. Metals,* **30**, (1942) p. 1202.
5. R.A. Grange, *Metall. Trans.,* **4** (1973) p. 2231.
6. C.B. Post, M.C. Fetzer and W.H. Fenstermacher, *Trans. Am Soc. Metals,* **35** (1945) p. 85.

CHAPTER 10

Hardenability of Steels—II

(*Correlation with Composition*)

1 INTRODUCTION

The concept of hardenability of steels and the methods for measurement and specification of hardenability were discussed in the previous chapter. Hardenability of a steel is generally specified in terms of its Ideal Critical Diameter, D_I, or Jominy curve. To design or choose a steel for a specific application in terms of its quench hardening characteristics, it is imperative that variation of hardenability (i.e., D_I or Jominy curve) with composition and other structural and operational parameters is known. Apart from composition, austenite grain size prior to quenching has a substantial effect on hardenability; as both the grain size and composition affect the kinetics of non-martensitic transformations from austenite. In addition, the hardening behaviour of a steel is also affected, to some extent, by the temperature and time of austenitizing prior to quenching. The (austenitizing) temperature, from which a steel is quenched, has an effect on the cooling rates during quenching and insufficient austenitizing time may affect the homogeneity of austenite. However, composition and grain size are the main factors that affect hardenability. Austenitizing temperatures for most commercial steels have been standardized and guidelines for austenitizing times, depending on prior structure and component sizes, also exist. In the present chapter, correlations between hardenability and the above mentioned factors, particularly composition and grain size, are discussed in detail.

2 NON-COMPOSITIONAL FACTORS

2.1 AUSTENITIZING TEMPERATURE AND TIME

To realize the full hardenability of a steel, it is essential that austenitizing temperature and time be adequate to attain complete dissolution of all the alloying elements in austenite and that the austenite be homogeneous in composition. Of course, too high a austenitizing temperature and/or long austenitizing times are avoided to limit grain coarsening, as it adversely affects other machanical properties, particularly toughness. Formation of austenite has been discussed earlier in Chapter VII. In deciding the austenitizing temperature and time, the following factor should generally be kept in mind:

(*i*) Uniform structures, like pearlite, transform to austenite and homogenize faster than duplex structures, like ferrite-pearlite and cementite-pearlite.

(*ii*) A coarse starting structure transforms to austenite, and homogenizes, at a slower rate than a finer structure.

(*iii*) Alloy carbides dissolve relatively slowly in austenite, as diffusion of the alloying elements is involved.

(*iv*) In thick sections, centre of the work piece heats up at a slower rate than the surface.

Figure 10.1 shows the results of Jominy End-Quench tests for a Cr-Mn steel (AISI-4150) austenitized at different temperatures. At lower austenitizing temperatures, the dissolution of carbides is not complete and/or homogeneous austenite is not attained, resulting in poor hardenability. In non-homogeneous austenite, the non-martensitic transformations start early, and occur faster, in the carbon and/or alloying-element poor regions, thus reducing the hardenability of the steel. In addition, when carbides are not completely dissolved, carbon in solution in austenite is lower and the undissolved carbides also act as additional heterogeneous nucleation sites for the formation of non-martensitic products during cooling. Both these factors accelerate the kinetics of decomposition of austenite to non-martensitic products, and hence, reduce the hardenability of the steel.

Figure 10.2 shows the effect of different starting structures and austenitizing times on the hardenability of AISI-4340 steel. At lower austenitizing times, complete austenitization and/or homogenization is not attained in coarser structures, like, fully annealed and spheroidized structures, resulting in a poor hardenability. However, for relatively fine starting structures, like normalized, quenched and hot rolled structures, almost full hardenability is attained after very short austenitizing times.

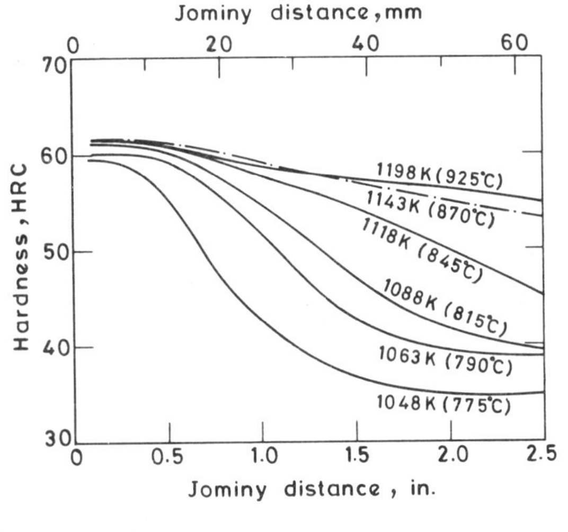

Fig. 10.1. Effect of austenitizing temperature on the hardenability of AISI-4150 steel (from Ref. 1).

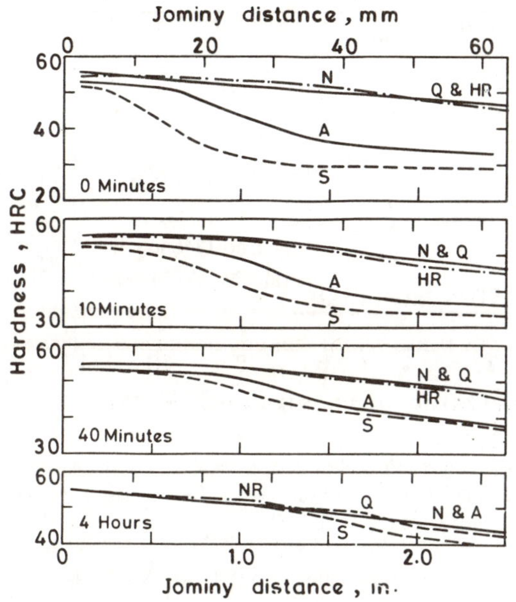

Fig. 10.2. Effect of initial structure and austenitizing time on the hardenability of AISI-4340 steel. HR: hot-rolled, N: Normalized, A: fully annealed, S: spheroidized, Q: quenched, [from J. Welchner, E.S. Rowland and J.E. Ubben, *Trans ASM*, **32**, 1944, p. 521.]

Apart from the above discussed factors, when austenitizing temperature is higher and the steel is quenched from a higher (austenitizing) temperature, more heat has to be extracted during quenching, and hence, all other factors being same, a lower effective hardenability would be observed.

Recommended austenitizing temperatures for commercial steels can be found in various handbooks on heat treatment of steels. The time of austenitizing treatment usually depends on the size of the work piece being heat treated and the starting microstructure, and could vary from few minutes to few hours. It is a normal practice to give normalizing treatment to steel components before austenitizing for quench hardening, to obtain finer starting structures.

2.2 GRAIN SIZE

Austenite grain size prior to quenching has a substantial effect on the hardenability of steels. Austenite grain boundaries act as heterogeneous nucleation sites for the formation of non-martensitic transformation products in steels, i.e. ferrite, cementite, pearlite and bainite transformations. Therefore, with larger grain boundary area, i.e. smaller grain size, non-martensitic transformations occur faster. Consequently, the hardenability of steels decreases with the decrease in austenite grain size, i.e. with increase in grain boundary area. Figure 10.3 shows the effect of austenite grain size

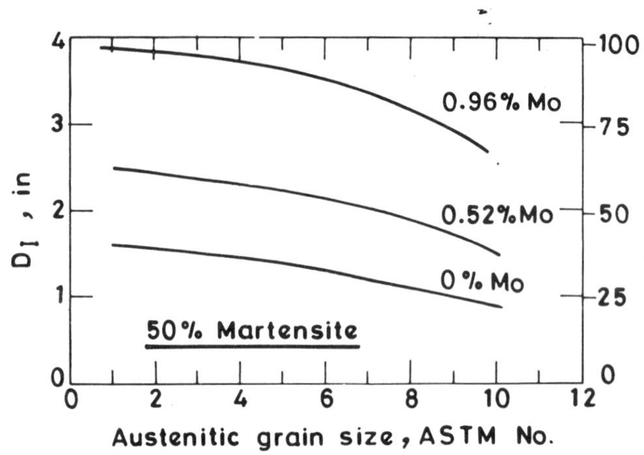

Fig. 10.3. Effect of grain size and Mo content on ideal critical diameter of 0.43C–0.50Mn–0.30Si steel [from R.V. Fostini and F.J. Schoen, *in* Symposium on Transformations and Hardenability in Steels, Climax Molybdenum Company, 1967, p. 195].

and Mo content on ideal critical diameter of a 0.43%C steel. Ideal critical diameter D_I, decreases with increasing ASTM grain size number, i.e., decreasing grain size. Grossmann (Ref. 1) has developed a useful diagram relating grain size to ideal critical diameter in steels. The diagram is reproduced in Fig. 10.4.

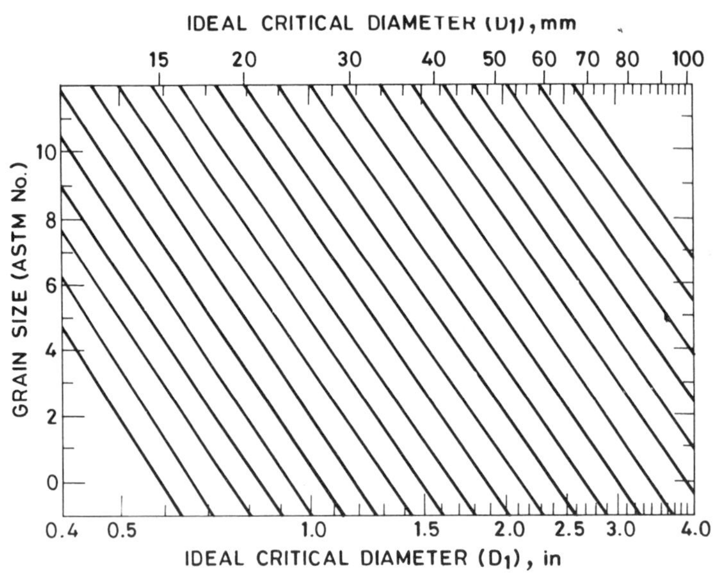

Fig. 10.4. Average relationship between ASTM grain size number and ideal critical diameter (from Ref. 1).

In most hardenability correlations, discussed later in this chapter, the effects of grain size and carbon content on the hardenability of steels are generally lumped together. From practical point of view, though it is possible to increase the hardenability of a steel by coarsening the prior austenite grain size, a large grain size has deleterious effect on other mechanical properties, particularly toughness, and hence, is generally avoided.

3 HARDENABILITY CORRELATIONS WITH COMPOSITION

3.1 INTRODUCTION

Hardenability of a steel is primarily a function of its composition and grain size. Carbon is one element which is present in all hardenable steels. Carbon content of a steel also determines the maximum hardness attainable upon quenching. Hardness of martensite in low alloy steels is essentially a function of their carbon content. In considering the effect of alloying elements on hardenability, it is necessary to "correct" the results for any variations in carbon content to ensure that, the observed hardness changes are due to change in hardenability rather than the differences in carbon concentration. Besides, carbon also contributes to the hardenability of steels.

Alloying elements affect the hardenability of steels in a complex manner and no single correlation has been found to satisfactorily explain the effect of alloying elements on hardenability over the whole range of steel compositions. The carbon and alloy contents of a steel determine the nature of non-martensitic austenite decomposition products on continuous cooling. At low carbon contents, ferrite is the main non-martensitic austenite decomposition product, whereas pearlite becomes the main product at higher carbon contents. As discussed in Chapter III, different alloying elements affect the kinetics of ferrite and pearlite transformations in different and complex manners. Also, in the presence of certain alloying elements, like, Mo and Cr, bainite may become the main non-martensitic transformation product on continuous cooling in certain range. Furthermore, the contributions of individual alloying elements are not always separable, in that, for the same addition of an alloying element, its total effect on transformations from austenite, and hence on hardenability, may depend on the presence or absence of certain other alloying elements in the steel, i.e. on the base composition of the steel.

In spite of the above mentioned complexities, relatively simple correlations for the effect of alloying elements on hardenability in steels have been worked out. These are based on the average effects, derived from large bank of empirical data. Necessarily, the correlations are different for different ranges of steel compositions. For these correlations, the steels are divided into three main categories, viz. (*i*) shallow hardening steels, (*ii*) medium-carbon low-alloy steels, and (*iii*) low carbon steels; and are separately discussed below.

3.2 SHALLOW HARDENING STEELS

Shallow hardening steels are defined as steels whose ideal critical diameter is less than ~25 mm (1.0 inch). Plain carbon steels containing small amounts of Mn and Si,

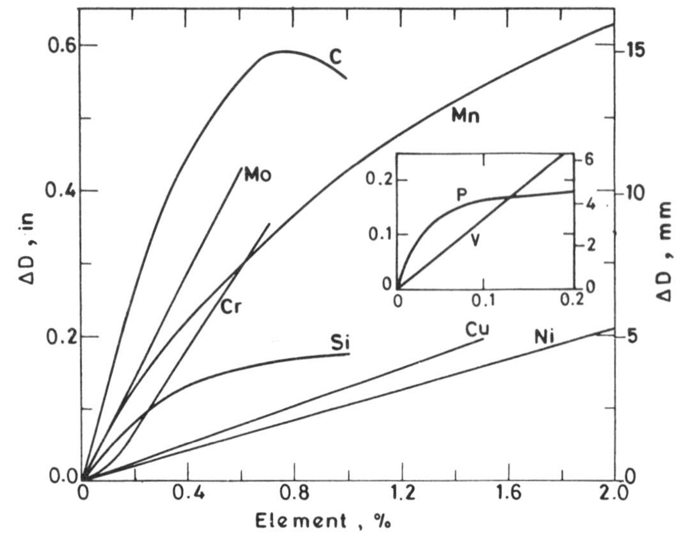

Fig. 10.5. Change in hardenable diameter (ΔD) with composition for shallow hardening steels, 90% martensite at centre on water quenching (from Ref. 5).

or other alloying elements, fall in this category. As discussed in the previous chapter, Grange (Ref. 5) has proposed a hot brine test for determining the hardenability of shallow hardening steels. He also systematically studied the effect of different alloying elements on hardenable diameter in shallow hardening steels. The hardenable diameter was defined as diameter of a cylinder at the centre of which 90% martensite is formed on quenching in water. It was found that the hardenable diameter, D_H, can be best represented by an additive formula of the type:

$$D_H = \Delta D_C + \Delta D_{Mn} + \Delta D_P + \Delta D_{Si} + \Delta D_{Cu} + \Delta D_{Ni} + \Delta D_{Cr} + \Delta D_{Mo} + \Delta D_V \quad (10.1)$$

where, ΔD_i's are contributions of individual elements to the total hardenable diameter. Data for use in Eq.(10.1) are given in Fig.10.5. These data are for prior austenite grain size of ASTM No. 4. Hardenable diameter for any other grain size is obtained with the help of Fig. 10.6, also developed by Grange [Ref. 5]. It must again be emphasized that the above correlation is valid only for shallow hardening steels, with ideal critical diameter less than ~25 mm (1.0 in).

3.3 MEDIUM-CARBON LOW-ALLOY STEELS

Most hardenable grade steels fall in this category. Hence, most work on hardenability of steels has been done on these steels. Grossmann (Ref.1-2) found that the effect of alloying elements on the hardenability of these steels can best be described by multiplicative formulae. Accordingly, the ideal critical diameter, D_I , of a steel is expressed as:

$$D_I = D_o \times M_{Mn} \times M_{Ni} \times M_{Cr} \times M_{Mo} \times M_{Si} \times .. = D_o \prod_{i=1}^{n} M_i \qquad (10.2)$$

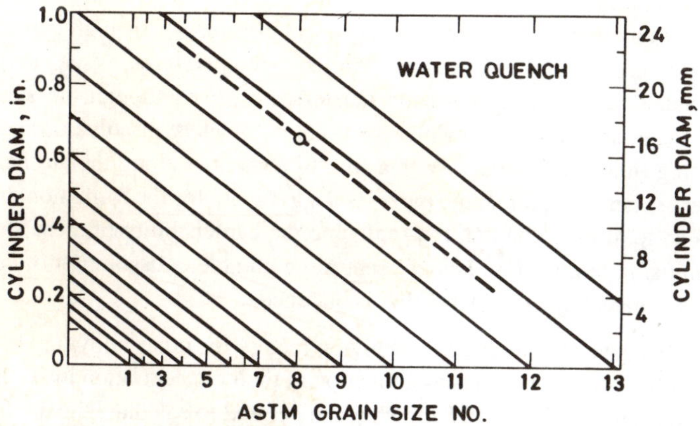

Fig. 10.6. Effect of grain size on hardenable diameter (90% martensite on water quenching) for shallow hardening steels (from Ref. 5).

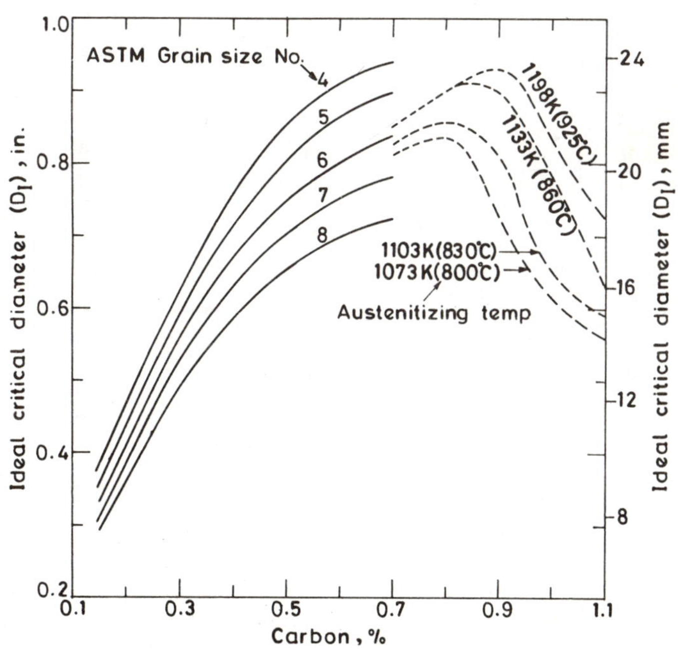

Fig. 10.7. Base hardenability (D_o) for carbon plus grain size (from Ref. 4).

where D_0 is carbon plus grain size factor, called base hardenability; and M_i's are multiplying factors for individual alloying elements. Multiplication is carried over all the alloying elements present in the steel. Figure 10.7 gives base hardenability D_0, i.e. ideal critical diameter for carbon plus grain size. Base hardenability increases with increase in austenite grain size; and with increase in carbon content, it increases up to around eutectoid composition and then decreases, as pro-eutectoid cementite appears as transformation product at higher temperatures. In high-carbon steels, hardenability is also very sensitive to austenitizing temperatures, as seen in Fig. 10.7. In these steels, at lower austenitizing temperatures, even though the steel in the austenite range above A_{cm}, cementite may not completely dissolve during normal austenitizing times, leaving a very thin film of cementite along the austenite grain boundaries. These tiny cementite particles act as nuclei for the formation of cementite, or pearlite, during cooling, thus reducing the hardenability of these steels. As the austenitising temperature is increased, more complete dissolution of cementite occurs and, hence, higher hardenability is obtained.

Figure 10.8 gives the average multiplying factors for other alloying elements in medium-carbon low-alloy steels as a function of their concentration in steels. Now, the data from Figs. 10.7 and 10.8 together can be used to calculate the hardenability of a steel of given composition via Eq. (10.2).

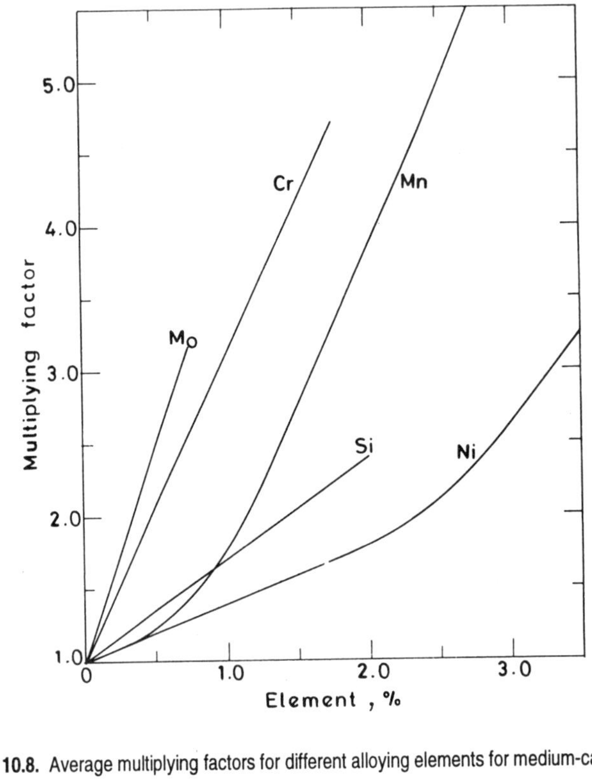

Fig. 10.8. Average multiplying factors for different alloying elements for medium-carbon steels.

Multiplying factors given in Fig. 10.8 for different alloying elements represent only the average effect of these elements on the hardenability of steels. They do not take into account all the possible alloy interaction effects on the hardenability of steels, that may exist. As an example, Fig. 10.9 shows multiplying factors for nickel as determined by different investigators. The differences are due to different base compositions of steels used for investigating the effect of nickel and not due to experimental errors. Another example of alloy interaction effects is shown in Fig. 10.10. Here, the multiplying factors for Mo vary differently in steels containing Ni and Cr. Again, the differences are significant and cannot be attributed to variations in experimental conditions. These example clearly illustrate the complex alloy interaction effects on the hardenability of steels. Hence, the hardenabilities calculated by using Figs. 10.7 and 10.8 represent only a first approximation and should be treated as such.

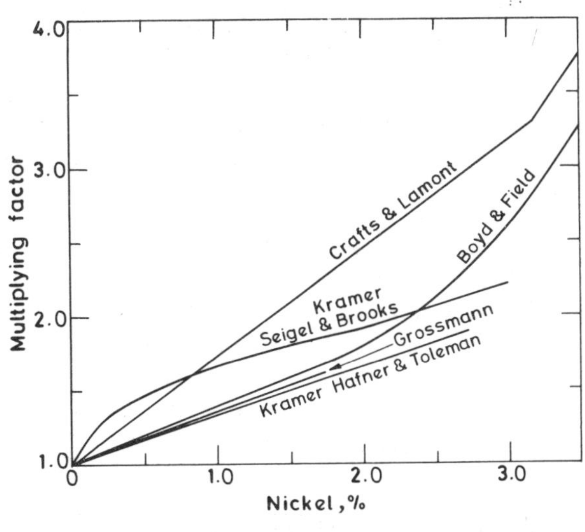

Fig. 10.9. Effect of nickel on hardenability, as determined by different investigators (from Ref. 1).

3.4 LOW-CARBON STEELS "CORE HARDENABILITY"

Effect of alloying elements on the hardenability of low-carbon steels is different from their effect on the hardenability of medium-carbon steels. Carburizing grade steels are essentially low-carbon steels, containing 0.15% to 0.25% carbon. Hardening behaviour of the core of carburized components, of original low-carbon composition, is an important factor in the design considerations of these components. In low-carbon steels, the main austenite decomposition product at slower cooling rates is ferrite, as opposed to pearlite in medium and high-carbon steels. Different alloying elements affect the kinetics of ferrite and pearlite transformations differently, as discussed in Chapter 3. It is, therefore, expected that the hardenability multiplying factors for different alloying elements for low and medium carbon steels would be different.

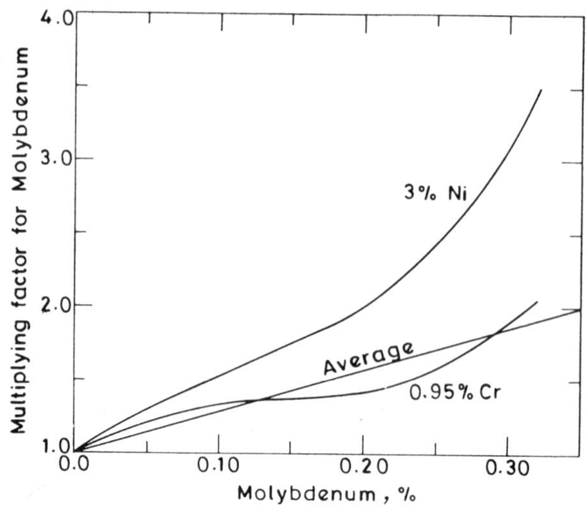

Fig. 10.10. Effect of molybdenum on hardenability in steels containing 3%Ni and 0.95%Cr [from J.M. Hodge, J.L. Giove and R. G. Strom, *J. Metals*, March 1950, **1**, sec. 3].

Hardenability of low-carbon steels has also been correlated by Grossmann's method of multiplying factors, as in Eq. (10.2). However, the average multiplying factors for different alloying elements for low-carbon steels are different from the ones for medium-carbon low-alloy steels. The multiplying factors for different alloying elements in low-carbon carburizing grade steels are given in Fig. 10.11 and should be used when the carbon content of a steel is less than ~ 0.25%. The base hardenability, i.e. the carbon plus grain size factor, is the same as for medium-carbon steels, given in Fig. 10.7. Here again, the multiplying factors given in Fig. 10.11 are only the average values.

The need for a different set of multiplying factors for low-carbon steels is demonstrated by comparing the multiplying factors in Fig. 10.11 with those for medium-carbon steels given in Fig.10.8. The multiplying factors for Mn in Fig. 10.8 are lower than in Fig. 10.11, whereas the multiplying factors for Si are higher in Fig. 10.8. Si has virtually no effect on the hardenability of low-carbon steels up to ~ 0.6% additions. Similarly, other differences can be noted. Also, for low-carbon steels, the interaction between Ni and Mo could not be averaged, and hence, the need for separate Mo factors for low- and high-Ni steels.

3.5 EFFECT OF MICROALLOYING ON HARDENABILITY

Strong carbide-forming elements, like, V, Nb, Ti, etc., are normally added in very small quantities in HSLA steels. With increasing interest in these steels, the effect of minor additions of V, Nb, Ti, etc., on the hardenability of steels has generated some interest. Since these elements are very strong carbide forming elements, their effect on hardenability is very sensitive to austenitizing temperature and time. To realize the full hardenability effect of these elements, the alloy carbides must be

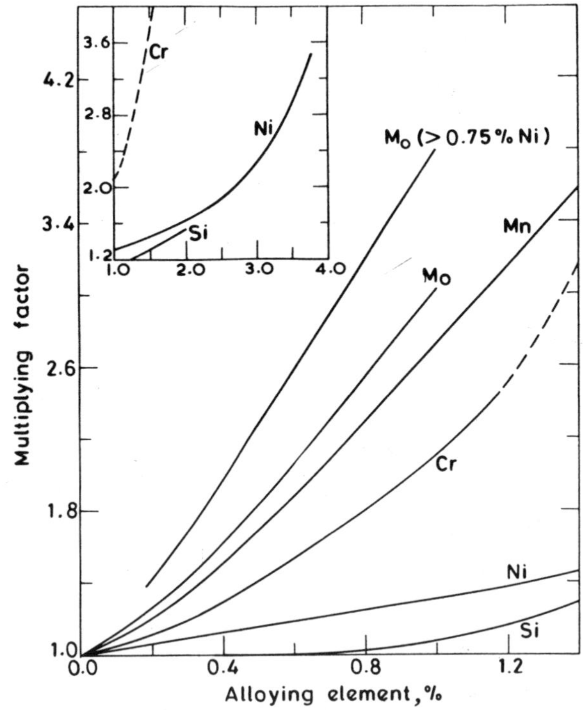

Fig. 10.11. Average multiplying factors for different alloying elements in low alloy steels containing 0.15 to 0.25 per cent carbon [after A.F. deRetana and D.V. Doane, *Metal Progress*, No. **100**, Sept. 1971, p 65].

completely dissolved during austenitization. Normally, very high austenitizing temperatures are required to completely dissolve these carbide. If these elements are present in higher concentrations, complete dissolution of carbides may not be possible even with high austenitizing temperatures. When carbides are not completely dissolved, the hardenability is lower for two reasons. First, the carbon and alloying element concentrations in solution in austenite are lower, due to these elements being tied up in the carbides, thus decreasing the carbon and alloying element hardenability factors . Secondly, the undissolved carbides may act as nuclei for the formation of non-martensitic transformation products, further reducing the hardenability of the steel. Very high austenitizing temperatures, in general, may not be acceptable because of their effect in increasing the austenite grain size.

Figure 10.12 shows the effect of V on the hardenability of steels for two different austenitizing temperatures. Note the higher mulitiplying factors for higher austenitizing temperature. Fig. 10.13 shows the results of a recent study on the effect of V, Nb and Ti on hardenability in steels (Ref. 6). The austenitizing temperature of 1473K (1200°C) was used. Even with such a high austenitizing temperature, effect of Ti on the hardenability is either nil or negative and that of V becomes negatives beyond ~0.1% additions.

As would be obvious from the brief discussion above, these elements are normally not added for increasing the hardenability of steels. However, they may be present

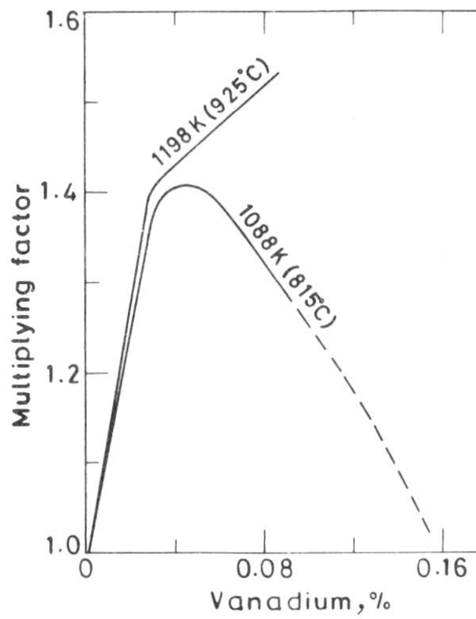

Fig. 10.12. Effect of V on the hardenability of steels for two different austenitizing temperatures (from Ref. 1).

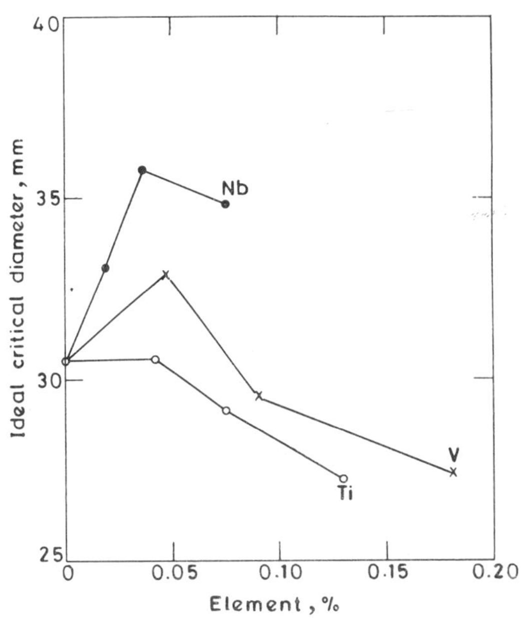

Fig. 10.13. Effect of micro-alloying elements, Ti, V and Nb, on the hardenability of steels (from Ref. 6).

in the steel for other reasons and their effect on the hardenability should be known for proper heat treatment design.

4 BORON HARDENABILITY

4.1 INTRODUCTION

Boron is added to steels primarily to increase their hardenability. Effect of boron on the hardenability of steels is unique in a number of respects: (*i*) very small additions of boron, approx. 5 to 30 ppm by weight, have a relatively large effect on hardenability; (*ii*) there exists an optimum boron level, beyond which the boron hardenability effect decreases with further increase in boron content; (*iii*) hardenability effect of boron varies considerably with carbon and alloying content of the steel, and (*iv*) boron hardenability is greatly affected by the presence of free nitrogen and the type of deoxidizers used during steel making. Boron as an alloying element in steels has not been discussed earlier in this book; therefore, a relatively more detailed discussion on various aspects of boron hardenability is given here.

4.2 EFFECT ON PHASE TRANSFORMATIONS

Boron, in amounts normally added in hardenable steels, does not have any measurable effect on the Ae_3 and Ae_1 transformation temperatures. As a consequence, to a first approximation boron does not affect the thermodynamic driving force for ferrite/bainite and pearlite transformations. Boron has limited solubility in pure iron, varying from ~0.001% at 1173K (900°C) to ~0.0045% at 1373K (1100°C). At higher boron contents, Fe_2B in precipitated in Fe-B alloys. However, in steels, in the presence of carbon, the phase that is formed at higher boron contents is borocarbide, $Fe_{23}(BC)_6$, rather than Fe_2B. In $Fe_{23}(BC)_6$, boron may substitute for upto 80% of carbon, and Mo and Cr, if present, partly substitute for Fe. Borocementite, $Fe_3(BC)$, is less stable than $Fe_{23}(BC)_6$ and is not formed at higher temperatures. However, at lower temperatures, below ~873K (600°C), $Fe_3(BC)$ may precipitate as a metastable phase.

During austenite decomposition, boron in solution in austenite has the largest retardation effect on ferrite transformation, whereas, it has little or no effect on pearlite transformation. Furthermore, the presence of boron only retards the nucleation of ferrite and does not affect the growth rates. Figure 10.14 shows the retardation effect of boron (40 ppm) on the nucleation rate of ferrite in 0.10% C – 1.0% Mn steel. The actual mechanism of nucleation retardation by boron is still a subject of controversy, and is discussed briefly later in this section (see sec. 4.8).

4.3 OPTIMUM BORON CONTENT

As has been mentioned earlier, to utilize boron hardenability effect to the maximum, boron must be present in steel in an optimum concentration. Figure 10.15 shows the effect of boron content on the hardenability of a low-carbon low-alloy steel as obtained by Kapadia *et al.* According to this, the optimum boron content is ~0.001% (or 10 ppm by weight). At higher boron concentrations, the hardenability effect gradually falls off. Various other investigators have reported the optimum boron content in the range of 0.0005 to 0.0030% boron, i.e. 5 to 30 ppm boron by weight. Some of this variation is due to the possibility that the reported boron content is not fully effective. For boron to be effective as a hardenability agent, it must be in "free"

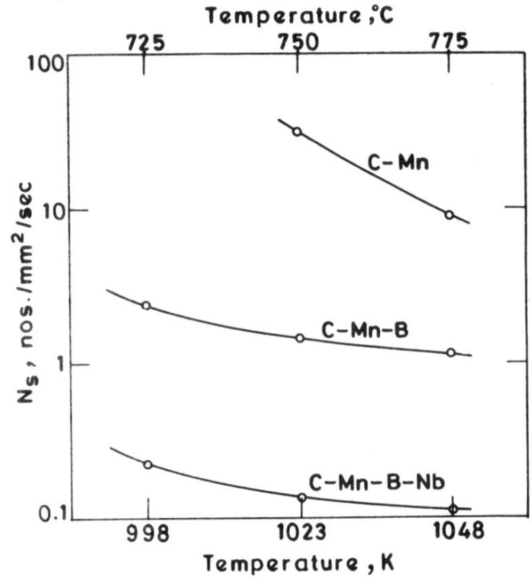

Fig. 10.14. Effect of boron on ferrite nucleation rate as number of nuclei per unit grain boundary area as a function of transformation temperature (from Ref. 7).

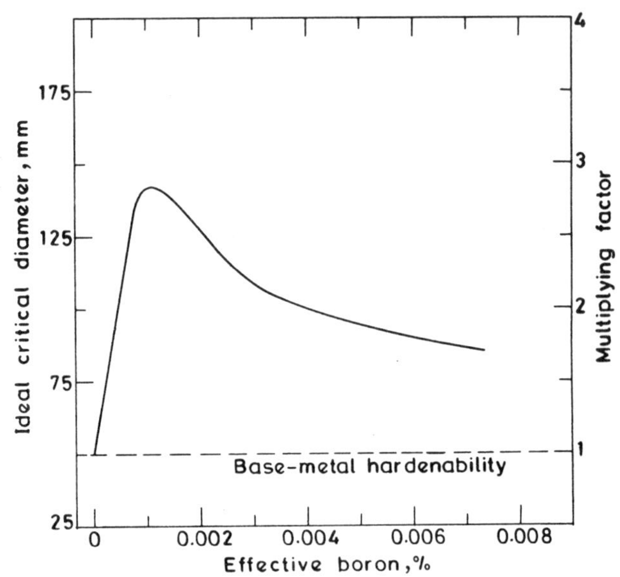

Fig. 10.15. Effect of boron concentration on the hardenability of a low-carbon low-alloy steel (from B.M. Kapadia, R.M. Brown and W. J. Murphy, *Trans AIME*, **242** (1968) p. 1689).

form and not in the combined from, i.e. it must be in solution in austenite. Because of its high affinity for oxygen and nitrogen, boron readily combines with these elements to form B_2O_3 and BN respectively. This combined boron is not effective as a hardenability agent, as these compounds do not decompose even at high austenitizing temperatures. Therefore, boron in steels must be properly ''protected'' from reacting with oxygen and nitrogen for it to be an effective hardenability agent. Thus, adequate deoxidation must be achieved by additions of Si, Al or other deoxidizers, prior to adding boron, to prevent the formation of B_2O_3. Also, strong nitride forming elements, like, Ti, Zr, etc., must be added to combine with free nitrogen to form TiN, ZrN, etc. respectively, to prevent the formation of BN. AlN is of comparable stability to BN and is not always very effective in preventing the formation of BN. If strong nitride formers, like, Ti, Zr, etc., are not be to added, then, enough boron should be added so that desirable ''free'' boron levels are available after some of it has combined with existing nitrogen to form BN.

Some of the discrepancies in reported optimum level of boron exist because a proper account of the above mentioned factors has not been taken into consideration and the hardenability effect of boron is plotted against the added/analyzed boron content rather than ''free'' boron. The actual optimum level is generally believed to be somewhere between 0.001% to 0.002% boron, i.e. 10 to 20 ppm boron by weight. Boron hardenability effect gradually drop off when boron content is increased beyond the optimum level. During the production of hardenable boron steels, ''free'' boron aimed at should be slightly beyond the optimum level to attain more consistent results. At boron levels lower than the optimum, hardenability effect falls off more rapidly, almost linearly with decreasing boron concentration (see Fig. 10.15).

4.4 EFFECT OF CARBON

Even when the optimum level of boron is present in a steel, the boron hardenability factor varies substantially with the composition of steel, particularly its carbon content. In general, boron hardenability factor decreases with increase in carbon content, to approximately nil around the eutectoid composition and may actually be negative beyond it. Figure 10.16 shows the optimum boron hardenability factor as a

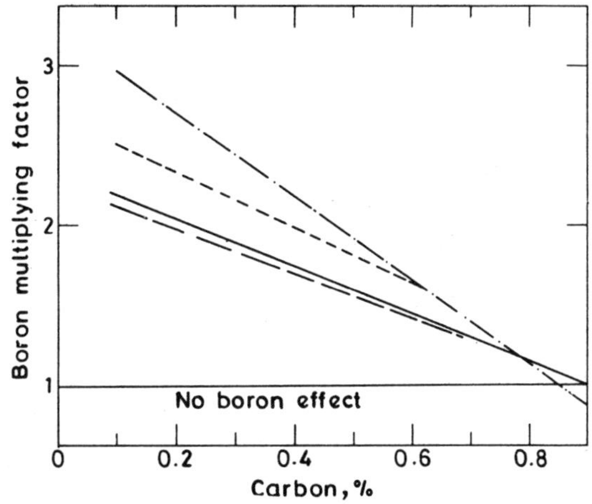

Fig. 10.16. Effect of carbon content on boron hardenability, from different investigations (from Ref. 8).

function of carbon content from different studies. As is obvious from this figure, boron is most effective in increasing the hardenability of low-carbon steels only.

The differences in boron hardenability factors at a given carbon level in Fig. 10.16 are due to different base compositions of steels used by different investigators for studying the boron hardenability effect. When base steel composition is kept constant and only carbon content is varied, the optimum boron hardenability factor continuously decreases with increase in carbon content without much scatter, as shown in Fig. 10.17.

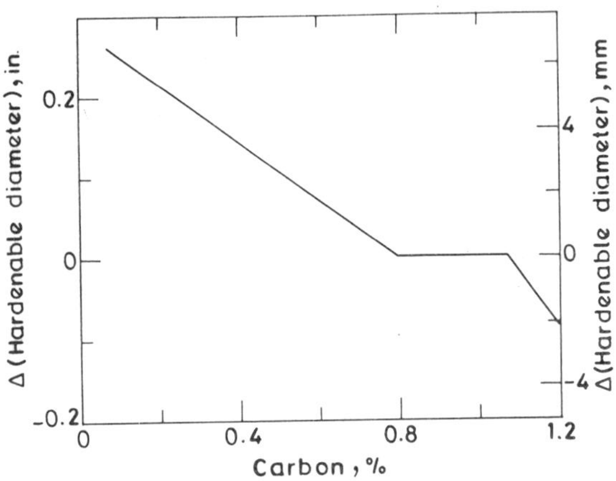

Fig. 10.17. Optimum boron hardenability effect in Fe–0.5%Mn steel as a function of carbon content (R.A. Grange quoted in Ref. 8).

4.5 EFFECT OF ALLOYING

The optimum boron hardenability factor also changes with the alloying content of a steel, apart from its carbon level. Most alloying elements decrease the eutectoid carbon content of steels. Since, boron has no retardation effect on pearlite transformation, it would be expected that for the same carbon level, the alloying elements would decrease the optimum boron multiplying factor. Figure 10.18 shows optimum boron multiplying factors, at two different carbon levels, for steels containing different concentrations of Mn and Cr. With increase in Mn and Cr contents, the optimum boron hardenability factor decreases and is almost nil even in 0.17% C steel containing 1.35% Mn and 1.55% Cr. Additions of Mn and Cr to steels also increase their hardenability. Therefore, it would seem that boron is more effective in low hardenability steels than in high hardenability steels of the same carbon levels. Mo, however, is an exception to this. In the presence of Mo, the effect of boron is further enhanced.

4.6 EFFECT OF GRAIN SIZE

Boron increases the hardenability of steels primarily by retarding the nucleation of ferrite, and ferrite nucleates heterogeneously at the austenite grain boundaries.

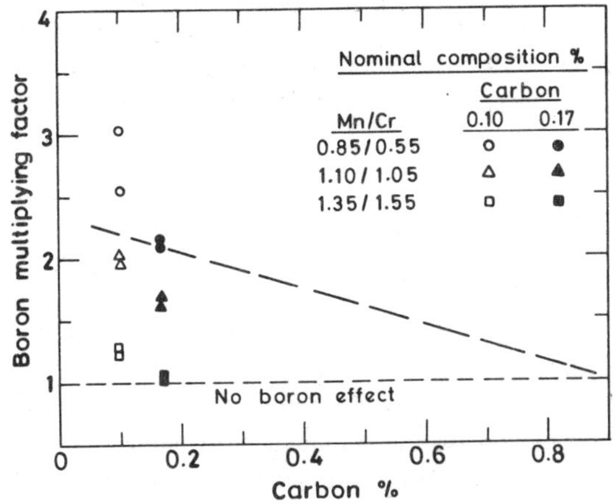

Fig. 10.18. Variation of boron hardenability factor with carbon content in steels of varying alloy (Mn/Cr) content (from Ref. 8).

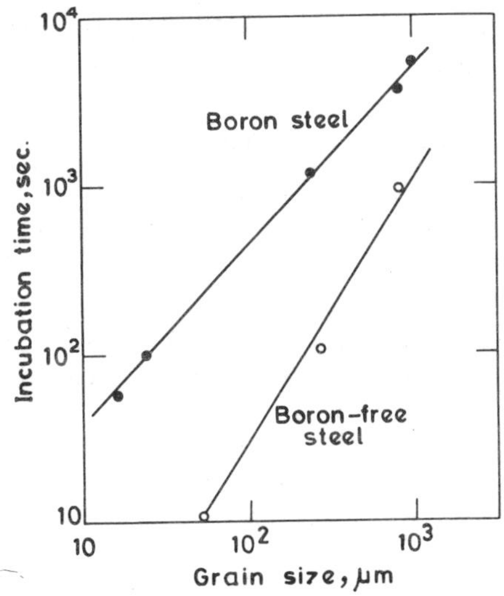

Fig. 10.19. Variation of effective incubation time for ferrite transformation as a function of grain size in boron-free and boron-treated low-carbon steel. [from Ph. Maitrepierre, D. Thivellier and R. Tricot, *Metall. Trans.*, **6A** (1975) p. 287)].

Because of this, boron diminishes the hardenability effect of grain size to some extent. Figure 10.19 shows incubation time for the grain boundary nucleated-ferrite transformation at 873K (600°C) as a function of austenite grain size in a boron-free and boron-treated low-carbon steel. The relative change in incubation time due to boron addition decreases as austenite grain size increases, i.e. boron is relatively more effective in increasing the hardenability of fine grain steels.

Grain size also affects the optimum boron level required for maximum hardenability effect to some extent. Since, boron acts in some manner at the austenite grain boundaries to inhibit the nucleation of ferrite, it can be argued that the optimum boron level should depend on the total grain boundary area per unit volume. It has been experimentally observed that the boron level which is too low to cause a marked increase in hardenability in fine grained steels, becomes more effective as grain size is increased by increasing the austenitizing temperature.

4.7 EFFECT OF AUSTENITIZING TEMPERATURE

Austenitizing temperature affects prior austenite grain size and to that extent would affect the boron hardenability factor as discussed above. Apart from this, some other effects of austenitizing temperature on boron hardenability have been reported. It has been generally observed that boron hardenability is maximum when austenitizing temperature is ~1173K (900°C) and decreases with increase in austenitizing temperature. This has been associated with the dissolution of some matrix boro-carbides at higher temperatures, thus increasing the average boron level beyond the optimum level. On the other hand, some investigators have reported an increase in boron hardenability effect with increasing austenitizing temperature. The lower effectiveness of boron in high-carbon steels is partly attributed to low austenitizing temperatures, normally used for these steels, where most of the boron could be present in the form of undissolved boro-carbides. This explains why the case hardenability of carburized boron steels is better if quenched from ~1173K (900°C) in accordance with single quench treatment than quenched from 1073-1103K (800–830°C) in conventional double quench treatment.

Apart from all this, partial or total loss of boron hardenability effect occurs on prolonged heating at very high temperatures, higher than ~1373K (1100°C). This loss of boron hardenability is permanent and is commonly known as boron "fade". Boron "fade" is faster in steels where boron is "protected" from nitrogen by additions of Al, V, or Nb, whereas it is considerably delayed when Ti or Zr is used for nitrogen protection, as seen in Fig. 10.20. The time required for boron "fade"

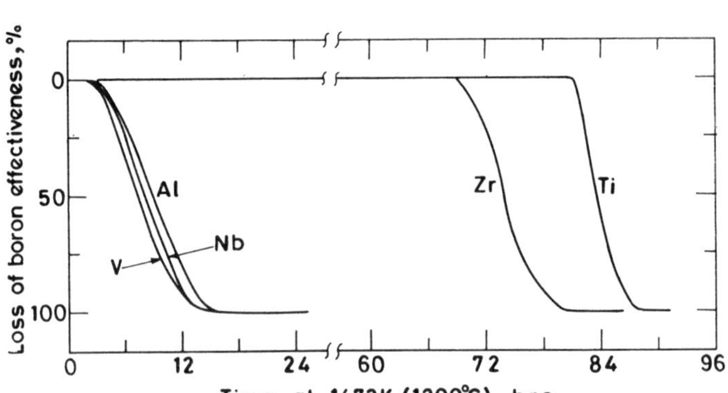

Fig. 10.20. Relative effectivenness of various elements in protecting boron hardenability effect after prolonged heating at elevated temperature. [from G.F. Melloy and J.C. Russ, *Metal Progress*, **90** (1966) p. 82].

decreases with increasing austenitizing temperature. It appears that, on prolonged heating at high temperatures, the nitrogen "protection" provided by these elements is slowly lost, resulting in the permanent loss of "free" boron to formation of BN, and hence, of boron hardenability effect.

4.8 MECHANISM OF BORON HARDENABILITY

As has been stated earlier, presence of boron affects the kinetics of ferrite transformation by retarding the nucleation of ferrite at austenite grain boundaries and has virtually no effect on pearlite transformation. Earlier studies on boron effect postulated that boron segregates at the austenite grain boundaries, sufficiently lowering their energy to give a strong nucleation retardation effect. Lowering of austenite grain boundary energy with the segregation of boron has been experimentally confirmed.

An alternative hypothesis on the mechanism of boron effect has been recently proposed. According to this hypothesis, during austenitizing and/or cooling from austenitizing temperatures, very fine precipitation of borocarbide, $Fe_{23}(BC)_6$, occurs at the austenite grain boundaries. These carbide precipitates are coherent with at least one of the austenite grains. Nucleation of ferrite on coherent side of these precipitates is prevented because of very low interfacial energy. In this manner, the ferrite nucleation is considerably retarded. However, if these carbides are allowed to grow to larger size, the coherency between $Fe_{23}(BC)_6$ precipitates and austenite is lost and nucleation can occur on incoherent carbide/austenite interfaces also. Precipitation of $Fe_{23}(BC)_6$ and selective nucleation of ferrite only on one side of the austenite grain boundaries has been experimentally observed.

The ineffectiveness of boron in retarding the pearlite transformation may be explained as follows. With increase in carbon content of steel, borocementite, $Fe_3(BC)$, may form at the austenite grain boundaries during cooling. These $Fe_3(BC)$ precipitates can then act as nuclei for cementite and/or pearlite transformations, thereby even accelerating these transformations to some extent. Thus, boron can even have a small negative effect on the hardenability of hypereutectoid steels, as has been observed.

4.9 JOMINY CURVES OF BORON STEELS

Jominy curves of boron steels are characteristically different from those of boron-free steels of equivalent hardenability. An example of this is given in Fig. 10.21. In a boron steel, hardness falls off more rapidly in the vicinity of the inflection point of the Jominy curve than in the boron-free steel of approximately the same hardenability, as seen in Fig. 10.21. This is due to the characteristic manner in which boron affects the kinetics of austenite decomposition reactions. In boron steels, only the nucleation rate of ferrite is affected, whereas, in an alloy steel of equivalent hardenability, alloying elements retard both the nucleation and growth rates of austenite decomposition products. Therefore, though boron and alloying elements both delay the start of transformations, once started, the transformations occur relatively more rapidly in boron steels than in alloy steels of equivalent hardenability. This is reflected in the faster drop in hardness (or faster increase in non-martensitic products) with Jominy distance in boron steels. Higher hardness gradients obtained

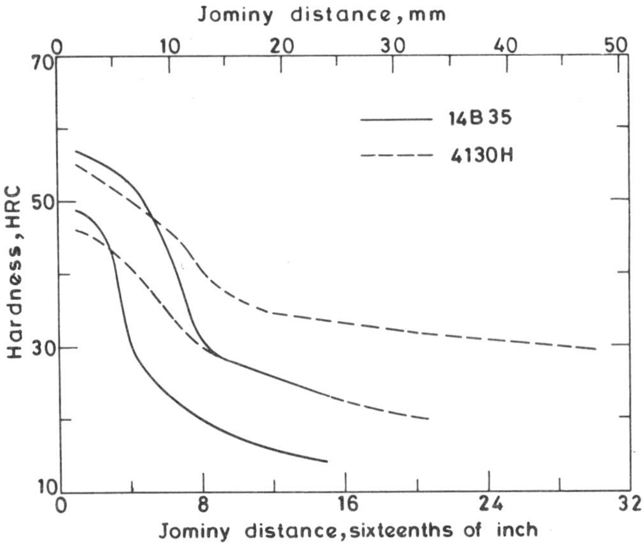

Fig. 10.21. Jominy hardenability bands for a boron-treated (14B35) and boron-free (4130H) steels of equivalent hardenability. [from M. C. Udy, Proceedings of the AIME Electric Furnance Conference, 9 (1951) p. 39].

in boron steels may not always be desirable and boron as a hardenability agent may be preferred only for sections where through hardening is desired.

5 OTHER HARDENABILITY CORRELATIONS

5.1 PREDICTION OF HARDENABILITY FROM CCT DIAGRAMS

Continuous Cooling Transformation (CCT) diagrams of steels give microstructures and hardness as a function of the cooling rate from austenite. If the cooling rates at different points in a component are known (calculated or measured), then, its hardening behaviour can be predicted from CCT diagram of the steel. Use of CCT diagrams in predicting the hardening behaviour of high hardenability steels is common, as briefly mentioned in the previous chapter. Use of CCT diagrams to predict the hardenability of steels, in general, would require a method for predicting the CCT diagrams as a function of composition and grain size. Recently, some empirical and semi-empirical methods have been developed to predict CCT diagrams with reasonable success. In this section, an empirical method developed by Maynier *et al.* (Refs. 9-10) is briefly discussed to illustrate the general methodology.

CCT diagram of a steel may be characterized by a set of critical cooling curves required to obtain given combinations of microstructural products on continuous cooling, as shown in Fig. 10.22. Here, the cooling curves have been characterized by instant cooling rates at 973K (700°C). The CCT diagram is then represented as % transformation vs cooling rate plot as in Fig. 10.23. Hardness as a function of

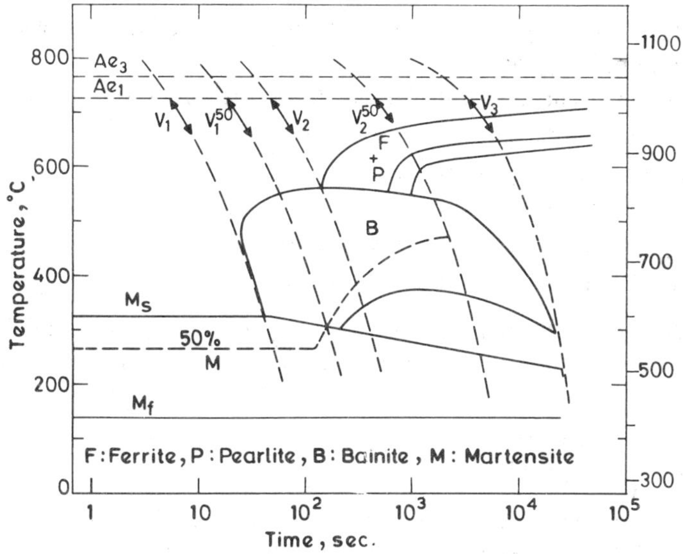

Fig. 10.22. CCT diagram of a steel. (from Ref. 9-10).

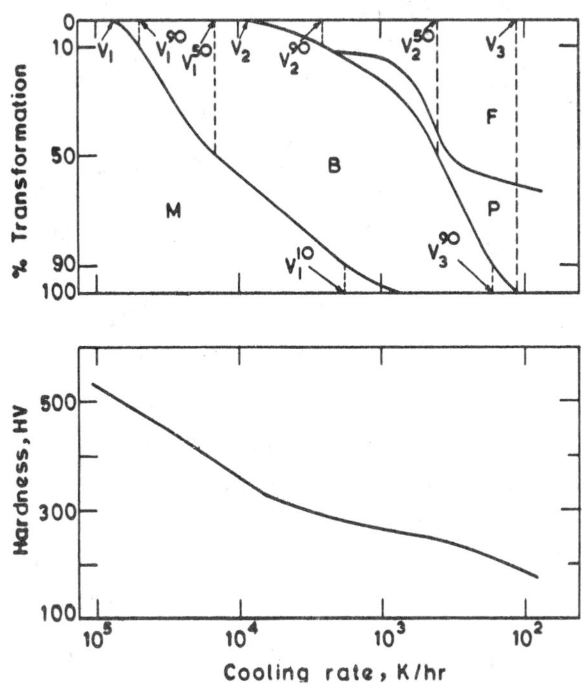

Fig. 10.23. CCT diagram in Fig. 10.22 plotted as % microstructural transformation vs cooling rate. (from Ref. 9-10).

cooling rate is also plotted in the same figure. The set of critical cooling rates chosen for correlation are as follows:

V_1 : minimum cooling rate to obtain 100% martensite,

V_2 : minimum cooling rate to avoid any ferrite and/or pearlite, i.e. to obtain 100% bainite plus martensite,
V_3 : maximum cooling rate that gives 100% ferrite plus pearlite,
V_1^{90}: cooling rate that gives 90% martensite,
V_1^{50}: cooling rate that gives 50% martensite,
V_2^{90}: cooling rate that gives 10% ferrite-pearlite,
V_2^{50}: cooling rate that gives 50% ferrite-pearlite, and
V_3^{90}: cooling rate that gives 90% ferrite-pearlite.

Now, these critical cooling rates for a large number of steels are correlated to composition and grain size by regression analyses. For grain size an austenitizing parameter, P_a, is used:

$$P_a = \left(\frac{1}{T} - \frac{R}{Q}(\ln t)\right)^{-1} \tag{10.3}$$

where T is austenitizing temperature in degrees Kelvin; t is time in hr; R is gas constant; and Q is activation energy for grain growth in austenite and is ~460 kJ/mole. Parameter, P_a, is developed on the assumption that grain size is a function of austenitizing temperature and time only, and was found suitable to account for the grain size effect.

The results of correlations of critical cooling rates with composition and P_a, for a large number of hardenable low alloy steels are given in the following (Refs. 9-10):

$$\log V_1 = 9.81 - (4.62\text{C}\%+1.05\text{Mn}\%+0.54\text{Ni}\%+0.50\text{Cr}\%+0.66\text{Mo}\%+0.00183P_a)$$

$$\log V_2 = 10.17 - (3.80\text{C}\%+1.07\text{Mn}\%+0.70\text{Ni}\%+0.57\text{Cr}\%+1.58\text{Mo}\%+0.0032P_a)$$

$$\log V_3 = 6.36 - (0.43\text{C}\%+0.49\text{Mn}\%+0.78\text{Ni}\%+0.27\text{Cr}\%+0.38\text{Mo}\% + 2\sqrt{\text{Mo}\%} + 0.0019P_a)$$

$$\log V_1^{90} = 8.76 - (4.04\text{C}\%+0.96\text{Mn}\%+0.49\text{Ni}\%+0.58\text{Cr}\%+0.97\text{Mo}\%+0.0010P_a)$$

$$\log V_1^{50} = 8.50 - (4.12\text{C}\%+0.86\text{Mn}\%+0.57\text{Ni}\%+0.41\text{Cr}\%+0.94\text{Mo}\%+0.0012P_a)$$

$$\log V_2^{90} = 10.55 - (3.65\text{C}\%+1.08\text{Mn}\%+0.77\text{Ni}\%+0.61\text{Cr}\%+1.60\text{Mo}\%+0.0032P_a)$$

$$\log V_2^{50} = 8.74 - (2.23\text{C}\%+0.86\text{Mn}\%+0.56\text{Ni}\%+0.59\text{Cr}\%+1.60\text{Mo}\%+0.0032P_a)$$

$$\log V_3^{90} = 7.51 - (1.38\text{C}\%+0.35\text{Mn}\%+0.93\text{Ni}\%+0.11\text{Cr}\% +2.31\text{Mo}\% +0.0033P_a) \tag{10.4}$$

where cooling velocities are in K/hr and compositions in wt%. These equations can now be used to predict the CCT diagram of any steel, in the form shown in Fig. 10.23. To obtain the hardening behaviour of steels, microstructures at different cooling rates are obtained with the help of predicted CCT diagrams and the hardness is calculated as a weighted average of the hardness of different microstructual constituents. Hardness of martensite, bainite and ferrite-pearlite is also empirically correlated to composition, grain size and cooling rate by regression analysis of the hardness data. The results are given in the following [Ref. 9-10]:

$$HV(\text{martensite}) = 127 + 949\text{C}\% + 27\text{Si}\% + 11\text{Mn}\% + 8\text{Ni}\% + 16\text{Cr}\% + 21(\log V_r)$$

$$HV(\text{bainite}) = 323 + 185\text{C\%} + 330\text{Si\%} + 153\text{Mn\%} + 65\text{Ni\%} + 144\text{Cr\%} + 191\text{Mo\%} + \log V_r\,(89+53\text{C\%}-55\text{Si\%}-22\text{Mn\%} -10\text{Ni\%}-20\text{Cr\%}-33\text{Mo\%})$$

and

$$HV(\text{ferrite-pearlite}) = 42 + 223\text{C\%} + 53\text{Si\%} + 30\text{Mn\%} + 12.6\text{Ni\%} + 7\text{Cr\%} + 19\text{Mo\%} + \log V_r\,(10-19\text{Si\%}+4\text{Ni\%}+8\text{Cr\%}+130\text{V\%}) \qquad (10.5)$$

where, HV is Vicker's hardness number and V_r is cooling rate. The set of Eqs. (10.4) and (10.5) can now be used to predict the complete hardening behaviour of a given steel. This system has an added advantage that microstructure at any point is also predicted in the process.

5.2 REGRESSION ANALYSIS

Early work on hardenability correlations was done without the aid of computers. Regression analysis with large data banks and complex equations was not easily possible. The emphasis, therefore, was on developing simple correlations for easy handling, sacrificing accuracy to some extent. Now that computers are available to handle complicated equations, more work in recent years has been done with the help of computers. Development of regression equations to predict microstructures and hardness of quenched steels from CCT diagrams data, discussed in the previous section, is an example of one such analysis. Another example, of such an analysis, is the equation developed by Just (Ref.11) for predicting hardness as a function of Jominy distance; given below:

$$\text{HRC at } J_{4-40} = 88(\sqrt{C}\,) - 0.0135E^2(\sqrt{C}\,) + 19\text{Cr} + 6.3\text{ Ni} + 16\text{Mn} + 35\text{Mo} + 5\text{Si} - 0.82G - 20(\sqrt{E}\,) + 2.11E - 2\text{HRC} \qquad (10.6)$$

where, HRC is hardness in Rockwell-C at J distances in the range 4 to 40 sixteenths of an inch from the quenched end; element symbols represent composition in wt%; E is distance from the quench end in sixteenths of an inch; and G is ASTM grain size number.

Still another example is the equations developed by Breen *et al*, (Ref. 12) for Jominy curves of boron steels in terms of hardness at different Jominy distances, j_i's, as a function of composition, given in the following:

$$\begin{aligned}
J_1 &= 39.5 + 37.5\text{C}\\
J_2 &= 38.6 + 37.9\text{C}\\
J_3 &= 38.1 + 37.8\text{C}\\
J_4 &= 36.3 + 41.1\text{C}\\
J_5 &= 23.6 + 44.6\text{C} + 8\text{Mn} + 10.2\text{Cr}\\
J_6 &= 5.3 + 58.0\text{C} + 16.2\text{Mn} + 30.4\text{Cr}\\
J_7 &= -27.6 + 65.5\text{C} + 35.1\text{Mn} + 66.0\text{Cr}\\
J_8 &= -40.7 + 54.4\text{C} + 42.0\text{Mn} + 93.6\text{Cr}\\
J_{10} &= -37.5 + 39.2\text{C} + 37.3\text{Mn} + 73.9\text{Cr}\\
J_{12} &= -31.2 + 37.5\text{C} + 29.9\text{Mn} + 54.8\text{Cr} \qquad (10.7)
\end{aligned}$$

where J_n is hardness in Rockwell-C at n sixteenths of an inch from the quenched end. The equations are valid in the composition range; C: 0.25–0.35%, Mn: 1.20–1.38%, Si: 0.23–0.35%, Ni: 0.02–0.04%,Cr: 0.02–0.12%, Mo: 0.01–0.02%, and 0.0005%B minimum.

Given above are just a few examples of application of rgression analysis with the aid of computers to hardenability calculations. Regression analysis can be used to more accurately calibrate the hardenability predictions in a narrow required range of compositions and/or to accurately caliberate a certain steel mill data. With the use of computers one is neither limited by the number of equations that may be used nor by their complexity.

5.3 SEMI-EMPIRICAL PREDICTIONS OF HARDENABILITY

In principle, one should be able to arrive at the CCT diagram, and hence, the hardening behaviour, of a steel from the theory of phase trnasformations in steels and heat flow analyses during cooling. However, in practice it has not been possible because of the gaps that exist in our understanding of phase transformations in multicomponent systems and the lack of complete quantitative matching between theory and experimental results. Still, some semi-empirical formalisms to predict the hardenability of steels from first principles have been developed. Here, the general correlative equations are derived from the theory of phase transformations; however, these contain some adjustable parameters that are optimized with respect to the empirical data. These correlations are not discussed in this book. The interested reader may refer to some of the articles in Ref. 3.

6 UTILIZATION OF HARDENABILITY DATA

6.1 HARDENABILITY BANDS

In commercial production of steels, exact chemical composition cannot be reproduced from one heat to another, and the same is true for hardenability grade steels. In commercial specifications, therefore, a composition range is normally quoted. This composition range for a given grade of steel gives rise to a hardenability range. When buying a hardennability grade steel one may prefer to specifying hardenability range, rather than composition range, to protect oneself against an odd heat of excessively low, or high, hardenability. For hardenability grade commercial steels, hardenability range in terms of Jominy hardenability bands is generally specified and is used to select a steel for given requirements. Figures 10.24 and 10.25 show Jominy hardenability bands of two commercial hardenability grade steels.

6.2 JOMINY EQUIVALENT CONDITION (Jec)

To determine the hardenability requirements for a given part, one must be able to relate the quenching behaviour of the part in actual production to standard Jominy test. This may be done by using the concept of equivalent cooling rates. Two cooling

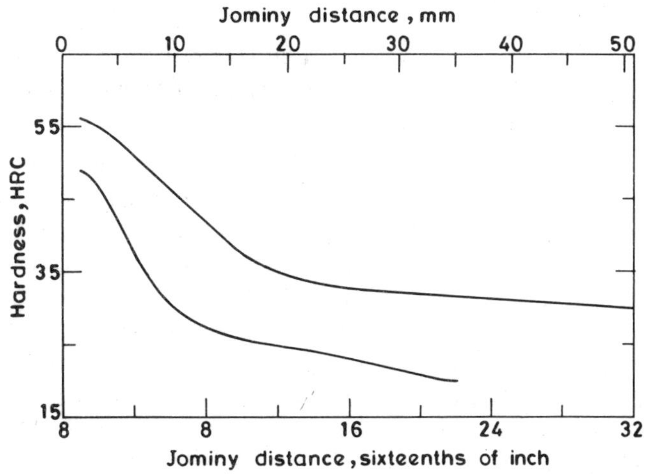

Fig. 10.24. Hardenability band of 4130H steel. (C: 027–0.33, Mn: 0.3–0.7, Si: 0.15–0.30, Cr: 0.75–1.20, Mo: 0.15–0.25).

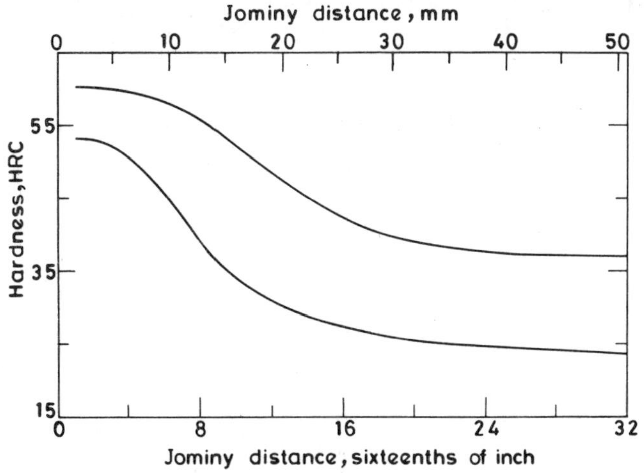

Fig. 10.25. Hardenability band of 8640H steel (C: 0.37–0.44, Mn: 0.7–1.05, Si: 0.15–0.30, Ni: 0.35–0.75, Cr: 0.35–0.65, Mo: 0.15–0.25).

curves are considered equivalent, if they produce same microstructure and hardness in a steel. The cooling curves may be obtained by heat flow analysis or by experimentation. Two cooling curves are considered equivalent, if,

(*i*) *the Half-Cooling Times,* the times to cool from Ae_3 to $(Ae_3+298K)/2$, a temperature half way between Ae_3 and room temperature (298K), are same; or,

(*ii*) *the Times to Cool From 1073K (800°C) to 773K (500°C)* are same; or, (*iii*) *the Instant Cooling Velocities at 973K (700°C)* are same.

All these criteria for equivalent cooling rates work reasonably well and there is nothing much to prefer one over the others. The half-cooling time criterion is, however, most commonly used.

Another method for determining the equivalence between the part to be produced and the Jominy curve, is to experimentally determine the Jominy equivalent condition, (Jec). A part made of some steel is quenched under the same conditions that are to be used in actual production and the hardness distribution in the part is measured. A standard Jominy test on the same steel from the same stock is also carried out. Now, any position in the part can be described by a Jominy equivalent condition, in terms of Jominy distance, where same hardness is obtained. The process is schematically illustrated in Fig. 10.26. Once, the "Jec" for the part is known, the hardenability requirements of the steel, from which it is to be eventually manufactured, can be set in terms of required Jominy hardenability curve.

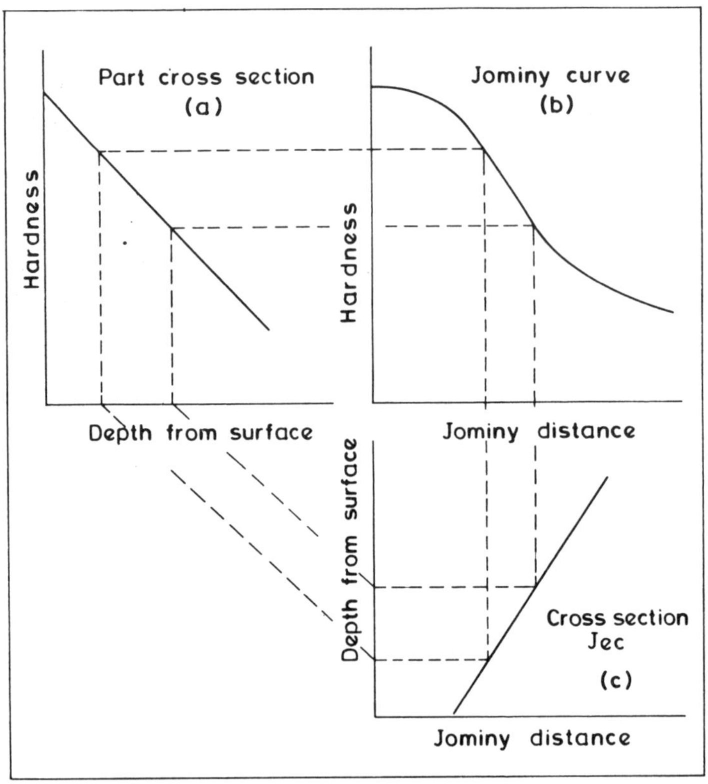

Fig. 10.26. Experimental procedure for determining the Jominy Equivalent condition (Jec).

6.3 ESTABLISHING HARDENABILITY REQUIREMENTS

Once the Jominy equivalent condition for a part has been determined and its hardness/strength requirements set, one can proceed to select/design a proper steel for the part. First step in the selection of a steel is to set the carbon level. It determines the maximum hardness attainable upon quenching. The hardness distribution as a function of Jominy distance is determined by the hardenability of steel.

Hardenability of a steel is usually calculated from Grossmann's multiplying factors in terms of ideal critical diameter. Ideal critical diameter, D_I , can be used to generate a Jominy curve with the help of Tables 10.1 and 10.2. Table 10.1 gives the maximum hardness attainable upon quenching as a function of carbon content of the steel and Table 10.2 gives the ratio of initial (maximum) hardness (IH) at the quenched end to hardness at any distance (DH) from quenched end of the Jominy bar, *IH/DH,* as a function of Jominy distance for different ideal critical diameters. Table 10.2 is for medium-carbon low-alloy steels. The *IH/DH* values for low-carbon carburizing grade steels are slightly different and are given in Table 10.3. The procedure for converting D_I to Jominy curve of a steel using these tables works reasonably well for most hardenability grade steels, except boron steels, where, for a given D_I the hardness drop is faster around the inflection point of the Jominy curve, as discussed earlier. The procedure described above may be used to select a steel from existing grades, or to design a new steel for specific requirements. All other factors which go into the selection of a steel for a given engineering component and the design of its heat treatment are beyond the scope of this book.

Table 10.1. Hardness of Fully Hardened Steel as a Function of Carbon Content

Carbon %	Maximum Hardness HRC	Carbon %	Maximum Hardness HRC	Carbon %	Maximum Hardness HRC	Carbon %	Maximum Hardness HRC
0.10	38	0.23	46	0.36	54	0.49	60
0.11	39	0.24	46	0.37	55	0.50	60
0.12	40	0.25	47	0.38	55	0.51	60
0.13	40	0.26	48	0.39	56	0.52	61
0.14	41	0.27	49	0.40	56	0.53	61
0.15	41	0.28	49	0.41	57	0.54	61
0.16	42	0.29	50	0.42	57	0.55	61
0.17	42	0.30	50	0.43	58	0.56	61
0.18	43	0.31	51	0.44	58	0.57	62
0.19	44	0.32	51	0,45	58	0.58	62
0.20	44	0.33	52	0.46	59	0.59	62
0.21	45	0.34	53	0.47	59	0.60	62
0.22	45	0.35	53	0.48	59		

Table 10.2. Initial-Hardness/Distance-Hardness (IH/DH) Ratios

D_I		Distance from quenched end, 1/16 in. (mm)																			
		(J1)	(J2)	(J3)	(J4)	(J5)	(J6)	(J7)	(J8)	(J9)	(J10)	(J11)	(J12)	(J13)	(J14)	(J15)	(J16)	(J20)	(J24)	(J28)	(J32)
in.	(mm)	(1.6)	(3.2)	(4.8)	(6.3)	(7.9)	(9.5)	(11)	(13)	(14)	(16)	(17)	(19)	(21)	(22)	(24)	(25)	(32)	(38)	(45)	(51)
1.00	(25)	1.00	1.29	1.91	2.48	2.72	2.93	3.14	3.33	3.60	3.87	4.13	4.40	—	—	—	—	—	—	—	—
1.10	(28)	1.00	1.22	1.65	2.17	2.43	2.63	2.84	3.08	3.29	3.50	3.72	3.93	4.14	4.34	4.55	4.75	5.70	—	—	—
1.20	(31)	1.00	1.18	1.56	1.96	2.22	2.42	2.63	2.86	3.06	3.25	3.44	3.60	3.79	3.95	4.11	4.15	4.58	5.00	6.00	—
1.30	(33)	1.00	1.15	1.47	1.80	2.01	2.21	2.42	2.66	2.83	2.99	3.16	3.32	3.44	3.55	3.67	3.78	4.13	4.40	4.72	5.25
1.40	(36)	1.00	1.11	1.39	1.67	1.88	2.09	2.29	2.49	2.66	2.82	2.97	3.10	3.23	3.34	3.44	3.53	3.77	4.02	4.26	4.53
1.50	(38)	1.00	1.08	1.31	1.57	1.76	1.97	2.16	2.34	2.49	2.64	2.78	2.93	3.02	3.12	3.21	3.30	3.53	3.73	3.91	4.10
1.60	(41)	1.00	1.06	1.24	1.49	1.69	1.87	2.06	2.21	2.36	2.50	2.63	2.75	2.85	2.94	3.03	3.10	3.33	3.51	3.67	3.83
1.70	(43)	1.00	1.04	1.18	1.43	1.63	1.82	1.96	2.11	2.23	2.35	2.47	2.59	2.68	2.76	2.85	2.93	3.16	3.33	3.47	3.59
1.80	(46)	1.00	1.04	1.17	1.38	1.56	1.74	1.86	2.01	2.12	2.23	2.35	2.45	2.55	2.63	2.72	2.80	3.00	3.17	3.29	3.40
1.90	(48)	1.00	1.04	1.16	1.34	1.50	1.66	1.80	1.91	2.02	2.12	2.23	2.33	2.42	2.51	2.59	2.68	2.88	3.04	3.14	3.25
2.00	(51)	1.00	1.03	1.14	1.30	1.44	1.59	1.71	1.83	1.94	2.03	2.13	2.23	2.32	2.41	2.50	2.58	2.78	2.92	3.02	3.11
2.10	(53)	1.00	1.02	1.12	1.26	1.38	1.52	1.63	1.75	1.85	1.94	2.04	2.13	2.22	2.32	2.41	2.50	2.69	2.82	2.91	3.00
2.20	(56)	1.00	1.01	1.11	1.24	1.36	1.48	1.58	1.69	1.79	1.88	1.97	2.06	2.15	2.25	2.33	2.42	2.61	2.73	2.83	2.91
2.30	(58)	1.00	1.00	1.11	1.22	1.34	1.45	1.54	1.64	1.73	1.82	1.91	1.99	2.09	2.18	2.26	2.35	2.53	2.65	2.75	2.83
2.40	(61)	1.00	1.00	1.10	1.20	1.30	1.40	1.50	1.60	1.69	1.76	1.85	1.93	2.02	2.10	2.19	2.27	2.47	2.58	2.67	2.75
2.50	(64)	1.00	1.00	1.09	1.18	1.28	1.37	1.46	1.55	1.63	1.72	1.80	1.88	1.97	2.05	2.14	2.22	2.40	2.51	2.60	2.68
2.60	(66)	1.00	1.00	1.08	1.17	1.26	1.34	1.43	1.52	1.60	1.68	1.76	1.84	1.94	2.00	2.08	2.16	2.34	2.44	2.53	2.61
2.70	(69)	1.00	1.00	1.06	1.15	1.24	1.32	1.41	1.48	1.57	1.65	1.73	1.80	1.88	1.96	2.03	2.10	2.28	2.38	2.47	2.54

D_I		Distance from quenched end, 1/16 in. (mm)																			
		(J1)	(J2)	(J3)	(J4)	(J5)	(J6)	(J7)	(J8)	(J9)	(J10)	(J11)	(J12)	(J13)	(J14)	(J15)	(J16)	(J20)	(J24)	(J28)	(J32)
in.	(mm)	(1.6)	(3.2)	(4.8)	(6.3)	(7.9)	(9.5)	(11)	(13)	(14)	(16)	(17)	(19)	(21)	(22)	(24)	(25)	(32)	(38)	(45)	(51)
2.80	(71)	1.00	1.00	1.06	1.14	1.22	1.30	1.38	1.45	1.54	1.61	1.69	1.76	1.84	1.91	1.98	2.05	2.23	2.33	2.41	2.48
2.90	(74)	1.00	1.00	1.05	1.13	1.21	1.28	1.36	1.42	1.50	1.58	1.65	1.72	1.8	1.87	1.94	2.00	2.18	2.28	2.35	2.42
3.00	(76)	1.00	1.00	1.05	1.11	1.18	1.25	1.32	1.39	1.46	1.54	1.60	1.68	1.75	1.81	1.88	1.94	2.12	2.22	2.28	2.36
3.10	(79)	1.00	1.00	1.04	1.10	1.17	1.24	1.30	1.37	1.44	1.50	1.57	1.65	1.7	1.77	1.84	1.90	2.08	2.18	2.24	2.32
3.20	(81)	1.00	1.00	1.03	1.09	1.16	1.23	1.29	1.35	1.41	1.48	1.54	1.61	1.67	1.73	1.80	1.86	2.08	2.13	2.20	2.32
3.30	(84)	1.00	1.00	1.03	1.08	1.15	1.21	1.27	1.33	1.40	1.46	1.52	1.58	1.65	1.71	1.77	1.83	2.00	2.08	2.15	2.22
3.40	(86)	1.00	1.00	1.02	1.07	1.13	1.19	1.25	1.31	1.37	1.44	1.50	1.55	1.60	1.66	1.73	1.80	1.95	2.04	2.11	2.17
3.50	(89)	1.00	1.00	1.02	1.07	1.13	1.19	1.24	1.29	1.35	1.40	1.45	1.51	1.56	1.62	1.69	1.76	1.91	2.00	2.07	2.13
3.60	(91)	1.00	1.00	1.02	1.06	1.11	1.17	1.22	1.27	1.32	1.39	1.43	1.48	1.55	1.60	1.66	1.72	1.87	1.96	2.03	2.08
3.70	(94)	1.00	1.00	1.01	1.06	1.11	1.15	1.20	1.25	1.30	1.35	1.40	1.46	1.51	1.56	1.62	1.68	1.83	1.92	1.98	2.04
3.80	(97)	1.00	1.00	1.01	1.05	1.10	1.14	1.19	1.23	1.28	1.33	1.38	1.43	1.48	1.53	1.59	1.65	1.80	1.88	1.94	2.00
3.90	(99)	1.00	1.00	1.01	1.05	1.09	1.14	1.18	1.22	1.27	1.31	1.36	1.41	1.46	1.51	1.56	1.62	1.76	1.84	1.90	1.96
4.00	(102)	1.00	1.00	1.00	1.04	1.08	1.12	1.16	1.20	1.25	1.29	1.33	1.38	1.43	1.48	1.53	1.59	1.72	1.80	1.86	1.92
4.10	(104)	1.00	1.00	1.00	1.04	1.08	1.11	1.15	1.18	1.23	1.28	1.32	1.36	1.41	1.46	1.51	1.56	1.68	1.77	1.82	1.88
4.20	(107)	1.00	1.00	1.00	1.03	1.06	1.10	1.14	1.17	1.22	1.25	1.29	1.34	1.38	1.42	1.48	1.53	1.65	1.73	1.78	1.84
4.30	(109)	1.00	1.00	1.00	1.03	1.06	1.10	1.13	1.16	1.20	1.24	1.28	1.32	1.37	1.41	1.46	1.50	1.62	1.70	1.75	1.80
4.40	(112)	1.00	1.00	1.00	1.02	1.05	1.09	1.12	1.15	1.19	1.23	1.27	1.30	1.35	1.39	1.43	1.47	1.58	1.66	1.72	1.76
4.50	(114)	1.00	1.00	1.00	1.02	1.05	1.08	1.11	1.14	1.18	1.22	1.25	1.28	1.32	1.36	1.40	1.44	1.55	1.63	1.68	1.73
4.60	(117)	1.00	1.00	1.00	1.02	1.05	1.07	1.10	1.12	1.15	1.19	1.22	1.26	1.29	1.33	1.37	1.41	1.52	1.59	1.64	1.69

D_I		Distance from quenched end, 1/16 in. (mm)																			
in.	(mm)	(J1) (1.6)	(J2) (3.2)	(J3) (4.8)	(J4) (6.3)	(J5) (7.9)	(J6) (9.5)	(J7) (11)	(J8) (13)	(J9) (14)	(J10) (16)	(J11) (17)	(J12) (19)	(J13) (21)	(J14) (22)	(J15) (24)	(J16) (25)	(J20) (32)	(J24) (38)	(J28) (45)	(J32) (51)
4.70	(119)	1.00	1.00	1.00	1.01	1.04	1.06	1.09	1.11	1.14	1.17	1.20	1.24	1.28	1.31	1.35	1.38	1.49	1.56	1.61	1.65
4.80	(122)	1.00	1.00	1.00	1.01	1.02	1.05	1.07	1.10	1.13	1.16	1.19	1.22	1.25	1.28	1.32	1.36	1.46	1.53	1.57	1.62
4.90	(125)	1.00	1.00	1.00	1.00	1.00	1.03	1.06	1.08	1.11	1.14	1.17	1.20	1.23	1.26	1.29	1.33	1.43	1.49	1.53	1.58
5.00	(127)	1.00	1.00	1.00	1.00	1.00	1.02	1.05	1.07	1.10	1.13	1.15	1.18	1.2	1.25	1.28	1.31	1.40	1.46	1.50	1.54
5.10	(130)	1.00	1.00	1.00	1.00	1.00	1.01	1.04	1.06	1.09	1.11	1.14	1.17	1.19	1.22	1.25	1.28	1.37	1.43	1.47	1.51
5.20	(132)	1.00	1.00	1.00	1.00	1.00	1.00	1.03	1.05	1.08	1.10	1.13	1.15	1.18	1.20	1.23	1.25	1.34	1.39	1.43	1.47
5.30	(135)	1.00	1.00	1.00	1.00	1.00	1.00	1.02	1.04	1.06	1.09	1.11	1.13	1.16	1.18	1.21	1.23	1.31	1.36	1.39	1.43
5.40	(137)	1.00	1.00	1.00	1.00	1.00	1.00	1.02	1.03	1.05	1.08	1.11	1.12	1.15	1.18	1.20	1.21	1.28	1.33	1.36	1.40
5.50	(140)	1.00	1.00	1.00	1.00	1.00	1.00	1.01	1.03	1.05	1.07	1.08	1.10	1.12	1.13	1.15	1.18	1.25	1.29	1.33	1.37
5.60	(142)	1.00	1.00	1.00	1.00	1.00	1.00	1.01	1.02	1.04	1.05	1.07	1.09	1.10	1.12	1.14	1.16	1.22	1.26	1.28	1.33
5.70	(145)	1.00	1.00	1.00	1.00	1.00	1.00	1.01	1.02	1.03	1.04	1.06	1.07	1.09	1.10	1.11	1.13	1.19	1.23	1.25	1.29
5.80	(147)	1.00	1.00	1.00	1.00	1.00	1.00	1.00	1.01	1.02	1.04	1.05	1.06	1.07	1.09	1.10	1.11	1.17	1.19	1.22	1.25
5.90	(149)	1.00	1.00	1.00	1.00	1.00	1.00	1.00	1.01	1.01	1.02	1.03	1.04	1.05	1.06	1.08	1.09	1.13	1.16	1.18	1.21
6.00	(152)	1.00	1.00	1.00	1.00	1.00	1.00	1.00	1.00	1.01	1.01	1.02	1.03	1.04	1.05	1.06	1.07	1.10	1.13	1.15	1.18

Table 10.3. Initial Hardness/Distance Hardness (IH/DH) Ratios in Carburizing Steels

D_I		IH/DH								
in.	(mm)	J1 (1.6)	J2 (3.2)	J3 (4.8)	J4 (6.4)	J6 (9.5)	J8 (13)	J10 (16)	J12 (19)	J16 (25)
0.8	(20.3)	1.14	1.48	2.28	2.79	3.57	4.32	5.14	5.88	7.75
0.9	(22.9)	1.10	1.36	2.00	2.47	3.16	3.79	4.46	5.09	6.61
1.0	(25.4)	1.08	1.27	1.78	2.81	2.81	3.34	3.88	4.41	5.64
1.1	(27.9)	1.06	1.20	1.60	1.97	2.52	2.96	3.40	3.84	4.82
1.2	(30.5)	1.04	1.15	1.45	1.78	2.27	2.64	3.00	3.37	4.14
1.3	(33.0)	1.03	1.12	1.34	1.63	2.06	2.38	2.67	2.97	3.58
1.4	(35.6)	1.03	1.09	1.26	1.50	1.89	2.16	2.40	2.65	3.13
1.5	(38.1)	1.02	1.08	1.20	1.40	1.75	1.98	2.18	2.39	2.77
1.6	(40.6)	1.02	1.07	1.16	1.33	1.64	1.84	2.01	2.19	2.48
1.7	(43.2)	1.02	1.06	1.13	1.27	1.55	1.73	1.88	2.03	2.27
1.8	(45.7)	1.02	1.05	1.11	1.23	1.48	1.65	1.79	1.91	2.10
1.9	(48.3)	1.02	1.05	1.09	1.19	1.42	1.59	1.71	1.82	1.98
2.0	(50.8)	1.02	1.05	1.09	1.17	1.38	1.54	1.66	1.77	1.90
2.1	(53.3)	1.02	1.04	1.08	1.15	1.35	1.50	1.63	1.74	1.84
2.2	(55.9)	1.01	1.04	1.08	1.14	1.32	1.47	1.60	1.71	1.81
2.3	(58.4)	1.01	1.04	1.08	1.13	1.30	1.45	1.58	1.68	1.78
2.4	(61.0)	1.01	1.03	1.08	1.12	1.29	1.44	1.56	1.66	1.75
2.5	(63.5)	1.01	1.03	1.07	1.10	1.28	1.42	1.54	1.63	1.72
2.6	(66.0)	1.01	1.02	1.07	1.09	1.26	1.40	1.51	1.60	1.69
2.7	(68.6)	1.01	1.02	1.06	1.08	1.25	1.38	1.48	1.57	1.66
2.8	(71.1)	1.00	1.02	1.06	1.07	1.23	1.36	1.46	1.54	1.63
2.9	(73.7)	1.00	1.01	1.05	1.06	1.22	1.34	1.43	1.51	1.60
3.0	(76.2)	1.00	1.01	1.04	1.06	1.20	1.32	1.41	1.48	1.57
3.1	(78.7)	1.00	1.01	1.03	1.05	1.19	1.29	1.38	1.46	1.54
3.2	(81.3)	1.00	1.01	1.02	1.05	1.18	1.27	1.36	1.43	1.51
3.3	(83.8)	1.00	1.01	1.02	1.04	1.16	1.25	1.33	1.40	1.48
3.4	(86.4)	1.00	1.01	1.02	1.04	1.15	1.23	1.31	1.37	1.45
3.5	(88.9)	1.00	1.01	1.02	1.04	1.13	1.21	1.28	1.34	1.41
3.6	(91.4)	1.00	1.01	1.02	1.03	1.12	1.19	1.26	1.31	1.38
3.7	(94.0)	1.00	1.00	1.01	1.02	1.10	1.17	1.23	1.28	1.35

REFERENCES

1. M.A. Grossman, *Elements of Hardenability*, American Society for Metals, Metals Parks, Ohio, 1952.
2. M.A. Grossman, *Principles of Heat Treatment,* American Society for Metals, Metals Park, Ohio, 1955.
3. *Hadenability Concepts with Application to Steels* (Eds. D.V. Doane and J. S. Kirkaldy), The Metallurgical Society of AIME, Warrendale, Pa, 1978.
4. C.A. Siebert, D.V. Doane and D.H. Breen, *The Hardenability of Steels*, American Society for Metals, Metals Park, Ohio, 1977.

5. R.A. Grange, *Metall. Trans.*, **4** (1973) p. 2231.
6. G.T. Eldis and W.C. Haget, Ref. 3, p. 397.
7. Ph. Maitrepierre, D. Thivellier, J. Rofes-Vernis, D. Rousseau and R. Tricot, Ref. 3, p. 421.
8. Behram M. Kapadia, Ref. 3, p. 448.
9. Ph. Maynier, J. Dollet and P. Bastien, Ref. 3, p. 163.
10. Ph. Maynier, B. Jungman and J. Dollet, Ref. 3, p. 518.
11. E. Just, *Metal Prog.* **96**, (Nov. 1969), p. 87.
12. D.H. Breen, G.H. Walter and J.T. Sponzilli, *Metal Prog.*, **104**, (Nov. 1973) p. 43.

CHAPTER 11

Carburizing and Carbonitriding

1 INTRODUCTION

Components for some engineering applications must have relatively hard, wear-resistant surfaces and must also possess high toughness. Such a combination of properties is usually not possible by heat treating the steel components by quench hardening and tempering. To obtain high surface hardness upon quenching, a steel must have relatively high carbon content. Hardness of quenched steels is basically a function of their carbon content. However, as the carbon content of a steel is increased, its toughness is greatly reduced. A combination of high surface hardness as well as high toughness may, however, be achieved, if surface of the component made from a low-carbon steel is enriched in carbon up to certain depth. Upon quench hardening, such a component would have high surface hardness, due to the formation of high carbon martensite near the surface, as well as high toughness, because of the relatively soft low-carbon steel core.

Carbon enrichment of the surface layer of a low carbon steel component may be achieved by bringing the component into contact with an environment of high carbon activity in the austenite stability range. Under these conditions, carbon is absorbed at the surface and diffuses inwards, enriching the surface layer with carbon. Maximum carbon content at the surface during this process is essentially controlled by carbon activity of the environment, whereas, depth of carbon penetration below the surface is controlled by carbon diffusion and is a function of temperature and time of the treatment. The carbon-enriched surface layer is generally called ''case'' and the low carbon interior is known as ''core'', and the process is called carburizing. In carburizing, steel components made of steels containing 0.1–0.25% carbon are carburized in the austenite stability range, normally at 1073K (800°C) to 1223K (950°C), to attain maximum surface carbon content of 0.6% to 1.1%. The case depth, depending upon the requirements, could vary from fraction of a mm to few mm. Carbonitriding is very similar to carburizing, except that in carbonitriding, in addition to carbon, nitrogen is also introduced into the surface layer. To produce hard, wear-resistant surfaces, carburized and carbonitrided components are normally quench hardened. Carburizing and carbonitriding are two of the several case (or surface) hardening processes of steels. Other surface (case) hardening processes are covered in subsequent chapters.

2 THEORY OF CARBURIZING

2.1 SURFACE CARBON CONTENT

When a low-carbon steel is brought into contact with an environment of high carbon activity at high temperatures in the austenite range, carbon is absorbed at the surface of steel. The surface carbon content of steel, in solution in austenite, increases till carbon activity at the surface equals the activity of carbon in the surrounding environment. However, if carbon activity of the environment is higher than the solubility limit of carbon in austenite at the carburizing temperature, then, the maximum surface carbon content is limited to the solubility limit of carbon in austenite. In Fe-C alloys, solubility limit of carbon in austenite is given by A_{cm} line in the Fe-C phase diagram, as shown in Fig. 11.1. Figure 11.1 also gives the carbon solubility limits in austenite of some other carburizing grade low alloy steels. Solubility limit of carbon in austenite increases with increasing temperature.

Hardness of martensite increases with increasing carbon content upto ~0.8% carbon. Beyond that, hardness of martensite does not increase, whereas upon quenching, retained austenite keeps increasing with increasing carbon content. Retained austenite is generally undesirable as it leads to lower hardness values and dimensional and microstructural instabilities. Therefore, the desired surface carbon content during carburizing is generally lower than the solubility limit of carbon in austenite at carburizing temperatures.

To summarize, the maximum surface carbon content during carburizing is limited by carbon activity of the environment, or, the solubility limit of carbon in austenite at carburizing temperature, whichever is lower.

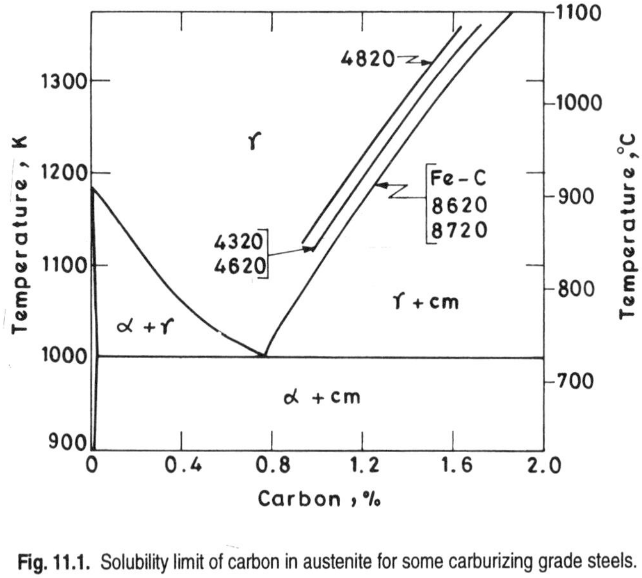

Fig. 11.1. Solubility limit of carbon in austenite for some carburizing grade steels.

2.2 MECHANISM OF CARBURIZING

In carburizing, a low carbon steel is brought into contact with an atmosphere of high carbon potential (activity) in the austenite stability range. The development of carbon rich surface layer during carburizing can be divided into two steps: (*i*) absorption of carbon at the surface, and (*ii*) diffusion of carbon from the surface to interior. Driving force for the absorption of carbon at the surface is the difference in carbon potential (activity) between carburizing atmosphere and the steel surface. With the absorption of carbon at the surface, a concentration gradient is set up between the surface and interior, and carbon diffuses inwards. In the initial stages, carbon potential difference between carburizing atmosphere and the steel surface is large, and hence, the rate of carbon absorption at the surface is high. As carbon concentration at the surface builds up, the rate of carbon absorption diminishes due to decreasing difference in carbon potential between the atmosphere and the surface. On the other hand, driving force for carbon diffusion to the interior increases with increase in carbon concentration at the surface. Carbon diffusion would occur at a maximum rate when surface carbon concentration builds up to the maximum possible level. In most carburizing processes, the maximum possible surface carbon content, determined by carbon activity of the atmosphere, or, the solubility limit of carbon in austenite; is attained in a relatively short time and is maintained at this value from then onwards. Depth of carburizing is, then, essentially controlled by the rate of carbon diffusion from the surface to interior.

2.3 CASE DEPTH

Depth of carburizing as a function of time can be easily estimated by assuming carbon diffusion control and making some simplifying assumptions. It is assumed that:

(*i*) surface carbon concentration reaches the maximum possible value, C_1, instantly, and is maintained at this value for the duration of carburizing;

(*ii*) carbon concentration far away from the surface is equal to the original carbon concentration of steel, C_o; and

(*iii*) the surface of steel is essentially flat and one-dimensional diffusion of carbon occurs from the surface to interior.

If, it is further assumed that at any time, t, greater than zero, the carbon concentration varies linearly from C_1 at the surface ($x = 0$), to C_o at distance x from the surface to which carbon has penetrated (see Fig. 11.2), then, the carbon diffusion flux, J, from the surface to interior is given by:

$$J = -D_C \left[\frac{dC}{dx}\right]_{x=0} = D_C \left[\frac{C_1 - C_o}{x}\right] \tag{11.1}$$

where D_C is diffusion coefficient of carbon in austenite; C refers to carbon concentration in austenite; and C_1, C_o and x are as defined above and schematically shown in Fig. 11.2. Now, let the case depth increase from x to $x + dx$ as time increases from t to $t + dt$. For an increase in case depth by dx, from x to $x + dx$, an amount of carbon

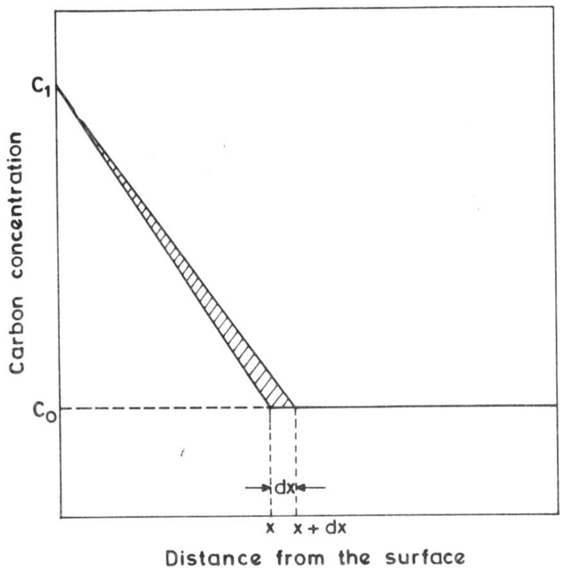

Fig. 11.2. Approximate carbon concentration profile during carburizing.

shown by the shaded area in Fig. 11.2 must be added to steel per unit area of steel surface. This carbon is supplied by diffusion from the surface in time dt, given by Jdt, hence,

$$Jdt = \frac{(C_1 - C_o)\ (x + dx)}{2} - \frac{(C_1 - C_o)\, x}{2} \tag{11.2}$$

where right hand side of Eq. (11.2) gives the shaded area in Fig.11.2. Substituting for J from Eq. (11.1) into Eq. (11.2) and rearranging, we get,

$$x\, dx = 2D_C\, dt$$

which, upon integration, gives:

$$x = 2\sqrt{D_C\, t} \tag{11.3}$$

Eq. (11.3), then, gives the depth of carburizing, x, as a function of carburizing time, t. Eq. (11.3) is an approximate solution to the diffusion problem defined above. A more rigorous solution, using Fick's Second Law of diffusion, gives the following expression for carbon concentration as a function of time and distance:

$$\frac{C_x - C_1}{C_o - C_1} = \text{erf}\,[x/(2\sqrt{D_C\, t})] \tag{11.4}$$

where C_x is carbon concentration at distance x from the surface and other terms are as defined earlier. Figure 11.3 schematically shows carbon concentration as a function of x, at a given time, t, according to Eq. (11.4). Though C_x is exactly equal to C_o only at x equal to infinity, it falls very close to C_o at some finite distance from the surface. If a linear carbon concentration profile is drawn in Fig. 11.3 in a manner

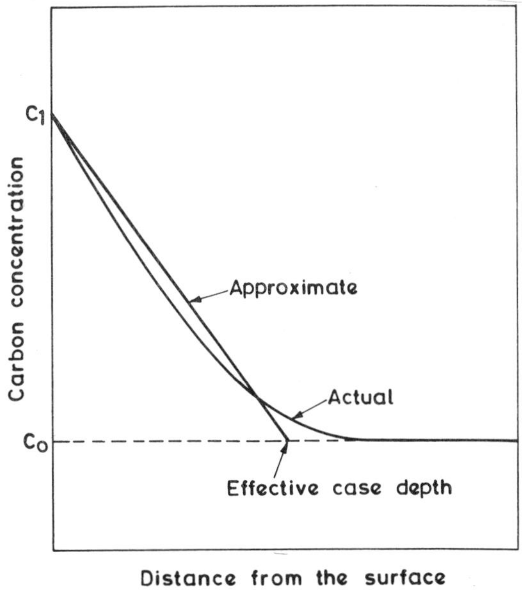

Fig. 11.3. Actual and approximate carbon concentration profiles during carburizing.

such that, the total carbon added to steel in time t is same as given by Eq. (11.4), then, the distance x at which such a straight line would meet the C_o line is given by:

$$x = \frac{4}{\sqrt{\pi}} \sqrt{D_C t} \cong 2.26 \sqrt{D_C t} \tag{11.5}$$

Such a linear distribution is also shown in Fig. 11.3 and is a reasonably good approximation to the actual carbon distribution. Equations (11.3) and (11.5) both give depth of carbon penetration (carburizing) as proportional to square root of $D_C t$, with the constant of proportionality of approximately two. Hence, either of the two equations may be used to estimate the depth of carburizing.

Equation (11.3), or (11.5), gives the depth of carbon penetration during carburizing when the surface of steel is planar and carbon diffuses inwards in a direction perpendicular to the surface. For curved surfaces, these equations are not strictly valid. For relatively simple cases of cylindrical and spherical surfaces, the diffusion problem can be solved easily. These solutions are not discussed here. In most practical carburizing situations, depth of carburizing is much smaller as compared to the radii of curvature of the surfaces involved. Under these conditions, Eq. (11.4), or Eq. (11.5), can be used without incurring much error. Furthermore, in actual practice, cold work load is normally charged into the carburizing furnaces maintained at carburizing temperatures. Time taken for the work load to reach carburizing temperatures can be substantial. Not much carbon penetration occurs during this period, as diffusion coefficient is exponentially dependent upon temperature. Therefore, Eq. (11.3), or Eq. (11.5), is only used as a guide and the actual carburizing time to attain a specific case depth is experimentally determined for given operating conditions. The case depth, d, in general, can be written as:

$$d = \phi \sqrt{t} \tag{11.6}$$

where ϕ is a constant at a given temperature. Figure 11.4 shows ϕ as a function of temperature and can be used as a first approximation in determining the carburizing times.

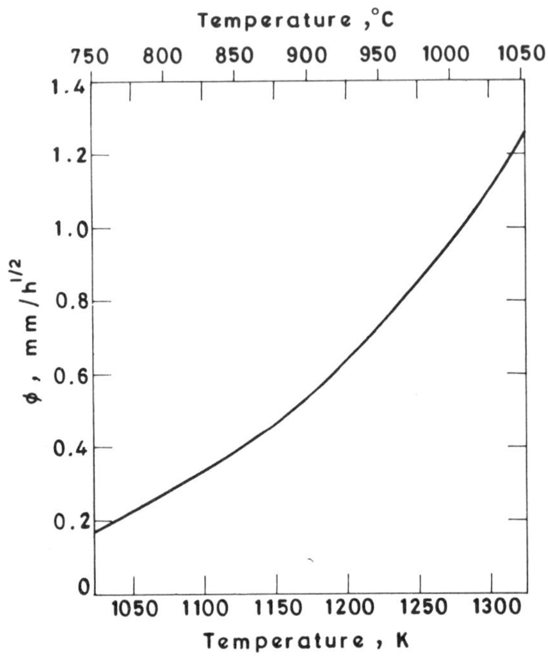

Fig. 11.4. Parameter ϕ in Eq. (11.6) as a function temperature.

3 METHODS OF CARBURIZING

A carburizing process requires the generation of an atmosphere of high carbon activity around the component to be carburized, at carburizing temperatures. Furthermore, the carburizing atmosphere should be able to react at the surface of steel to introduce carbon at a sufficiently rapid rate. If introduction of carbon at the surface is too slow relative to the diffusion of carbon away from the surface, carbon concentration at the surface may not build up to desired levels. In most carburizing processes, absorption of carbon at the surface is rapid enough to attain near maximum possible levels, determined by thermodynamic equilibrium with the environment.

Different methods of carburizing of steels may be divided into three main categories depending upon the nature of carburizing atmosphere, i.e. (*i*) Pack carburizing, (*ii*) Liquid carburizing, and (*iii*) Gas carburizing. In pack carburizing, work pieces are packed in solid carburizing mixture and heated to the carburizing temperature, whereas in liquid and gas carburizing, work pieces are surrounded by liquid and gaseous carburizing atmospheres respectively. Of these methods, gas carburizing is the most versatile in terms of process controls, and is most widely used. However, other methods also have certain advantages in some circumstances and are also often used in practice. Lately some new methods of carburizing have been developed. These include vacuum carburizing, plasma carburizing and fluidized bed carburizing. In vacuum carburizing, the work load is heated in a vacuum furnace to carburizing temperatures and then carburized by introducing small amounts of carburizing gases at low pressures. Plasma carburzing is done in a plasma generated by ionization of carburizing gases at low pressures, whereas in fluidized bed carburizing, the components are heated in fluidized beds in gaseous carburizing atmospheres. Different carburizing methods are discussed in detail in the following sections, emphasizing basic processes occurring during carburizing, carbon control, and their relative advantages and disadvantages.

4 PACK CARBURIZING

4.1 BASIC PROCESS

In pack carburizing, steel components to be carburized are packed in a solid carburizing mixture, containing hardwood charcoal, which acts as a source of carbon; $BaCO_3$, which acts as energizer; and coke, which acts as a filler and also increases thermal conductivity of the mixture. Components are packed in the carburizing mixture in a suitable container, which is then sealed and heated to carburizing temperatures, normally by putting it in a furnace that has been preheated to desired carburizing temperature. Typical composition of a pack carburizing mixture is given in Table 11.1.

Table 11.1. Typical Composition of Pack Carburizing Mixture

Component	Composition (wt%)
Hardwood charcoal	53 – 55
Coke	30 – 32
Barium carbonate	10 – 12
Sodium carbonate	2 – 3
Calcium carbonate	3 – 4

Although charcoal is the basic source of carbon during pack carburizing, transfer of carbon from carburizing mixture to the surface of steel does not occur directly by solid-solid reaction. Air entrapped in the box reacts with carbon to form carbon monoxide, which then reacts at the surface of steel to enrich it with carbon according to the reaction:

$$2CO + (Fe) \longrightarrow C(Fe) + CO_2 \quad (11.7)$$

CO_2, thus produced, further reacts with carbon (charcoal) to form CO again:

$$C + CO_2 \longrightarrow 2CO \quad (11.8)$$

At carburizing temperatures, reaction (11.8) always goes to right. $BaCO_3$ in the carburizing mixture also decomposes at carburizing temperatures to give BaO and CO_2. This ensures enough supply of CO_2 for reaction (11.8), and hence, enough CO for reaction (11.7). It is for this reason that $BaCO_3$ is called energizer.

4.2 SURFACE CARBON CONTENT AND CASE DEPTH

In pack carburizing, surface carbon content given by the solubility limit of carbon in austenite at carburizing temperature is normally obtained (see Fig.11.1). Only means of controlling the surface carbon content is, then, to use appropriate carburizing temperature. Sometimes, surface carbon content lower than the solubility limit of carbon in austenite may be obtained by making some changes in composition of the carburizing mixture, like, lowering the amount of energizer ($BaCO_3$) and/or additions of iron silicide, chromium chloride, etc. However, accurate control of surface carbon concentration is not possible in pack carburizing.

Equation (11.6) may be used as a first approximation to estimate the carburizing times for required case depths. Actual carburizing times are determined by further experimentation. It is generally difficult to control case depths during pack carburizing to close tolerances. This is mainly because of relatively long heating and cooling times involved, which make the accurate control of actual carburizing temperature and time difficult. In pack carburizing, along with the parts to be carburized, carburizing mixture and the container are also heated and cooled during the carburizing cycle. This additional load considerably slows down the heating and cooling processes. In general, it is difficult to control case dpeth to an accuracy better than ± 0.25 mm. Because of this inherent problem, pack carburizing is normally not used for shallow case depths (less than ~1.0 mm).

5 LIQUID CARBURIZING

5.1 CARBURIZING BATHS

In liquid carburizing, work pieces to be carburized are immersed in molten salt baths maintained at carburizing temperatures. These baths contain sodium cyanide as a carburizing agent. Liquid carburizing baths can be divided into two categories: (*i*) Low-temperature baths, and (*ii*) High-temperature baths. They not only differ with respect to temperatures of carburizing, but the compositions of these baths and the mechanisms (chemistry) of carburizing are also different. Table 11.2 gives compositions of these baths. Recently, some non-cyanide liquid carburizing baths have also been developed.

5.2 CHEMISTRY OF CARBURIZING

(*i*) *Low-Temperature Baths*: These are normally operated at 1123–1173K (850–900°C) and are best suited for producing shallow case depths (~0.075 to 0.75 mm). Typical composition of low-temperature carburizing baths is given in Table 11.2.

Table 11.2. Compositions of Liquid Carburizing Baths (in wt %)

Constituent	Low Temperature Baths	High Temperature Baths
Sodium cyanide	10 – 23	6 – 16
Barium chloride	–	30 – 55
Salts of alkaline earths	0 – 10	0 – 10
Potassium chloride	0 – 25	0 – 20
Sodium chloride	20 – 40	0 – 20
Sodium carbonate	40 max.	30 max.
Other accelerators	0 – 5	0 – 2
Sodium cyanate	1.0 max.	0.5 max.
Density:	1760 kg/m^3 (at 1173K)	2000 kg/m^3 (at 1198K)

Chemistry of carburizing in low-temparature baths is rather complex. The main reactions involved are as follows:

$$2NaCN \longrightarrow Na_2CN_2 + C \text{ (``Cynamide shift'')} \tag{11.9}$$

and, either

$$2NaCN + O_2 \longrightarrow 2NaNCO \text{ (Cyanate formation)}$$

or

$$NaCN + CO_2 \longrightarrow NaNCO + CO \text{ (Cyanate formation)} \tag{11.10}$$

The cyanate (NaNCO) thus produced, further reacts to give:

$$NaNCO + C \longrightarrow NaCN + CO \tag{11.11}$$

$$4NaNCO + 2O_2 \longrightarrow 2Na_2CO_3 + 2CO + 4N \tag{11.12}$$

and

$$4NaNCO + 4CO_2 \longrightarrow 2Na_2CO_3 + 6CO + 4N \tag{11.13}$$

CO and C produced by reactions (11.9) to (11.13) react with Fe at the steel surface to enrich it with carbon as,

$$2CO + (Fe) \rightarrow C(Fe) + CO_2 \tag{11.14}$$

and

$$C + (Fe) \rightarrow C(Fe) \tag{11.15}$$

Reactions (11.12) and (11.13) deplete the activity of the bath and lead to an eventual loss of carburization potential, unless suitable replenishment is done.

(*ii*) *High-Temperature Baths*: These are normally operated at 1173–1223K (900–950°C). Typical composition of high-temperature baths is given in Table 11.2. High-temperature baths are used for producing deeper case depths, in the range of 0.5 to 3.0 mm. Apart from cyanide, these baths contain a major amount of barium chloride. Although reactions given above for low-temperature baths occur here also to some degree, the principal reactions in high-temperature baths are:

$$2NaCN + BaCl_2 \longrightarrow Ba(CN)_2 + 2NaCl \tag{11.16}$$

$$Ba(CN)_2 \longrightarrow BaCN_2 + C \tag{11.17}$$

and

$$C + (Fe) \longrightarrow C(Fe) \tag{11.18}$$

Surface carbon content of the case during liquid carburizing can be controlled by controlling the cyanide content of the bath. Low-temperature baths operate at higher cyanide contents than high-temperature baths. Both, the high as well as low temperature baths may be operated with varying cyanide contents, through which the carbon activity of the bath can be controlled to some extent. Table 11.3 gives preferred operating cyanide contents at different temperatures. Lower end of the cyanide content range, at a given temperature, would normally produce a hypo-eutectoid case, whereas, a hyper-eutectoid case is obtained with cyanide content near the upper limit.

Table 11.3. Sodium Cyanide Content in Liquid Carburizing Baths at Different Operating Temperatures

Temperature K (°C)	Sodium cyanide, %		
	Maximum	Preferred	Minimum
1088 (815)	23	18	14
1113 (840)	20	16	12
1143 (870)	18	14	11
1173 (900)	16	12	10
1198 (925)	14	10	8
1228 (955)	12	8	6

Reactions (11.12) and (11.13) show that, there is also nascent nitrogen present in the carburizing baths to some extent. This nitrogen is also absorbed at the surface of steel and diffuses inwards. However, at cyanide concentrations of carburizing baths, nitrogen activity of the bath is relatively low and only very little nitrogen diffuses into the steel. Activity of nitrogen is higher at higher end of the cyanide content range at given temperature.

(iii) Other Liquid Carburizing Baths: Liquid carburizing salt baths, not containing any cyanide, have also been developed for commerical use in some places. Here, a special grade of carbon in the form of small particles is dispersed in molten salt baths by mechanical agitation. The baths are operated in the temperature range 1173–1223K (900–950°C). The chemistry involved is not fully understood.

6 GAS CARBURIZING

6.1 INTRODUCTION

Gas carburizing is most commonly used method of carburizing in industry. In gas carburizing, the parts to be carburized are heated in a furnace, where a gaseous carburizing atmosphere is maintained. The most common carburizing agent used in gas carburizing is methane (CH_4), normally in the form of natural gas. Other gaseous or liquid hydrocarbons may also be used as carburizing agents. Carburizing agent is diluted by a carrier gas before it enters the carburizing furnance. The carrier gas itself is normally made by controlled burning of CH_4 or some other hydrocarbon gas. Most commonly used carrier gas is endothermic base, obtained by controlled burning of CH_4 in air, with air-to-gas ratio of 2:5, to give:

$$2CH_4 + O_2(air) \longrightarrow 2CO + 4H_2 \tag{11.19}$$

Endothermic carrier gas, then, contains the remaining nitrogen from air, CO and H_2 as by products of Eq. (11.19) and small amounts of CO_2 and H_2O, that may form during the production of carrier gas. Composition of the carrier gas is then: 39–40% N_2, 20–21% CO, 38–39% H_2, and small amounts of CH_4, CO_2 and H_2O (all in vol%). Sometimes, commercially pure nitrogen available at cheap rates is also used as a carrier gas. Ratio of hydrocarbon gas (carburizing agent) to carrier gas in a carburizing gas mixture could vary from about 1:8 to 1:30, depending upon the desired surface carbon content, temperature of carburizing, and other considerations.

6.2 CARBURIZING REACTIONS

The specific reactions that occur during gas carburizing would depend on the nature of carburizing gases, i.e. carrier gas and the carburizing agent used. Under most conditions, various reactions occurring in a gaseous atmosphere at carburizing temperatures may be considered to be in thermodynamic equilibrium. In the following, the reactions that occur when CH_4 is used as a carburizing agent with endothermic carrier gas, discussed above, are given in some detail. Reactions occurring in other carburizing atmospheres can be easily inferred from the nature of gases present. The main carburizing reactions occurring during gas carburizing with CH_4 and endothermic carrier gas mixtures are:

$$(Fe) + 2CO \longrightarrow C(Fe) + CO_2 \tag{11.20}$$

$$(Fe) + CH_4 \longrightarrow C(Fe) + 2H_2 \tag{11.21}$$

$$(Fe) + CO + H_2 \longrightarrow C(Fe) + H_2O \tag{11.22}$$

As CO_2 and H_2O in the atmosphere [reactions (11.20) and (11.22)] increase, carbon potential of the atmosphere falls. CO_2 and H_2O are both decarburizing agents. To counteract this, CH_4 in the carburizing gas mixture reacts with CO_2 and H_2O to give:

$$CH_4 + CO_2 \longrightarrow 2CO + 2H_2 \tag{11.23}$$

and

$$CH_4 + H_2O \longrightarrow CO + 3H_2 \tag{11.24}$$

and CO and H_2 in the atmosphere increase again. CO and H_2 produced by reactions (11.23) and (11.24) again react at the surface of steel to give surface carbon enrichment via reactions (11.20) and (11.22). Hence, CH_4 is the ultimate source of carbon during gas carburizing.

6.3 CARBON POTENTIAL OF THE ATMOSPHERE

During gas carburizing, all gases present in the furnace atmosphere may be considered to be in thermodynamic equilibrium. Now, consider the following reaction:

$$CO_2 + C(Fe) \Longleftrightarrow 2CO \tag{11.25}$$

where, C(Fe) is carbon dissolved at the surface of steel. The equilibrium constant, K_1, for reaction (11.25) is given by:

$$K_1 = \frac{p_{CO}^2}{a_C \, p_{CO_2}} \tag{11.26}$$

where, a_C is activity of carbon at the surface of steel with respect to pure graphite; and p_{CO} and p_{CO_2} are partial pressures of CO and CO_2 respectively, in the gas atmosphere. The equilibrium constant, K_1, is a function of temperature only and is given by:

$$K_1 = \exp\left(-\frac{\Delta G^o}{RT}\right) \tag{11.27}$$

where, ΔG^o is standard Gibbs energy for reaction (11.25); and R and T are gas constant and temperature respectively. From thermodynamic data, K_1 is given as:

$$\log K_1 = -\frac{8918}{T} + 9.1148 \tag{11.28}$$

Now, carbon activity, a_C, at the steel surface in equilibrium with the gaseous atmosphere, from Eq. (11.26), can be written as:

$$a_C = \frac{p_{CO}^2}{K_1 \, p_{CO_2}} \tag{11.29}$$

Hence, at a given temperature of carburizing, if p_{CO} and p_{CO_2} in the gaseous atmosphere are known, carbon potential (activity) of the atmosphere, a_C, can be calculated using Eqs. (11.28) and (11.29).

6.4 MEASUREMENT OF CARBON POTENTIAL

Equation (11.29) forms the basis of different methods of measuring the carbon potential of gaseous atmospheres. These method are briefly mentioned below.

(*i*) *CO_2 Partial Pressure Measurements*: To obtain carbon potential of a gaseous carburizing atmosphere from Eq. (11.29), both p_{CO_2} and p_{CO} must be known. However, endothermic carrier gas-based carburizing atmospheres normally contain about 20-22% CO, whereas CO_2 content is in the range of 0-2%. Therefore, small variations in the partial pressure of CO_2 would affect the carbon potential of the atmosphere much more than small variations in p_{CO}. Hence, measurement of CO_2 content of the atmosphere is normally sufficient to estimate the carbon potential of such carburizing atmosphere. For a given carburizing atmosphere, $p_{CO} + p_{CO_2}$ is first estimated, and then, any measurement, or control, of carbon potential is carried out by measuring CO_2 content of the atmosphere. CO_2 content in gaseous atmospheres is easily measured by infrared spectroscopy.

Figure 11.5 shows carbon potential of gaseous atmospheres as a function of CO_2 content and temperature, when (%CO + %CO_2) = 20; and Fig. 11.6 gives carbon potential of gaseous atmospheres as a function of CO_2 and CO contents of the atmosphere at different temperatures. In Figs. 11.5 and 11.6, carbon potential is

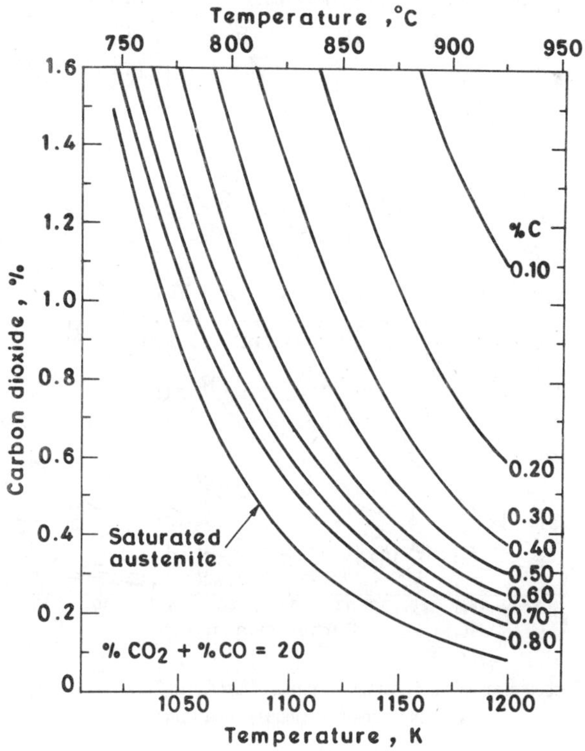

Fig. 11.5. Carbon potential (as % carbon in iron) as a function of temperature and $\%CO_2$ in gaseous atmosphere, when $\%CO + \%CO_2 = 20$.

expressed in terms of carbon in solution in pure iron in equilibrium with the atmosphere.

(*ii*) *Dew Point Measurements*: Another method of measuring carbon potential of a gaseous atmosphere is to measure dew point of the atmosphere. Carburizing gases also contains H_2 and H_2O; and a definite relationship exists between p_{H_2}/p_{H_2O} and p_{CO}/p_{CO_2} ratios. Consider the following reaction (also known as water-gas reaction):

$$CO + H_2O \Longleftrightarrow CO_2 + H_2 \tag{11.30}$$

The equilibrium constant, K_2, for this reaction is given by:

$$\log K_2 = \log\left[\frac{p_{CO_2}\, p_{H_2}}{p_{H_2O}\, p_{CO}}\right] = \frac{1901}{T} - 1.672 \tag{11.31}$$

Hence, the ratios of partial pressı res of CO to CO_2 and H_2 to H_2O in the gaseous atmosphere are related via Eq. (11 31).

Dew point measurements give % H_2O content of the atmosphere, as shown in Fig. 11.7. As H_2 in the furnance atmosphere is approximately constant (~**40% for en-**

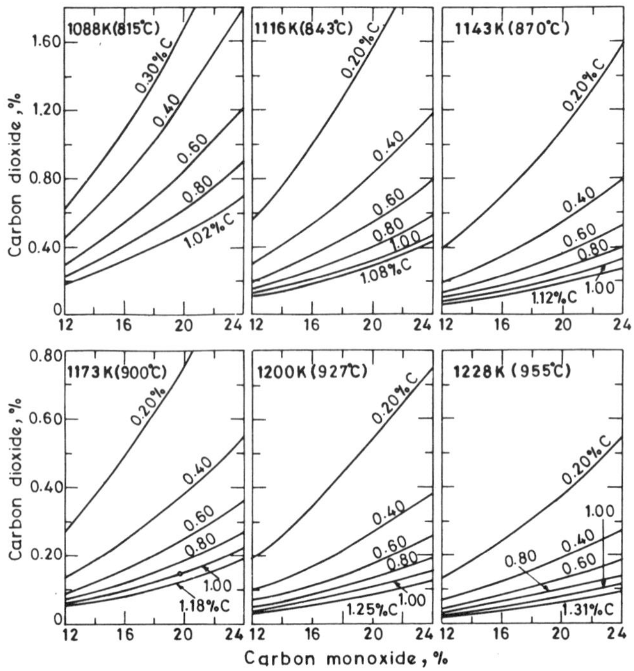

Fig. 11.6. Carbon potential (as % carbon in iron) as a function of CO and CO_2 contents of gaseous atmosphere at various temperatures.

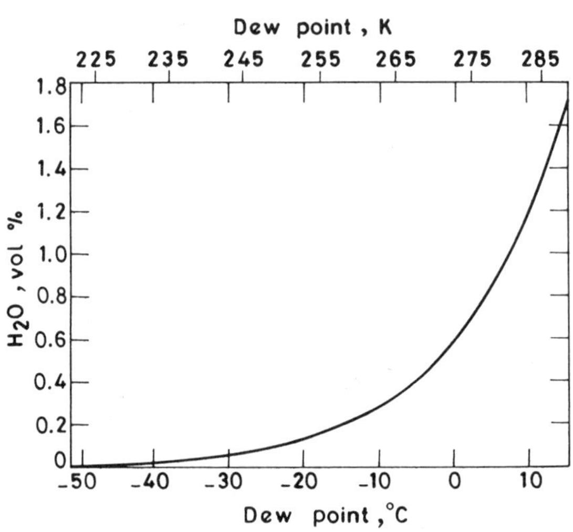

Fig. 11.7. Dew point as a function of $\%H_2O$ in the gaseous atmosphere.

dothermic carrier gas discussed in the previous section), p_{H_2O}/p_{H_2} ratio can be easily estimated, if partial pressure of H_2O is known. The p_{H_2O}/p_{H_2} ratio is related to the p_{CO}/p_{CO_2} ratio by Eq. (11.31). Therefore, from dew point measurements, carbon potential of the atmosphere can be easily determined from Eq. (11.29), when (%H_2 + %H_2O) and (%CO+%CO_2) are known. Figure 11.8 shows the relation between dew point and carbon potential for a given carrier gas as a function of temperature.

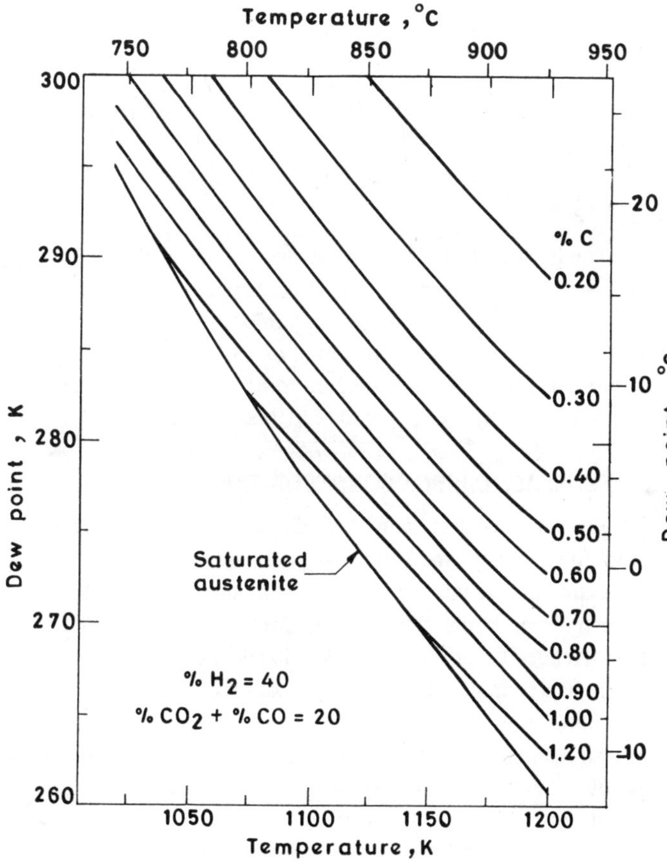

Fig. 11.8. Carbon potential (as % carbon in iron) as a function of dew point of the atmosphere and temperature.

(iii) Oxygen Probe: Carbon potential of a gaseous atmosphere can also be calculated from partial pressure of oxygen in the atmosphere. Consider the following equilibrium reactions:

$$CO + \frac{1}{2} O_2 \rightleftarrows CO_2 ; \qquad K_3 = \frac{p_{CO_2}}{p_{CO}\, p_{O_2}^{1/2}} \tag{11.32}$$

and

$$H_2 + \frac{1}{2} O_2 \rightleftarrows H_2 ; \qquad K_4 = \frac{p_{H_2O}}{p_{H_2}\, p_{O_2}^{1/2}} \tag{11.33}$$

Values of the equilibrium constants K_3 and K_4 for reactions (11.32) and (11.33) are given as:

$$\log K_3 = \frac{14752}{T} - 4.5347 \tag{11.34}$$

and

$$\log K_4 = \frac{12850}{T} - 2.8626 \tag{11.35}$$

Hence, from the partial pressure of oxygen in the carburizing gaseous atmosphere, p_{CO}/p_{CO_2} or p_{H_2}/p_{H_2O} ratio in the atmosphere can be calculated, and then, carbon potential is arrived at, as discussed earlier. Solid electrolyte oxygen probe is normally used for p_{O_2} measurements.

(*iv*) *Hot Wire Test*: Hot wire test is a direct measurement of the carbon potential of an atmosphere. A thin wire of pure iron is carburized in the given carburizing atmosphere for sufficiently long time to obtain homogeneous carburization. Carbon analysis of the wire then gives carbon potential of the atmosphere. This method is also suitable for measuring carbon potential of liquid carburizing baths. Continuous monitoring of carbon potential is not possible by hot wire test.

6.5 CONTROL OF SURFACE CARBON CONCENTRATION

During gas carburizing, carbon potential of the furnace atmosphere can be continuously monitored by various methods, discussed above. Carbon potential during gas carburizing can then be controlled by regulating the flow of carburizing agents, i.e. CH_4 or other hydrocarbons. This can be done manually or by an automated feedback system. Hence, the activity of carbon that is obtained at the surface of steel during carburizing can be controlled. To obtain desired surface carbon concentration during gas carburizing of a steel of given composition, relationship between carbon concentration and carbon activity as a function of composition and temperature must be known. Activity of carbon in austenite varies not only with carbon concentration and temperature, but also with the concentration of other alloying elements present in the steel.

Activity of carbon, a_C, in austenite containing a number of alloying elements can be written as:

$$a_C = \psi_C Z_C \tag{11.36}$$

where

$$\ln \psi_C = \ln \psi_C^o + \theta_C^C Y_C + \sum_{j=1}^{n} \theta_C^j Y_j \tag{11.37}$$

with

$$Y_C = \frac{X_C}{1 - X_C}, \quad Y_j = \frac{X_j}{1 - X_C}, \quad \text{and } Z_C = \frac{Y_C}{1 - Y_C}$$

where C stands for carbon and $j = 1, 2, ..., n$, for other alloying elements; X_C and X_j are mole fractions of carbon and alloying element j in austenite, respectively; and

ψ_C^o, θ_C^C and θ_C^j are thermodynamic constants, independent of composition. ln ψ_C^o in Eq. (11.37) is given by:

$$\ln \psi_C^o = \frac{5297}{T} - 2.12 \tag{11.38}$$

and θ_C^C, and θ_C^j for some common alloying elements are given in Table 11.4.

Table 11.4. θ_C^j for Some Common Alloying Elements in Austenite

j	θ_C^j
C	$8890/T$
Ni	$4606/T + 0.69$
Mn	$-5070/T$
Cr	$-21879/T + 7.02$
Mo	$-21879/T + 5.76$

From the data given above, activity of carbon in austenite at carburizing temperature may be calculated for desired surface carbon concentration, and then used for controlling the carbon potential of the carburizing atmosphere, as discussed in the previous section.

6.6 TWO-STEP GAS CARBURIZING PROCESS

When carburizing is done under constant carbon potential of the atmosphere for a given length of time, a characteristic carbon concentration profile as shown in Fig. 11.9(a) is obtained. Carbon concentration drops continuously from the surface to

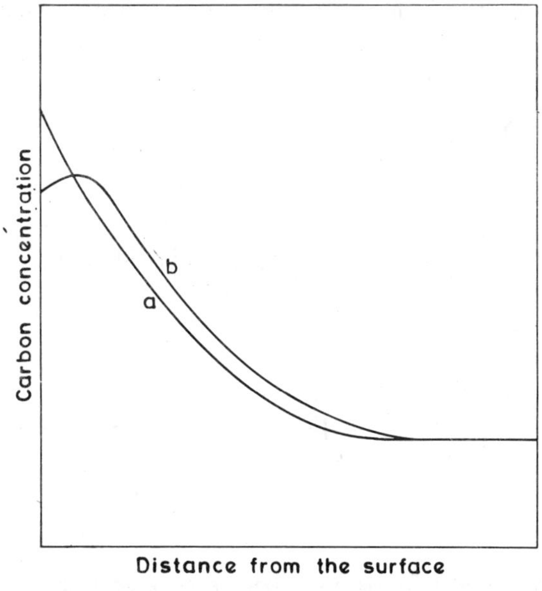

Fig. 11.9. Carbon concentration profiles during two-stage carburizing process (a) after carburizing stage (b) after diffusion stage.

interior. For some applications it may be more desirable to have a relatively uniform carbon concentration, and hence hardness, up to cartain depth from the surface. This can be easily achieved in gas carburizing by two-stage carburizing process. In the first stage, called carburizing stage, work piece is carburized for a certain length of time in an atmosphere of higher carbon potential than dictated by the required surface carbon content. Then, in the second stage, called diffusion stage, carbon potential of the atmosphere is lowered to the desired level and the process is continued for some more time. During carburizing stage, normal carbon concentration gradient, as shown in Fig. 11.9(a), is obtained. Then, during the diffusion stage, carbon close to the surface diffuses back into the atmosphere, due to lowered surface carbon concentration, whereas inwards diffusion of carbon continues further below the surface. This modifies the carbon concentration gradient up to certain depth below the surface, as shown in Fig. 11.9(b). The two-step process can be carried out either in a batch furnace, by lowering the carbon potential of the atmosphere after the carburizing period, or, in a single continuous furnace, where different carbon potentials are maintained in different zones. Relative durations of the two stages can be estimated by diffusion analysis, or determined experimentally.

6.7 FLUIDIZED BED CARBURIZING

Fluidized bed carburizing is a gas carburizing process, in which gas used for fluidization is also the source of carbon (or in the case of carbonitriding, of carbon and nitrogren). Figure 11.10 shows the flow chart of a fluidized bed carburization process in which nitrogen/methanol atmosphere with hydrocarbon additions has been used for carburization. Components to be carburized are kept in the bed retort, which also contains fine alumina powder used for fluidization. Liquid methanol is vaporized, and mixed with nitrogen and enrichment gases in bottom chamber of the bed. In the furnance retort, number of reactions occur. Main reactions are as follows. The methanol cracks according to:

$$CH_3OH \longrightarrow 2H_2 + CO \qquad (11.39)$$

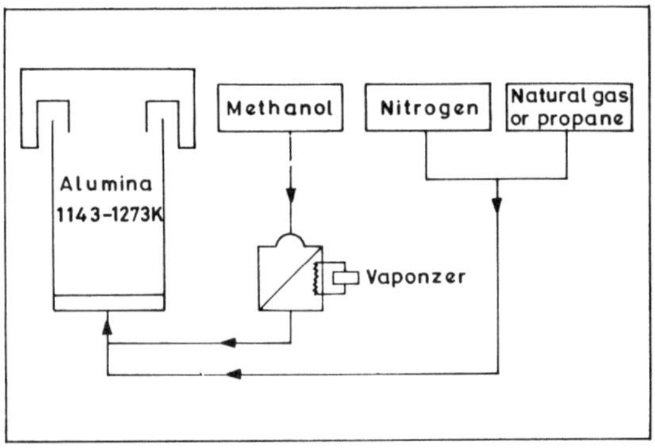

Fig. 10.10. Schematic illustration of a fluidized bed carburizing set-up with nitrogen/methanol atmosphere. [from Ref. 3].

and carburization takes place according to:

$$2CO + (Fe) \Longleftrightarrow C(Fe) + CO_2 \qquad (11.40)$$

Carbon potential is controlled via hydrocarbon (say CH_4) addition:

$$CH_4 + CO_2 \Longleftrightarrow 2CO + 2H_2 \qquad (11.41)$$

All these reactions apply equally to conventional gas carburizing, carried out in the same atmosphere. However, with normal fluidization velocities, the average residence time of gases in the retort is only about 15-20 seconds. Nonetheless, it has been shown that near equilibrium conditions do exist in the fluidized bed. It is possible that, due to large surface area of alumina powder in the retort, equilibrium is attained more efficiently. Hence, carbon potential during fluidized bed carburizing may be controlled in the same manner as in conventional gas carburizing. Other gas carburizing atmospheres, like, natural-gas/air, propane/air or endothermic carrier gas (discussed earlier), may equally be used in fluidized bed carburizing. The two-step carburization process, consisting of carburizing period and diffusion period, can be carried in fluidized beds as well. Fluidized bed carburizing has the following advantages over conventional gas carburizing:

(*a*) Heat transfer in fluidized bed furnances is much faster.

(*b*) Carbon potential in the bed reaches its final value within few minutes and can be altered quickly.

(*c*) Due to high gas flows, necessary for fluidization, variations in surface area of the charge has no measurable effect on carbon pickup.

(*d*) Carburization process is not impaired even if soot precipitation occurs from the atmosphere. Soot is continuously removed by the high velocity gases. Hence, it is possible to have maximum possible surface carbon content during the carburization period in a two-step process. Soot precipitation is the precipitation of solid carbon from gaseous atmosphere, when activity of carbon in the atmosphere exceeds unity.

(*e*) Since the furnance retort is gas tight, it is possible to have inert treatment with pure nitrogen without decarburization. For example, during diffusion period in the two-step process, only pure nitrogen may be passed to lower the surface carbon content and to moderate the carbon concentration gradients close to the surface.

7 VACUUM CARBURIZING

7.1 BASIC PROCESS

Vacuum carburizing refers to carburizing of steel components in vacuum furnances with the introduction of controlled amounts of carburizing gaseous mixtures, usually a mixture of nitrogen and a hydrocarbon gas (normally CH_4 or C_2H_8), at relatively low pressures. Heating steel components in vacuum furnaces provides excellent oxidation and decarburization resistance. A vacuum furnace may be back filled with a carburizing gas mixture after the load has been heated to desired carburizing temperature, usually 1173-1323K (900–1050°C). Vacuum furnaces are specifically suited for high temperature carburizing (also see sec. 9). Carburizing gas mixtures containing oxygen compounds are generally not used in vacuum carburizing, as CO and H_2O react with the traditional vacuum furnace materials, such as graphite and molybdenum. Hydrocarbons present in the back filled carburizing gas mixtures crack at the surface of steel and provide carbon to the steel surface, i.e.:

$$CH_4 \longrightarrow 2H_2 + C(Fe) \qquad (11.42)$$

or

$$C_2H_8 \longrightarrow 4H_2 + 2C(Fe) \qquad (11.43)$$

Carbon produced by these cracking reactions is highly reactive and is easily absorbed at the surface of steel. As a result of cracking of the hydrocarbons, the gas mixture in the furnace consists of N_2, CH_4 (or C_2H_8) and H_2. Such an atmosphere has a tendency to produce soot.

Carbon pickup during vacuum caburizing depends on the initial partial pressure of hydrocarbons in the back filled gases and the temperature and time of carburizing. Figure 11.11 shows typical carbon pickup during vacuum carburizing in ($N_2 + CH_4$) atmospheres at various partial pressures of CH_4 and carburizing times, at 1313K (1040°C).

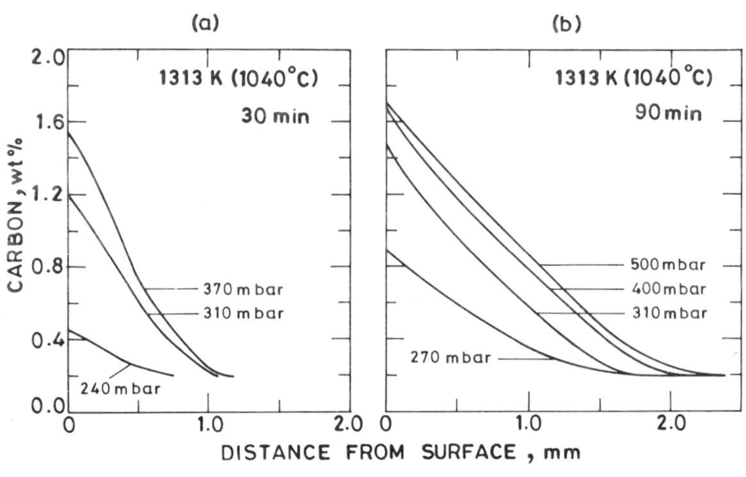

Fig. 11.11. Carbon pickup during vaccum carburizing at 1313K (1040°C) in $N_2 + CH_4$ atmosphere at various partial pressures of CH_4, total pressure 610 mbar [from Ref. 4].

7.2 CONTROL OF CARBON SUPPLY AND CASE DEPTH

With no chemical equilibrium available as a control parameter, the carburizing process during vacuum carburizing is controlled by controlling the process variables, i.e. the partial pressure of hydrocarbon gas in the back filled gas mixture, and the temperature and time of carburizing. Shallow cases, that are formed in less than 20 to 30 min., can be obtained by time control only, i.e. fixed amount of hydrocarbon gas is introduced and carburization is carried out for a predetermined time. For deeper cases and to allow for more accurate surface carbon control, a two-step process, consisting of a boost period and a diffusion period is used. During the boost period, sufficient hydrocarbon gas is introduced to obtain saturated carbon levels without undue sooting of the furnace or components. Subsequently, the furnace is evacuated of all gases and diffusion is allowed to occur. Under vacuum heating, during the diffusion period, decarburization at the surface does not occur. The existing carbon is redistributed, lowering the surface carbon and increasing the depth of carburizing. Figure 11.12 shows typical results obtained by a two-step process. The relative durations of boost and diffusion steps depend on the desired surface carbon content and depth of carburizing, and are empirically determined.

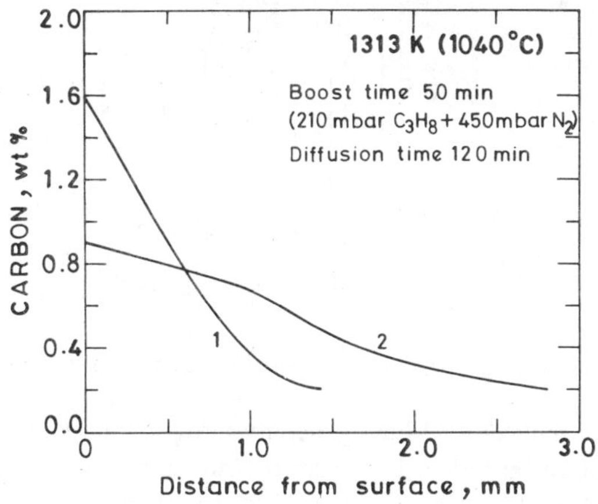

Fig. 11.12. Carbon concentration profiles after (1) boost stage, and (2) diffusion stage, in a two-step vacuum carburizing of AISI-1022 steel at 1313K (1040°C) [from Ref. 4].

Reproducibility of the two-step boost-diffusion method during vacuum carburizing depends on the carbon supply during the boost period. The other two parameters, time and temperature can be easily and accurately controlled. Carbon supply is most easily controlled when sufficient hydrocarbon gas is used to maintain the surface carbon content close to saturation level of carbon in austenite. However, excess partial pressure of the carburizing gas may give rise to soot formation, which is undesirable. Recently, a soot sensor has been developed to control the supply of hydrocarbon gases during vacuum carburizing. This allows for accurate carbon control, without undue sooting of the furnace parts or the components.

8 PLASMA (ION) CARBURIZING

Plasma (ion) carburizing, also known as "glow discharge" carburizing, is a method of carburizing where partial heating of the parts and their carburization is carried out in a plasma of low-pressure ionized gases. The workpiece to be carburized is made cathode of the glow discharge, with a suitable d.c. voltage impressed between the cathode and the anode. An atmosphere of a hydrocarbon gas, say methane (CH_4), at a proper pressure is provided as a conducting atmosphere to support a stable glow as well as to act as a carburizing agent. Figure 11.13 schematically shows a plasma carburization chamber. The chamber is evacuated and then back filled with a

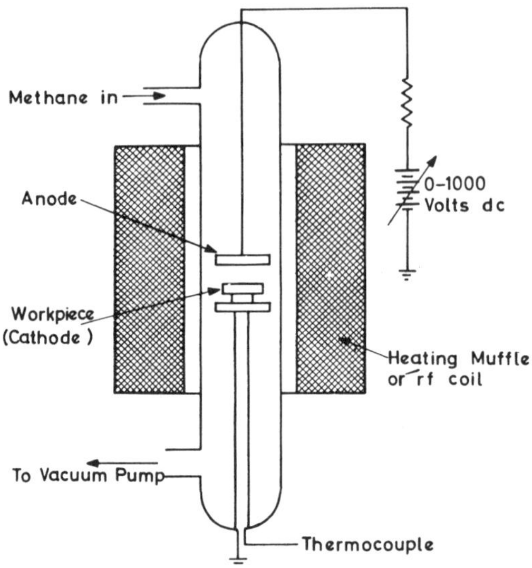

Fig. 11.13. Schematic illustration of a plasma carburizing set-up [from Ref. 5].

hydrocarbon gas at reduced pressure, generally in the range of 0.1 to 2.7 kPa. A continuous flow of gas at reduced pressure is maintained during the carburization (boost) cycle. Figure 11.14 shows glow discharge voltage-current characteristic curve. While, 500 to 1000 volts may be required to strike the plasma, depending upon the pressure of gases in the chamber; once initiated, approx. 400 volts will

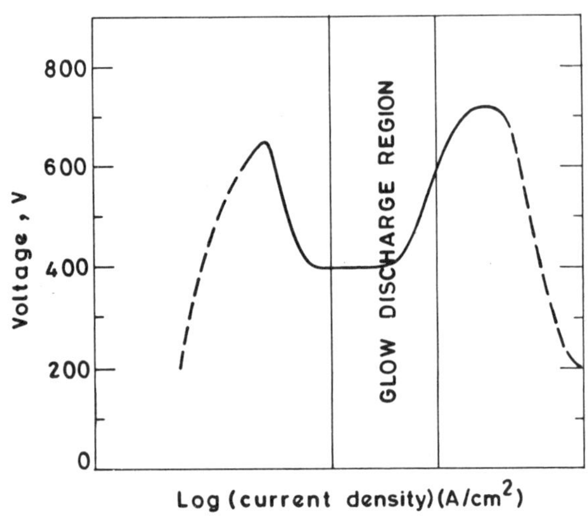

Fig. 11.14. Glow discharge voltage-current characteristic curve.

sustain the plasma in a methane atmosphere of ~2.7 kPa. Under these conditions, a "tight" thin plasma completely envelops the workpiece and closely follows its contours, even if the surface is quite irregular. It is within this thin plasma envelop that methane is dissociated and a high carbon potential is established at the workpiece surface, even though the total pressure in the furnace is relatively low.

The plasma consists of ionized gases and electrons. Positively charged ions of the type CH_i^{+n} (i = 0 to 3) accelerate towards the cathode (workpiece) and introduce carbon at the surface, whereas electrons accelerate to the anode. In the process, both cathode and anode also get heated. However, unlike in plasma nitriding (discussed in the next chapter), heating of the workpiece by plasma is insufficient to heat it to the carburizing temperatures of 1223–1323K (950–1050°C). Thus an auxilliary induction or radiation heating source (see Fig. 11.13) is used to keep the workpiece at appropriate carburizing temperature.

In plasma carburizing, high rates of carburization, as compared to vacuum or conventional gas carburization, are normally obtained. Within the glow discharge plasma, the electron temperature may be of the order of 100 times that of average gaseous molecules, and therefore, some chemical reactions may occur, which would not occur under normal thermodynamic equilibrium. These electrons help to break chemical bonds and thereby dissociate methane to provide necessary carbon at the surface. Hydrogen generated by dissociation of CH_4 and ion bombardment of the surface may also dissociate surface oxides, and thus remove potential barrier to quick introduction of carbon at the surface. These factors accelerate uniform introduction of carbon and the attainment of saturation level of carbon at the surface. Plasma carburizing, like vacuum carburizing, is normally carried out in two steps. In the first step, carbon is introduced at the surface by methane plasma and the second step is carried out by further heating the workpiece in vacuum to decrease surface carbon to the desired level and to increase the case depth by diffusional processes. As the

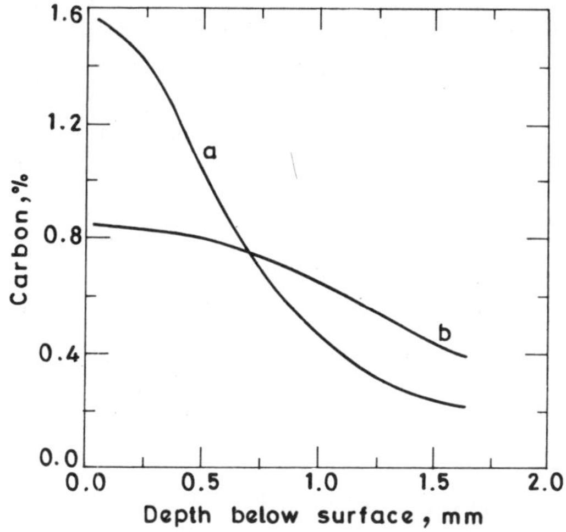

Fig. 11.15. Carbon concentration profiles in AISI-1018 steel, plasma carburized at 1323K (1050°C), (a) after plasma carburizing for 10 min., (b) after additional diffusion period of 30 min. [from Ref.5].

second step is carried out in vacuum, no decarburization at the surface occurs, only redistribution of carbon by diffusion takes place. Figure 11.15 shows carbon profiles obtained in AISI-1018 steel on plasma carburizing for 10 min. at 1323K (1050°C), followed by a diffusion period of 30 min. at the same temperature. Like vacuum carburizing, consumption of gases in plasma carburizing is much less as compared to conventional gas carburizing. Furthermore, since thin plasma envelops the workpiece surface, closely following its contours, very uniform case depths are obtained in plasma carburizing.

Another advantage of plasma carburizing, over vacuum carburizing, is the much reduced possibility of soot formation. Since methane present in the chamber is dissociated principally within the plasma, close to the workpiece surface, high carbon potential exists only in this region. In other regions, outside the inter-electrode space, carbon potential is simultaneously very low. Thus, the tendency to form free carbon (soot) in areas remote from the workpiece is greatly diminished.

9 HIGH-TEMPERATURE CARBURIZING

In conventional carburizing processes i.e. pack, liquid, and gas carburizing, carburizing is normally done in the temperature range 1073–1223K (800–950°C). Temperature of carburizing is partly restricted due to the fact that, with increasing temperature the furnace life sharply decreases. However, furnace materials are now available which can stand higher temperatures, to make high temperature carburizing economical. Vacuum and plasma carburizing are specifically suited for high temperature carburization. The time required to achieve a specific case depth decreases sharply with increasing temperature [see Eq. (11.6) and Fig. 11.4], as diffusion coefficient of carbon increases exponentially with temperature. Hence, considerable savings in cost and time may be achieved by high temperature carburizing, in the range of 1273–1323K (1000–1050°C).

However, before deciding on high temperature carburizing, the suitability of a particular steel for high temperature carburizing must be ascertained. There exists a possibility of substantial grain growth occurring at higher temperatures, which may adversely affect impact properties of the components. Different steels respond differently to grain growth at higher temperatures, and this must be experimentally ascertained for a given steel for the desired carburizing temperature and time. In general, more grain growth is likely to occur in a plain carbon steel than in an alloy steel. The grain growth problem may be partly corrected by reheating and quenching, rather than direct quenching of components, during subsequent heat treatment (see Sec. 12).

10 SELECTIVE CARBURIZING

Some components, because of their intended use, must be selectively carburized, i.e. carburized only on certain surfaces. During carburizing of such components, the surfaces that are not to be carburized must be suitably protected.

The most common method to protect or "stop off" selected surface regions from carburizing atmosphere is to plate copper on these regions. During the plating of copper, to prevent deposition of copper on other regions, they are coated with high temperature microcrystalline wax or chemically resistant lacquer, which is removed before carburizing. Copper plating is relatively easy to apply and to machine or remove after carburizing. Copper is also a good conductor of heat. After carburizing, copper may be removed in a chromic acid bath, or other suitable stripping solution. Copper plating may also be removed by subsequent machining or grinding operations.

Sometimes ceramic coatings or paints are used to protect surfaces from carburizing. The primary requirement for these coatings is that, they must be impervious and stick to the workpiece during carburizing at high temperatures, and handling of workpieces. Also, they should be such as could easily be stripped off after carburizing.

The most positive method of ensuring that a specific area is free of carburization, is to design the component is such a manner that the carburized layer from this area can be machined off after carburization. Machining to remove the carburized layer is done before the subsequent hardening operation.

11 HOMOGENEOUS CARBURIZATION

In homogeneous carburization, a component is carburized to a given carbon level uniformly throughout its cross-section. Homogeneous carburization is economically feasible only for parts with small cross-sections, ~5 mm or less. The process offers the advantage of making the components from easily formable low-carbon steels, and then, carburizing them uniformly to a desired carbon level to attain higher strength. For homogeneous carburization, sufficient time must be given to obtain uniform carbon concentration throughout the component. Carburization time should be greater than $\sim(5x^2/D_C)$, where, x is maximum cross-sectional thickness of the component and D_C is diffusion coefficient of carbon in austenite at the carburizing temperature.

12 HEAT TREATMENT OF CARBURIZED PARTS

12.1 QUENCH HARDENING

After carburizing, carburized components are normally quenched from the austenite temperature range to obtain maximum hardness at the surface. A carburized component may either be quenched directly from carburizing temperature, or, reheated (after slow cooling) to appropriate austenitizing temperature and quenched. Mildest possible quench, consistent with desired hardening, is normally used to minimize the possibility of quenching cracks and distortion of the components during quenching. Whenever possible, direct quenching from carburizing temperature is done to minimize operational time and costs. After pack carburizing, direct quenching is not possible, and hence, the components have to be reheated for quench hardening.

12.2 REHEATING AND QUENCHING

Sometimes, even the parts carburized by gas and liquid carburizing are slow cooled to room temperature, and then, reheated for quench hardening. This may be done for one or more of the following reasons:

(*i*) Some carburized components may require some machining before the hardening operation. In such cases, parts are slowly cooled and machined in the soft state, before quench hardening.

(*ii*) When grain coarsening has occurred during carburizing, it is desirable to reheat the components for quench hardening to refine the grain size to some extent.

(*iii*) Surface carbon concentration of pack carburized components is normally at saturation level, and that may be higher than the desired value. Liquid carburized components may also at times have higher surface carbon content than desired. Such components, when quenched directly, would have relatively higher retained austenite levels, and consequently lower hardness values, near the surface, as shown in Fig. 11.16. Furthermore, high retained austenite levels near the surface lead to problems during the grinding of these components. It may be recalled that retained austenite increases with increasing carbon content. Generally, the retained austenite should be less than ~15%. When carburized components are reheated for hardening, carbon gradient near the surface gets somewhat moderated by carbon

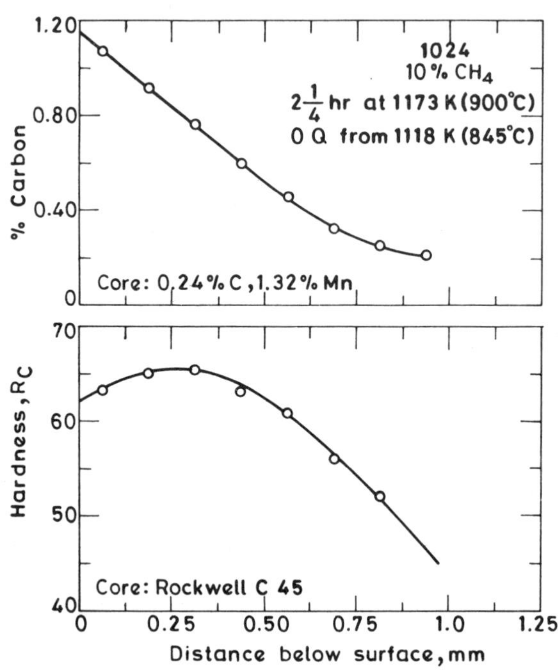

Fig. 11.16. Carbon and hardness profiles in AISI-1024 steel, carburized to high surface carbon content.

diffusion and the surface carbon concentration is somewhat reduced, leading to reduced retained austenite.

12.3 COLD TREATMENT

At times, the carburized components are given cold treatment after quenching. This is done by cooling the quenched components further below room temperature, either in ice, or dry ice, depending on the requirements. The purpose of cold treatment is to reduce or eliminate retained austenite in the surface layer by further transformation of austenite to martensite.

12.4 TEMPERING

After quenching, the carburized components are normally tempered at temperatures up to ~473K (200°C). The purpose of tempering is to increase the toughness of case and to reduced its susceptibility to cracking during grinding, without greatly affecting its hardness.

13 CARBONITRIDING

13.1 INTRODUCTION

In carbonitriding, the surface layer of steel components is enriched simultaneously with carbon and nitrogen in the austenite temperature range, with the same purpose in mind as carburizing, i.e. to produce hard wear-resistant surface layer on engineering components. Carbonitriding is normally carried out in the temperature range 1023–1173K (750–900°C), and is done by adding ammonia gas (2–12%) to gaseous carburizing atmospheres. Ammonia decomposes at the surface of steel to give nascent nitrogen, which is absorbed at the surface and diffuses inwards. It gives nitrogen enrichmennt of the surface layer alongwith carbon enrichment. Hence, carbonitriding is also sometimes called modified gas carburizing.

13.2 CHEMISTRY OF CARBONITRIDING

With the presence of ammonia in the gaseous carburizing atmosphere, nitrogen is also introduced at the surface of steel, in accordance with the reaction:

$$NH_3 + (Fe) \Longleftrightarrow N(Fe) + \frac{3}{2}H_2 \tag{11.43}$$

whose equilibrium constant K is given by:

$$\log K = \log\left[\frac{a_N\, p_{H_2}^{3/2}}{p_{NH_3}}\right] = -\frac{2817}{T} + 6.083 \tag{11.44}$$

At high temperatures, ammonia also decomposes according to the reaction:

$$NH_3 \longrightarrow \frac{1}{2}N_2 + \frac{3}{2}H_2 \tag{11.45}$$

N_2, thus produced, does not cor tribute to thc absorption of nitrogen at the steel surface, as the dissociation of N_2 at these temperature, which is essential for the absorption of nitrogen in the steel, is negligible. As reaction (11.45) proceeds, partial pressure of ammonia in the atmosphere decreases, and consequently, nitrogen potential of the atmosphere also decreases [see Eq. (11.44)]. Furthermore, reaction (11.45) is slow and does not reach equilibrium during carbonitriding. It may be at various stages of completion depending upon the temperature and residence time of the gases. Hence, nitrogen activity of the atmosphere not only depends on the initial volume % of NH_3 added to the atmosphere, but also on the stage of its decomposition. Decomposition of NH_3 is higher at higher temperatures and low turnovers, i.e. large residence time of gases in the furnace. This must be kept in mind while determining the NH_3 requirements to attain desired nitrogen activity. Apart from this, reactions (11.43) and (11.45) increase H_2 and N_2 contents of the gaseous atmosphere and that would affect carbon potential of the atmosphere also.

The reactions discussed above are in addition to the carburizing reactions discussed in Sec.6, as carbonitriding atmosphere is obtained by adding small amounts of NH_3 to the carburizing gaseous mixtures. Hence, during carbonitriding, absorption of both nitrogen and carbon occur at the surface.

13.3 CASE DEPTH AND CONCENTRATION GRADIENTS

While case depth depends on the temperature and time of carbonitriding, the surface carbon and nitrogen concentrations depend on the composition of the gaseous atmosphere. Figure 11.17 shows case depths obtained upon carbonitriding as a function of time at various temperatures, based on the industrial data. Surface nitrogen concentration depends on the temperature of carbonitriding and NH_3 content of the gaseous atmosphere. At higher temperatures, lower surface nitrogen concentrations are obtained for the same inlet percentage of ammonia in the atmosphere, due to higher decomposition of ammonia to H_2 and N_2. Therefore, carbonitriding is

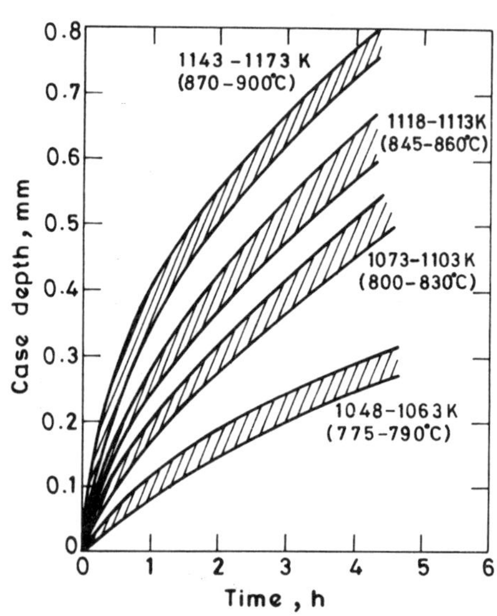

Fig. 11.17. Typical case depths during carbonitriding.

generally done at temperatures lower than normal carburizing temperatures. Figure 11.18 shows carbon and nitrogen concentration gradients and case hardness for typical carbonitrided cases. Figure 11.19 shows the effect of % inlet ammonia and dew point of the atmosphere on nitrogen penetration curves.

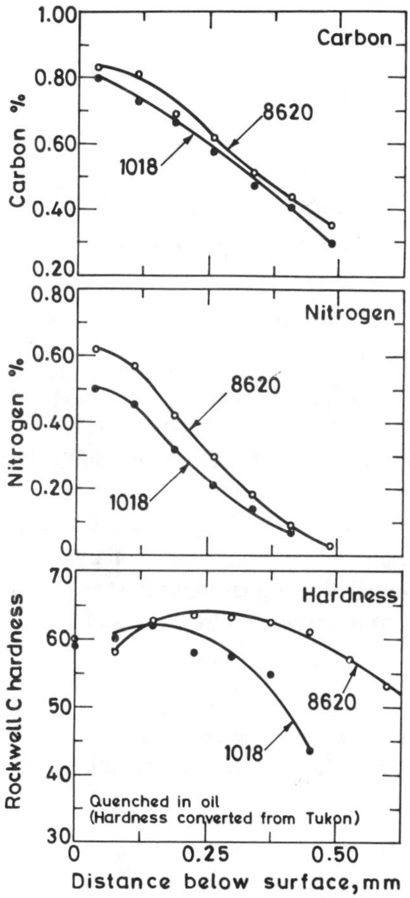

Fig. 11.18. Carbon, nitrogen and hardness profiles in AISI 1018 and 8620 steels, carbonitrided at 1118K (845°C) for 4 h.

The desired case depths are governed by service applications. Case depths of 0.025 to 0.075 mm are commonly applied to thin parts that require wear resistance under light loads. Case depths of up to 0.75 mm may be applied to parts for resisting high compressive loads.

13.4 HEAT TREATMENT OF CARBONITRIDED COMPONENTS

Carbonitrided components are heat treated essentially in the same manner as carburized parts, i.e. by quench hardening and tempering. The presence of nitrogen in

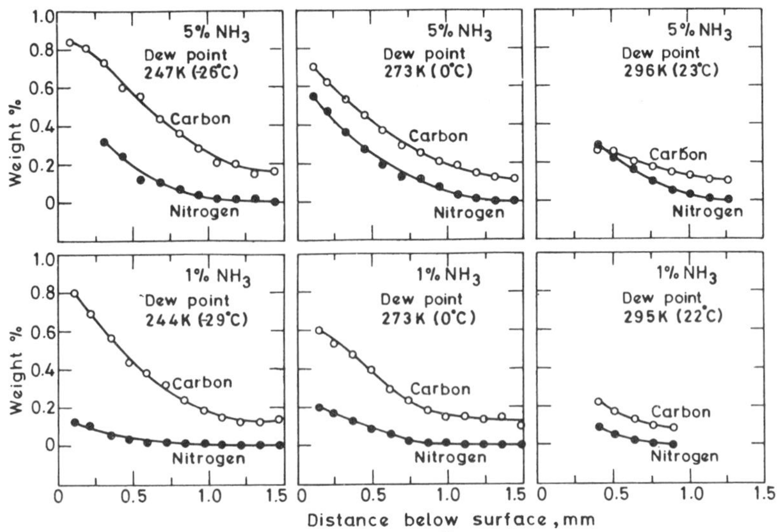

Fig. 11.19. Effect of ammonia concentration and inlet gas dew point on carbon and nitrogen profiles in AISI-1020 steel, carbonitrided for 4 h at 1118K (845°C).

carbonitrided cases significantly increases their hardenability. Because of increased hardenability of the case, plain carbon steels can be used in place of low-alloy steels when core properties are not critical. Furthermore, because of increased hardenability of the case in the presence of nitrogen, usually a milder quench can be used. This minimizes the possibility of quenching cracks and distortion on quenching. Small parts may even be quenched by stream of cooled atmosphere gases.

Nitrogen also lowers the M_s temperature in steels. Therefore, upon quenching, a carbonitrided case usually contains more retained austenite than a carburized case of similar carbon content. To reduce retained austenite, quenched carbonitrided components are usually given cold treatment by further cooling to 233 to 173K (–40 to –100°C).

14 CYANIDING

Cyaniding, sometimes also called liquid carbonitriding, is a case hardening process where surface layer enriched in carbon and nitrogen is produced by dipping steel components in liquid cyanide baths at austenite temperatures. Liquid cyaniding baths usually contain higher percentages of sodium cyanide than liquid carburizing baths. This gives higher nitrogen and relatively lower carbon activity in the baths, and hence, higher nitrogen and relatively lower carbon in the surface layer. Typical composition of a cyaniding bath is: 30% NaCN, 40% Na_2CO_3, and 30% NaCl. In some cases even higher cyanide contents may be used. NaCN in the bath reacts with atmospheric air to form cyanate (NaNCO), i.e.

$$2NaCN + O_2 \longrightarrow 2NaNCO \tag{11.46}$$

Cyanate (NaNCO) then decomposes to give:

$$4NaNCO \longrightarrow Na_2CO_3 + 2NaCN + CO + 2N \quad (11.47)$$

Nascent nitrogen and CO produced by reaction (11.47) lead to absorption of nitrogen and carbon at the surface. When CO reacts at the steel surface to introduce carbon in solution, CO_2 is produced, which again reacts with NaCN to provide CO:

$$NaCN + CO_2 \longrightarrow NaNCO + CO \quad (11.48)$$

Usually, the formation and decomposition of cyanate increases with increasing temperature. Hence, bath activity is higher at higher temperatures. Air is sometimes bubbled through the bath to accelerate cyanate formation. Cyaniding baths are usually operated in the temperature range 1023–1173K (750–900°C) to produce very thin cases, usually only up to ~0.25 mm. Lower operating temperatures are generally preferred to minimise distortion upon quenching. Cases produced by cyaniding have the same advantages and disadvantages as those produced by gas carbonitriding, and are heat treated in a similar manner.

REFERENCES

1. *Metals Handbook,* Vol. 2, 8th Edition, American Society for Metals, Metals Park, Ohio, 1964.
2. *Carburizing and Carbonitriding*, American Society for Metals, Metals Park, Ohio, USA, 1977.
3. P. Sommer, *Heat Treat of Met.*, **14** (1987) p. 7.
4. C.H. Luiten, F. Limque and F. Bless, in *Heat Treatment* '79, The Metals Society, London, 1979, p. 69.
5. W.L. Grube and J.G. Gay, *Metall. Trans. A.*, **9A** (1978) p. 1421.

CHAPTER 12

Nitriding of Steels

1 INTRODUCTION

Nitriding is a surface hardening treatment, where nitrogen is introduced at the surface of steel at temperatures lower than Ae_1 temperature. Nitriding is carried out by bringing the steel components into contact with an environment of high nitrogen activity in the ferrite stability range, normally at 773–848 K (500–575°C). At these temperatures, structure of a steel is normally ferrite plus carbides and hardening of the surface layer occurs by internal precipitation of alloy nitrides in ferrite. Hence, normally steels containing strong nitride-forming elements, like, Al, Cr, Mo, Ti, V, Nb, etc., may only be surface hardened by nitriding. As hardening of the surface layer is due to the internal precipitation of alloy nitrides, no quenching is required after nitriding treatment. Core properties of the components must be developed before nitriding, by quenching and tempering, if necessary. Tempering temperature used for developing core properties must be at least 40K higher than the intended nitriding temperature, so that no changes in the core properties take place during nitriding treatment.

As nitriding is done at relatively lower temperatures and no quenching is required after nitriding, distortion of the components is minimal. However, certain dimensional changes do occur during nitriding and these must be taken into consideration when close tolerances are desired. Mainly due to lower temperatures used for nitriding, relatively more time is required to develop requisite case depths during nitriding as compared to other case hardening processes like carburizing, carbonitriding, induction hardening, etc. Normally it takes 50–100 h of nitriding time to develop ~1.0 mm thick case depth. Also, more expensive ammonia gas is used for nitriding and special alloy steels, containing nitride-forming elements, are required for nitrided components. For these reasons, nitriding as a case hardening process is more expensive as compared to carburizing or carbonitriding. However, higher surface hardness can be developed in nitrided components. Furthermore, nitrided components usually have greatly improved fatigue life, due to the compressive stresses set up in the surface layer during nitriding. Hence, nitriding may be more useful for certain applications.

2 MECHANISM OF NITRIDING

Nitrogen in pure iron acts as an austenite stabilizing element and its solubility in austenite is much higher than in ferrite. At higher nitrogen concentrations, beyond the solubility limit of nitrogen in iron, three intermediate compounds are formed in the Fe–N binary system. Figure 12.1 shows relevent portion of the Fe–N phase diagram and Table 12.1 gives more information about the intermediate phases. When a steel, which does not contain any strong nitride forming elements, is exposed to an atmosphere of high nitrogen activity in the ferrite stability range, iron nitrides are formed at the surface whenever nitrogen activity exceeds the solubility limit of nitrogen in ferrite. The iron nitride layer, thus formed, is generally brittle and no advantage in properties is normally obtained.

Table 12.1. Intermediate Phases formed in the Fe–N System

Phase	Formula	Crystal Symmetry
γ'	Fe_4N	Cubic
δ	Fe_2N	Orthorhombic
ε	$Fe_{2-3}N$	Hexagonal

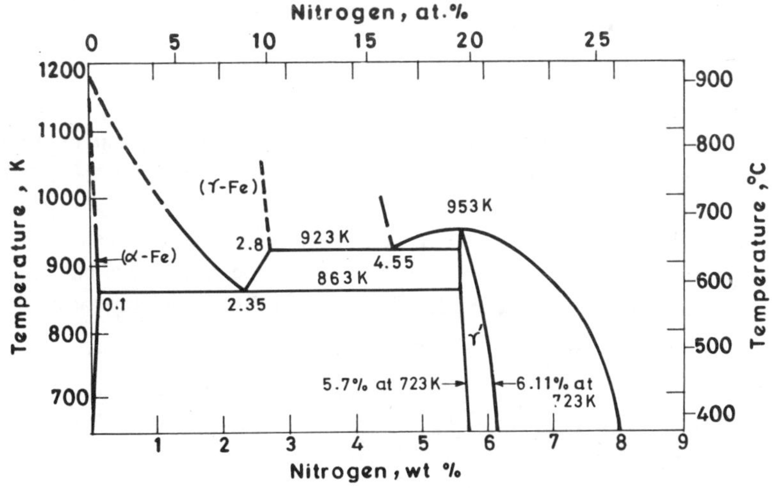

Fig. 12.1. The Fe–N phase diagram.

In steels containing strong nitride-forming elements, like, Al, Mo, Cr, Ti, V, Nb, etc., strength (hardness) of the surface layer is increased due to precipitation hardening effect of the internally precipitated alloy nitride precipitates. Table 12.2 gives general information about the nitride phases that precipitate during nitriding of steels in the presence of these elements.

The extent of increase in surface hardness on nitriding depends on the size, distribution and volume fraction of the alloy nitride precipitates. Precipitation of alloy nitrides during nitriding involves diffusion of nitrogen from the surface and that of

Table 12.2. Particulars of Nitride Phases of Commonly Used Elements in Nitriding Steels

Element	Nitride Phase	Crystal Structure	Unit cell Dimensions (nm)	Heat of Formation (kJ/mole)
Al	AlN	Hexagonal	$a = 0.3110$ $c = 0.4975$	335
Ti	TiN	Face centred cubic	$a = 0.4244$	300
V	VN	-do-	$a = 0.4139$	218
Cr	CrN	-do-	$a = 0.4149$	125
Mo	Mo_2N	-do-	$a = 0.4169$	80
W	W_2N	-do-	$a = 0.4126$	71

nitride-forming elements within the ferrite matrix. At nitriding temperatures, diffusivity of nitrogen in ferrite is orders of magnitude higher than that of the alloying elements. Hence, the extent of alloy nitride precipitation is controlled by the diffusion of nitrogen, whereas, the precipitate size is essentially controlled by the diffusion of alloying elements. The volume fraction of nitride precipitates is proportional to the concentration of nitride-forming elements in the steel. At normal nitriding temperatures, 773–848K (500–575°C), the precipitate size is sufficiently fine to give substantial precipitation hardening effect.

3 THEORY OF NITRIDING

3.1 GROWTH RATE AND CASE DEPTH

Case depth and hardness distribution, developed upon nitriding, depend on the diffusivity of nitrogen in ferrite and on the nature and amount of nitride-forming elements present in the steel. Under some simplifying assumptions, case depth as a function of nitriding time may be arrived at as follows. Let there be a single strong nitride-forming element (M) present in the steel, which precipitates out as M_nN nitride during nitriding. In addition, let us make the following assumptions:

(i) the solubility product of M_nN nitride in ferrite is essentially zero;

(ii) M_nN precipitates nucleate homogeneously in ferrite and the activation energy for nucleation is negligible, i.e. essentially no supersaturation is required for the precipitation of M_nN;

(iii) diffusivity of nitrogen, D_N, in ferrite is much higher than the diffusivity of alloying element, D_M, in ferrite, i.e. $D_N >> D_M$; and

(iv) the surface nitrogen concentration is maintained at a fixed value, [N], determined by the nitrogen activity of the surrounding environment, or the solubility limit of nitrogen in iron, whichever is lower.

Assumption (iii) implies that the depth of nitriding is essentially controlled by the diffusion of nitrogen and assumptions (i) and (ii) suggest that nitrogen readily combines with alloying element, M, to precipitate out as M_nN nitrides, till all the alloying element is exhausted. Hence, nitrogen concentration at any point below the surface remains essentially zero till all of the alloying element at that point has precipitated out as M_nN. This, combined with assumption (iv), would give a linear nitrogen concentration profile for nitrogen in solution in ferrite, from [N] at the surface to zero at depth to which nitriding has occurred, as shown in Fig. 12.2. In the nitrided region, all the alloying element would have precipitated out as M_nN. Let the depth of nitriding at any time t be x and let us say that it increases to $x + dx$ as time increases from t to $t + dt$ (see Fig. 12.2). The rate of nitrogen diffusion into the steel at time t is given by:

$$J = -D_N \left(\frac{dC_N}{dx} \right) = D_N \left(\frac{[N]}{x} \right) \tag{12.1}$$

where, J is nitrogen diffusion flux; D_N is diffusion coefficient of nitrogen in ferrite; C_N represents concentration of nitrogen in solution; and [N] is nitrogen concentration in solution at the surface, i.e. at $x = 0$. The diffusivity of nitrogen in ferrite is given by:

$$D_N = 7.7. \times 10^{-3} \exp \left(-\frac{9470}{T} \right) \text{ cm}^2\text{/s} \tag{12.2}$$

In time dt, depth of nitriding increases by dx. For depth of nitriding to increase by dx, all the alloying element, M, present between x and $x + dx$ must precipitate out as M_nN. The amount of nitrogen, ΔN, required for this is:

$$\Delta N = \frac{[M]}{n} dx \tag{12.3}$$

where, [M] is concentration of alloying element in steel in at% and n is stoichiometric factor for M_nN nitride. This amount of nitrogen, ΔN, is obtained by diffusion of nitrogen from the surface in time dt, i.e.

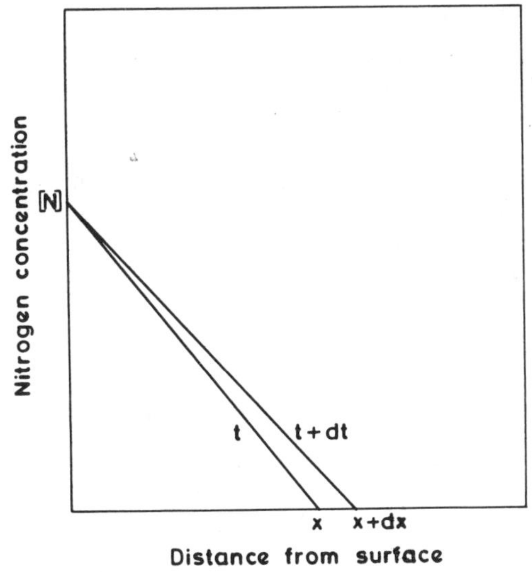

Fig. 12.2. Nitrogen in solution in ferrite during nitriding under ideal conditions.

$$\Delta N = J\ dt$$

or

$$\frac{[M]}{n}\ dx = D_N \frac{[N]}{x}\ dt \tag{12.4}$$

Rearranging and integrating eq. (12.4), we obtain:

$$x^2 = 2n \frac{[N]}{[M]} D_N\ t \tag{12.5}$$

where [N] and [M] are surface nitrogen concentration in solution and initial alloying element concentration in ferrite respectively, in atomic fraction or at%. Equation (12.5) then gives case depth as a function of time under the assumptions made above. Figure 12.3 schematically shows concentration distribution of different constrituents and the expected hardness distribution under these conditions as a function of distance from the surface. Note that, the concentrations [M] and [M_nN], and the hardness are essentially step functions. This is a consequence of assumptions (i) and

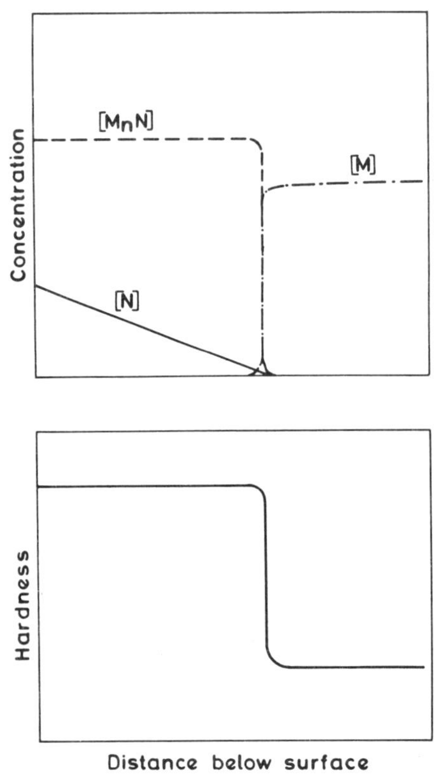

Fig. 12.3. Expected distribution of [M], [N] and [M_nN] concentrations, and hardness after nitriding under idealized conditions.

(ii), which envisage no solubility of M_nN in ferrite and easy nucleation of M_nN precipitates, requiring no supersaturation.

In general, the activation energy for nucleation of alloy nitride precipitates is not negligible. Therefore, nitrogen must build up to a certain level, before nitride precipitation can occur. Most of the alloy nitrides with fcc structure (see Table 12.2) do nucleate homogeneously with coherent or semicoherent interfaces with Bain orientation with bcc ferrite. AlN (with hexagonal structure) nucleates heterogeneously on dislocations. Depending upon the solubility product of the precipitating nitride (nitrides with higher enthalpy of formation (Table 12.2) would have lower solubility product), and the ease with which it nucleates, nitriding behaviour of steels containing different nitride-forming elements may be classified as follows.

(a) *Strong interaction with Easy Nucleation*: In the presence of elements which form very stable nitrides, and which can also homogeneously nucleate with little supersaturation, all the assumptions made above are generally satisfied. Then, the case depth is given by Eq. (12.5) and the concentration and hardness distribution would be as shown in Fig.12.3. Titanium falls in this category. Figure 12.4 shows hardness distribution obtained on nitriding of Fe–Ti alloys.

(b) *Weak Interaction and Difficult Nucleation*: If nucleation of alloy nitrides is relatively more difficult, requiring higher activation energy, large supersaturation must build up before any precipitation of nitrides occurs. Such a behaviour is observed in steels containing Mo, W and Al. Variation of concentrations of different

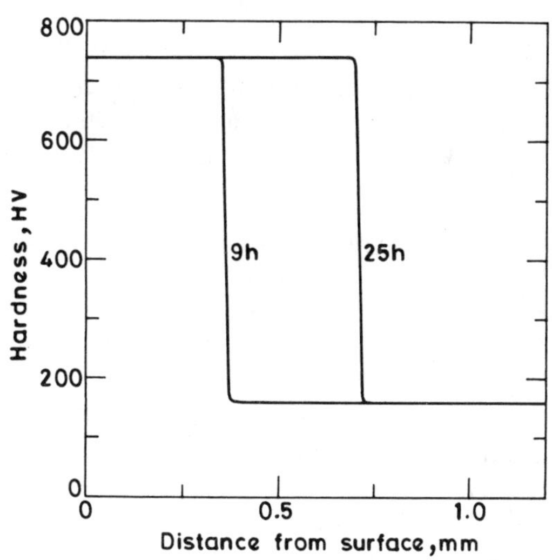

Fig. 12.4. Hardness distribution in Fe–0.94Ti alloy nitrided at 853K (580°C) in $8NH_3/92H_2$ atmosphere [from D.H. Jack et al., in 'Chemical Metallurgy of iron and Steel', The Iron and Steel Institute, London, 1973, p. 374].

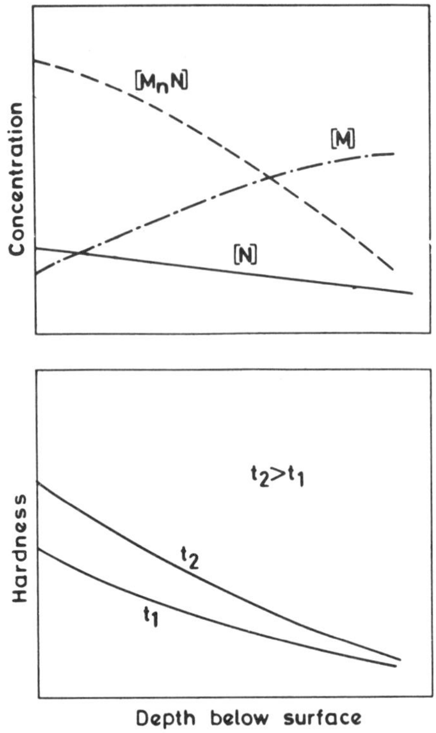

Fig. 12.5. Concentration and hardness distribution during nitriding in weak interacting systems (schematic).

constituents and of hardness obtained upon nitriding of these alloys is schematically shown in Fig.12.5. Here, the surface hardness is time dependent and it decreases gradually below the surface. In alloys containing Al, nucleation of AlN precipitates also depends on the dislocation density, as AlN preferentially nucleates on dislocations.

(c) *Intermediate Interaction*: Nitriding response of Fe–Cr alloys is intermediate to the two extreme situations discussed above. The critical solubility product, [%Cr][%N], for homogeneous nucleation of CrN precipitates is higher than for the precipitation of TiN, but not as high as for the precipitation of nitrides of Mo, W, or Al. Here, [%Cr] and [%N] refer, respectively, to concentrations Cr and N in solution in ferrite. Nitriding response of Fe–Cr alloys is schematically shown in Fig. 12.6. Diffuseness of the interface, measured by Δx in Fig.12.6, is a function of chromium content of the steel, surface nitrogen concentration and the temperature and time of nitriding. $\Delta x/d$, where d is total depth of nitriding (see Fig. 12.6), is directly proportional to the solubility product of CrN in ferrite and inversely proportional to maximum possible [%Cr][%N] product, i.e.:

$$\frac{\Delta x}{d} \propto \frac{K_s}{[\%\text{Cr}]\,[\%\text{N}]} \tag{12.6}$$

where, K_s is solubility product of CrN in ferrite; and [%Cr] and [%N] are initial chromium concentration in the alloy and surface (maximum) nitrogen concentration in solution, respectively. The total nitriding depth, *d*, to a first approximation can be estimated by Eq. (12.5). Thus, the interface is more diffused at higher temperatures (K_s increases with temperature), low chromium contents and at lower nitrogen activities of the nitriding atmosphere. Figure 12.7 shows the effect of these variables on the hardness profiles of nitrided Fe–Cr alloys.

3.2 HARDNESS OF THE CASE

Hardening of the surface layer upon nitriding is due to precipitation hardening effect of the alloy nitride precipitates. Hence, hardness of a nitrided case at any point depends on the volume fraction and average size of the alloy nitride precipitates. Volume fraction of the precipitates is directly proportional to the concentration of nitride-forming elements present in the steel, whereas, average size of the precipitates is essentially determined by their diffusivity in ferrite. Therefore, average precipitate size is smaller at lower nitriding temperatures. Hence, higher surface hardness would be obtained at higher concentrations of nitride-forming ele-

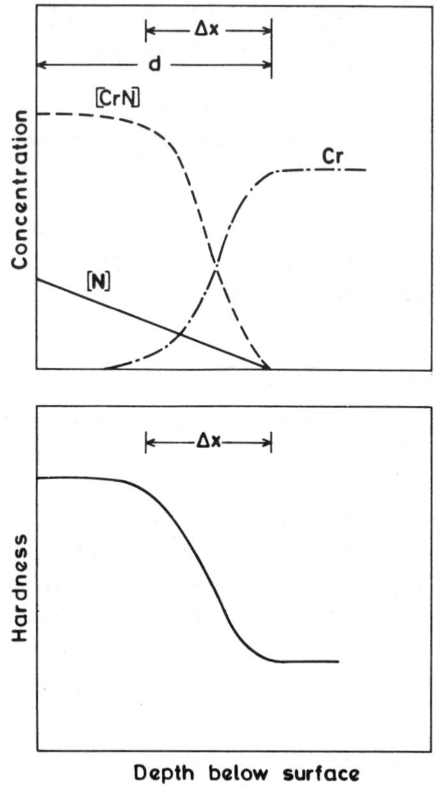

Fig. 12.6. Schematic nitriding behaviour of Fe–Cr alloys.

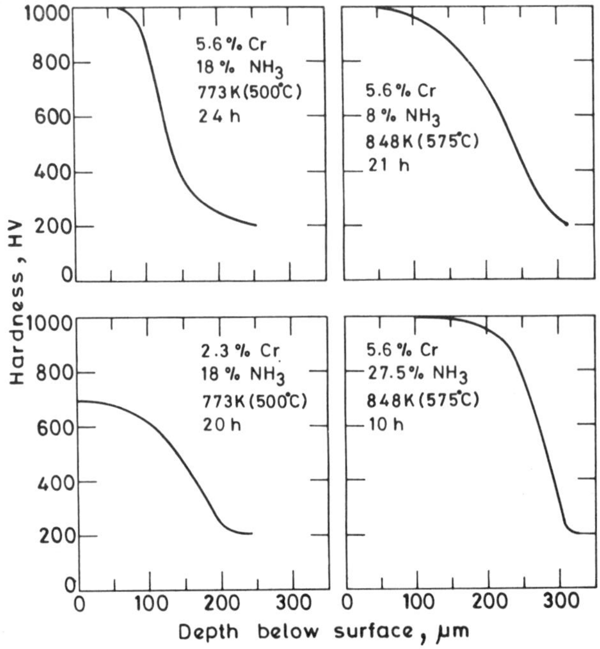

Fig. 12.7. Effect of temperature, nitrogen activity and chromium content on the surface hardness and diffuseness of the case on nitriding of Fe–Cr alloys [from B.J. Lightfoot and D.H. Jack, *Heat Treatment* '73, The Metals Society, London, p. 59].

ments and lower nitriding temperatures. Effect of alloy content on maximum surface hardness can be seen in Fig. 12.7, however, the temperature variation is not large enough to show significant temperature effect.

4 EFFECT OF CARBON ON NITRIDING

All commercial nitriding steels, apart from nitride forming elements, also contain some carbon. Most nitride forming elements, with the exception of Al, also form alloy carbides, or preferentially segregate to cementite when alloy carbides are not formed. Before nitriding, steel components are normally quenched and tempered to develop requisite core properties. During the prior quenching and tempering operation, the tempering temperature should be at least 40K higher than the intended nitriding temperature to guard against deterioration of core properties during nitriding. Depending upon the time and temperature of prior tempering process, structure of steel before nitriding may consist of ferrite plus cementite, or ferrite plus alloy carbides.

When structure before nitriding is ferrite plus cementite, the nitride forming elements may have preferentially segregated to cementite. During nitriding, cementite decomposes and alloy nitrides precipitate in the nitriding zone. The alloying element,

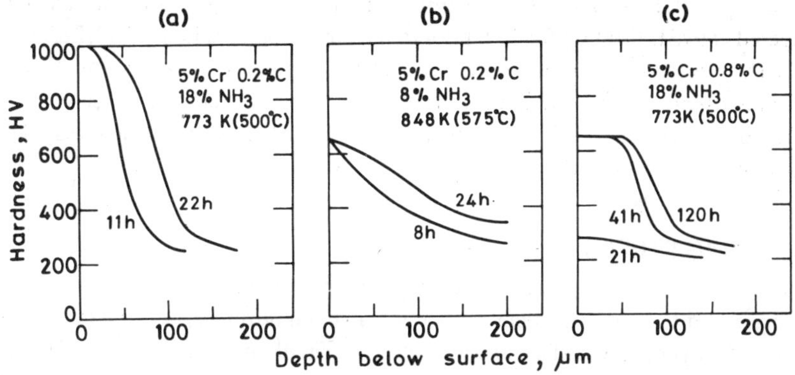

Fig. 12.8. Effect of carbon and prior tempering temperature on nitriding of Fe–Cr alloys [from B.J. Lighfoot and D.H. Jack, *Heat Treatment* '73, The Metals Society, London, p. 59].

upon decomposition of cementite, can easily dissolve in the surrounding ferrite, whereas carbon must diffuse away from the nitriding front and precipitate out as cementite, or alloy carbides, ahead of the front. Under these circumstances, kinetics of nitriding is affected by the kinetics of cementite decomposition. This effect is stronger when steel is overaged and the alloying elements must diffuse over larger distances upon decomposition of cementite.

When nitride forming elements have precipitated out as alloy carbides during prior tempering, the situation is little different. Alloy carbides, in general, are more stable than cementite and also have higher concentrations of alloying elements. Dissolution of alloy carbides is considerably slower than that of cementite, and hence, the kinetics of nitriding is considerably slowed down. Furthermore, if alloy carbides do not completely dissolve during nitriding, then, lower case hardness is obtained upon nitriding, due to lower volume fraction of the nitride precipitates.

Finally, if prior tempering temperature is not substantially higher than the intended nitriding temperature, then, tempering processes may continue during nitriding, complicating it further. Figure 12.8 shows the effect of carbon and prior tempering process on the nitriding of Fe–5%Cr alloy. Figures 12.8(a) and 12.8(b) show the effect of nitriding temperature on the hardness profiles in Fe–5%Cr–0.2%C alloy, quenched and tempered for 1 h at 873 K (600°C) prior to nitriding. On nitriding at 773K (500°C), maximum hardness and hardness profile essentially similar to nitriding of carbon-free Fe–Cr alloy of similar Cr concentration is obtained, i.e. carbon has virtually no effect on the nitriding process [Fig. 12.8(a)]. However, on nitriding the alloy with the same prior treatment at 848K (575°C), the nitriding response is typical of more dilute Fe–Cr alloys [Fig. 12.8(b)]. At 848K (575°C), the steel continues to temper ahead of the reaction front and carbides become richer in chromium. These chromium-rich carbides also act as heterogeneous nucleation sites for the formation of relatively large non-hardening CrN precipitates. Hence, effective chromium content of the alloy contributing to hardening upon nitriding is substantially reduced. Figure 12.8(c) shows nitriding response of Fe–5%Cr–0.8%C alloy that has been tempered at 973K (700°C) for 50 h prior to nitriding. On nitriding at 773K (500°C), the surface hardness is time dependent and relatively low. In this case, due to precipitation of chromum-rich alloy carbides during prior tempering, the effective chromium concentration has been reduced to a level at which it behaves like a weakly interacting system.

5 NITRIDING STEELS

As discussed earlier, only steels containing strong nitride forming elements may be case hardened by nitriding. Plain carbon steels, upon nitriding, develop only brittle iron nitride layer at the surface and are, hence, normally unsuitable for case hardening by nitriding. Nitriding steels, therefore, must contain nitride forming elements, like, Al, Cr, Mo, V, Ti, etc. Maximum surface hardness developed upon nitriding is proportional to the concentration of nitride forming elements in the steel. Of the commercially available low alloy steels, only those containing Cr and Mo, Like, 41XX, 43XX, 86XX, etc. may be nitrided. However, maximum surface hardness that is obtained in these steels is limited to about 40–50 HRC, as these steels contain only up to 1–2% Cr and up to ~0.5% Mo. To obtain higher surface hardness values, special nitriding steels containing higher amounts of nitride forming elements have been developed. In these steels, surface hardness in excess of 70 HRC may be obtained upon nitriding. Table 12.3 lists the compositions and maximum hardness on nitriding of some commercial nitriding steels. In addition to these, certain tool steels, stainless steels and cast irons containing nitride forming elements respond very well to surface hardening by nitriding.

Table 12.3. Composition of Some Nitriding Steels*

Alloy	C	Cr	Mo	Al	Max. Hardness, HRC
Nitroalloy–125	.2–.3	.9–1.4	.15–.25	.85–1.2	70+
Nitroalloy–135	.3–.4	.9–1.4	.15–.25	.85–1.2	70+
Nitroalloy–N	.2–.3	1.0–1.3	.2–.3	.85–1.2	70+
Nitroalloy–230	.25–.35	–	.6–1.0	.85–1.2	70+
AISI–4340	.38–.43	.7–.9	.2–.3	–	45
AISI–8640	.38–.43	.4–.6	.15–.25	–	40
H11 Tool Steel	.35	5.0	1.5	–	(.4V) 70+

*Only concentration of nitride forming elements is given in the Table. These steels also contain small amounts of Mn, Ni, Si, etc.

6 NITRIDING METHODS

6.1 GAS NITRIDING

Gas nitriding is the most common method of nitriding, where the components to be nitrided are heated in an atmosphere of dissociated ammonia gas. At nitriding temperatures, 773–848K (500–575°C), ammonia reacts at the surface of steel to introduce nitrogen in solution in iron, i.e.:

$$NH_3 = N\,(Fe) + \frac{3}{2}\,H_2 \tag{12.6}$$

with an equilibrium constant,

$$K = \frac{a_N\, p_{H_2}^{3/2}}{p_{NH_3}} \quad \text{or} \quad \%N \cong \frac{K_1\, p_{NH_3}}{p_{H_2}^{3/2}} \tag{12.7}$$

where, K and K_1 are constants at a given temperature, a_N is activity of nitrogen in iron; and %N refers to nitrogen dissolved in iron. In arriving at %N dissolved in steel in Eq. (12.7), it has been assumed that activity of nitrogen in ferrite is directly proportional to its concentration. During nitriding, %N at the surface in solution is given by Eq. (12.7) only when it does not exceed the solubility limit of nitrogen in steel at the nitriding temperature. Actual surface nitrogen concentration is given by Eq. (12.7) or the maximum solubility of nitrogen in ferrite, whichever is lower.

Ammonia gas is itself unstable at nitriding temperatures and dissociates according to reaction:

$$NH_3 \longrightarrow \frac{1}{2}\,N_2 + \frac{3}{2}\,H_2 \tag{12.8}$$

Reaction (12.8) is relatively slow. During an actual nitriding process, ammonia gas may be partially cracked in a separate reaction chamber and the resulting mixture of gases (NH_3, N_2 and H_2) fed into the nitriding furnace, or alternatively, decomposition of ammonia may be controlled by controlling the turnover time of gases in the nitriding furnance itself. A check on nitrogen potential of the atmosphere is kept by analyzing the exit gases.

Molecular nitrogen present in the gas atmosphere may also decompose at the surface of steel to introduce nitrogen in steel, i.e.:

$$\frac{1}{2}\,N_2 = N\,(Fe), \qquad \%N = K_2\, p_{N_2}^{1/2} \tag{12.9}$$

However, at nitriding temperatures, the constant K_2 is orders of magnitude smaller than K_1 in Eq. (12.7). NH_3–H_2 mixture containing 18% NH_3 and 82% H_2 (total pressure 1 atm) gives the same percentage nitrogen dissolved in iron as 5×10^3 atm of N_2 at 773K (500°C). Hence, it is not practical to use nitrogen gas for nitriding.

Whenever nitrogen potential of the atmosphere exceeds the solubility limit of nitrogen in iron, iron nitrides (γ–Fe_4N and/or ε–$Fe_{2-3}N$) form at the surface of steel (see Fe–N phase diagram in Fig. 12.1). Figure 12.9 shows appropriate conditions for the formation of these compounds as a function of nitrogen activity of the atmosphere and temperature. Commerical nitriding in dissociated ammonia atmosphere is normally carried out at high nitrogen potentials, where iron nitride layer is generally formed at the surface. This layer is referred to as ''white layer'' (due to its colour) or ''compound layer'', and is removed after nitriding. Even when nitriding is done under saturated conditions, depending upon the concentration of nitride forming

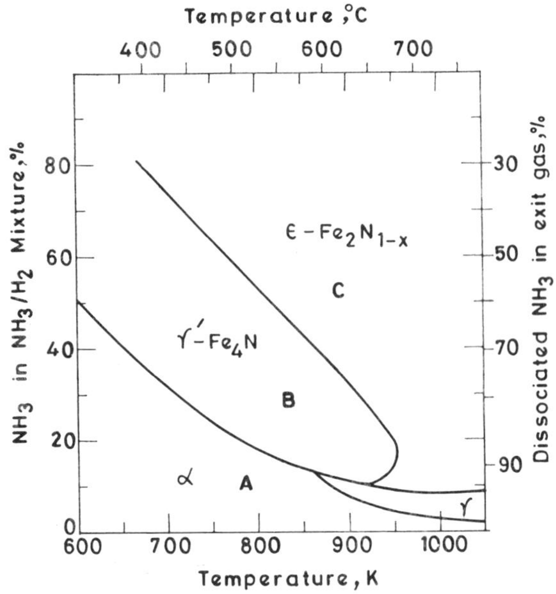

Fig. 12.9. Nitrogen potential diagram for the Fe–N system.

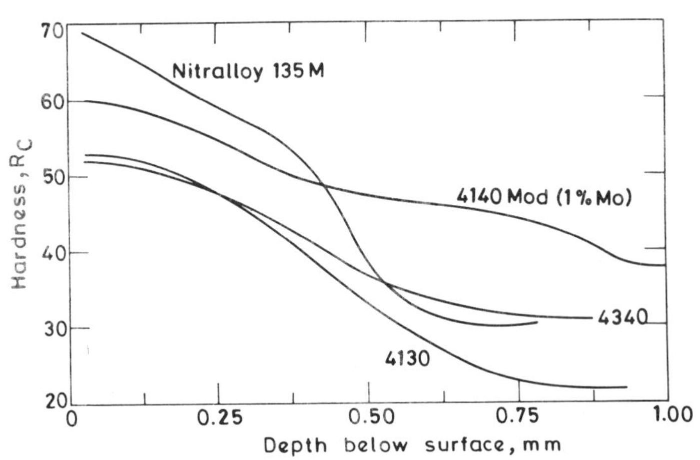

Fig. 12.10. Hardness distribution in some commercial steels nitrided at 840K (575°C) for 72 h.

elements and temperature, it takes anywhere from 50 to 100 h to develop ~1.0 mm thick nitrided case. Figure 12.10 shows hardness distribution in some commercial nitriding steels after 72 h of gas nitriding at 840K (567°C).

6.2 LIQUID NITRIDING

Molten salt nitriding baths, containing approximately one-third each of sodium cyanide (NaCN), sodium cyanate (NaCNO) and sodium carbonate (Na_2CO_3) are used for nitriding tools and other small components. The bath composition may be obtained by melting and aging sodium cyanide (NaCN) for 24–48 h at nitriding temperatures, prior to nitriding. During aging of the bath, the following reactions occur:

$$2NaCN + O_2 \longrightarrow 2NaCNO \tag{12.10}$$

$$4NaCNO \longrightarrow Na_2CO_3 + 2NaCN + CO + 2N \tag{12.11}$$

Nitrogen provided by reaction (12.11) is absorbed at the surface of steel. Nitrogen activity of the bath is essentially a function of its NaCNO content. Baths are dredged periodically to remove sodium carbonate (which eventually forms a sludge) and fresh sodium cyanide is added. KCl is sometimes added to the bath to act as a diluting agent to increase fluidity. Typically, a working nitriding bath may contain 12–25% sodium cyanide, 12–25% sodium cyanate, 25–30% potassium chloride and the balance, sodium carbonate.

6.3 ION (PLASMA) NITRIDING

In ion nitriding, also known as "glow discharge" or "plasma" nitriding, workpiece to be nitrided is made cathode of the glow discharge with a suitable voltage impressed between the cathode and the anode. An atmosphere of nitrogen plus hydrogen at a proper pressure is provided as the conducting atmosphere to support a stable glow and to perform the process of ion nitriding. Figure 12.11 schematically shows an ion nitriding apparatus. The specimen chamber is evacuated and then backfilled with N_2 and H_2 gas mixture at reduced pressures (generally 1–10 torr). A d.c. voltage is then impressed and increased till the glow is established. Once a stable glow is established and it completely envelops the workpiece, nitriding of the workpiece occurs. Figure 12.12 shows characteristic voltage-current curve for glow discharge. Ion nitriding is performed at current densites typically from 0.5×10^{-3} A/cm^2 to 3.0×10^{-3} A/cm^2 (Fig. 12.12). The workpiece is heated by the glow discharge and the anode is kept cool by circulating water around it. Temperature of the workpiece can be controlled by controlling the current density and/or pressure of the gases. The glow discharge consists of different types of ions, i.e. H^+, N^+, NH^+, NH_2^+, etc. Absorption of nitrogen at the steel surface occurs mainly due to the presence of partially dissociated ammonia ions (NH^+, NH_2^+ , etc.) in the glow. Activity of nitrogen in the glow may be controlled by controlling the partial pressure of N_2 in the back filled gases. Once absorbed at the surface, nitrogen diffuses inwards forming a nitrided layer. The penetration rates of nitrogen during ion nitriding have been generally found to be faster than during conventional gas nitriding. Figure 12.13 shows case depth as a function of time during ion nitriding of some steels at 773K(500°C). The 'white layer' formed during ion nitriding is generally thinner than in conventional gas nitriding and may, in some cases, be completely eliminated.

One of the problems often experienced in ion nitriding is in the establishment of a stable glow, i.e. to avoid the deterioration of a glow into an arc. Establishment of a stable glow becomes more difficult when trapped gases, moisture, oxides and other contaminants are present at the surface of the workpiece and are released upon evacuation. Therefore, it is essential that, before the workpiece is introduced into the

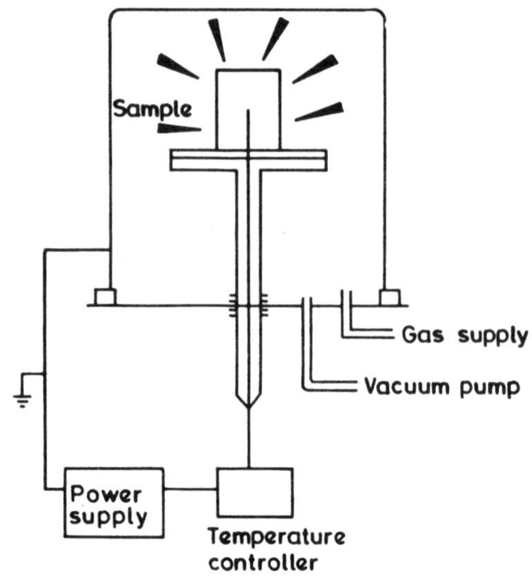

Fig. 12.11. Ion nitriding apparatus (schematic).

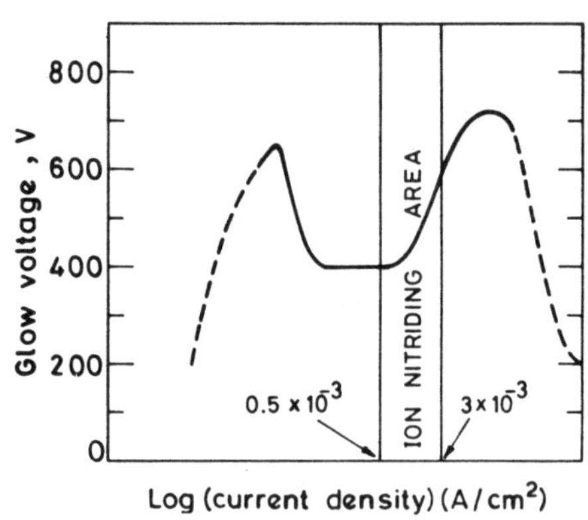

Fig. 12.12. Glow discharge characteristic curve.

ion nitriding apparatus, it is properly cleaned and degassed. Additionally, an unfiltered full wave rectified a.c. output may be used to excite the glow. This controls the ignition and extinguishing points of the glow as shown in Fig. 12.14. The glow is extinguished every 1/200th s, for a period long enough for the ions to recombine, which otherwise might trigger an arc.

7 "WHITE LAYER" AND ITS PREVENTION

7.1 FORMATION OF "WHITE LAYER"

During industrial gas nitriding, nitrogen potential of the atmosphere is generally kept higher than the solubility limit of nitrogen in iron, normally in region "C" in Fig.

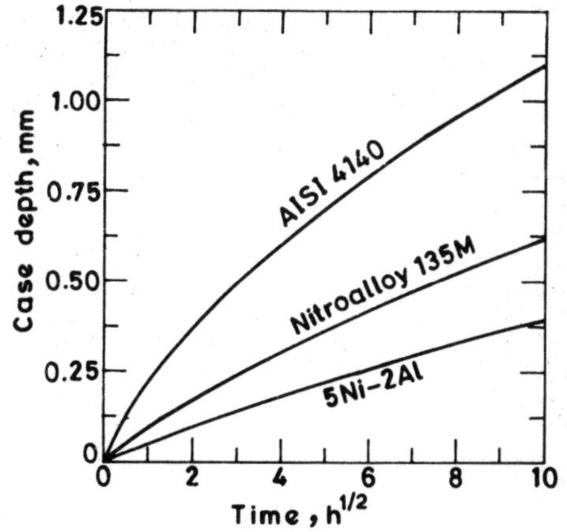

Fig. 12.13. Case depth versus time upon ion nitriding of some steels at 773K (500°C) [from C.K. Jones, S.W. Martin, D.J. Sturges and M. Hudis, *Heat Treatment'73*, The Metals Society, London, p. 71].

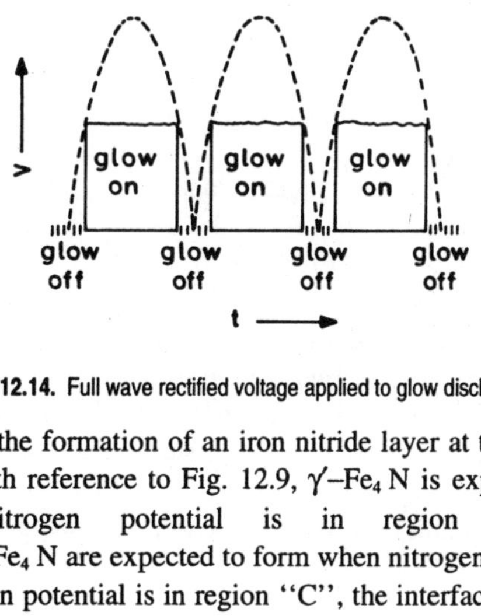

Fig. 12.14. Full wave rectified voltage applied to glow discharge.

12.9. This leads to the formation of an iron nitride layer at the surface, known as "white layer". With reference to Fig. 12.9, γ'–Fe_4N is expected to form at the surface when nitrogen potential is in region "B", and both ε–Fe_2N_{1-x} and γ'–Fe_4N are expected to form when nitrogen potential is in region "C". When nitrogen potential is in region "C", the interface equilibria would be expected to be:

$$\text{Gas} \Leftrightarrow \varepsilon\,(\text{high} - \text{N})\,;\quad \varepsilon(\text{low} - \text{N}) \Leftrightarrow \gamma'\text{–Fe}_4\text{N}\,;\quad \text{and}\quad \gamma'\text{–Fe}_4\text{N} \Leftrightarrow \alpha\text{–Fe}$$

γ'–Fe_4N phase has a large incubation period for nucleation and does not easily form. When nitrogen activity is in region "C" in Fig. 12.9, ε–Fe_2N_{1-x} easily forms at the surface and grows with time. γ'–Fe_4N may later, after a considerable incubation period, nucleate under it and grow. In an atmosphere of high nitrogen activity in region "C" in Fig. 12.9, the nitriding rate is relatively faster till the appearance of γ'–Fe_4N. In the beginning, when no iron nitrides have formed, surface nitrogen concentration is relatively high, given by nitrogen activity of the atmosphere. Soon, ε-nitride is formed at the surface and surface nitrogen concentration, in solution, is reduced to the solubility limit of metastable ε-nitride in ferrite. Later, when γ'–Fe_4N appears between ε-nitride and ferrite, surface nitrogen concentration in solution further falls to the solubility limit of γ' – Fe_4N in ferrite, and consequently, the nitriding rate also falls. Note that, the solubility of metastable ε-nitride in ferrite is always higher than that of the more stable γ'-nitride, and the nitriding rate [see Eq.(12.5)] is directly proportional to nitrogen concentration in solution at the surface. Therefore, to achieve faster growth of the nitrided layer, nitriding is generally carried out in high nitrogen potential, in region "C" in Fig. 12.9. The brittle composite iron nitride layer ("white layer") formed in the process is removed in the subsequent operations.

Under most industrial nitriding conditions, the "white layer" (composite iron nitride layer) may form to depths up to 0.05 mm on the outer surface of nitrided parts. "White layer" is generally brittle and may spall under service loads, leading to siezure and/or cracking. Appearance of these cracks greatly reduces fatigue life of the components. Therefore, "white layer" must be either completely removed or greatly reduced, before nitrided parts may be used in service.

7.2 REMOVAL OF "WHITE LAYER"

After nitriding, the "white layer" may be removed either by grinding or by chemical dissolution. Removal of white layer by grinding is of limited utility as only relatively smooth surfaces may be ground to remove the "white layer". Chemical dissolution of "white layer" is, therefore, more widely used. Removal of "white layer" by chemical means involves soaking of nitrided parts in hot alkaline solution (100 g of NaOH in a liter of water heated to 348–363K (75–90°C) for short periods, which makes the white layer friable, followed by blast cleaning by Al_2O_3 particles of 220 mesh grit at 80 psi pressure. Vapour blasting and blast cleaning with fine glass beads at various pressures may also be used in order to satisfy the specific surface finish requirements. The total soaking time required in hot alkaline solution may be up to 8 h. The method produces "white layer" free surfaces at extremely low cost, while simultaneously performing a copper-stripping operation in selectively nitrided components. Selective nitriding is normally done in the same manner as selective carburizing (see Chapter 11, Sec. 10).

7.3 TWO-STEP GAS NITRIDING (FLOE PROCESS)

"White layer" can be considerably reduced by using a two-step gas nitriding process, also known as Floe process. In the first step, nitriding is carried out under normal gas atmospheres of high nitrogen activity (~20% dissociated ammonia) to achieve faster growth rates. Once requisite case depth has been achieved, the components are further treated for few hours at the same temperature in an atmosphere of low nitrogen activity (~80% dissociated ammonia). During the second step, the activiity of nitrogen is lower than required for the formation of iron nitrides. Therefore, iron nitrides dissociate during this period and thickness of the "white layer" reduces. By this process, "white layer" may be reduced from its normal thickness of ~0.05 mm to less than ~0.01 mm. If the second step is carried out for longer times to completely eliminate ''white layer'', some nitrogen from the underlying nitrided layer may also escape, leading to a fall in the surface hardness.

7.4 ION NITRIDING WITHOUT "WHITE LAYER"

In ion nitriding, the process variables, i.e. voltage, current, partial pressures of H_2 and N_2, etc., are more amenable for easy and accurate control as compared to the process variables during gas nitriding. In ion nitriding, nitrided surfaces almost free of ''white layer'' may be obtained in two ways. The first method involves nitriding in an atmosphere where nitrogen activity is not high enough to form ''white layer''. This is achieved by controlling the partial pressure of nitrogen in the atmosphere. It is important that maximum nitrogen level consistent with the requirement of ''no white-layer formation'' is used. This is essential to attain maximum surface hardness and high nitriding rates.

The second method employed to obtain ''white layer'' free nitrided surfaces during ion nitriding is similar to Floe process. First, nitriding is carried out in saturated nitrogen atmosphere and then the nitrided specimen is heated in an inert plasma of a non-nitriding gas, such as H_2 or Ar, for about 2–4 h (the exact time to be experimentally determined). This completely removes the ''white layer'' by dissociation of iron nitrides. In the second step, some nitrogen may also escape from the underlying nitrided case, leading to softening of the surface. This is rectified in the subsequent third step, where nitriding is carried out again for a short period to fully re-nitride the depleted layer. Hardly any ''white layer'' forms during the short re-nitriding period.

8 NITRIDING OF PLAIN CARBON STEELS

Traditionally, nitriding has been used as a surface hardening process for components made from so-called nitriding steels. However, nitriding may also be used to improve the surface properties of components made of plain carbon steels. Plain carbon steels are normally nitrided for short periods, 2 to 4 h at 773–843K(500–570°C), in the ferrite stability range. This treatment increases the scuffing and wear resistance of the components, and also improves their fatigue life. Furthermore, corrosion resistance of the components is also enhanced.

Nitriding of plain carbon steels for 2 to 4 h gives an iron nitride compound layer at the surface and a nitrogen diffusion zone below it. The compound layer is generally less than 20 μm thick and consists mainly of ε–Fe_2N_{1-x}. The depth of nitrogen diffusion zone, below the compounds layer, is of the order of 1.0 mm. After nitriding, the components are usually oil, or water, quenched to retain nitrogen in the diffusion zone in solid solution. Figure 12.15 shows nitrogen distribution in a nitrided plain carbon steel and Fig. 12.16 gives the resulting hardness distribution. The initial apparent low hardness is due to porosity in the compound layer.

The main property improvements achieved by nitriding plain carbon non-alloyed steels are in the scuffing and wear resistance under small loads and in fatigue proper-

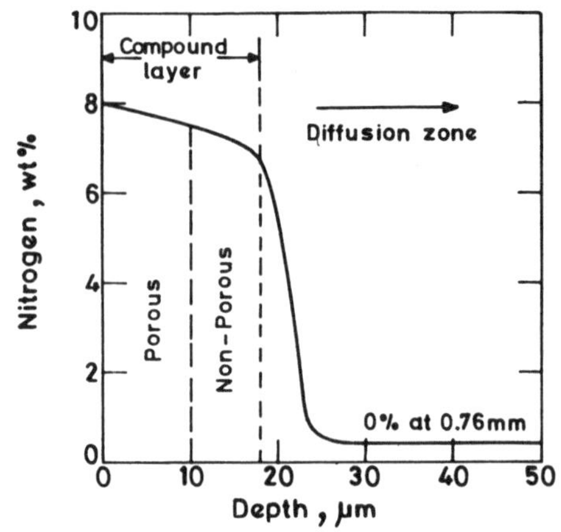

Fig. 12.15. Nitrogen distribution in a plain carbon steel nitrided at 843K (570°C) for 2 h [from C. Dawes, D.F. Tranter and C.G. Smith, *Heat Treatment* '79, The Metals Society, London, p. 60].

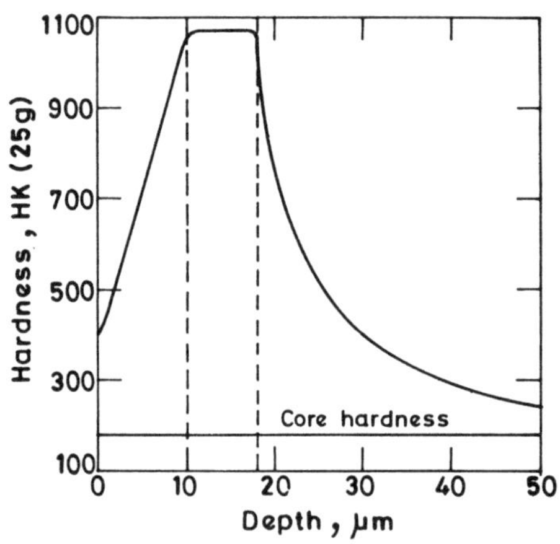

Fig. 12.16. Hardness profile (knoop Hardness) in the nitrided plain carbon steel in Fig. 12.15 [from C. Dawes, D.F. Tranter and C.G. Smith, *Heat Treatment* '79, The Metals Society, London, p. 60].

ties. Iron nitride compound layer, mainly consisting of ε–$Fe_2 N_{1-x}$, at thicknesses of up to ~ 20 μm, achieved during 2–4 h of nitriding of these steels, is very hard and adherent, and does not spall easily. The scuffing and wear resistance increases with increasing thickness of the compound layer up to ~15 μm, and then, saturates. The improvement in fatigue resistance is essentially due to the compressive stresses set up in the surface layer by nitrogen in solid solution, and hence, is a function of the diffusion zone thickness. With ~1.0 mm nitrogen diffusion zone 50 to 100% improvement in endurance limit may be achieved. The surface iron nitride layer also improves the corrosion resistance of steels in certain environments. No advantage is accrued by nitriding plain carbon steels for longer time, as the thick iron nitride compound layer, thus formed, is generally brittle.

REFERENCES

1. *Heat Treatment* '73, The Metals Society, London, 1973.
2. *Heat Treatment* '76, The Metals Society, London, 1976.
3. *Heat Treatment* '79, The Metals Society, London, 1979.
4. *Metals Handbook*, Vol.2, 8th Edition, American Society for Metals, Metals Park, Ohio, 1964.

• CHAPTER 13

Induction and Flame Hardening

1 INTRODUCTION

Induction and flame hardening are used for producing hard and wear resistant surfaces in steel components by rapidly heating the surface layer to austenite temperatures, and then quenching it to form martensite. Material below the hardened surface layer remains at relatively lower temperatures. In these processes, heating of the surface layer is sufficiently rapid to heat it into the austenite range, while heat conduction to interior of the part during this short period is minimal and it remains at relatively lower temperatures. Rapid heating of the surface layer is achieved by high frequency induction heating in induction hardening and by high-temperature flame heating in flame hardening. Maximum hardness of the surface layer is limited by the carbon content of steel, as hardness of martensite is essentially a function of its carbon content. Hence, substantial surface hardening by these processes is possible only in medium and high carbon steels.

Case hardening by induction or flame hardening is generally preferred over carburizing or carbonitriding, whenever feasible. Since only the surface layer is heated during induction or flame hardening; the overall power consumption is much lower as well as distortion of the parts on quenching is minimal. Furthermore, small areas in large parts can be easily surface hardened without heating the whole part. However, the initial equipment capital costs, particularly for induction hardening, are high. Hence, induction hardening is economical only where large number of parts are to be heat treated. Automobile axle shafts, hydraulic piston rods, steering knuckles, certain gears, etc., are some of the parts that are normally induction hardened. Flame hardening is normally used for hardening cylindrical pins, gear teeth, etc.

2 INDUCTION HARDENING

2.1 HEATING BY INDUCTION

Any electrical conductor can be heated by electromagnetic induction. Figure 13.1 shows patterns of heating obtained by different induction coils. As alternating current flows through the work coil, a highly concentrated magnetic field is established within the coil. The magnetic field, thus established, induces an electric potential in the part. Since, the part represents a closed circuit, induced voltage causes flow of current and heating of the part occurs by resistance heating. Rate of heating depends

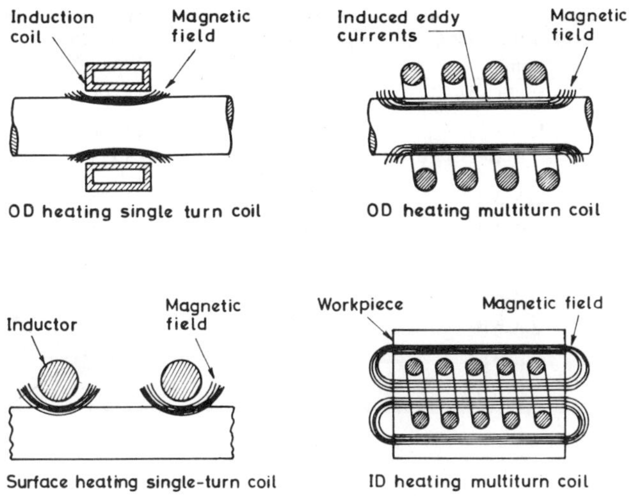

Fig. 13.1. Patterns of magnetic field and induced current produced by various induction coils.

on the strength of the magnetic field to which the part is exposed. Magnetic field, and hence, the induced current and resistance heating of the part, is maximum at the surface and decreases rapidly below it. The effective penetration of current below the surface decreases with increasing frequency of the a.c. current passing through the work coil. Heat is also conducted from the surface layer to interior due to temperature gradients set up during induction heating. Therefore, actual depth of heating (temperature profile) depends on the duration of induction heating, power density of the coil and frequency of the a.c. current. High frequency currents and high power densities are used for shallow hardening, whereas low frequency currents and lower power densities are used for deeper case depths, with appropriate power and time requirements normally established by experimentation. Table 13.1 gives general guidelines for frequency selection for different depths of hardening. For a given depth of hardening, power input, time and frequency of the a.c. current should be such that the surface does not overheat in the time austenite is obtained to required depth from the surface. At the same time, heating should not be too slow to heat the component to larger depths than required, by the time proper austenitizing temperature is reached in the surface region.

Success of any induction hardening operation partly depends on the proper selection and design of the induction coil. Coils are usually made from copper tubes and are water cooled during induction heating. For most rapid heating, the induction coils are designed to provide maximum flow of current in the inductor and closest possible coupling, i.e. minimum possible gap between the coil and steel surface without any physical contact. Figure 13.2 [1–5a & 5b] shows some typical designs of working coils used for induction hardening. While designing a coil for an irregularly shaped component, it must be kept in mind that surface closest to the coil will usually be in the strongest magnetic field, and hence, will heat most rapidly.

Table 13.1. Guidelines for Frequency Selection during Induction Hardening

Depth of Hardening (mm)	Frequency kHz	Power Input (W/mm^2)
0.375–1.125	500	11–18.5
1.125–2.25	500	4.5–12.5
1.5–2.25	10	12.5–25
2.25–3.0	10	8–23
3.0–4.0	10	8–21.5
2.25–3.0	3	15.5–26.5
3.0–4.0	3	8–25
4.0–5.0	3	8–21.5
5.0–7.0	1	8–18.5
7.0–9.0	1	8–18.5

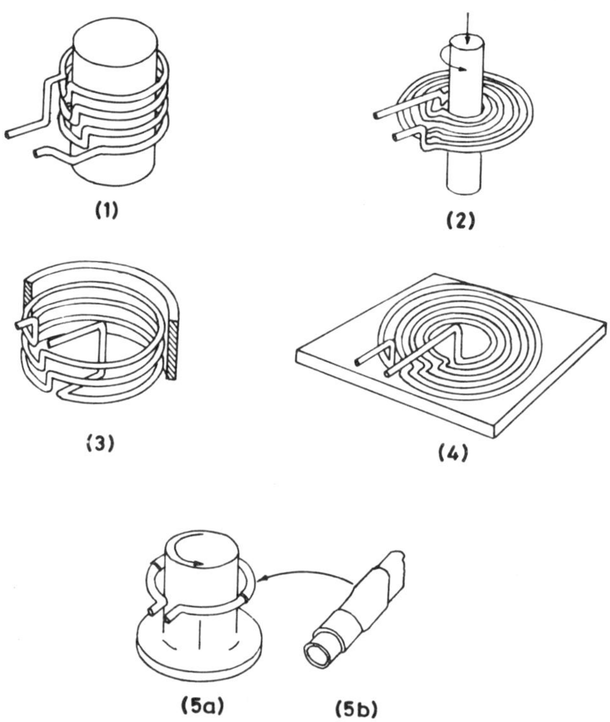

Fig. 13.2. Typical designs of high-frequency induction hardening systems.

2.2 QUENCHING

To obtain hardened surface layer, induction heated surface layer is quenched from austenite temperatures to form martensite. Generally, water is used as a quenching medium. Occasionally, other quenching media, like, oil, brine, compressed air, etc., may also be used. The following types of quenching arrangements are generally used during induction hardening.

(i) Part is heated in the induction coil, and then, manually, or mechanically, lifted and quenched.

(ii) Part is spray quenched in position, after induction heating.

(iii) When induction heating is done by horizontal or vertical scanning of the parts, quenching system is an integral part of the induction coil assembly. It moves behind the coil at the same speed and the part is spray quenched.

(iv) "Self-quenching": When the part being surface hardened is very large, specifically in direction normal to the surface, heat may be rapidly absorbed by unheated mass below the surface at a rapid enough rate to form martensite in the austenitized surface layer. This is referred to as self-quenching. No external quenching is required in such cases. Self-quenching ability of a part depends on its size and hardenability of the steel.

(v) A modified self-quenching is sometimes adopted, where compressed air blast is used to accelerate cooling of the heated surface layer.

2.3 METALLURGICAL FACTORS

Austenitizing times during induction hardening are of the order of few seconds, as compared to a few minutes to about an hour or more in conventional quench hardening treatments. Therefore, prior microstructure and composition of steel have a far greater influence on its response to induction hardening, and hence on the choice of induction hardening parameters.

The temperature above Ae_3 at which a steel is completely transformed to austenite on continuous heating depends on the heating rate and microstructure of the steel, in addition to its composition. This temperature is known as Ac_3 temperature. A steel with a fine and uniform prior microstructure is more easily austenitized as compared to a steel with coarse and duplex structure. For example, a fully pearlitic steel is more easily austenitized than a ferrite-pearlite or cementite-pearlite steel. Similarly, a steel in quenched and tempered state, where carbides are finely dispersed, is more easily austenitized as compared to a normalized or fully annealed steel, and a normalized structure is more easily austenitized than fully annealed structure. Spheroidized structures, where carbides are present in relatively large sized spheroidal particles, are most difficult to austenitize, as large carbide particles do not dissolve easily. These factors are reflected in the effective Ac_3 temperature of a steel at a given heat rate.

Figure 13.3 shows Ac_3 temperatures of AISI-1042 steel as a function of heating rate and prior microstructure. Ac_3 temperature is higher at higher heating rates and for coarser microstructures. Hence, on induction hardening the same steel under similar conditions, lower case depth is obtained when starting structure is coarse. Figure 13.4 gives an example of the effect of prior microstructures on hardening response during induction hardening. Figure 13.4 also shows the temperature profile obtained during induction hardening and the Ac_3 temperatures for different

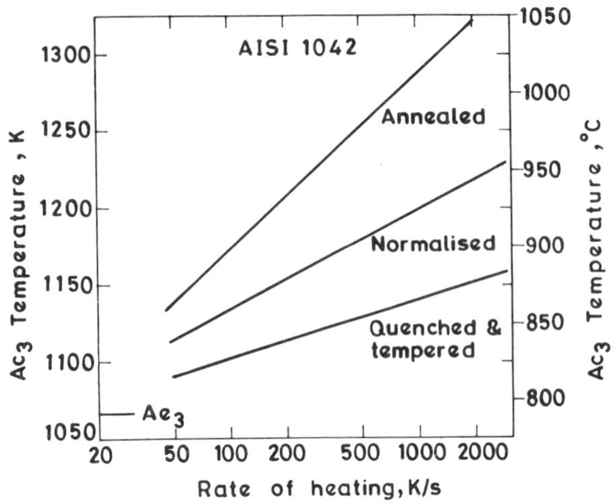

Fig. 13.3. Effect of prior microstructure and rate of heating on Ac_3 temperatures of AISI-1042 steel [from Ref. 1].

microstructures at this heating rate. Relationship between Ac_3 temperature, prior microstructure and the case depth is obvious. The Ac_3 temperature increases and the case depth decreases as we go from finer to coarser prior microstructures. Also, in the case of prior quenched and tempered steel, some sc'tening occurs in the region next to the hardened region (Fig. 13.4). Region next to the fully austenitized region is at relatively higher temperatures, though lower than Ac_3. Softening occurs in this region in the prior quenched and tempered steel, due to coarsening of carbide precipitates at these temepratures, i.e. by further continuation of martensite tempering processes. This is called heat affected zone. A small softening effect is also observed in the normalized steel, but does not exist in the fully annealed steel.

The example given above sufficiently illustrates the effect of prior microstructures on the induction hardening response of steels. Therefore, while deciding on the austenitizing temperature and other parameters during induction hardening, thermal history of the part must be taken into consideration. For induction hardening, higher austenitizing temperatures are generally chosen than recommended for conventional austenitizing and quenching treatment. This is because of the higher Ac_3 temperatures due to rapid heating rates during induction hardening and short austenitizing times. For plain carbon steels, having a suitable prior microstructure, austenitizing temperatures about 30K higher than recommended for conventional treatment are quite adequate.

In alloy steels, the response to induction hardening treatment is further affected by carbide-forming elements, like Cr, Mo,V, W, etc., if present in the steel. Presence of alloy carbides in these steels, which are relatively more difficult to dissolve, greatly affects the induction hardening response of these steels. Figure 13.5 shows induction hardening response of different steels under the same operating conditions.

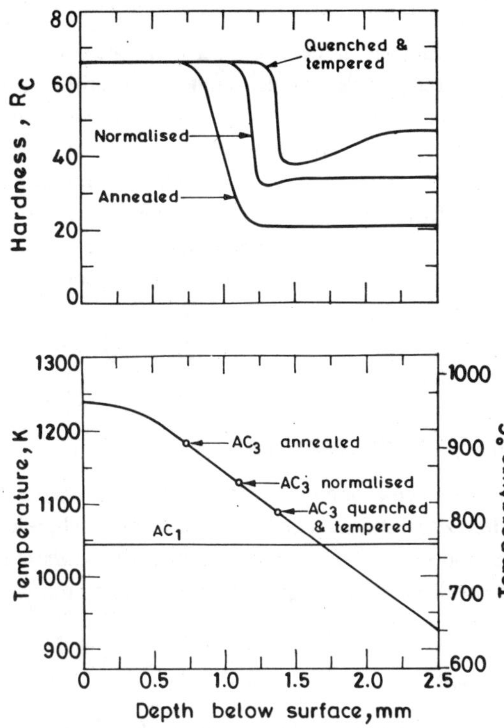

Fig. 13.4. Effect of prior structures on the induction hardening response of AISI-1070 steel at 450 kHz [from Ref. 1].

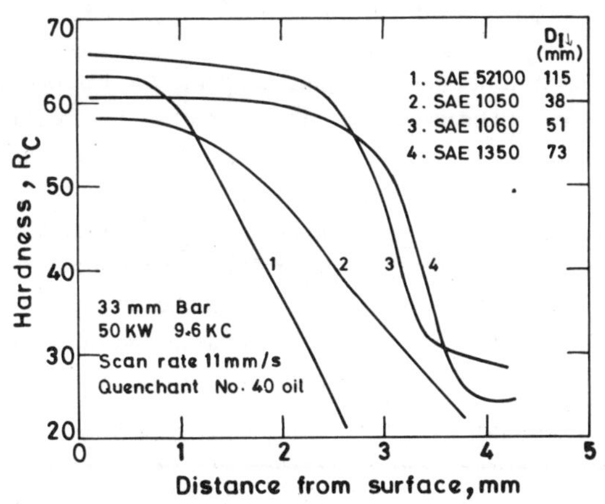

Fig. 13.5. Relative response to induction hardening of a few steels [from C.A. Siebert, D.V. Doane and D.H. Breen. The Hardenability of Steels, American Society for Metals, 1977].

Hardenability of these steels, in terms of ideal critical diameters, D_I, is also given in Fig. 13.5. Depth of hardening, in general, increases with increasing D_I, as expected, except for SAE-52100 steel. This steel, a high hardenability steel by normal criteria, responds poorly to induction hardening treatment because it contains ~1.5% chromium. During induction hardening, chromium-rich carbides present in the steel are not easily dissolved, and hence it responds poorly to induction hardening treatment. In applications where hardness gradient is the only engineering requirement, alloy steels containing strong carbide forming elements should not be chosen for induction hardening. However, if such alloying elements have to be present for some other reasons and these steels are to be induction hardened, relatively higher austenitizing temperatures should be chosen to obtain good hardening response. When carbide forming elements are present in a steel, the hardening temperature should be about 50 to 100K higher than recommended for conventional austenitizing and quenching treatment.

2.4 THROUGH HARDENING AND TEMPERING

Induction heating can also be economically used for through hardening and tempering applications. Here, the parts must be heated uniformly. Therefore, low frequencies and low power inputs are used. Low frequencies give higher penetration of the magnetic field and lower power inputs prevent overheating of the surface.

3 FLAME HARDENING

Flame hardening is similar to induction hardening in that surface layer of the part to be case hardened is rapidly heated by high temperature flame, and then quenched. Depths of hardening from 0.8 mm to 6 mm, or more, can be obtained by flame hardening, depending upon the fuel gas used, design of the flame head, duration of heating, method of quenching and the hardenability of steel. For shallow hardening (case depths less than ~2 mm), high calorific value fuel gases with oxygen as a burning agent are used to obtain high flame temperatures. For deeper case depths, air, instead of oxygen, may be used to burn the fuel gas, so that the flame temperature is lower and overheating of the surface is prevented. Hence, for shallow case depths oxy-acetylene flame is normally used, whereas for deeper case depths other gases of lower calorific value, like natural gas, propane, etc., may be used along with oxygen or air as a burning agent. Table 13.2 gives flame temperatures for different fuel gases burned with oxygen and air. Apart from flame temperature, design of the flame head, gap between flame head and the surface, and duration of heating are used to control the heating pattern of the part.

Table 13.2. Flame Temperature for Different Fuel Gases

	Flame Temperature, K(°C)	
Fuel Gas	With oxygen	With air
Acetylene	3373 (3100)	2598 (2325)
City gas	2813 (2540)	2258 (1985)
Natural gas (CH_4)	2973 (2700)	2148 (1875)
Propane	2908 (2635)	2198 (1925)

In a flame hardening operation, a part may be spot heated and quenched, or it may be progressively heated and quenched with the help of a moving flame head and spray quenching system, depending upon the requirements. Very large parts, in which only a small area is to be hardened, may "self-quench". As in induction hardening, flame hardening also involves short heating times with high intensity heating source, and therefore, prior microstructures and composition affect the hardening response in the same manner as in induction hardening. Flame hardening is generally used for one or more of the following reasons:

(i) Part are so large that conventional furnace heating and quenching is impractical or uneconomical. Typical examples include large gears, machine-ways, large dies and rolls, etc.

(ii) Only a small segment or section of the part requires hardening.

(iii) Dimensional accuracy of the part is difficult to maintain or control by furnace heating and quenching, due to distortion.

REFERENCES

1. *Metals Handbook,* Vol. 2, 8th Edition, American Society for Metals, 1964.

CHAPTER 14

Miscellaneous Thermal and Thermo-mechanical Treatments

1 AUSTEMPERING

1.1 AUSTEMPERING TREATMENT

When a steel component is quenched and tempered to a desired hardness (strength) level, at times there is a possibility of producing cracks during quenching which adversely affect ductility and toughness of the component. Hardness/strength levels equivalent to those of a quenched and tempered steel may also be produced by isothermally transforming the steel to bainite (preferably lower bainite) at an appropriate temperature. This process is called austempering. An austempered steel usually has better ductility and toughness as compared to quenched and tempered steel of equivalent hardness. Figure 14.1 schematically illustrates the austempering, and quenching and tempering treatments; and Table 14.1 compares properties of a steel which has been austempered, and quenched and tempered to approximately the same hardness levels. Notice the distinct superior ductility and toughness achieved by austempering.

Table 14.1. Properties of Austempered, and Quenched and Tempered 0.74% Carbon Steel*. [from Davenport, Roff and Bain. Trans Am. Soc. of Metals *22* (1934) p 289]

Property	Austempered	Quenched & Tempered
Hardness, HRC	50.4	50.2
Ultimate Strength, MPa	1950.0	1700.0
Yield Strength, MPa	1040.0	840.0
Elongation, % (in 15 cm sample)	1.9	0.3
Reduction in Area, %	34.5	0.7
Impact value, J	48.0	4.0

**Austemper*: Austenitized at 1061K (788°C) and austempered at 577K (304°C) for 15 min and quenched into water.

Quench & Temper: Austenitized at 1061K (788°C), quenched in oil and tempered for 30 min at 589K (316°C).

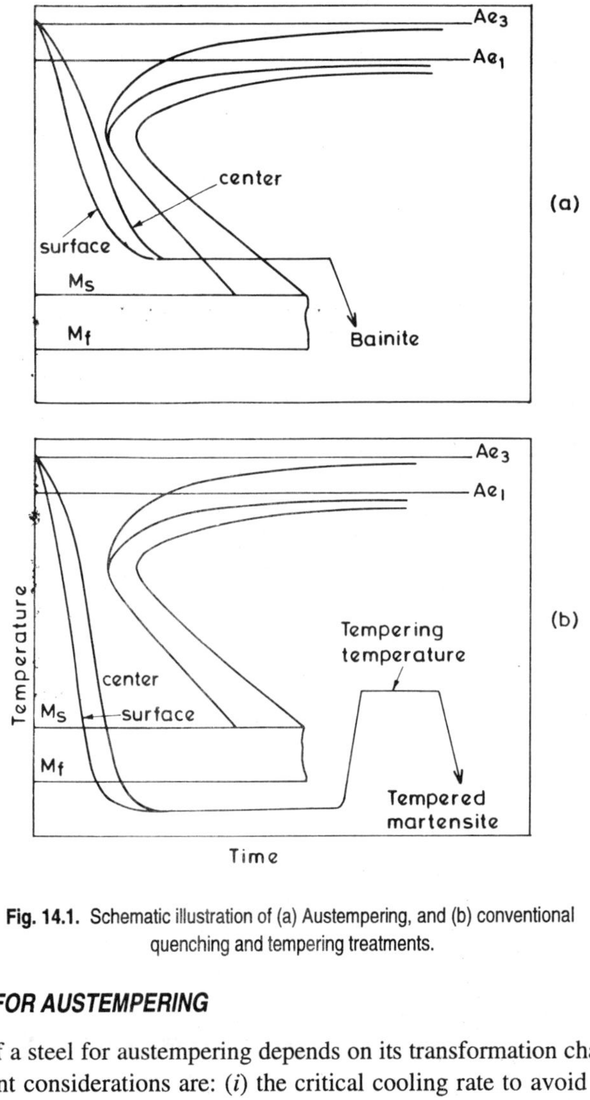

Fig. 14.1. Schematic illustration of (a) Austempering, and (b) conventional quenching and tempering treatments.

1.2 STEELS FOR AUSTEMPERING

Suitability of a steel for austempering depends on its transformation characteristics. The important considerations are: (*i*) the critical cooling rate to avoid any ferrite–pearlite transformation should not be too high; (*ii*) time required to complete the γ to bainite transformation at austempering temperatures should be reasonable; and (*iii*) M_s temperature should be lower than the intended austempering temperature.

Maximum thickness of a steel part that can be uniformly austempered, depends on its ability to avoid ferrite–pearlite transformation during quenching to austempering temperatures. During quenching of steel parts from austenitizing to austempering temperatures, the cooling rate is maximum at the surface and minimum at the center of the part. Furthermore, cooling rate at the center decreases with increasing thickness of the part. For uniform austempering, center of the part should be able to avoid any ferrite–pearlite transformation during cooling. During austempering, steel parts are quenched into salt baths maintained at austempering temperatures, i.e. at 573–673K (300–400°C). Therefore, cooling rates during quenching to austempering temperatures are much slower as compared to the ones obtained during direct quenching to room temperature. Hence, the maximum thickness of a steel that can be uniformly austempered is substantially smaller than that can be quenched to room temperature for uniform hardening.

For example, for AISI–1080 steel, whose IT diagram is shown in Fig. 14.2, the maximum size that can be uniformly austempered is limited to ~5 mm. Plain carbon

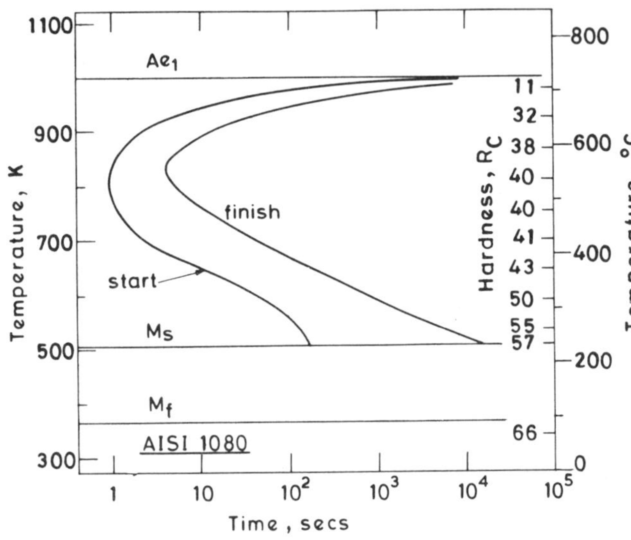

Fig. 14.2. IT diagram of AISI-1080 steel.

steels of lower carbon contents are generally unsuitable for austempering, due to still faster kinetics of ferrite and pearlite transformations in these steels. Low alloy steels of higher hardenability, particularly the ones with double-C curve IT diagrams, are generally suitable for austempering. Figure 14.3 shows IT diagram of a low-alloy steel, AISI-5140, which is well suited for austempering. In some alloy steels, though the ferrite–pearlite transformation is easily avoided during quenching to austempering temperatures, the times required for the completion of bainite transformation at austempering temperatures may be excessively long. Such steels are normally not selected for austempering applications.

2 MARTEMPERING

When a steel part of certain size is quenched from austenite for through hardening, the martensite transformation in different regions of the part occurs at different times. It occurs first at the surface, where the cooling rate is fastest, and occurs last at the

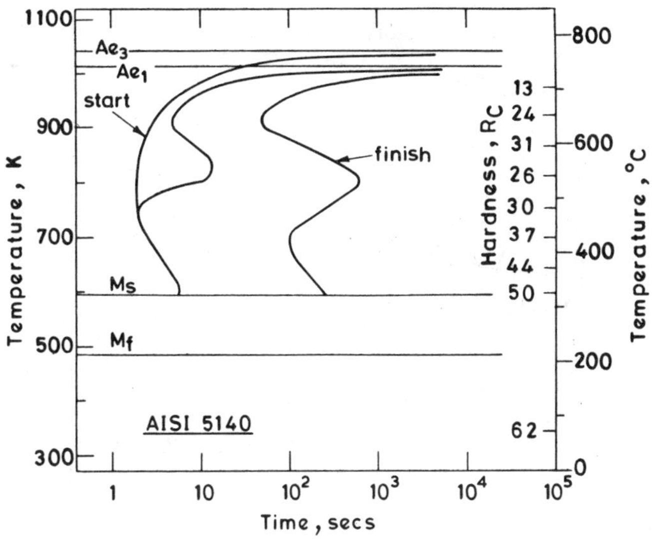

Fig. 14.3. IT diagram of AISI-5140 steel.

center, where the cooling is slowest; as schematically shown in Fig. 14.1(b). In some cases, transformation at the surface may be over, even before it starts at the center. As γ to martensite transformation is accompanied by an increase in specific volume (~4%), substantial internal stresses are built up in the components upon quenching, partly due to differential transformation in different regions, as discussed above. Differential transformation also increases the probability of distortion of the parts during quenching. Internal stresses and distortion of the parts during quenching can, however, be minimized by making the martensite transformation to occur more uniformly, i.e. simultaneously throughout the cross-section of the part. This is achieved by quenching the part to a temperature just above the M_s temperature, holding it there till uniform temperature is attained throughout the part, and then cooling it slowly (say in air) through the martensite transformation range. This process is called martempering, and is schematically shown in Fig. 14.4.

For martempering, a steel should have relatively higher hardenability, as the cooling rates on quenching to just above the M_s temperature are slower than during direct quenching to room temperature. Thickness of the part which can be successfully martempered is, therefore, smaller than what could be hardened by direct quenching to room temperature; and it depends on the hardenability of the steel. For steels with marginal hardenability, or for thicker sections, a modified martempering process may be used. Here, the part is quenched to a temperature in between the M_s and M_f temperatures, held there till the temperature is homogeneous throughout the part, followed by slow cooling. The process is schematically shown in Fig. 14.5. In modified martempering process also, internal stresses and distortion of the parts are lower than during direct quenching. Furthermore, because of lower quenching

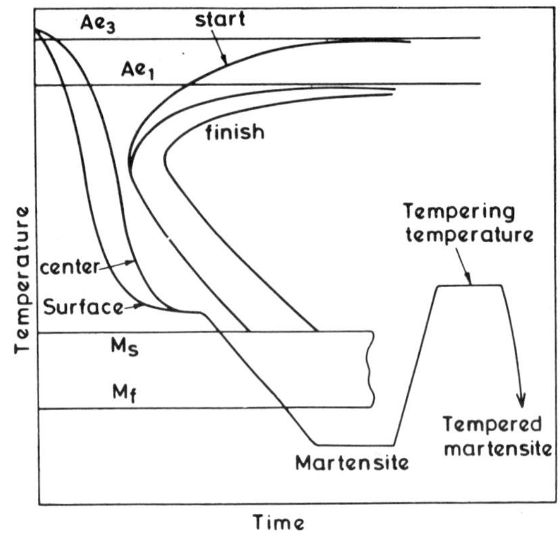

Fig. 14.4. Schematic illustration of martempering process.

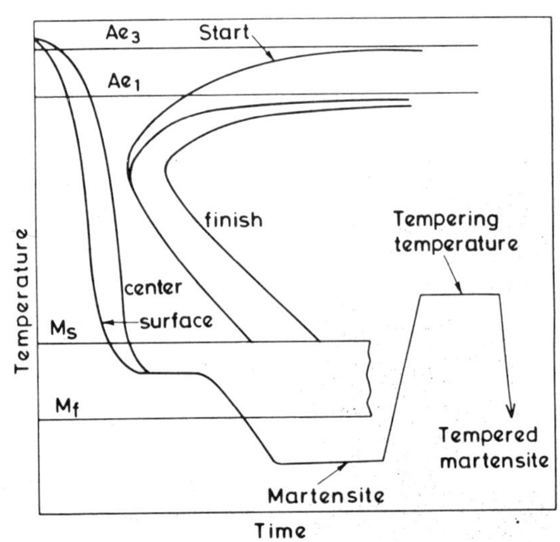

Fig. 14.5. Modified martempering process.

temperatures as compared to martempering, hot oil baths in place of low temperature salt baths may be used as quenching media.

Martempered steels are tempered in the same way as quenched steels. Because of lower internal stresses developed during martempering, probability of quenching cracks is considerably reduced, resulting in improved ductility and toughness. Furthermore, distortion of the parts during martempering is considerably less, requiring little or no straightening.

3 THERMO-MECHANICAL TREATMENTS

3.1 HIGH-TEMPERATURE THERMO-MECHANICAL TREATMENT

In high-temperature thermo-mechanical treatment (HTMT), steel is deformed in the stable austenite range, just above Ae_3 temperature, before being quenched to martensite, as schematically illustrated in Fig. 14.6. Best results are obtained when martensite is formed from well developed polygonized structure in austenite. Martensite formed from such a structure fully inherits the dislocation sub-boundaries of austenite. As a result of the fragmentation of martensite crystals by subgrain boundaries, the yield and ultimate strength of quenched and tempered steels are increased, without adversely affecting its ductility. Though the improvement in strength by HTMT is relatively small, a considerable increase in toughness is obtained. Furthermore, the proneness of the steel to temper embrittlement is considerably reduced.

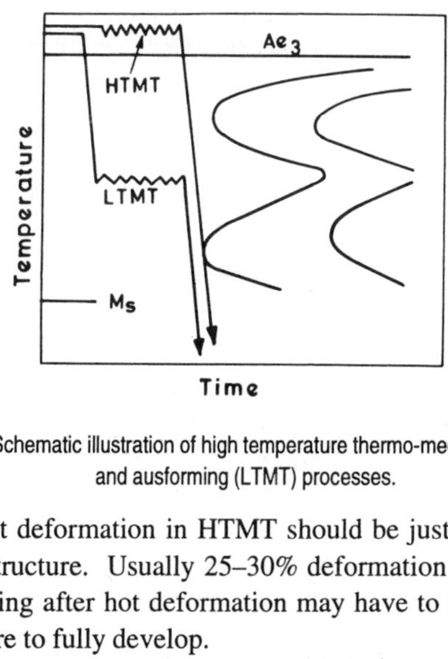

Fig. 14.6. Schematic illustration of high temperature thermo-mechanical (HTMT) and ausforming (LTMT) processes.

The degree of hot deformation in HTMT should be just sufficient to develop a fully polygonized structure. Usually 25–30% deformation is optimum. In certain alloy steels, quenching after hot deformation may have to be delayed to allow the polygonized structure to fully develop.

3.2 AUSFORMING

Ausforming, or low temperature thermo-mechanical treatment (LTMT), of a steel is a thermo-mechanical process, where, austenite is deformed (over 50%) in 673–873K (400–600°C) temperature range, in metastable austenitic state, before being quenched to martensite, as schematically illustrated in Fig. 14.6. Steels with a deep bay in IT diagrams in this temperature range can only be ausformed. Hence, steels containing relatively larger amounts of molybdenum and chromium are only suitable for ausforming, as deep bay is formed in the IT diagrams of these steels. Martensite formed after ausforming treatment needs to be tempered to increase its toughness, just as in normal quenching and tempering treatment. Tempered martensite obtained after ausforming treatment has higher yield and tensile strengths as compared to normal tempered martensite. The increase in strength is proportional to the amount of deformation given during the ausforming treatment. Strengthening is usually in the range of 4 to 9 MPa for each 1% deformation. Presence of carbon (minimum of about 0.05–0.1%) is essential to obtain the increase in strength by ausforming. In the absence of carbon, the strengthening effect is small. The following structural changes occur in martensite due to the deformation of metastable austenite prior to quenching:

(*i*) refinement of martensite packets or plates;

(*ii*) possible change (increase) in the dislocation density in martensite;

(*iii*) change in the size, amount and distribution of carbides; and

(*iv*) development of texture in martensite.

During deformation, the austenite grains get elongated in the direction of rolling. Therefore, on quenching, martensite plates in the direction normal to the rolling plane are refined due to reduced grain size in this direction, whereas in other directions they are relatively longer. Apart from the overall refinement of martensite structure, this also introduces directional properties (texture) in the steel. Deformation may also induce precipitation of carbides in metastable austenite in the presence of strong carbide forming elements, like, molybdenum, vanadium, chromium, etc. These carbides strengthen the martensite matrix by dispersion hardening and also contribute to the refinement of martensite structure by restricting the growth of martensite plates. Some of the dislocations produced during the deformation of austenite are also inherited by the martensite, increasing its dislocation density. All these structural changes contribute to the strengthening of martensite. Since, not much strengthening is observed in carbon-free ausformed steels, it seems that major contribution to the strengthening of martensite on ausforming is due to the precipitation of carbides. Note that, normally the steels containing Mo, Cr, etc., the elements that contribute to the formation of deep bay in the IT diagrams, are only suitable for ausforming, and these are also strong carbide forming elements.

3.3 ISOFORMING

Isoforming is a thermo-mechanical treatment, where, deformation of steel is carried out while it is isothermally transforming from austenite to ferrite–pearlite structure, as schematically illustrated in Fig. 14.7. Simultaneous deformation with pearlite transformation produces very fine subgrain structure together with small spheroidal carbides in place of lamellar pearlite. The temperature at which isoforming is carried out must be high enough for polygonization to occur, i.e. in the range 873–973K (600–700°C), and over 60% deformation is generally necessary to produce satisfactory structure. Only a small improvement in strength is obtained by isoforming, depending upon the final subgrain size. However, the main advantage of isoforming is in the considerably increased toughness, with greatly reduced impact transition temperature. This is due to the formation of spheroidal carbides in place of lamellar cementite structure obtained in the absence of deformation.

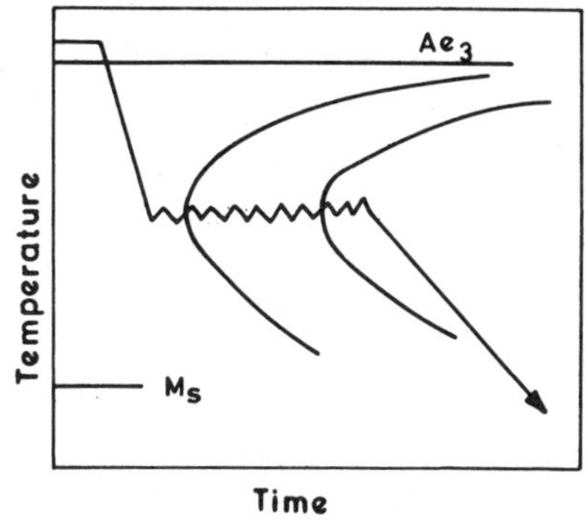

Fig. 14.7. Isoforming process (schematic).

Deforming of a steel during isothermal transformation to bainite also leads to a marked increase in strength, but, with a detrimental effect on ductility and toughness.

4 CONTROLLED ROLLING OF HSLA STEELS

4.1 INTRODUCTION

The high strength low alloy (HSLA), or micro-alloyed, steels are essentially low carbon low alloy steels containing small amounts (generally less than 0.1%) of so-called micro-alloying elements, i.e., titanium, niobium and/or vanadium. These steels are control-rolled in the austenite temperature range and very fine ferrite grain size (of the order of few micrometres) is obtained on transformation to ferrite on subsequent cooling. Controlled rolling of these steels refers to a process where the purpose of rolling is not only to achieve the reduction in thickness and required cross-sections but also to attain an ultrafine grain structure in ferrite on cooling by controlling the process of rolling, i.e. the temperature and reduction sequence followed during rolling.

The combination of relatively low carbon (low pearlite content) and ultrafine ferrite grain size in control rolled HSLA steels provides a good combination of strength and toughness in these steels as well as relatively good weldability, owing to low carbon and low alloy content.

Micro-alloying elements help in the attainment of ultrafine ferrite grain size, primarily by modifying the recrystallization and grain growth behaviour of austenite at hot rolling temperatures. The carbides and nitrides of micro-alloying elements are very stable and have only limited solubility in austenite. Hence, they precipitate in austenite at relatively high temperatures. TiN is the most stable of these precipitates and usually forms during solidification or at relatively higher temperatures, 1473–1573K (1200–1300°C), during soaking prior to rolling. TiN precipitates restrict the austenite grain size at soaking temperatures and during dynamic recrystallization of austenite at rolling temperatures. Niobium carbides and carbonitrides precipitate during the hot deformation of austenite in the temperature range 1073–1323K (800–

1050°C). Niobium is also most effective in modifying the recrystallization behaviour of austenite during hot rolling, and hence is the most important micro-alloying element for proper controlled rolling of HSLA steels. Carbides and nitrides of vanadium generally precipitate at lower temperatures, either during the austenite to ferrite transformation or in ferrite itself. These precipitates mainly contribute to the strength of steel by precipitation hardening.

4.2 HOT ROLLING OF AUSTENITE

Figure 14.8 schematically shows the grain structure of austenite at different stages of hot rolling and the resulting ferrite grain structure on further cooling to room temperature, when rolling is finished at various temperatures. When austenite is rolled at relatively high temperatures, it dynamically recrystallizes and grain growth occurs between two rolling passes. If rolling is finished at these high temperatures, then, austenite is completely recrystallized. Its grain structure is equiaxed and the

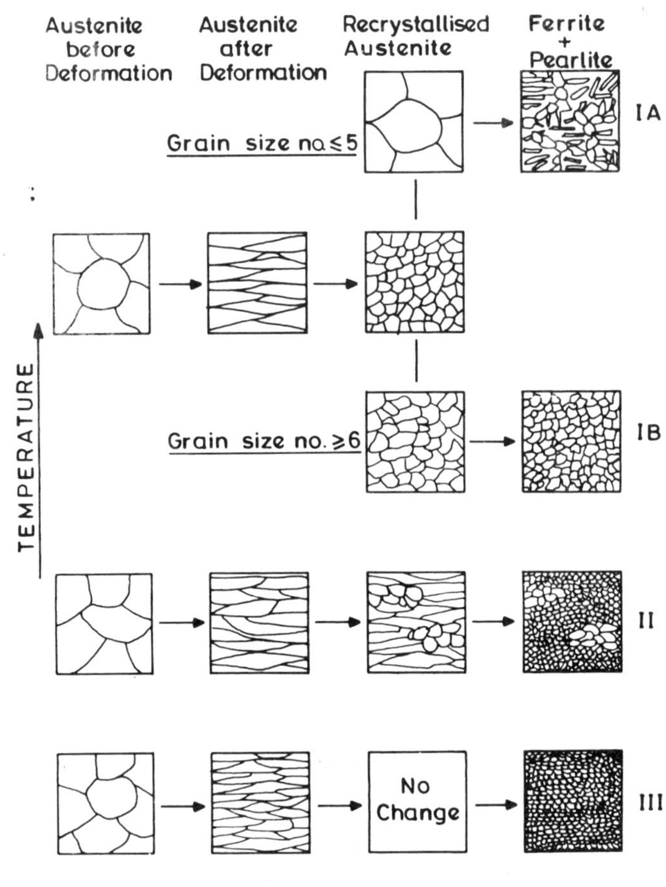

Fig. 14.8. Schematic illustration of development of grain structures during hot deformation of steels followed by cooling to room temperature.

grain size depends on the finishing temperature. With relatively high finishing temperatures, where austenite grain size is relatively large (ASTM grain size No. ≤ 5), coarse grained ferrite and Widmanstätten structure is obtained on subsequent cooling to room temperature (structure IA in Fig. 14.8). With decreasing finishing temperature, the recrystallized austenite grain size decreases and equiaxed ferrite is obtained on subsequent cooling (structure IB in Fig. 14.8), when austenite grain size is less than about ASTM grain size No. 6. This is the normal structure after usual hot rolling of steels.

As the finishing temperature of rolling is further decreased, austenite may only partially recrystallize and the resulting ferrite would be a duplex structure, consisting of regions of two different grain sizes, i.e. structure II in Fig. 14.8. Coarse ferrite grain size is obtained in completely recrystallized regions, whereas finer ferrite grains are obtained in the unrecrystallized regions. This type of structure is normally undesirable. On rolling at still lower temperatures, austenite does not recrystallize and the ferrite formed from deformed elongated austenite grains has a very small grain size (structure III in Fig. 14.8). Ferrite grains, which nucleate at prior austenite grain boundaries, very soon impinge upon each other in the direction perpendicular to the rolling plane, due to thin elongated nature of the deformed austenite grains, thus producing an ultrafine ferrite grain size. Hence, ultrafine grained ferrite can be obtained by controlling the rolling process.

4.3 EFFECT OF MICROALLOYING

Niobium is the most effective micro-alloying element in obtaining ultrafine ferrite grain sizes by controlled rolling of steels. Niobium modifies the recrystallization behaviour of austenite during hot rolling of steels. Niobium carbonitrides precipitate in austenite in the temperature range 1073–1273K (800–1000°C) and their precipitation is strongly aided by the deformation processing of austenite, as shown in Fig. 14.9. These precipitates, along with the TiN precipitates (if present), help to restrict the grain growth of recrystallized austenite grains, and hence, in the attainment of successively smaller austenite grain sizes with decreasing rolling temperatures. More importantly, niobium also retards the recrystallization of austenite at hot rolling temperatures. Figure 14.10 compares the time required for recrystallization of austenite as a function of temperature for a niobium-containing and a niobium-free low carbon steel, after 50% deformation at a given temperature. As seen in Fig. 14.10, niobium considerably retards the austenite recrystallization kinetics. Therefore, unrecrystallized thin elongated austenite grains on hot rolling, essential for attaining ultrafine ferrite grain size, can be obtained at relatively higher finishing temperatures. In plain C-Mn steels, austenite recystallization occurs very rapidly down to temperatures where austenite is already metastable with respect to ferrite. Figure 14.11 gives finishing temperatures for attaining different types of structures, shown in Fig. 14.8, for plain C-Mn and micro-alloyed steels. Note that, niobium-containing steels can be finished rolled in the stable austenite range, around 1123K (850°C), to attain the type III structure in Fig. 14.8, essential for obtaining ultrafine ferrite grain sizes.

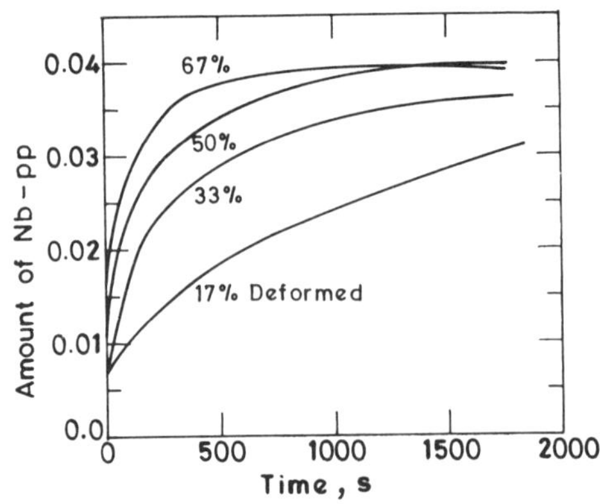

Fig. 14.9. Kinetics of niobium carbonitride precipitation after given amount of deformation at 1173K (900°C) in a steel containing 0.06% C, 0.041% Nb and 0.004% N. (from T.M. Hoogendoorn and M.J. Spanraft, in Ref 3, p 75)

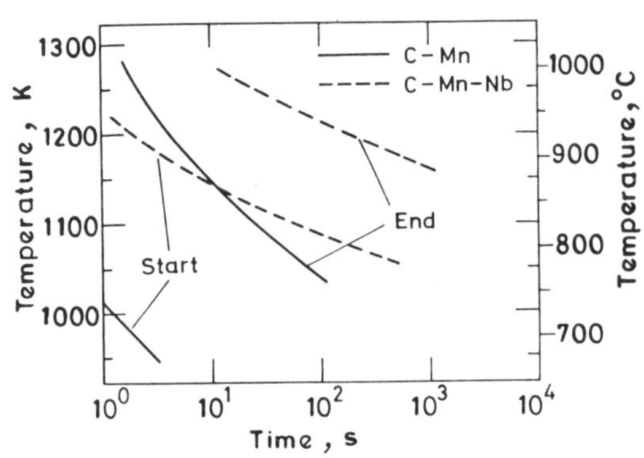

Fig. 14.10. Recrystallization kinetics of austenite in C-Mn and C-Mn-Nb steels at high temperatures, after 50% deformation. (from T.M. Hoogendoorn and M.J. Spanraft, in Ref 3, p 75)

4.4 FINAL FERRITE GRAIN SIZE

The main aim of controlled rolling of HSLA steels is to attain ultrafine ferrite grain size. The following factors affect the final ferrite grain size of control-rolled HSLA steels.

(i) Austenite Grain Size: Finer equiaxed austenite grains prior to the final rolling pass would give thinner elongated austenite grains during the final pass (see Fig. 14.8), thus leading to a finer ferrite grain size on subsequent cooling. Size of equi-axed austenite grains prior to the final pass depends on the deformation sequence at higher temperature. Also, carbides and nitrides of micro-alloying elements restrict the grain growth in austenite, and thus help to attain finer equiaxed austenite grain size prior to the final rolling pass.

(ii) Deformation during the Final Pass : The amount of deformation during the final pass, to attain unrecrystallized thin elongated austenite grain structure (''pan-

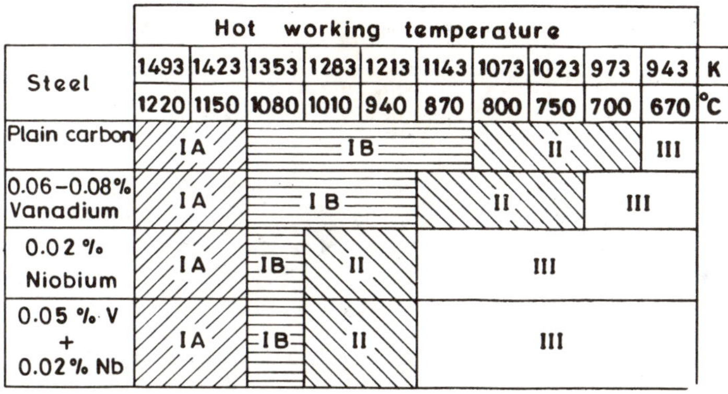

Fig. 14.11. Type of structure (as defined in Fig. 14.8) obtained on hot working at various temperatures [heated to 1523K (1250°C) and defomed 75% at that temperature] (from Ref 3).

cake structure''), is very critical in achieving ultrafine ferrite grain size. Higher reduction in the final pass leads to thinner elongated grains. Deformation reduction in the final pass should normally be over 50% to attain ultrafine ferrite grains.

(iii) Cooling Rate : At faster cooling rates from austenite, the austenite to ferrite transformation occurs at higher undercoolings, which gives a finer ferrite grain size.

(iv) Alloying Elements : Alloying elements generally lower the temperatures at which austenite to ferrite transformation occurs on cooling, and hence, decrease the final ferrite grain size. With the addition of certain alloying elements, like, Mo, Mo-B, etc., austenite may transform to accicular ferrite, or bainite, on cooling. This further increases the strength of steel; however, it is at the cost of decreased ductility and toughness.

By controlled rolling of HSLA steels, ferrite grain size of the order of 8–10 μm in thick plates and of the order of ~5 μm in thin plates has been obtained in industry; and a grain size of 1–2 μm has been obtained under laboratory conditions. This is to be compared with a grain size of 16–30 μm (ASTM grain size No. 9–7) in fine grained hot rolled C-Mn steels.

5. DUAL-PHASE STEELS

5.1 INTRODUCTION

Dual-phase steels consist of a dispersion of martensite icelands (a hard phase) in soft ferrite matrix. These are produced by inter-critical annealing of low-carbon steels, followed by quenching. In inter-critical annealing, a steel is held at a temperature in between the Ae_1 and Ae_3 temperatures to attain $(\alpha + \gamma)$ structure, and then, quenched to transform the austenite regions to martensite. The main advantage of dual-phase steels over ferrite–pearlite, or quenched and tempered steels, is that for comparable strength levels, dual-phase steels show higher ductility. Furthermore, dual-phase steels are free from yield point elongation and also have a low yield point in com-

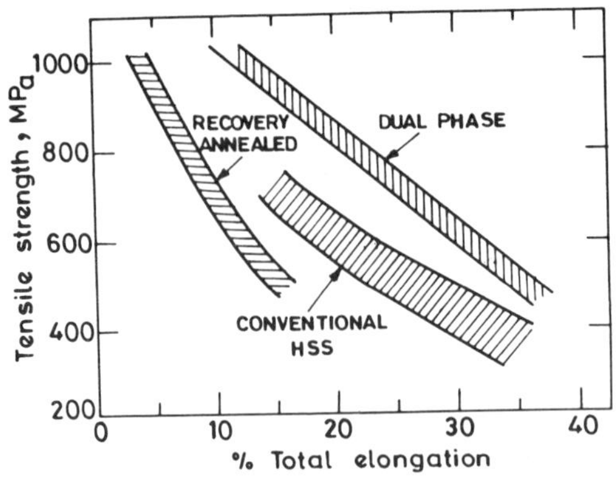

Fig. 14.12. Strength vs ductility relationship for dual-phase, recovery annealed and conventional high strength steels.

bination with high initial work hardening rates. Hence, these steels combine high strength with good formability, and are potential materials for certain automotive parts. Figure 14.12 compares the strength vs ductility relationship of dual-phase steels with that of recovery annealed ferrite–pearlite and high strength steels.

5.2 INTER-CRITICAL ANNEALING

Dual-phase steels may be produced by inter-critical annealing by any of the following methods, also schematically shown in Fig. 14.13.

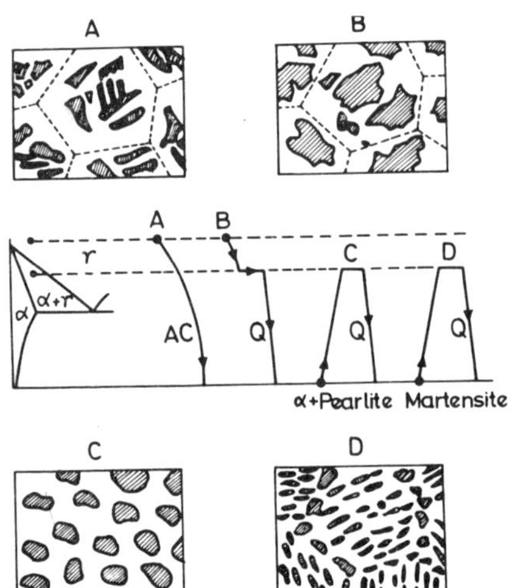

Fig. 14.13. Schematic illustration of different methods of obtaining dual-phase steels. A: air cooling (ferrite-pearlite), B: step quenching, C: intermediate normalizing, D: intermediate quenching.

(i) Step quenching: Steel is isothermally transformed from austenite at the inter-critical annealing temperature till the two-phase ($\alpha + \gamma$) equilibrium structure is obtained and then quenched. During inter-critical annealing, ferrite nucleates at prior austenite grain boundaries and grows inwards till equilibrium amount of ferrite has formed. On quenching, the remaining austenite transforms to martensite. Relatively coarse ferrite–martensite structure is obtained by this method.

(ii) Intermediate Normalizing: The steel is first air-cooled from austenite (i.e. normalized) to obtain a relatively fine ferrite–pearlite structure and then heated to the inter-critical annealing temperature. It is held there till equilibrium is attained, and then, quenched to produce dual-phase steel. On heating, the pearlite transforms to austenite first, in a relatively short period, and then, it grows into ferrite, till equilibrium is reached. On quenching, the austenite transforms to martensite. The dual-phase structure produced by this method is finer as compared to the one produced by step-quenching.

(iii) Intermediate Quenching: Here, the steel is first quenched to form martensite, and then, reheated to the inter-critical annealing temperature. Once, equilibrium is attained at this temperature, it is quenched again to form dual-phase steel. During inter-critical annealing, austenite apparently nucleates at former boundaries of martensite plates and grows along them. The resulting dual-phase structure is fibrous, consisting of elongated martensite particles in ferrite matrix.

5.3 STRUCTURE AND PROPERTIES

The dual-phase steels consist of relatively hard martensitic regions dispersed in a soft ferrite matrix. The strength of a dual-phase steel, to a first approximation, is given by the law of mixtures, i.e.

$$\sigma = \sigma_f (1 - V_m) + \sigma_m V_m \tag{14.1}$$

where σ is strength of the dual-phase steel; σ_f and σ_m are the strengths of ferrite and martensite, respectively, and V_m is the volume fraction of martensite in the dual-phase steel. Hence, the strength of a dual-phase steel increases linearly with volume fraction of martensite in the steel. Volume fraction of martensite in a dual phase steel can be controlled by changing the composition and/or inter-critical annealing temperature.

As compared to ferrite–pearlite steels, dual-phase steels show higher ductility for the same strength levels as well as have a low yield point and are free from yield point elongation. Figure 14.14 compares the stress-strain curve of a dual-phase steel with that of a ferrite–pearlite steel of the same composition; illustrating the above mentioned characteristics. Ductility of these steels can be considered to be essentially proportional to the volume fraction of the ferrite phase. However, since martensite is harder than pearlite, higher strength levels are obtained in dual-phase steels. The low yield point in dual-phase steels is due to the excess dislocations in ferrite surrounding the martensite regions, formed due to volume expansion (of ~4%) during the austenite to martensite transformation. These dislocations are highly mobile, and

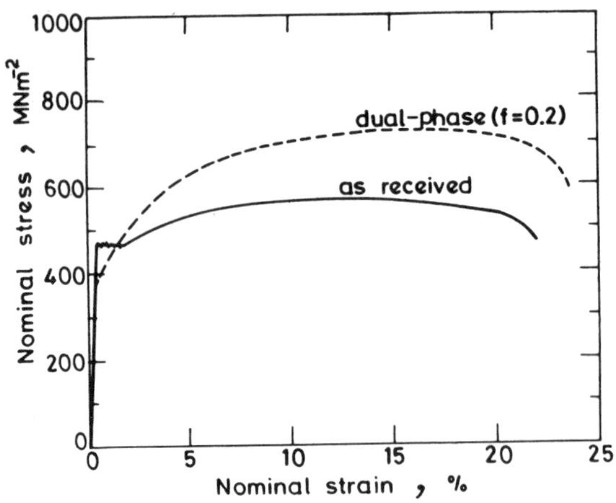

Fig. 14.14. Stress-strain curves of (ferrite-pearlite) and dual-phase (V_m=0.2) steels of the same composition (0.11% C, 1.17% Mn).

hence, give a low yield point and prevent yield point elongation. The increased dislocation density also leads to higher initial work hardening rates.

REFERENCES

1. M.J. May and D.J. Latham, in *Towards Improved Ductility and Toughness*, Climax Molybdenum Company Symp., Kyoto, Japan, 1971.
2. *Metals Handbook*, 8th Edition, Volume 2, American Society for Metals, Metals Park, 1964.
3. *Microalloying* '75, Union Carbide Corporation, New York, 1976.
4. *Structure and Properties of Dual-Phase Steels — Conference Proceedings*, (Eds. R.A. Kot and J.W. Morris), The Metallurgical Society of AIME, Warrendale, Pa, 1979.

CHAPTER 15

Tool Steels and their Heat Treatment

1 CLASSIFICATION AND USES

Tool steels refer to a large group of steels used as tools for working and shaping of other materials, including metals. Uses of tool steels include: hand tools, such as chisels, punches, hammers, etc; tools intended for cutting metals and other materials; and dies for deep drawing, extrusion, forging, die casting, hot drawing, etc. The large variety of steels used as tools, makes their classification difficult. The AISI system of classification of tool steels — based on quenching methods, applications, special characteristics and applications for particular industries — is given in Table 15.1. Depending upon the application, one or more of the following properties may be important for the selection of a tool steel for a given application: hardness, wear resistance, toughness, warpage, depth hardening (hardenability) and resistance to softening at elevated temperatures. Table 15.2 lists the various characteristics of different types of tool steels.[1]

The choice of a tool steel depends on the requirements of a particular application and the steel chosen should be no more expensive than needed to meet the specific requirements. Tools for relatively simple applications, like files, wood working tools, axes, taps, reamers and some drill bits, can be satisfactorily made from water-hardening tool steels. Battering tools, such as chisels, punches and rivet sets, have shock resistance as their main requirement and are made from shock-resisting tool steels. Steels for moulds for plastics are soft to facilitate machining and are carburized for wear resistance. The cold work tool steels, used for stamping and trimming dies, punches, thread rolling dies, shear blades, etc., are hardenable by cooling in air, or by oil quenching, to minimize distortion and cracking during heat treatment. These steels must be finish-machined to close tolerances before heat treatment and these tolerances must be maintained after heat treatment. Hot work tool steels are used for forging dies, piercing tools, extrusion dies, die casting dies, etc., where resistance to softening, deformation and cracking under thermal shock are important requirements. Hence, these steals have low carbon and high alloy content. The most complex and important type of the tool steels are high speed tool steels. They maintain their hardness at elevated temperatures, are deep hardening, and quite resistant to wear. They contain relatively large amounts of tungsten and molybdenum, along with chromium, cobalt and vanadium. These are used as lathe tools, milling cutters, end mills and other cutting tools which remove metal at high rates, and therefore, must withstand the resulting high temperatures.

Table 15.1. Tool Steel Types and their Nominal Composition

Water-Hardening Tool Steels (Symbol W)

Type	C	Cr	V	Applications
W1	0.6–1.4	–	–	
W2	0.6–1.4	–	0.25	General purpose
W5	1.10	0.5	–	

Shock-Resisting Tool Steels (Symbol S)

Type	C	Mn	Si	W	Mo	Cr	Applications
S1	0.50	–	–	2.50	–	1.50	Chisels, punches, shears, heading dies
S2	0.50	–	1.00	–	0.50	–	
S5	0.55	0.80	2.00	–	0.40	–	
S6	0.45	1.40	2.25	–	0.40	1.50	
S7	0.50	–	–	–	1.40	3.25	

Mould Steels (Symbol P)

Type	C	Mo	Cr	Ni	Al	Applications
P2	0.07	0.20	2.00	0.50	–	Carburized hubbed and cut moulds
P3	0.10	–	0.60	1.25	–	
P4	0.07	0.75	5.00	–	–	
P5	0.10	–	2.25	–	–	
P6	0.10	–	1.50	3.50	–	
P20	0.35	0.40	1.70	–	–	
P21	0.20	–	–	4.00	1.20	

Cold Work Tool Steels (Symbol D, high-C high-Cr)

Type	C	Mo	Cr	V	Co	Applications
D2	1.50	1.00	12.00	1.00	–	Rolls, mandrels, punches, dies, shears, (high wear resistance)
D3	2.25	–	12.00	–	–	
D4	2.25	1.00	12.00	–	–	
D5	1.50	1.00	12.00	–	3.0	
D7	2.35	1.00	12.00	4.00	–	

Cold Work Tool Steels (Symbol O, oil-hardening)

Type	C	Mn	Si	W	Mo	Cr	Applications
O1	0.90	1.00	–	0.50	–	0.50	General purpose tools, dies, broaches
O2	0.90	1.60	–	–	–	–	
O6	1.45	0.80	1.00	–	0.25	–	
O7	1.20	–	–	1.75	–	0.75	

Cold Work Tool Steels (Symbol A, medium alloy air-hardening)

Type	C	Mn	Si	W	Mo	Cr	V	Ni	Applications
A2	1.00	–	–	–	1.00	5.00	–	–	
A3	1.25	–	–	–	1.00	5.00	1.00	–	Similar to type O, less distortion than type O

	C	Mn	Si	W	Mo	Cr	V	Ni
A4	1.00	2.00	–	–	1.00	1.00	–	–
A6	0.70	2.00	–	–	1.25	1.00	–	–
A7	2.25	–	–	1.00	5.00	5.25	4.75	–
A8	0.55	–	–	1.25	1.25	5.00	–	–
A9	0.50	–	–	–	1.40	5.00	1.00	1.50
A10	1.35	1.80	1.25	–	1.50	–	–	1.80

Hot Work Tool Steels (Symbol H)

	C	W	Mo	Cr	V	Co	
Chromium types							
H10	0.40	–	2.50	3.25	0.40	–	Gripper, bending and
H11	0.35	–	1.50	5.00	0.40	–	heading dies,
H12	0.35	1.50	1.50	5.00	0.40	–	light work up to
H13	0.35	–	1.50	5.00	1.00	–	598K (325°C)
H14	0.40	5.00	–	5.00	–	–	
H19	0.40	4.25	–	4.25	2.00	4.25	
Tungsten types							
H21	0.35	9.00	–	3.50	–	–	Blanking, forming,
H22	0.35	11.00	–	2.00	–	–	extrusion, casting
H23	0.30	12.00	–	12.00	–	–	dies up to 823K (550°C)
H24	0.45	15.00	–	3.00	–	–	
H25	0.25	15.00	–	4.00	–	–	
H26	0.50	18.00	–	4.00	1.00	–	
Molybdenum type							
H42	0.60	6.00	5.0	4.00	2.00	–	Same as above

High Speed Tool Steels (Tungsten Type, Symbol T)

	C	W	Mo	Cr	V	Co	
T1	0.75	18.00	–	4.00	1.00	–	
T2	0.80	18.00	–	4.00	2.00	–	Cutting tools
T4	0.75	18.00	–	4.00	1.00	5.00	all types,
T5	0.80	18.00	–	4.00	2.00	8.00	severe hot work
T6	0.80	20.00	–	4.50	1.50	12.00	
T8	0.75	14.00	–	4.00	2.00	5.00	
T15	1.50	12.00	–	4.00	5.00	5.00	

High Speed Tool Steels (Molybdenum type, Symbol M)

	C	W	Mo	Cr	V	Co	
M1	0.85	1.50	8.50	4.00	1.00	–	
M2	0.85 to 1.0	6.00	5.00	4.00	2.00	–	
M3(1)	1.05	6.00	5.00	4.00	2.40	–	Cutting tools
M3(2)	1.20	6.00	5.00	4.00	3.00	–	all types,
M4	1.30	5.50	4.50	4.00	4.00	–	severe hot work
M6	0.80	4.00	5.00	4.00	1.50	12.0	
M7	1.00	1.75	8.75	4.00	2.00	–	
M10	1.00	–	8.00	4.00	2.00	–	
M30	0.80	2.00	8.00	4.00	1.25	5.00	

	C	W	Mo	Cr	V	Co
M33	0.90	1.50	9.50	4.00	1.15	8.00
M34	0.90	2.00	8.00	4.00	2.00	8.00
M36	0.80	6.00	5.00	4.00	2.00	8.00
M41	1.10	6.75	3.75	4.25	2.00	5.00
M42	1.10	1.50	9.50	3.75	1.15	8.00
M43	1.20	2.75	8.00	3.75	1.60	8.25
M44	1.15	5.25	6.25	4.25	2.00	12.00
M46	1.25	2.00	8.25	4.00	3.20	8.25
M47	1.10	1.50	9.50	3.75	1.25	5.00

2. HEAT TREATMENT

2.1 AUSTENITIZATION

Tool steels are generally sold in annealed condition and the user is responsible for their heat treatment. Tool steels are generally heat treated by austenitizing, quenching and tempering sequence to attain desired properties. Table 15.3 gives general heat treatment conditions for different types of tool steels.

The austenitizing temperature for a steel should generally be high enough to dissolve all the carbides and to attain a reasonably homogeneous austenite. In hot

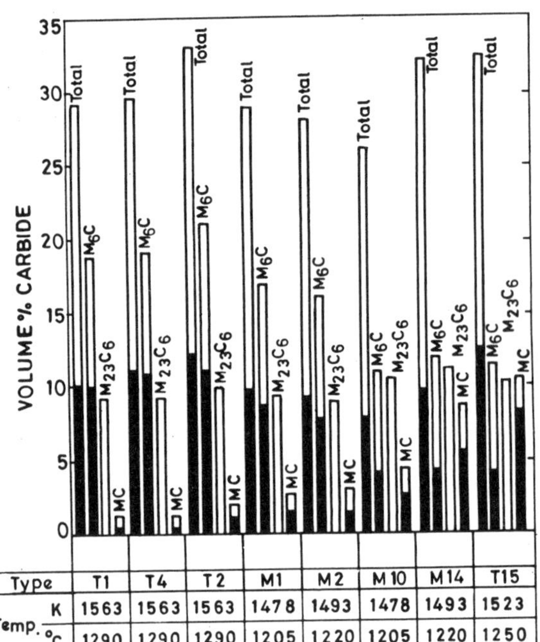

Fig. 15.1. Carbides in high-speed steels in annealed condition (open bars) and at normal austenitizing temperatures (solid bars).

work and high-speed tool steels it is generally not possible to dissolve all the carbides; however, high enough temperatures are used to dissolve sufficient carbides, so that they respond well to secondary hardening during the subsequent tempering treatment after quenching. Table 15.3 gives austenitizing temperatures used for different types of tool steels. In high speed steels, carbides occupy up to 30 to 40% of the total volume under annealed condition and it may still be about 10% at austenitizing temperatures. Figure 15.1 shows the carbide volume percentage in different high speed steels under annealed conditions and at recommended austenitizing temperatures. Relatively large particles of undissolved carbides in these steels, mostly M_6C and MC types, serve to enhance the wear resistance of the tools as well as restrict grain growth, to some extent, at high austenitizing temperatures.

Table 15.2. Characteristics of Tool Steels

Type	Group	Quench medium	Wear resistance	Toughness	Warpage	Hardness depth	Resistance to softening
W	Water hardening	Water/ brine	Fair to good	Good	Poor	Shallow	Poor
S	Shock resisting	Oil/ water	Fair	Best	O:Fair W:Poor	Medium	Fair
P	Mould steels	Air/ oil/ water	Good	Good	Good	Shallow	Poor
D	Cold work High-C High-Cr	Air/ oil	Best	Poor	A:Best O:Very good	Deep	Good
O	Cold work Oil hardening	Oil	Good	Fair	Very good	Medium	Poor
A	Cold work Air hardening	Air	Good	Fair	Best	Deep	Fair
H	Hot work						
	Cr type	Air/ oil	Fair	Good	A:Good O:Fair	Deep	Good
	W type	Air/ oil	Fair to good	Good	A:Good O:Fair	Deep	Very good
	Mo type	Oil/air/ salt	Good	Poor	O:Fair A:Good S:Good	Deep	Very good
M	High speed (Mo type)	Oil/ air/ salt	Very good	Poor	Good	Deep	Very good
T	High speed (W type)	Oil/air/ salt	Very good	Poor	Good	Deep	Best

Table 15.3. Heat Treating Conditions for Various Types of Tool Steels

Type	Quenchant	Austenitizing temperature K(°C)	Hardness on quenching (HRC)	Tempering temperature K(°C)	Hardness on tempering (HRC)
W1	Water	1043–1063 (770–790)	65–67	448–548 (175–275)	65–56
W2	Water	1043–1088 (770–815)	65–67	448–548 (175–275)	65–56
S1	Oil	1173–1253 (900–980)	57–59	423–808 (150–535)	57–45
S2	Water	1118–1128 (845–855)	60–62	423–533 (150–260)	57–45
	Oil	1143–1158 (870–885)	58–60	423–533 (150–260)	58–54
S5	Water	1118–1143 (845–870)	60–62	423–618 (150–345)	60–54
	Oil	1143–1188 (870–915)	58–60	423–618 (150–345)	58–54
O1	Oil	1063–1088 (790–815)	63–65	423–698 (150–425)	62–50
O2	Oil	1043–1063 (770–790)	63–65	463–533 (190–260)	62–57
O6	Oil	1063–1088 (790–815)	63–65	423–698 (150–425)	63–50
A2	Air	1213–1243 (940–970)	61–63	478–643 (205–370)	60–57
D2	Air	1253–1293 (980–1025)	61–63	478–643 (205–370)	60–58
D3	Oil	1228–1253 (955–980)	62–64	478–643 (205–370)	62–58
D5	Air	1253–1298 (980–1025)	60–62	478–643 (205–370)	59–63
D7	Air	1283–1338 (1010–1065)	63–65	423–533 (150–260)	65–63
				728–813 (455–540)	62–58
H1	Air	1268–1298 (995–1025)	53–55	813–868 (540–595)	51–43
H12	Oil, Air	1253–1313 (980–1040)	53–55	813–868 (540–595)	51–43
H13	Air	1268–1298 (995–1025)	53–55	813–868 (540–595)	51–43
H21	Oil, Air	1423–1448 (1150–1175)	50–52	783–893 (510–620)	50–47
T1	Oil, Air, Salt	1533–1573 (1260–1300)	63–65	823–868 (550–595)	65–63
T2	Oil, Air, Salt	1533–1573 (1260–1300)	63–65	823–868 (550–595)	65–63
T4	Oil, Air, Salt	1533–1573 (1260–1300)	63–65	823–868 (550–595)	65–63
T5	Oil, Air, Salt	1533–1588 (1260–1315)	63–65	838–868 (565–595)	65–63
T8	Oil, Air, Salt	1533–1573 (1260–1300)	63–65	823–868 (550–595)	65–63
M1	Oil, Air, Salt	1448–1503 (1175–1230)	63–65	823–838 (550–565)	65–63
M2	Oil, Air, Salt	1463–1503 (1190–1230)	63–65	823–853 (550–580)	65–63
M3	Oil, Air Salt	1448–1493 (1175–1220)	63–65	823–853 (550–580)	65–63
M4	Oil, Air, Salt	1448–1493 (1175–1220)	63–65	823–853 (550–580)	65–63

Performance of tools largely depends on their surface condition and properties close to the surface. Therefore, both carburizing and decarburizing must be avoided during any heat treatment of tools. Neutral salt baths are generally used for heat treatment of tools to avoid any carburization or decarburization. When tools are to be austenitized at relatively high temperatures, greater than ~1323K (1050°C), then they are generally preheated, particularly if they are large and/or irregularly shaped. They are preheated to ~1073K (800°C), before being transferred to the high temperature austenitizing baths. The purpose of preheating is to have slow and uniform heating to minimize distortion.

2.2 QUENCHING

With the exception of water-hardening types, tool steels generally have sufficiently high hardenability and they need not be quenched drastically (see Table 15.3). Figures 15.2 to 15.5 show isothermal transformation (IT) diagrams for some representative tool steels. IT diagrams of type D, H, M and T tool steels, containing larger amounts of Mo and Cr, generally show a very deep bay in the temperature range 673 to 873K (400 to 600°C). In these steels, cooling can be considerably delayed in this temperature range. These steels are generally air hardening. However, it is not always desirable to air-cool these steels for hardening. In some of these steels, specifically in high speed steels, carbide precipitation in austenite may occur during slow cooling in the temperature range 1023–1173K (750–900°C). Because of the deep bay in their IT diagrams, high speed steels may be quenched into salt or lead baths maintained at 773 to 873K (500 to 600°C), allowed to attain uniform temperature and then cooled in air to form martensite. This relieves most of the thermal stresses as well as avoids the precipitation of carbides.

Tool steels containing high carbon and/or high alloy content may contain as much as 20–25% retained austenite on quenching to room temperature. This does permit the straightening of tools immediately after quenching; however, retained austenite must be considerably reduced to maximize the hardness and wear resistance of the

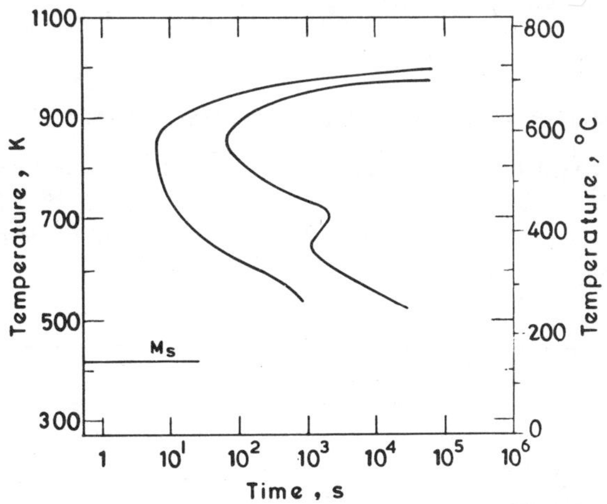

Fig. 15.2. IT diagram of 02 steel (0.87C–1.78Mn–0.29Si–0.15Ni–0.2Cr–0.03Mo)

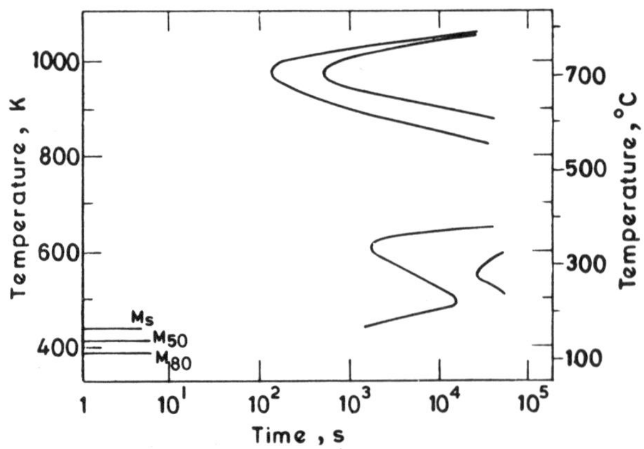

Fig. 15.3. IT diagram of D4 steel (2.25C–11.5Cr–0.8Mo–0.2V).

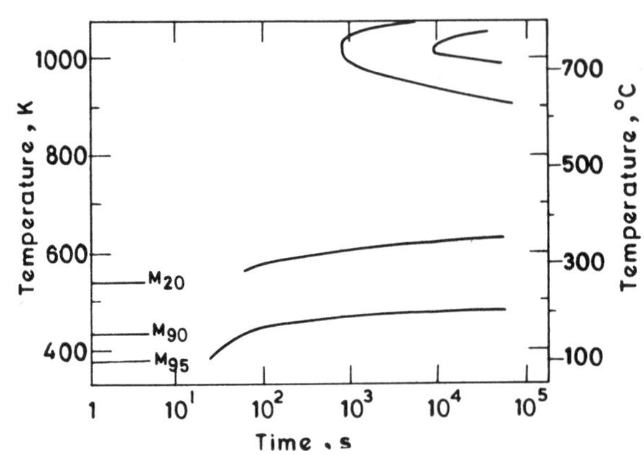

Fig. 15.4. IT diagram of H12 steel (0.32C–0.35Mn–0.95Si–4.86Cr–1.29W–1.45MO).

tools. This may be achieved by multiple tempering, as discussed later. After quenching, the tools are immediately tempered to reduce the chances of delayed quench cracking. However, they must be allowed to completely cool to room temperature to minimize retained austenite.

2.3 TEMPERING TEMPERATURES

Table 15.3 gives the tempering temperatures used for different types tool steels. Tool steels which are used at ambient temperatures, i.e water-hardening (W), shock-resisting (S), mould (P), and cold work (D, O and A) types, are tempered at 423 to 623K (150–350°C). The choice of tempering temperature is dictated by the compromise between strength (hardness) and toughness. The temperature chosen is nor-

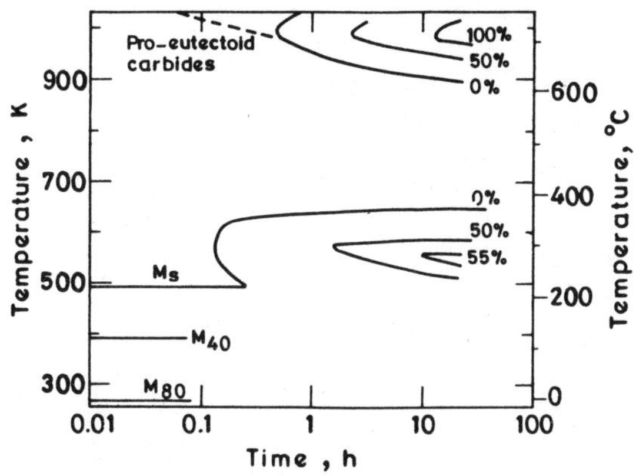

Fig. 15.5. IT diagram of M2 steel (0.81C–0.24Mn–0.26Si–4.1Cr–4.69Mo–5.95W–1.64V)

mally such that maximum toughness is obtained without significantly reducing the hardness levels.

Tools for high temperature applications, i.e. hot work (H) and high speed (M and T) types, are tempered at 773 to 873K (500–600°C) to promote secondary hardening by alloy carbide precipitation. Hardness levels equal to, or higher than, those for as-quenched condition, with higher toughness and wear resistance, can be obtained in these steels on secondary hardening. The basic principles of secondary hardening have already been discussed in Chapter V. Figure 15.6 shows secondary hardening in a M2 high speed steel austenitized at different temperatures. Note that, higher secondary hardness peak is obtained with increasing austenitizing temperature as more of the alloy carbides go into solution during austenitizing treatment and reprecipitate as fine particles during secondary hardening.

2.4 MULTIPLE TEMPERING

On quenching to room temperature, high speed steels may contain 20–25% retained austenite. When these are tempered for secondary hardening at 773 to 873K (500–600°C), there is very little tendency for the retained austenite to transform due to the deep bay in the IT diagrams of these steels in this temperature range (for example see Fig. 15.5). However, during the tempering operation, the austenite is said to be "conditioned", for at least some of it transforms to martensite on cooling from the tempering temperatures. The nature of this "conditioning" is not well understood. The generally accepted explanation is that the austenite becomes more susceptible to martensite transformation by losing some of its carbon to prior martensite regions. These become sinks for carbon because of the precipitation of alloy carbides during tempering. Additional martensite, formed on cooling from the tempering temperature, must be tempered by a second heating to the tempering temperature. Double tempering is usually sufficient, but sometimes three or four tempers may be required to reduce the retained austenite to acceptable levels.

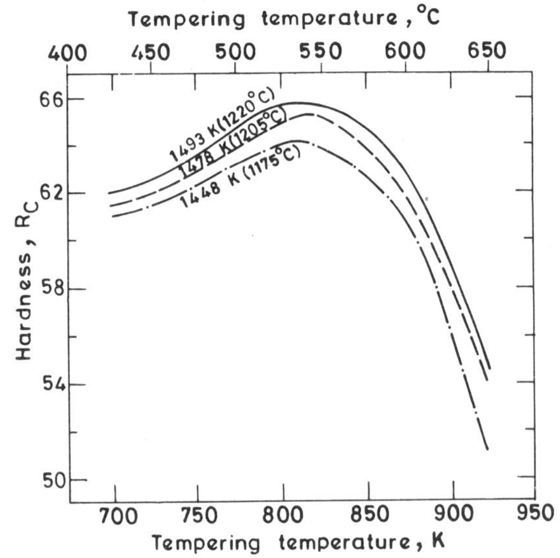

Fig. 15.6. Effect of austenitizing temperature on secondary hardness peak in M2 high-speed steel.

2.5 CARBIDE PRECIPITATION AND SECONDARY HARDENING

Properties of a high speed tool steel are critically dependent on the types of carbides present in the steel and their hardness, as well as on whether these are primary carbides formed during solidification and/or precipitation from austenite, or, secondary carbides precipitated from martensite during tempering. Table 15.4 gives approximate hardness values of different carbides formed in these steels, along with the maximum hardness obtained in martensite. MC, the hardest carbide encountered in steels, is essentially a carbide of vanadium, with molybdenum and tungsten in solution; M_2C is a carbide of tungsten and molybdenum, containing some vanadium; $M_{23}C_6$ and M_6C are W-Mo-Fe carbides, and M_3C is essentially Fe_3C with chromium and other alloying elements dissolved in it. MC is also the most stable of all the carbides present. MC may directly form from the liquid during solidification. During tempering for secondary hardening, the principal hardening agent is MC and it precipitates first. M_2C precipitates next, during overaging beyond the hardness peak, followed by M_6C and $M_{23}C_6$.

Table 15.4. Hardness of Various Carbides in High Speed Steels

Carbide type	MC	M_2C	M_6C	$M_{23}C_6$	Fe_3C	Martensite
Hardness (HV, 0.02 kg)	3000	2000	1500	1100	850	800

Non-uniform distribution of carbide particles is a persistent problem in the production of tool steels. This occurs due to large temperature differences between the liquidus and solidus temperatures, as much as 130K for M2 type steel, and the consequent segregation of alloying elements during solidification. However, highly uniform dispersion of fine carbide particles can be achieved by processing the steel by powder metallurgy route, i.e. atomizing the tapping stream by gas jet, screening the resulting powder, compacting it by isostatic pressing, followed by sintering.

Hardness of tempered martensite is easily measured at room temperature; however, for hot work and high speed steels, the hardness of interest is that existing at service temperatures. Payson has given a useful correlation between hardness at room temperature and several elevated temperatures for hot work and high speed steels. This correlation is shown in Fig. 15.7.

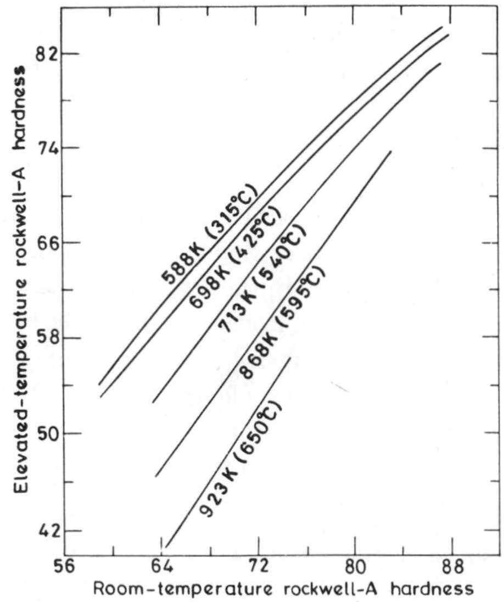

Fig. 15.7. Correlation between room temperature and elevated temperature hardnesses of tempered martensite in tool steels [from P. Payson, *Trans. ASM*, **50** (1959) p. 60].

REFERENCES

1. *AISI Steel Products Manual, Tool Steels*, 1976.
2. *Atlas of Isothermal Transformation Diagrams,* American Society of Metals, Metals Park, Ohio, 1977.
3. E. Haberling, A. Rose and H.H. Weigand, *Stahi Eisen*, 93 (1973), p. 645.

CHAPTER 16

Cast Irons and Their Heat Treatment

1 INTRODUCTION

Cast irons refer to a large group of ferrous alloys containing more than 2% carbon. These alloys are normally cast into shape, and hence, the name cast irons. A large number of engineering components are made by cast iron castings. Apart from higher carbon contents, cast irons differ from steels in that the excess carbon in cast irons may be present either in the combined form as cementite (Fe_3C), same as in steels, or as graphite (pure carbon), or a combination of these two forms. Graphite is generally formed at higher carbon contents, slower cooling (solidification) rates and in the presence of certain alloying elements. Thermodynamically, graphite in iron is more stable than cementite.

Figure 16.1 shows stable Fe-graphite and metastable Fe–Fe_3C phase diagrams. In the high carbon range, Fe–Fe_3C has a eutectic at 4.3% carbon and 1421K (1148°C), whereas, Fe-graphite eutectic is at 4.26% carbon and 1427K (1154°C). During the solidification of Fe–C alloys, it is Fe_3C which is normally formed, even though graphite is the more stable phase. Thermodynamic driving force for the formation of graphite is always higher than for the formation of cementite, as schematically shown in Fig. 16.2. However, graphite is more difficult to nucleate than cementite, from the liquid phase as well as from austenite.

According to the iron-carbon phase diagram (Fig. 16.1), in the eutectic and hypoeutectic alloys between 1421K (1148°C) and 1427K (1154°C) and in the hypereutectic alloys between graphite and cementite liquidus only graphite can form on solidification. Formation of cementite in this range is thermodynamically not possible. However, at lower temperatures, both graphite and cementite are thermodynamically stable and can form during solidification. Relative difference in the thermodynamic driving force for the formation of graphite and cementite from the liquid phase is large at small undercoolings and it decreases with increasing undercooling, i.e with decreasing temperature. Furthermore, it is much easier to nucleate cementite than to nucleate graphite. Therefore, during solidification, graphite is more likely to form at small undercoolings (i.e. slow cooling rates) for thermodynamic reasons, whereas cementite formation is favoured at higher undercoolings (i.e. faster cooling rates) for kinetic reasons. During transformations from

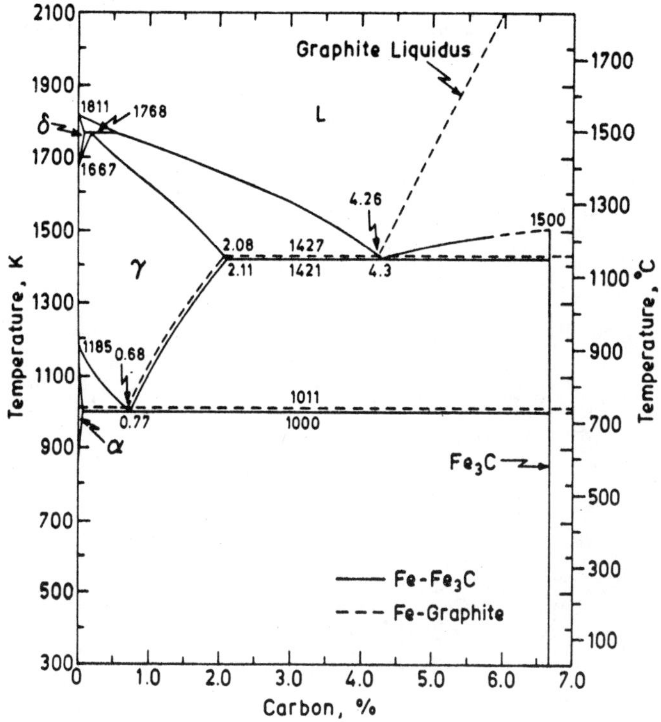

Fig. 16.1. Stable Fe-graphite and metastable Fe-Fe_3C phase diagrams.

austenite, on further cooling in solid state, there is no clear evidence that graphite precipitates from homogeneous austenite. However, if graphite is already present in austenite, either due to its formation during solidification, or graphitization of cementite in austenite at higher temperatures, carbon can precipitate as graphite from austenite on existing graphite particles during cooling to room temperature.

In addition to carbon, commercial cast irons also contain other elements, like, silicon, manganese, sulphur and phosphorus, etc. Presence of these elements in cast irons substantially affects the conditions of graphitization, and hence their structure and properties. Silicon has a strong effect on the structure of cast irons; it enhances graphitization. Silicon content in cast irons may vary from 0.3 to 5.0%. Manganese, on the contrary, prevents graphitization. Sulfur is generally kept as low as possible and phosphorus, though has no effect on graphitization, is useful in cast irons as it improves the fluidity of these alloys. Apart from these, other alloying elements may be added to cast irons for various reasons. Such alloys are normally called alloy cast irons. Of the other alloying elements, carbide forming elements, like, chromium, vanadium, tungsten, molybdenum, etc., that generally segregate to cementite and/or form alloy carbides, inhibit graphitization, whereas non-carbide forming elements, like, nickel, aluminium and copper, promote graphitization, though not as much as silicon.

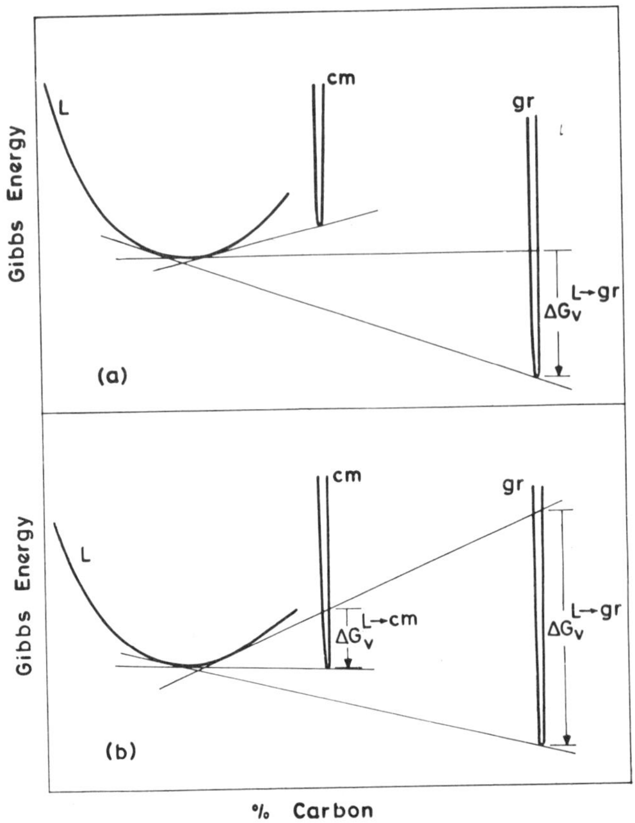

Fig. 16.2. Thermodynamic driving force, ΔG, for the formation of graphite and cementite from liquid Fe–C alloys, (a) between graphite and cementite liquidus, (b) below the cementite liquidus.

Cast irons are normally classified on the basis of the form in which carbon is present in these alloys and its morphology. Cast irons can also be heat treated to modify their structure and properties. Heat treatment operations in cast irons include stress relieving, annealing, quenching and tempering, and surface hardening. A full discussion on cast irons is beyond the scope of this book. However, classification, structure and properties, and heat treatment of cast irons are briefly discussed in this chapter.

2 CLASSIFICATION OF CAST IRONS

2.1 WHITE CAST IRONS

Cast irons in which all the excess carbon is present in combined form as Fe_3C and other carbides, are classified as white cast irons. White cast iron is generally very hard and brittle. Appearance of its fractured surface is dull white, and hence, the name white cast iron. White cast irons are further classified as hypo-eutectic, eutectic and hyper-eutectic, when the carbon content is, respectively less than, equal to and greater than the eutectic carbon content (4.3% carbon in binary Fe–C alloys). These alloys solidify according to the Fe–Fe_3C phase diagram (Fig. 16.1). Just below the eutectic temperature, a hypo-eutectic alloy would contain primary austenite and a eutectic mixture of austenite and cementite; a hyper-eutectic alloy, primary cementite and eutectic mixture; and the eutectic alloy, only the eutectic mixture of austenite and cementite. On further cooling, the carbon content of austenite decreases from ~2% at the eutectic temperature to the eutectoid value at Ae_1 temperature by further precipitation of carbon as cementite, mostly on the existing cementite particles. Below Ae_1 temperature, the austenite, of eutectoid carbon content, transforms to pearlite. Figure 16.3 shows typical microstructure of a hypo-eutectic white cast iron. Other elements, such as, manganese, silicon, sulphur and phosphorus etc., that may be present in white cast irons do not change the general character of phase relationships and microstructures discussed above; they only alter the temperatures of transformations and compositions of the phases to some extent. White cast irons generally contain lower amounts of silicon to prevent graphitization, whereas the presence of manganese, lower carbon content and faster cooling rates promote the formation of cementite.

White cast iron is very hard, about 350 to 500 Brinell, and is also excessively brittle. It is, therefore, not employed for any structural applications. However, it is useful in resisting wear by abrasion and is used for wearing plates, pump liners, parts of abrasion machinery, etc. White cast iron is very difficult to machine due to its high hardness. It is normally cast into near final shape and finished by grinding.

2.2 MALLEABLE CAST IRONS

Malleable cast irons are produced from white cast irons by dissociation of metastable cementite into more stable phases. i.e. graphite plus iron. In white cast irons contain-

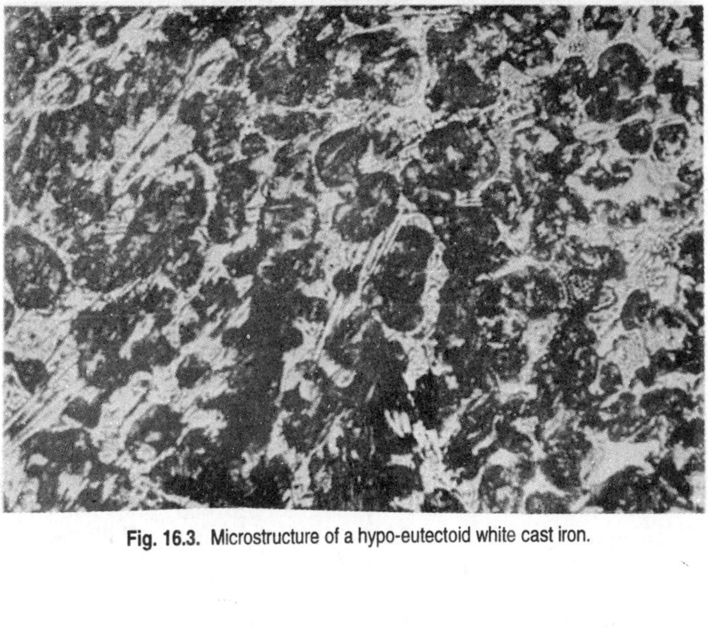

Fig. 16.3. Microstructure of a hypo-eutectoid white cast iron.

ing more than 2% carbon and some graphitizing elements, like, silicon, nickel, etc., cementite dissociates to austenite plus graphite on heating above the eutectoid temperature in accordance with the graphitization reaction:

$$Fe_3C \rightarrow 3Fe + C(\text{Graphite}) \tag{16.1}$$

White cast iron is malleabilized by heating it in the austenite plus graphite stability range between eutectoid and eutectic temperatures, normally at 1173K (900°C) to 1273K (1000°C). On heating in this temperature range, primary and eutectic cementite dissociates to austenite and graphite. Graphite normally nucleates at the cementite/austenite interfaces and grows at the expense of cementite in accordance with reaction (16.1). Complete dissociation of cementite at these temperatures normally takes about 24 to 32 h. At the end of complete graphitization at these temperatures, the alloy consists of graphite nodules dispersed in austenite matrix. It is then rapidly cooled to around 1023K (750°C), followed by slow cooling down to ~923K (650°C), at cooling rates of 4–6 K/h. During this second stage of malleabilizing treatment, the carbon in solution in austenite further precipitates as graphite on the existing graphite nodules to give a room temperature structure of ferrite plus graphite. If the alloy is cooled at a faster rate from the austenite range, then the austenite may transform to pearlite and a structure of pearlite plus graphite would be obtained. Figure 16.4 shows the microstructure of a fully malleabilized cast iron. The morphology of

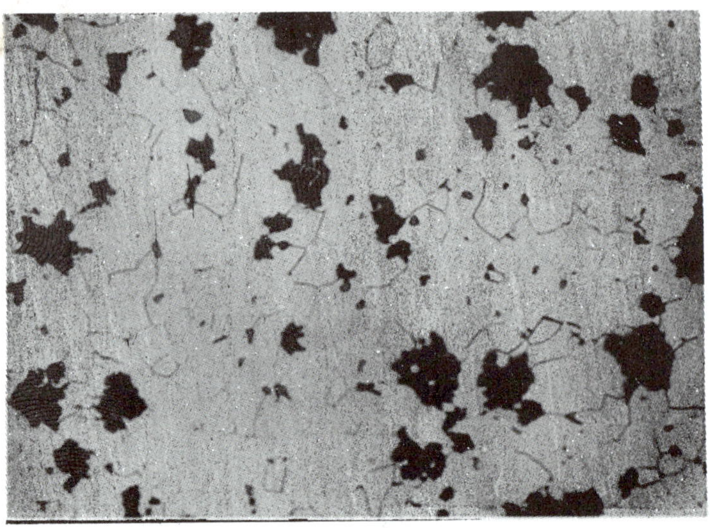

Fig. 16.4. Microstructure of a fully malleabilized cast iron.

graphite nodules in malleable cast iron is referred to as temper graphite. Malleable cast iron is ductile and tough, and is used in a number of automotive and other applications.

2.3 GRAY CAST IRONS

In gray cast irons the excess carbon precipitates as graphite, in lamellar (flake) graphite structure, directly from the liquid phase during solidification. Direct

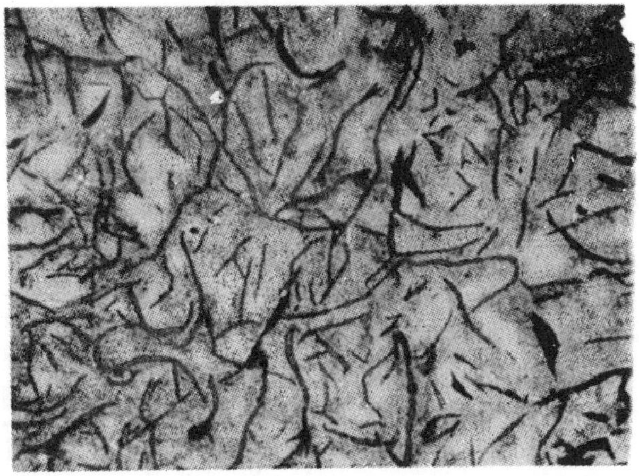

(a)

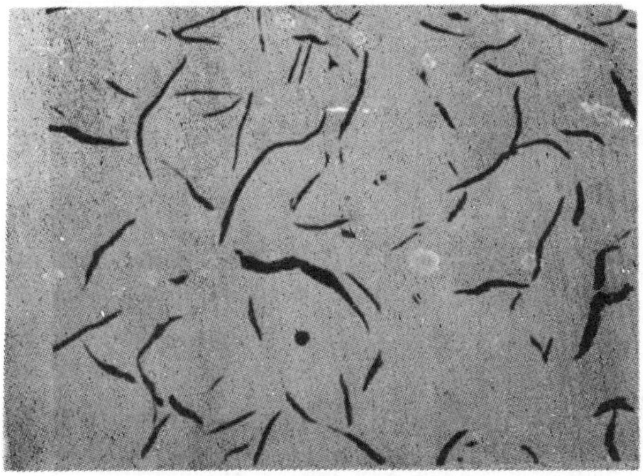

(b)

Fig. 16.5. Microstructure of gray cast iron, (a) ferritic gray cast iron, (b) pearlitic gray cast iron.

precipitation of graphite during solidification occurs in the presence of higher carbon contents, higher concentrations of graphitizing elements, particularly silicon, and slower solidification rates. Hence, gray cast irons normally contain higher amounts of graphitizing elements, like, Si, Ni, etc., and lower (or negligible) amounts of carbide forming elements, like, Mn, Cr, Mo, etc. In gray cast irons, a structure of austenite and lamellar graphite is obtained upon solidification. On further cooling to room temperature, austenite may transform to pearlite, giving a room temperature structure of graphite flakes in pearlite matrix (pearlitic gray cast iron), or, carbon may partially or fully precipitate as graphite on the existing graphite flakes to give a structure of graphite flakes in a matrix of ferrite-pearlite or 100% ferrite (ferritic gray

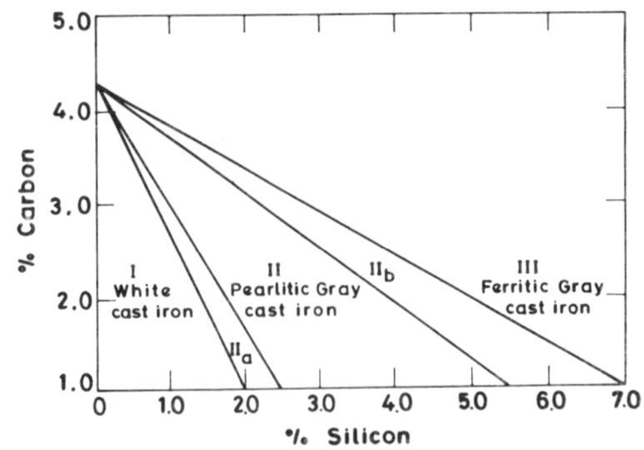

Fig. 16.6 Effect of carbon and silicon concentrations on the formation of different structures in Fe-C-Si alloys.

cast iron), respectively. Slower cooling rates, higher carbon contents and higher concentrations of silicon and other graphitizing elements promote the formation of ferritic cast iron. Figure 16.5 shows typical gray cast iron structures.

In cast irons, Si is the most important alloying element and is present in almost all cast irons. Fig. 16.6 shows the effect of composition and Fig. 16.7 that of the cooling rates on the formation of different gray cast iron structures in Fe–C–Si alloys. With reference to Fig. 16.7, note that the cooling rate decreases as thickness of the casting increases. Gray cast irons, then, contain flakes of graphite in a matrix of steel. The composition of the steel matrix, i.e. the relative amounts of pearlite and ferrite, depends on the composition and cooling rates, as discussed above.

Mechanical properties of gray cast irons depend on the strength of the steel matrix and the size and morphology of the graphite flakes. Since, eutectoid steels have the maximum strength, strongest gray cast irons are produced when the matrix is fully pearlitic. Mainly due to the presence of soft lamellar graphite flakes, gray cast irons, in general, have pure tensile ductility and low impact strength. However, these alloys have high compressive strength, and good damping capacity and high thermal conductivity, due to the presence of graphite flakes. Gray cast irons find extensive use for cylinders and pistons for internal combustion engines, locomotive cylinders, machine tool beds and frames, flywheels, etc., where good ductility is not essential and the high compressive strength, good thermal conductivity and/or damping capacity of gray cast iron are desirable.

2.4 NODULAR (DUCTILE) CAST IRONS

Nodular (or ductile) cast irons are produced by adding small amounts of Mg and/or Ce to gray cast irons. Presence of small amounts of Mg and/or Ce modifies the morphology of graphite during solidification. In nodular cast irons, excess carbon precipitates as essentially spheroidal graphite nodules during solidification, as opposed to lamellar (flake) graphite in gray cast irons. Figure 16.8 shows typical

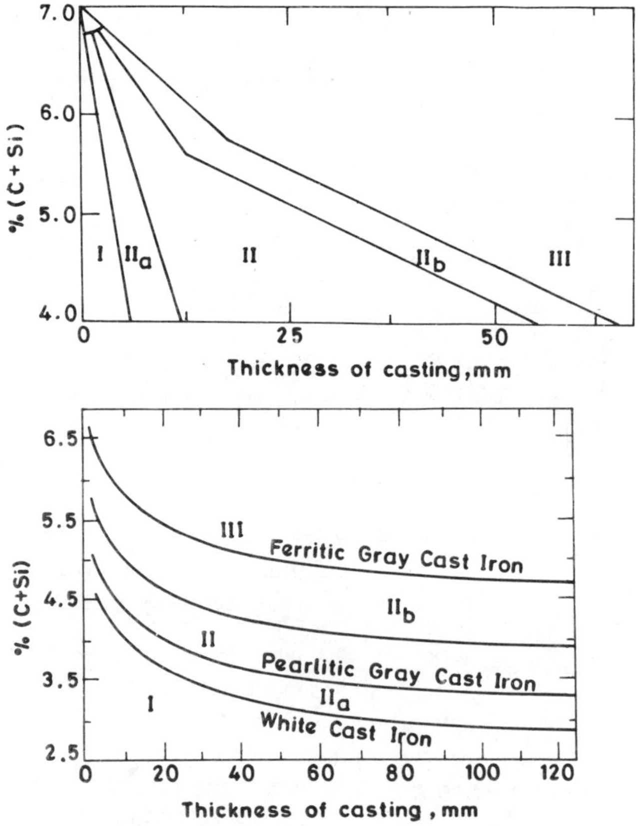

Fig. 16.7. Effect of cooling rate during casting on the formation different structures in Fe-C-Si alloys, (cooling rate decreases as thickness of the casting increases).

microstructures of a nodular cast irons. The matrix structure of a nodular cast iron could be pearlite, ferrite-pearlite or ferrite, and can be controlled in the same manner as in gray cast irons, i.e. by controlling the composition, particularly silicon content, and the solidification rates.

Ducitility and toughness of nodular cast irons are much higher than gray cast irons, essentially due to the presence of graphite as nodules, as opposed to flakes in gray cast irons. Graphite being a very soft phase hardly takes up any stress. Therefore, in gray cast irons, flakes essentially act as wide longitudinal voids in steel and the ductility and toughness are adversely affected due to high stress concentration at the tips of these voids (flakes). As graphite is present in nodular (spheroidal) form in nodular cast irons, stress concentration at the graphite/matrix interfaces is greatly reduced and a marked improvement in tensile ductility and toughness occurs. Nodular cast irons find use in a number of engineering components in machine tools, agricultural implements, automotive parts, earth moving machinery, etc.

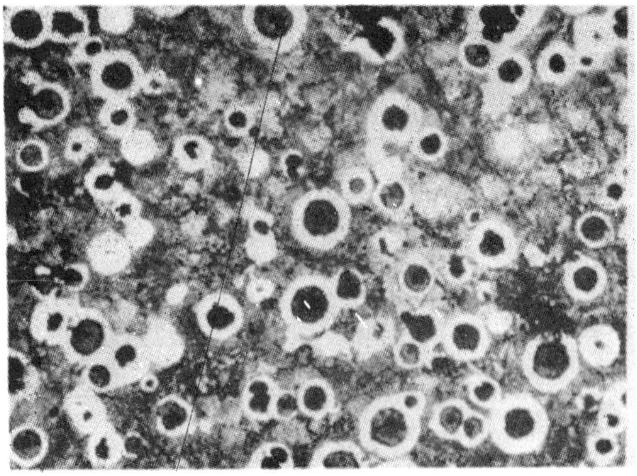

(a)

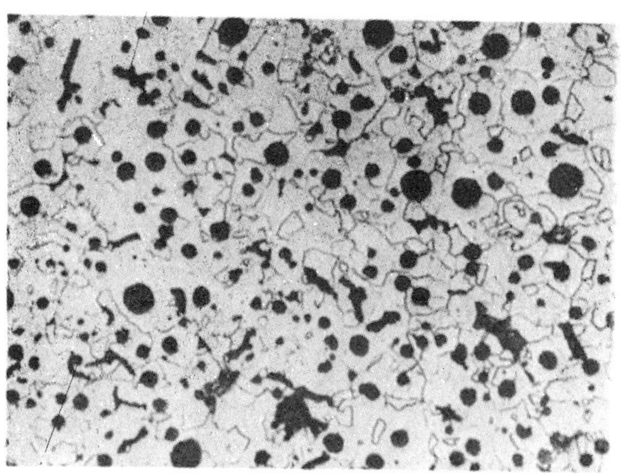

(b)

Fig. 16.8. Microstructure of nodular cast iron, (a) ferrite-pearlite matrix, (b) fully ferritic matrix.

2.5 COMPACTED/VERMICULAR GRAPHITE CAST IRONS

A structure intermediate to gray and nodular cast iron is called compacted graphite or vermicular graphite, cast iron. In compacted graphite cast irons, graphite is present as elongated chunkey particles of graphite with length to width ratio of 2 to 10 as compared to 1 to 2 in nodular cast irons and greater than 30 in a typical flake gray cast iron. Figure 16.9 shows microstructure of a compacted/vermicular graphite cast iron. Compacted graphite structure is obtained by controlled additions of spheroidizing elements, like, Mg, Ce, La, etc., and of anti-spheroidizing elements, like, Ti, Al, Sb, etc., and using low sulphur alloys. All the factors that control the graphite morphology in graphitic cast irons are not discussed here.

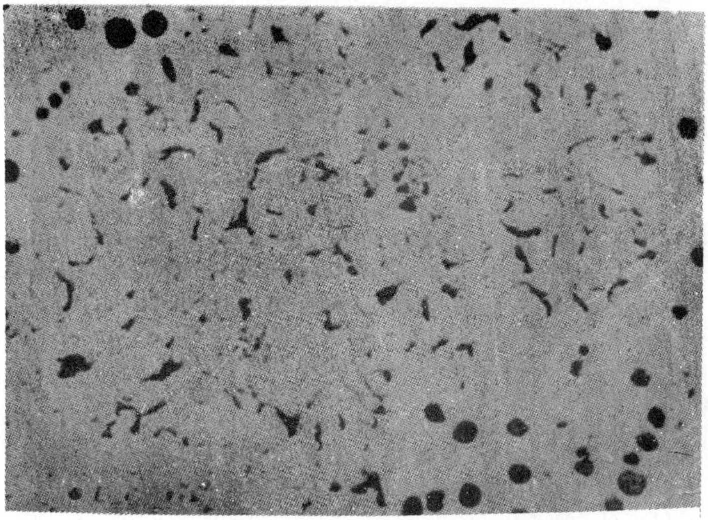

Fig. 16.9. Microstructure of a compacted/vermicular cast iron.

Compacted graphite cast irons have properties intermediate to gray and nodular cast irons. These alloys have much improved mechanical properties as compared to gray cast irons; and compared to nodular cast irons these are characterized by lower shrinkage and better fluidity during casting.

3 ALLOY CAST IRONS

3.1 LOW ALLOY CAST IRONS

Common alloying elements used in alloy cast irons are chromium, nickel, molybdenum, silicon, aluminium, copper etc. Addition of alloying elements to cast irons considerably extends the range of microstructures and properties that are obtained on solidification and/or subsequent heat treatments. Alloy cast irons are used for specific applications requiring higher strength, wear resistance and/or corrosion resistance. Excess carbon in alloy cast irons may precipitate as cementite and/or alloy carbides (alloy white cast irons), or, as flake or nodular graphite. The matrix structure could be pearlite, ferrite-pearlite, ferrite, bainite, martensite or austenite; depending upon the type and amount of alloying elements and the cooling rates.

Low alloy cast irons contain small amounts of Ni, Mo, Cr, etc., in addition to Si. These may be added to change the matrix structure and/or their response to heat treatment. For example, the matrix structure of gray and nodular cast irons can be changed from ferrite-pearlite to bainite or martensite by small additions of nickel and molybdenum.

3.2 CHROMIUM WHITE CAST IRONS

These alloys contain higher chromium and high carbon contents and small additions of other alloying elements. Chromium cast irons are normally classified into three categories:

(i) *Low Cr White Cast Irons*: Small additions of chromium to unalloyed white cast irons further stabilize the cementite phase and prevent graphitization during heat treatment and/or service. Chromium segregates to cementite in these alloys.

(ii) *14–28% Cr Cast Irons*: The as-cast structure of these alloys consists of $(FeCr)_7C_3$ carbides and austenite, which may partially transform to martensite during further cooling. They are normally heat treated to produce martensitic matrix for optimum abrasion resistance. In addition to chromium, these alloys may contain up to 2–3% molybdenum.

(iii) *33% Cr White Cast Irons*: These alloys, containing ~33% Cr and high carbon, have a structure of austenite plus carbides (some ferrite may also be present), and have applications mainly in conditions requiring oxidation resistance up to ~1323K (1050°C) or in mildly corrosive environments.

3.3 NI-HARD CAST IRONS

Commercial Ni-Hard cast irons contain ~4.5% Ni, 1.5–3.0% Cr, 2.8–3.5% C and small amounts of other elements, like, Si, Mn, etc. During casting, a structure of austenite plus cementite is obtained upon solidification and during further cooling to room temperature, austenite transforms to martensite. These alloys are used in applications requirement high abrasion resistance, in fields of applications comparable with high chromium cast irons.

3.4 NI-RESIST AUSTENITIC CAST IRONS

Ni-resist austenitic cast irons contain higher amounts of nickel (13–36%) and copper (to ~7%), with small addition of Cr, Mn and Si. With increase in nickel content, carbon precipitates as graphite during solidification and the austenite phase is stabilized to room temperature. These alloys are also called austenitic cast irons and show good corrosion and oxidation resistance in different environments. They can be produced in normal flake graphite structure or in spheroidal (nodular) graphite structure. Higher strength and ductility are obtained in nodular graphite alloys.

3.5 SILICON CAST IRONS

Silicon cast irons have ferritic matrix and can be produced either in flake graphite or spheroidal graphite structures. Increased silicon content improves the oxidation resistance and structural stability of cast irons. Silicon content is normally kept below ~6%. At higher silicon contents a proncunced decrease in toughness occurs. Heat-resistant, high silicon spheroidal graphite cast irons have composition in the range, 4–5% Si, 0.5–1.5% Mo and ~3%C. Mo additions lead to the presence of alloy carbides in the structure, which improve the high temperature strength. These alloys are used in exhaust manifolds, gas turbine components, glass moulds, etc.

High silicon gray cast irons containing 13–18% Si and 0–6% Mo are used where very high corrosion resistance is required. These alloys, however, have very poor mechanical properties.

3.6 ALUMINIUM ALLOYED CAST IRONS

With small additions of aluminium (upto ~5%), strength of gray cast irons is improved. Structure of gray cast iron with mixed ferrite-pearlite matrix is obtained in these alloys. With aluminium additions between 6 and 20%, white cast iron with Fe_3AlC_x carbide is obtained. Alloys containing 20–30% Al again give flake graphite structure, but with completely ferritic matrix and have good high temperature oxidation resistance.

4 HEAT TREATMENT OF CAST IRONS

4.1 INTRODUCTION

Various engineering components made of cast irons are produced by casting. Heat treatment of cast iron components includes relieving of stresses introduced during casting, annealing operations for softening and producing uniform structures, normalizing, quenching and tempering, and various surface hardening treatments. In certain respects, heat treatment of cast irons is similar to that of steels in that it involves the attainment different matrix structures by controlling the transformations from austenite. However, in cast irons, except in white cast irons, all or major portion of the carbon is present as graphite which significantly affects the kinetics of austenite formation. Furthermore, during cooling from austenite, carbon may precipitate as graphite or cementite, depending on the composition of cast iron and the cooling rates from austenite. In addition, due to high carbon contents of cast irons, austenite would always contain some undissolved graphite and/or carbides, which may act as nuclei for transformations during cooling. Notwithstanding these differences, the general principles of heat treatment of steels apply equally to the heat treatment of cast irons. In this chapter, different heat treatments given to cast irons are, therefore, briefly discussed, emphasizing only the special features with respect to cast irons. Heat treatment of white cast iron to obtain malleable cast iron is not discussed in this section, as it has already been dealt with in Sec. 2.2.

4.2 STRESS RELIEVING

Internal stresses are introduced in cast components during the cooling of castings from solidification temperatures due to differential cooling rates (and hence differential contraction during solidification) in different regions of the components, and also due to the volume changes accompanying the transformations from austenite. Level of internal stresses, therefore, strongly depend on the size and shape of the components and the cooling rates. Residual internal stresses are tensile in some regions and compressive in others. These stresses may contribute to premature failure of the components during service. In extreme cases, internal stresses may give rise to cracking and warpage of cast components.

Internal stresses may be reduced by stress relieving annealing treatment at higher temperatures. As the material is heated to higher temperatures, its flow stress decreases, and local plastic flow and other recovery processes occur. The internal stresses are, then, substantially reduced, depending upon the annealing temperature.

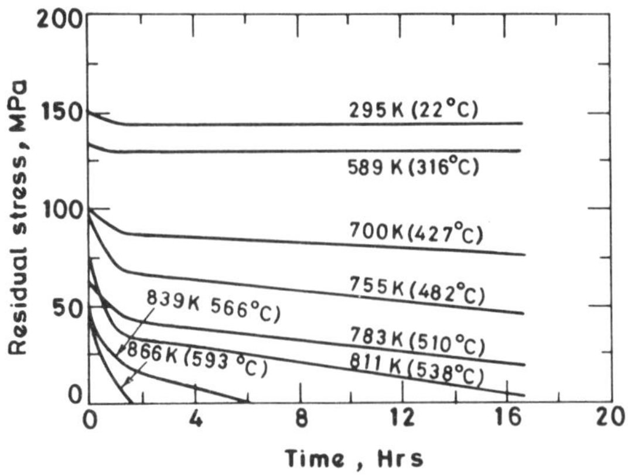

Fig. 16.10. Effect of stress relieving temperature and time on the residual stress in a gray cast iron casting.

Hence, internal stresses in cast iron castings are reduced by annealing them at appropriate temperatures, followed by slow uniform cooling. Annealing at ~723K (450°C) is normally recommended for reducing the chances of cracking and distortion, while complete stress relieving should be done at ~873K (600°C). Fig. 16.10 shows the effect of annealing temperature and time on residual stress in a typical gray cast iron casting.

Stress relieving heat treatment may also lead to some microstructural changes, like graphitization of pearlitic cementite, precipitation of secondary carbides in alloys containing Cr and Mo, etc., and the consequent changes in the mechanical properties. These factors must be kept in mind while designing a stress relieving operation.

4.3 ANNEALING OF GRAY CAST IRONS

Apart from the stress relieving operations, annealing treatments are most frequently used for softening gray and nodular cast irons, by graphitization of cementite (when present), to attain maximum ductility and better machinability. Normally one of the following three annealing treatments: *(i)* ferritizing anneal, *(ii)* full annealing, or *(iii)* graphitizing anneal, is used for softening gray and nodular cast irons. These treatments are briefly discussed below.

(i) Ferritizing Anneal: In ferritizing anneal, cast irons are heated below the eutectoid temperature to graphitize pearlitic cementite. When a gray or modular cast iron with partial or fully pearlitic matrix is heated to higher temperatures; insignificant graphitization occurs till ~873K (600°C). Above 873K (600°C), the rate at which iron carbide decomposes increases rapidly, reaching a maximum at around the eutectoid temperature. For unalloyed and low-alloy cast irons, when it is desired to only graphitize the pearlitic cementite to improve machinability and/or ductility, ferritizing anneal at 973K (700°C) to 1023K (750°C) would serve the purpose. The casting is held at the annealing temperature long enough for the decomposition of cementite to go to completion. The annealing time required for complete graphitization

depends on the temperature of annealing and alloy composition. It could vary from several minutes to about an hour or more, and normally has to be experimentally determined. Once complete graphitization has occurred, the rate of cooling from the annealing temperature is not of great importance. However, slow cooling rates, depending upon the complexity of the casting, are recommended to minimize the introduction of residual stresses that are automatically relieved during the ferritizing anneal.

(ii) Full Annealing: Full annealing is usually done when ferritizing anneal is ineffective in graphitizing the pearlitic cementite, mainly due to the presence of relatively higher concentrations of carbide forming elements. In full annealing, the alloy is heated above the eutectoid temperature, normally between 1073K (800°C) and 1173K (900°C); held at the temperature for sufficiently long time for all the pearlite and pro-eutectoid cementite, if any, to convert to austenite (half an hour to one hour is usually sufficient); followed by slow cooling. In full annealing, the alloy must be cooled very slowly through the eutectoid transformation range, i.e. from 1023K (750°C) to 923K (650°C), for the carbon in austenite to fully precipitate out as graphite on the pre-existing graphite flakes or nodules.

(iii) Graphitizing Anneal: If the microstructure of a gray/nodular cast iron casting contains massive carbide particles, then, still higher annealing temperatures are normally required to completely graphitize these carbides. Massive carbides in gray cast iron castings may form due to accidental faster cooling of a casting, or, in thin sections of a casting, which normally would cool at faster rates. To break down these carbides in a reasonable time, castings are annealed at 1173K (900°C) to 1223K (950°C). The annealing time could vary from few minutes to several hours, depending upon the alloy composition and annealing temperature. This normally has to be experimentally determined. Alloys containing higher carbon and higher silicon contents normally need less annealing times, whereas alloying elements like, chromium, manganese, vanadium, etc., that stabilize the carbides, increase the required annealing times. Desired cooling rates from the annealing temperatures depend on the final structure and properties that are desired. If the purpose of annealing treatment is to break down the massive carbides only, while retaining maximum strength and wear resistance, castings should be air cooled down to ~823K (550°C) to promote the formation of pearlitic matrix. However, if maximum machinability is desired, it has to be cooled slowly through the eutectoid transformation range to obtain a fully ferritic matrix, as in full annealing.

4.4 NORMALIZING OF GRAY CAST IRONS

Normalizing of cast irons is very similar to the normalizing of steels. In normalizing, cast irons are heated above the eutectoid temperature, normally around 1173K (900°C), for about one hour, and then, cooled to room temperature in still air. After normalizing treatment, a fine pearlite matrix structure is obtained. The purpose of normalizing treatment is to generally enhance the mechanical properties, such as hardness and tensile strength, or to restore as-cast properties of pearlitic gray (or nodular) cast irons, that may have been modified during other heating processes such as graphitization anneal, repair welding, etc.

4.5 HARDENING AND TEMPERING

Cast iron components can be hardened by quenching from austenite temperatures to form martensite. The basic principles of quench hardening of cast irons are the same as of steels. The quench hardened components are normally tempered at low temperatures, i.e. ~473K (200°C), to improve their toughness and structural stability, without significantly reducing their hardness. The main purpose of hardening and tempering treatment is to significantly enhance the hardness and wear resistance of these components.

Quench hardening process involves austenitization at higher temperatures, followed by quenching to form martensite. Austenitization kinetics in ferritic cast irons is generally much slower than in pearlitic cast irons. In an alloy with ferrite plus graphite structure (ferritic cast iron), on heating above Ae_1 temperature, austenite nucleates at ferrite/graphite interfaces, and then, grows by consuming both the ferrite and graphite. When ferrite is completely consumed, an inhomogeneous austenite, with carbon content given by the $\gamma/(\alpha + \gamma)$ phase boundary (Fig. 16.1) in regions where ferrite dissolves last, and equal to the solubility limit graphite in austenite next to the undissolved graphite particles, is obtained. With continued heating, austenite becomes more homogeneous and average carbon content of the austenite increases, approaching the solubility limit of graphite in austenite. The time required to obtain completely homogeneous austenite, then, depends on the size and distribution of graphite flakes/nodules, apart from the temperature of austenitization. In cast irons with pearlite matrix, on the other hand, the austenitization process is relatively faster. Here, pearlite fully transforms to austenite in a relatively short period (as in steels), and then, enrichment of austenite with further dissolution of graphite occurs.

Carbon content of austenite has an effect on the hardness, hardenability and retained austenite on quenching. On austenitization of cast irons, the amount of carbon in austenite is given by the solubility limit of graphite in austenite and it increases with increasing temperature (Fig. 16.1). Normally, austenitization of cast irons is done at ~100K higher than Ae_1 temperature. Note that, elements like Si, Mo, Cr, etc., increase the Ae_1 temperature, whereas Mn, Ni and Cu decrease it (see Chapter II). Furthermore, excessively high temperatures should be avoided, as it will increase the probability of distortion and cracking during quenching.

After austenitization, the components are quenched to form martensite. Oil quenching is most frequently used for cast irons. As a principle, least severe quenching medium consistent with the hardening requirements is used to minimize the probability of quench cracking and distortion. Quenched components are normally tempered at 423K (150°C) to 573K (400°C) for about one hour. On tempering, hardness marginally drops whereas ductility and toughness are improved.

4.6 AUSTEMPERING AND MARTEMPERING

Austempering and martempering of steels have been discussed in Chapter 14. Austempering and martempering treatments can also be given to cast iron components to obtained similar hardness values as by quench hardening and tempering treatment and with the same advantages and limitations of these treatments vis a vie quench hardening, as discussed for steels in Chapter 14.

4.7 SURFACE HARDENING TREATMENTS

Surface hardening treatments like induction and flame hardening, and nitriding can be applied to cast irons to increase the surface hardness and wear resistance of cast iron components. The basic principles of these treatments are the same as for steels. As cast irons already contain high carbon contents, carburization as a surface hardening treatment is not applicable to cast irons.

During flame and induction hardening, the surface of a component is rapidly heated to temperatures above Ae_1, and then quenched. The region that gets heated above Ae_1, partially, or fully, transforms to austenite during the heating process, and then, transforms to martensite on quenching. Flame and induction hardening of steels have been discussed in detail in Chapter 13. The same considerations apply to flame and induction hardening of cast irons, except for the effect of cast iron structure on the kinetics of austenitization.

In flame and induction hardening, the time allowed for austenite formation is relatively short, of the order of a few seconds. The matrix structure of cast iron, therefore, plays a critical role in flame and induction hardening response of these alloys. Cast irons with completely ferritic matrix do not respond well to flame and induction hardening, as the austenitization kinetics in these alloys is relatively slow. Furthermore, whatever austenite is formed, dissolves very little carbon during the short period for which the surface region is heated to high temperatures. Therefore, for proper surface hardening response by flame and induction hardening processes, the matrix structure of a cast iron must be fully or mostly pearlitic, i.e. it must contain an equivalent of ~0.5 to 0.7% carbon in iron in combined (cementite) form. Such alloys would respond to flame and induction hardening in the same manner as steels of similar carbon contents; and the hardness levels achieved would directly depend on the percentage carbon present in the combined form in the matrix. Flame and induction hardening is not recommended for alloys containing more than equivalent of ~0.8% carbon in combined form, because such alloys may crack during surface hardening. The amount of combined carbon in cast irons can be controlled by using alloying elements and control of cooling rates during casting. Malleable cast irons can be surface hardened in the same manner as gray and nodular cast irons.

Like steels, cast iron components can also be nitrided to produce high hardness wear and corrosion resistant surfaces. The same basic principles apply to the nitriding of cast iron also (see Chapter 12).

REFERENCES

1. *Metals Handbook*, Vol 2, 8th Edition, American Society for Metals, Metals, Park, 1964.
2. C.R. Brooks, *Heat Treatment of Ferrous Alloys*, Hemisphere Publishers, Washington, 1979.

Appendices

APPENDIX I

Conversion Factors

To Convert From	To	Multiply By
Angstrom (Å)	Metre (m)	1.000000×10^{-10}
atmosphere (Standard)	pascal (Pa)	1.013250×10^{5}
bar	pascal (Pa)	1.000000×10^{5}
calorie/cm s°C	watt/m K	4.184000×10^{2}
calorie	joule (J)	4.184000
day (mean solar)	second (s)	8.640000×10^{4}
dyne	newton (N)	1.000000×10^{-5}
dyne–cm	newton-metre (N.m)	1.000000×10^{-7}
dyne/cm^2	pascal (Pa)	1.000000×10^{-1}
electron volt (eV)	joule (J)	1.602190×10^{-19}
electron volt/atom	joule/mole (J/mol)	9.648659×10^{4}
erg	joule (J)	1.000000×10^{-7}
foot (ft)	metre (m)	3.048000×10^{-1}
foot-pound (ft–lb)	joule (J)	1.355818
gauss (G)	tesla (T)	1.000000×10^{-4}
kilogram force	newton (N)	9.806650
kilogram force/mm^2	pascal (Pa)	9.806650×10^{6}
kilopound	newton (N)	9.806650
ksi. in	MPa.m	1.098855
oersted	ampere/metre (A/m)	7.957747×10
pound avoirdupois	kilogram (kg)	4.535924×10^{-1}
pound/$foot^3$ (lb/ft^3)	kilogram/$metre^3$ (kg/m^3)	1.601846×10
pound/$inch^3$ (lb/in^3)	kilogram/$metre^3$ (kg/m^3)	2.767990×10^{4}
pound force/in^2 (psi)	pascal (Pa)	6.894757×10^{3}
tonne	kilogram (kg)	1.000000×10^{3}
torr	pascal (Pa)	1.333220×10^{4}
watt-hour (W.h)	joule (J)	3.600000×10^{3}
year (calender)	second (s)	3.153600×10^{7}

APPENDIX II

Physical Constants

Avogadro's number, *N*	6.022169×10^{23} mol^{-1}
Bohr magneton	9.274096×10^{-24} J.T.$^{-1}$
Boltzmann's constant, *k*	1.380622×10^{-23} J.K.$^{-1}$
Gas constant, *R*	8.31432 ± 0.00034 J.K.$^{-1}$ mol^{-1}
Planck's constant, *h*	$6.62517 \pm 0.00023 \times 10^{-34}$ J.s

APPENDIX III

Approximate Conversion of Hardness Values for Steels

Vickers hardness No. HV	Brinell* 3000 kg Load 10 mm ball HB	Rockwell C-scale 150 kg load diamond cone HRC	Rockwell A scale 60 kg load diamond cone HRA	Rockwell Superficial 30–N 30 kg load diamond cone
1	2	3	4	5
940	—	68.7	85.6	84.4
920	—	67.5	85.3	84.0
900	—	67.0	85.0	83.6
880	—	66.4	84.7	83.1
860	—	65.9	84.4	82.7
840	745	65.3	84.1	82.2
820	733	64.7	83.8	81.7
800	722	64.0	83.4	81.1
780	710	63.3	83.0	80.4
760	698	62.5	82.6	79.7
740	684	61.8	82.2	79.1
720	670	61.0	81.8	78.4
700	656	60.1	81.3	77.6
690	647	59.7	81.1	77.2
680	638	59.2	80.8	76.8
670	630	58.8	80.6	76.4
660	620	58.3	80.3	75.9
650	611	57.8	80.0	75.5
640	601	57.3	79.8	75.1
630	591	56.8	79.5	74.6
620	582	56.3	79.2	74.2
610	573	55.7	78.9	73.6
600	564	55.2	78.6	73.2
590	554	54.7	78.4	72.7
580	545	54.1	78.0	72.1

1	2	3	4	5
570	535	53.6	77.8	71.7
560	525	53.0	77.4	71.2
550	517	52.3	77.0	70.5
540	507	51.7	76.7	70.0
530	497	51.1	76.4	69.5
520	487	50.5	76.1	69.0
510	479	49.8	75.7	68.3
500	471	49.1	75.3	67.7
490	460	48.4	74.9	67.1
480	452	47.7	74.5	66.4
470	441	46.9	74.1	65.7
460	433	46.1	73.6	64.9
450	425	45.3	73.3	64.3
440	415	44.5	72.8	63.5
430	405	43.6	72.3	62.7
420	397	42.7	71.8	61.9
410	388	41.8	71.4	61.1
400	379	40.8	70.8	60.2
390	369	39.8	70.3	59.3
380	360	38.8	69.8	58.4
370	353	37.7	69.2	57.4
360	345	36.6	68.7	56.4
350	335	35.5	68.1	55.4
340	328	34.4	67.6	54.4
330	320	33.3	67.0	53.3
320	311	32.2	66.4	52.3
310	303	31.0	65.8	51.3
300	295	29.8	65.2	50.2
290	285	28.5	64.5	49.0
280	275	27.1	63.8	47.8
250	245	22.2	61.6	43.4
240	235	20.3	60.7	41.7
230	225	—	60.0	—
220	215	—	59.5	—
210	205	—	59.0	—
200	195	—	58.0	—
190	185	—	57.0	—
180	175	—	56.0	—
170	165	—	54.0	—
160	155	—	53.0	—

1	2	3	4	5
150	145	—	52.0	—
140	135	—	50.0	—
130	125	—	48.0	—
120	115	—	46.0	—
110	105	—	45.0	—
100	95	—	43.0	—

* Brinell figures higher than 480 are determined with a carbide ball.

APPENDIX IV

Methods of Measuring Case Depth

(SAE Recommended Practice J 423a June 1963 revision)

Case hardening may be defined as a process for hardening a ferrous material in such a manner that the surface layer, known as the case, is substantially harder than the remaining material, known as the core. The process embraces carburizing, nitriding, carbonitriding, cyaniding, and induction and flame hardening. In every instance, chemical composition or mechanical properties, or both, are affected by such practice.

This testing procedure describes various methods for measuring the depth to which change has been made in either chemical composition or mechanical properties. Each procedure has its own area of application established through proved practice, and no single method is advocated for all purposes. The relationship between case depths as determined by the different methods can vary extensively. Some of the factors that affect this relationship are case characteristics, parent steel composition, and quenching conditions.

Methods employed for determining the depth of case are chemical, mechanical or visual, and the specimens or parts may be subjected to the described test in either the soft or the hardened condition. The measured case depth may then be reported as either effective or total case depth on hardened specimens, and as total case depth on unhardened specimens.

Effective case depth is the perpendicular distance from the surface of a hardened case to the farthest point at which a specified level of hardness is maintained. The hardness criterion is Rockwell-C 50, except when otherwise specified. Effective case depth should always be determined on samples having a heat treated condition representative of the part under consideration.

Total case depth may be defined as the distance (measured perpendicularly) from the surface of a hardened or unhardened case to a point at which differences in chemical or physical properties of the case and core can no longer be distinguished.

CHEMICAL METHOD

This method generally is applicable only to carburized cases, but may also be used for cyanided or carbonitrided cases. The procedure consists in determining the carbon content (and nitrogen, when applicable) at various depths below the surface of a test specimen. This method is considered the most accurate for measuring total case depth on carburized cases.

Procedure for Carburized Cases: Test specimens shall normally be of the same grade of steel as parts being carburized. Test specimens may be actual parts, rings or bars, and should be straight or otherwise suitable for accurate machining of surface layers into chips for subsequent carbon analysis.

Test specimens shall be carburized with parts or in a manner representative of the procedure to be used for parts in question. Care should be exercised to avoid distortion and decarburization in cooling test specimens after carburizing. When parts and test specimens are quenched after carburizing, the specimens should be tempered at approximately 873–923 K (600–650°C) and straightened to 0.0015 max total indicator reading (TIR) before machining is attempted. The time of tempering should be minimized to avoid excessive carbon diffusion.

Test specimens must have clean surfaces and shall be machined dry in increments of predetermined depth. The analysis of machined chips will then accurately reveal the depth of carbon penetration. Chosen increments usually vary between 0.05 and 0.25 mm, depending on the accuracy desired and expected depth of the case.

Chips from each increment shall be kept separate and analyzed individually for carbon content by an accepted method. Total case depth is considered to be the distance from the surface equivalent to the depth of the last increment of machining whose chips analyze to a carbon content 0.04% higher than the established carbon content of the core.

MECHANICAL METHOD

This method consists of making a hardness traverse on the case and core of a specimen prepared by one of three procedures. It is considered the most accurate for measuring effective case depth, and may be used as a referee and control method applicable to either specimens or parts. This method is also preferred for measuring total case depth on nitrided parts.

For effective case depth measurement, read to point of specified hardness, which is Rockwell-C 50 (or approved equivalent) except for certain induction or flame hardened cases for which the following table applies:

Carbon content, %	Effective case depth hardness, HRC
0.28 to 0.32	35
0.33 to 0.42	40
0.43 to 0.52	45
0.53 and over	50

A plot of hardness versus depth from the surface will facilitate this reading. Figs. 1, 2, 3 and 4 illustrate the recommended procedures.

Hardness testes that produce small, shallow impressions should be used for all the following procedures, in order that the hardness values obtained will be representative of the surface or area being tested. Testers used to produce diamond pyramid or knoop hardness numbers are recommended, although testers using heavier loads, such as the Rockwell superficial, A or C scales, can be used in some instances on flame and induction hardened cases.

Considerable care should be exercised during preparation of specimens for case depth determination by any of the mechanical methods to insure against grinding or cutting burns. The use of an etchant for burn detection is recommended as a general precaution, because of the serious error that can be introduced by its presence.

Cross-section Procedure: Cut specimens perpendicular to the hardened surface at a critical location, being careful to avoid any cutting or grinding practice that would affect the original hardness. Grind and polish the specimen. The surface of the area to be traversed shall be polished finely enough so the hardness impressions are unaffected, that is, the lighter the indenter load, the finer the polish necessary.

The procedure illustrated by Fig. 1 is recommended for the measurement of light and medium cases. The alternative procedure illustrated in Fig. 2 is recommended for the measurement of medium and heavier cases.

The hardness traverse should be started for enough below the surface to insure proper support from the metal between the centre of the impression and the surface. Subsequent impressions are spaced far enough apart so as not to distort hardness values. The distance from the surface of case to the centre of the impression is measured on a calibrated optical instrument, micrometer stage, or other suitable means.

Taper-grind Procedure: This procedure illustrated by Fig. 3, is recommended for measurement of light and medium cases.

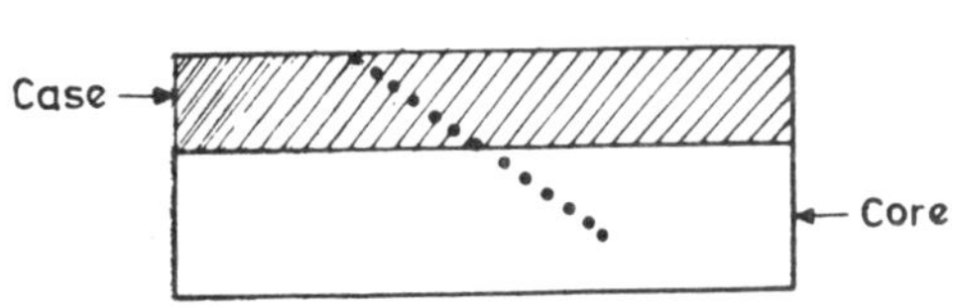

Fig. 1. Cross-sectioned specimen for hardness-transverse method for light and medium cases. Dots show location of hardness indenter impressions.

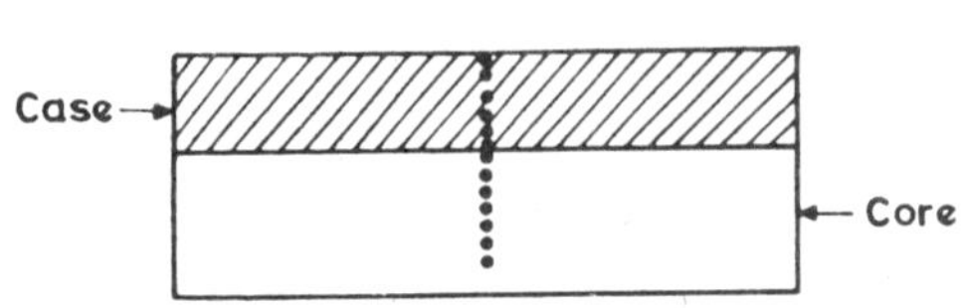

Fig. 2. Cross-sectioned specimen for hardness-transverse method for medium and heavy cases. Dots show location of hardness indenter impressions.

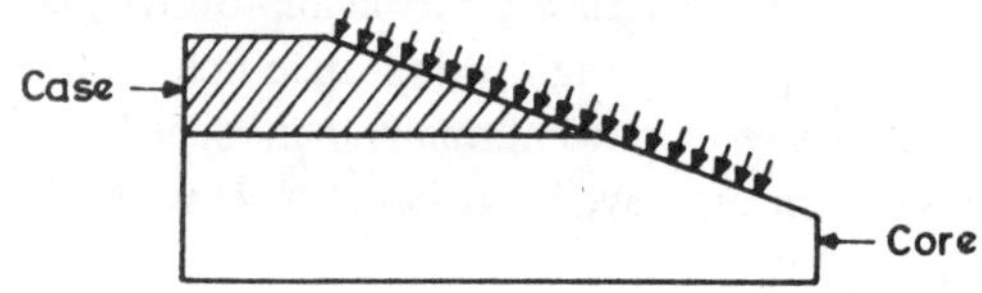

Fig. 3. Taper-ground specimen for hardness-transverse method for light and medium cases. Arrows show location of hardness indenter impressions.

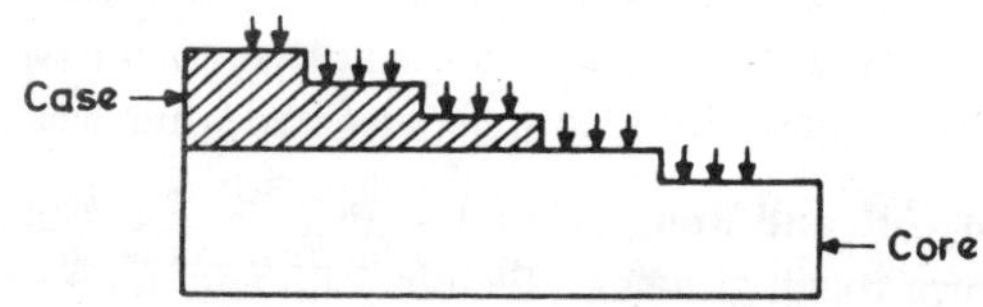

Fig. 4. Step-ground specimen for hardness-transverse method for medium and heavy cases. Arrows show location of hardness indenter impressions.

A shallow taper is ground through the case, and hardness measurements are made along the surface thus prepared. The angle is chosen so that readings spaced equal distances apart will represent the hardness at the desired increments below the surface of the case.

Unless special anvils are used, a parallel section should be prepared so that readings are taken at right angles to the surface. Care should be exercised in grinding, to prevent tempering or rehardening.

Step-grind Procedure: This procedure, illustrated by Fig. 4, is recommended for measurement of medium and heavy cases. It is essentially the same as the taper-grind procedure, with the exception that hardness readings are made on steps that are at known distances below the surface.

A variation in this procedure is the step-grind method in which two pre-determined depths are ground to insure that the effective case depth is within specified limits.

VISUAL METHODS

These methods employ any visual procedure, with or without the aid of magnification, for reading the depth of case produced by any of the various processes. Samples may be prepared by combinations of fracturing, cutting, grinding and polishing methods. Etching with a suitable reagent is normally required to produce a contrast between the case and core. Nital (concentrated nitric acid in alcohol) of various strengths is frequently used as the reagent for producing this contrast.

MACROSCOPIC VISUAL PROCEDURES

Magnification methods for determination of case depth measurement are recommended for routine process control, primarily because of the short time required for determinations, and the minimum of specialized equipment and trained personnel needed. They have the added advantage of being applicable to the measurement of all types of cases. However, the accuracy can be improved by correlation with other methods more in keeping with engineering specifications for the parts being processed. These methods are applied normally to hardened specimens. Except that a variety of etchants may be employed with equal success, the following procedures are typical and widely used.

1. Fracture — Prepare product or samples by fracturing. Examine at a magnification not to exceed 20 diameters, with no further preparation.

2. Fracture and Etch — Water quench samples directly from the carburizing temperature. Fracture, then etch in 20% nitric acid in water for a time established to develop maximum contrast. Rinse in water and read while wet.

3. Fracture or Cut, and Rough Grind — Prepare specimen by either fracturing or cutting, and then rough grinding. Etch in 10% nital for a period of time established to provide a sharp line of demarcation between case and core. Examine at magnification not to exceed 20 diameters (Brinell glass) and read all of the darkened area for approximate total case depth.

4. Fracture or Cut, and Polish or Grind — Prepare specimen by fracturing or cutting. Polish, or grind through No. 000 or finer metallographic emery paper, or both. Etch in 5% nital for approximately 1 min. Rinse in two clean alcohol or water rinses. Examine at magnification not to exceed 20 diameters (Brinell glass) and read all of the darkened zone. After correlation, effective case depth can be determined by reading from external surface of specimen to a selected line of the darkened zone.

MICROSCOPIC VISUAL PROCEDURE

Microscopic methods are generally for laboratory determination and require a complete metallographic polish and an etch suitable for the material and the process. The examination is made most commonly at 100 diameters.

Carburized Cases: The microscopic method may be used for laboratory determinations of total and effective case depths in the hardened condition. When the specimen is annealed properly, the total case depth and the depth of the various zones — hypereutectoid, eutectoid and hypoeutectoid — also can be determined quite precisely.

I. Procedure for Hardened Condition:

1. Fracture or cut specimen at right angle to the surface.
2. Prepare specimen for microscope and etch in 2 to 5% nital.
3. For effective case depth, read from surface to metallographic structures that have been shown to be equivalent to Rockwell-C 50.
4. For total case depth, read to the line of demarcation between the case and core. In alloy steels quenched from a high temperature, the line of demarcation is not sharp. Read all of the darkened zone that indicates a difference in carbon from the uniform core structure.

II. Procedure for Annealed Condition (For specimens previously hardened or not cooled under controlled conditions)

1. The specimen to be annealed may be protected by copper plate or any other suitable means for preventing loss of carbon.
2. Pack in small, thin-wall container with a suitable material such as charcoal.
3. Place container in furnace at 298–338K (26–65°C) above the upper critical temperature (Ae_3) of the core. (Generally, an annealing temperature of 1143–1198K (870–925°C) is satisfactory).
4. Leave the specimen in the furnace long enough to reach furnace temperature (but not for an excessive time, because carbon diffusion will increase total case depth).
5. Cooling Rates: A satisfactory cooling rate is obtained by cooling the container in mica, lime or other insulating material at a rate that will reduce the temperature to 698K(425°C) in 2.5 to 3 h. Cool as desired below this temperature. Slower cooling rates or isothermal transformations are required for alloy steels. If martensite is retained in the structure, better contrast after etching may be obtained by tempering the specimens at 813–873K(540–600°C). Cool as desired after tempering.
6. Section, prepare and etch specimen as described under 'Procedure for Hardened Conditions'. Etching time is usually longer.
7. For total case depth measurement, read the depth of carbon enrichment.

III. Procedure for Annealed Condition (For specimens cooled slowly after carburizing)

If the production carburizing cycle provides the proper cooling rate, or if the cooling rate is otherwise controlled as described above for the annealed condition, specimens may be prepared and examined without reheating after carburizing. This is often possible when the parts are cooled in solid compound when the boxes are not too small.

Carbonitrided Cases: Carbonitrided cases are measured for the total case depth in the hardened condition. High quenching temperature, high alloy content of the steel, and high carbon content of the core decrease the accuracy of readings obtained by this method.

Procedure: Section, prepare, etch and read as described above for carburized cases, in 'Procedure for Hardened Condition'.

Cyanided Cases: Cyanided cases are thin, and only the microscopic method is recommended for accurate case depth measurement. The usual cyanided case contains a light-etching layer followed by a totally martensitic constituent, which in turn is followed by martensite with increasing networks of other constituents, depending on the type of steel cyanided. Cyanided cases are read in hardened condition only and results reported as total case depth.

Procedure:

1. Section, prepare and etch specimen as described above for carburized cases, in 'Procedure for Hardened Condition'.
2. Read to the line of demarcation between the case and core. (When a sharp line of demarcation does not exist, the use of a hardness traverse such as described under 'Mechanical Method' is recommended).

Nitrided Cases: The microscopic method is used chiefly in those situations where the available sample cannot readily be prepared for the more desirable hardness-traverse method.

Procedure:

1. Section and prepare the specimen as described above the carburized cases, in 'Procedure for Hardened Condition'.
2. Etch in 10% nital.
3. Read all of the darkened zone for total case depth.

Flame or Induction Hardened Cases: Because no chemical change occurs in flame or induction hardening, readings must be made in the hardened or hardened-and-tempered condition only. A procedure for reading effective case depth nay be established by correlating microstructures with a hardness-traverse method. A minimum hardness of Rockwell-C 50 is commonly used, but some other point may be selected or required — for example, in lower-carbon steels that do not reach Rockwell-C 50 when fully hardened (see the table correlating carbon content with effective case depth hardness, under 'Mechanical Method'). The microstructure at the selected location will differ depending on steel composition, prior treatment (annealed, heat treated, or other treatments), and hardness level chosen.

Procedure:

1. Section, prepare and etch specimen as described above for carburized cases, in 'Procedure for Hardened Condition',
2. For total case depth, read the entire zone containing structures hardened by the process.
3. For effective case depth, read to the selected microstructure correlated with specified hardness.

APPENDIX V

Composition of AISI-SAE Standard Carbon and Alloy Steels

AISI/ SAE No.	Composition (%)							
	C	Mn	P (max)	S (max)	Si	Ni	Cr	Mo
1005	0.06 max	0.35 max	0.040	0.050				
1006	0.08 max	0.25–0.40	0.040	0.050				
1008	0.10 max	0.30–0.50	0.040	0.050				
1010	0.08–0.13	0.30–0.60	0.040	0.050				
1012	0.10–0.15	0.30–0.60	0.040	0.050				
1015	0.13–0.18	0.30–0.60	0.040	0.050				
1016	0.13–0.18	0.60–0.90	0.040	0.050				
1017	0.15–0.20	0.30–0.60	0.040	0.050				
1018	0.15–0.20	0.60–0.90	0.040	0.050				
1019	0.15–0.20	0.70–1.00	0.040	0.050				
1020	0.18–0.23	0.30–0.60	0.040	0.050				
1021	0.18–0.23	0.60–0.90	0.040	0.050				
1022	0.18–0.23	0.70–1.00	0.040	0.050				
1023	0.20–0.25	0.30–0.60	0.040	0.050				
1024	0.22–0.28	0.30–0.60	0.040	0.050				
1025	0.22–0.28	0.60–0.90	0.040	0.050				
1029	0.25–0.31	0.60–0.90	0.040	0.050				

AISI/ SAE No.	Composition (%)							
	C	Mn	P (max)	S (max)	Si	Ni	Cr	Mo
1030	0.28–0.34	0.60–0.90	0.040	0.050				
1035	0.32–0.38	0.60–0.90	0.040	0.050				
1037	0.32–0.38	0.70–1.00	0.040	0.050				
1038	0.35–0.42	0.60–0.90	0.040	0.050				
1039	0.37–0.44	0.70–1.00	0.040	0.050				
1040	0.37–0.44	0.60–0.90	0.040	0.050				
1042	0.40–0.47	0.60–0.90	0.040	0.050				
1043	0.40–0.47	0.70–1.00	0.040	0.050				
1044	0.43–0.50	0.30–0.60	0.040	0.050				
1045	0.43–0.50	0.60–0.90	0.040	0.050				
1046	0.43–0.50	0.70–1.00	0.040	0.050				
1049	0.46–0.53	0.60–0.90	0.040	0.050				
1050	0.48–0.55	0.60–0.90	0.040	0.050				
1053	0.48–0.55	0.70–1.00	0.040	0.050				
1055	0.50–0.60	0.60–0.90	0.040	0.050				
1059	0.55–0.65	0.50–0.80	0.040	0.050				
1060	0.55–0.65	0.60–0.90	0.040	0.050				
1070	0.65–0.75	0.60–0.90	0.040	0.050				
1078	0.72–0.85	0.30–0.60	0.040	0.050				

AISI/ SAE No.	Composition (%)							
	C	Mn	P (max)	S (max)	Si	Ni	Cr	Mo
1080	0.75–0.88	0.60–0.90	0.040	0.050				
1084	0.80–0.93	0.60–0.90	0.040	0.050				
1086	0.80–0.93	0.30–0.50	0.040	0.050				
1090	0.85–0.98	0.60–0.90	0.040	0.050				
1095	0.90–1.03	0.30–0.50	0.040	0.050				
1513	0.10–0.16	1.10–1.40	0.040	0.050				
1522	0.18–0.24	1.10–1.40	0.040	0.050				
1524	0.19–0.25	1.35–1.65	0.040	0.050				
1526	0.22–0.29	1.10–1.40	0.040	0.050				
1527	0.22–0.29	1.20–1.50	0.040	0.050				
1541	0.36–0.44	1.35–1.65	0.040	0.050				
1548	0.44–0.52	1.10–1.40	0.040	0.050				
1551	0.45–0.56	0.86–1.15	0.040	0.050				
1552	0.47–0.55	1.20–1.50	0.040	0.050				
1561	0.55–0.65	0.75–1.05	0.040	0.050				
1566	0.60–0.71	0.85–1.15	0.040	0.050				
1330	0.28–0.33	1.60–1.90	0.035	0.040	0.15–0.30			
1335	0.33–0.38	1.60–1.90	0.035	0.040	0.15–0.30			
1340	0.38–0.43	1.60–1.90	0.035	0.040	0.15–0.30			

AISI/ SAE No.	Composition (%)							
	C	Mn	P (max)	S (max)	Si	Ni	Cr	Mo
1345	0.43–0.48	1.60–1.90	0.035	0.040	0.15–0.30			
4023	0.20–0.25	0.70–0.90	0.035	0.040	0.15–0.30			0.20–0.30
4024	0.20–0.25	0.70–0.90	0.035	0.050	0.15–0.30			0.20–0.30
4027	0.25–0.30	0.70–0.90	0.035	0.040	0.15–0.30			0.20–0.30
4028	0.25–0.30	0.70–0.90	0.035	0.050	0.15–0.30			0.20–0.30
4037	0.35–0.40	0.70–0.90	0.035	0.040	0.15–0.30			0.20–0.30
4047	0.45–0.50	0.70–0.90	0.035	0.040	0.15–0.30			0.20–0.30
4118	0.18–0.23	0.70–0.90	0.035	0.040	0.15–0.30		0.40–0.60	0.08–0.15
4130	0.28–0.33	0.40–0.60	0.035	0.040	0.15–0.30		0.80–1.10	0.15–0.25
4137	0.35–0.40	0.70–0.90	0.035	0.040	0.15–0.30		0.80–1.10	0.15–0.25
4140	0.38–0.43	0.75–1.00	0.035	0.040	0.15–0.30		0.80–1.10	0.15–0.25
4142	0.40–0.45	0.75–1.00	0.035	0.040	0.15–0.30		0.80–1.10	0.15–0.25
4145	0.43–0.48	0.75–1.00	0.035	0.040	0.15–0.30		0.80–1.10	0.15–0.25
4147	0.45–0.50	0.75–1.00	0.035	0.040	0.15–0.30		0.80–1.10	0.15–0.25
4150	0.48–0.53	0.75–1.00	0.035	0.040	0.15–0.30		0.80–1.10	0.15–0.25
4161	0.56–0.64	0.75–1.00	0.035	0.040	0.15–0.30		0.70–0.90	0.15–0.25
4320	0.17–0.22	0.45–0.65	0.035	0.040	0.15–0.30	1.65–2.00	0.40–0.60	0.20–0.30
4340	0.38–0.43	0.60–0.80	0.035	0.040	0.15–0.30	1.65–2.00	0.70–0.90	0.20–0.30
E4340	0.38–0.43	0.65–0.85	0.025	0.025	0.15–0.30	1.65–2.00	0.70–0.90	0.20–0.30

AISI/ SAE No.	Composition (%)							
	C	Mn	P (max)	S (max)	Si	Ni	Cr	Mo
4615	0.13–0.18	0.45–0.65	0.035	0.040	0.15–0.30	1.65–2.00		0.20–0.30
4620	0.17–0.22	0.45–0.65	0.035	0.040	0.15–0.30	1.65–2.00		0.20–0.30
4626	0.24–0.29	0.45–0.65	0.035	0.040	0.15–0.30	0.70–1.00		0.15–0.25
4720	0.17–0.22	0.50–0.70	0.035	0.040	0.15–0.30	0.90–1.20	0.35–0.55	0.15–0.25
4815	0.13–0.18	0.40–0.60	0.035	0.040	0.15–0.30	3.25–3.75		0.20–0.30
4817	0.15–0.20	0.40–0.60	0.035	0.040	0.15–0.30	3.25–3.75		0.20–0.30
4820	0.18–0.23	0.50–0.70	0.035	0.040	0.15–0.30	3.25–3.75		0.20–0.30
5117	0.15–0.20	0.70–0.90	0.035	0.040	0.15–0.30		0.70–0.90	
5120	0.17–0.22	0.70–0.90	0.035	0.040	0.15–0.30		0.70–0.90	
5130	0.28–0.33	0.70–0.90	0.035	0.040	0.15–0.30		0.80–1.10	
5132	0.30–0.35	0.60–0.80	0.035	0.040	0.15–0.30		0.75–1.00	
5135	0.33–0.38	0.60–0.80	0.035	0.040	0.15–0.30		0.80–1.05	
5140	0.38–0.43	0.70–0.90	0.035	0.040	0.15–0.30		0.70–0.90	
5150	0.48–0.53	0.70–0.90	0.035	0.040	0.15–0.30		0.70–0.90	
5155	0.51–0.59	0.70–0.90	0.035	0.040	0.15–0.30		0.70–0.90	
5160	0.56–0.64	0.75–1.00	0.035	0.040	0.15–0.30		0.70–0.90	
E51100	0.98–1.10	0.25–0.45	0.025	0.025	0.15–0.30		0.90–1.15	
E52100	0.98–1.10	0.25–0.45	0.025	0.025	0.15–0.30		1.30–1.60	
6118	0.16–0.21	0.50–0.70	0.035	0.040	0.15–0.30		0.50–0.70	0.10–0.15 V

AISI/ SAE No.	Composition (%)							
	C	Mn	P (max)	S (max)	Si	Ni	Cr	Mo
6150	0.48–0.53	0.70–0.90	0.035	0.040	0.15–0.30		0.80–1.10	0.15V (min.)
8615	0.13–0.18	0.70–0.90	0.035	0.040	0.15–0.30	0.40–0.70	0.40–0.60	0.15–0.25
8617	0.15–0.20	0.70–0.90	0.035	0.040	0.15–0.30	0.40–0.70	0.40–0.60	0.15–0.25
8620	0.18–0.23	0.70–0.90	0.035	0.040	0.15–0.30	0.40–0.70	0.40–0.60	0.15–0.25
8622	0.20–0.25	0.70–0.90	0.035	0.040	0.15–0.30	0.40–0.70	0.40–0.60	0.15–0.25
8625	0.23–0.28	0.70–0.90	0.035	0.040	0.15–0.30	0.40–0.70	0.40–0.60	0.15–0.25
8627	0.25–0.30	0.70–0.90	0.035	0.040	0.15–0.30	0.40–0.70	0.40–0.60	0.15–0.25
8630	0.28–0.33	0.70–0.90	0.035	0.040	0.15–0.30	0.40–0.70	0.40–0.60	0.15–0.25
8637	0.35–0.40	0.75–1.00	0.035	0.040	0.15–0.30	0.40–0.70	0.40–0.60	0.15–0.25
8640	0.38–0.43	0.75–1.00	0.035	0.040	0.15–0.30	0.40–0.70	0.40–0.60	0.15–0.25
8642	0.40–0.45	0.75–1.00	0.035	0.040	0.15–0.30	0.40–0.70	0.40–0.60	0.15–0.25
8645	0.43–0.48	0.75–1.00	0.035	0.040	0.15–0.30	0.40–0.70	0.40–0.60	0.15–0.25
8655	0.51–0.59	0.75–1.00	0.035	0.040	0.15–0.30	0.40–0.70	0.40–0.60	0.15–0.25
8720	0.18–0.23	0.70–0.90	0.035	0.040	0.15–0.30	0.40–0.70	0.40–0.60	0.20–0.30
8740	0.38–0.43	0.75–1.00	0.035	0.040	0.15–0.30	0.40–0.70	0.40–0.60	0.20–0.30
8822	0.20–0.25	0.75–1.00	0.035	0.040	0.15–0.30	0.40–0.70	0.40–0.60	0.30–0.40
9260	0.56–0.64	0.75–1.00	0.035	0.040	1.80–2.00			

AISI/ SAE No.	Composition (%)							
	C	Mn	P (max)	S (max)	Si	Ni	Cr	Mo
Standard boron grades*								
50B44	0.43–0.48	0.75–1.00	0.035	0.040	0.15–0.30		0.40–0.60	
50B46	0.44–0.49	0.75–1.00	0.035	0.040	0.15–0.30		0.20–0.35	
50B50	0.48–0.53	0.75–1.00	0.035	0.040	0.15–0.30		0.40–0.60	
50B60	0.56–0.64	0.75–1.00	0.035	0.040	0.15–0.30		0.70–0.90	
81B45	0.43–0.48	0.75–1.00	0.035	0.040	0.15–0.30	0.20–0.40	0.35–0.55	0.08–0.15
94B17	0.15–0.20	0.75–1.00	0.035	0.040	0.15–0.30	0.30–0.60	0.30–0.50	0.08–0.15
94B30	0.28–0.33	0.75–1.00	0.035	0.040	0.15–0.30	0.30–0.60	0.30–0.50	0.08–0.15

* 0.0005 to 0.003 % boron

APPENDIX VI

Recommended Heat Treatment Temperatures for Some AISI-SAE Alloy Steels

Steel No.	Normalising Temp K(°C)	Annealing Temp. K(°C)	Hardening Temp. K(°C)	Quenching medium
1330	1143–1198(870–925)	1088–1143(815–870)	1103–1133(830–860)	water/oil
1335, 1340	—do—	1088–1143(815–870)	1103–1133(830–860)	oil
3130	—do—	–	1088–1118(815–845)	water/oil
3140	—do—	1063–1118(790–845)	1088–1118(815–845)	oil
4037, 4042	—do—	1103–1133(830–860)	1088–1133(815–860)	oil
4047	—do—	1063–1118(790–845)	1088–1133(815–860)	oil
4063	—do—	—do—	1073–1118(800–845)	oil
4130	—do—	—do—	1143–1173(870–900)	water/oil
4137, 4140	—do—	—do—	1118–1143(815–870)	water/oil
4145, 4150	—do—	—do—	1088–1143(815–870)	oil
4340	—do—	—do—	1073–1103(800–830)	oil
5046	—do—	—do—	1073–1088(800–815)	oil
5130, 5132	1173-1228(900-955)	—do—	1088–1118(815–845)	water/oil
5135, 5140, 5145	—do—	—do—	1088–1118(815–845)	oil
5147, 5150	—do—	—do—	1073–1118(800–845)	oil
50100	—do—	1008–1063(735–790)	1048–1073(775–800)	water
51100, 51200	—do—	1008–1063(735–790)	1088–1143(815–870)	oil
6150	1173-1228(900-955)	1118–1173(845–900)	1143–1173(870–900)	oil
9255, 9260, 9262	—do—	1118–1173(845–900)	1088–1173(815–900)	oil
8627, 8630	1143–1198(870–925)	1063–1118(790–845)	1118–1173(845–900)	water/oil
8637, 8640	—do—	—do—	1103–1133(830–860)	oil
8642, 8645, 8650	—do—	—do—	1088–1118(815–845)	oil
8655, 8660	1173–1228(900–955)	—do—	1073–1118(800–845)	oil
8735, 8740	1143–1198(870–925)	—do—	1103–1133(830–860)	oil
9840	—do—	—do—	1088–1118(815–845)	oil

Subject Index